American Voices:

A Historical Reader
Volume II

American Voices:
A Historical Reader
Volume II

Robert Marcus and David Burner
State University of New York at Stony Brook

Scott, Foresman and Company
Glenview, Illinois
Dallas, Tex.
Oakland, N.J.
Palo Alto, Cal.
Tucker, Ga.
London

Printed in the United States of America.

Library of Congress Cataloging in Publication Data

Main entry under title:

American voices.

1. United States—History—Sources. I. Marcus, Robert D., 1936– II. Burner, David, 1937–
E173.A759 973 78-17850
ISBN 0-673-15173-5 (v. 2)

1 2 3 4 5 6 7-RRC-84 83 82 81 80 79 78

Acknowledgments

Margaret Leech. "Arrival of a Westerner" (pp. 33–45) from REVEILLE IN WASHINGTON. Copyright 1941 by Margaret Leech Pulitzer. Reprinted by permission of Harper & Row, Publishers, Inc.

Helen Hunt Jackson. A CENTURY OF DISHONOR (1881).

Edward Bellamy. LOOKING BACKWARD (Boston: Houghton Mifflin Co.), 1898.

Frederick Jackson Turner. "The Significance of the Frontier in American History" from ANNUAL REPORT FOR 1893, American Historical Association, pp. 199–227.

Andy Adams. LOG OF A COWBOY (1903).

Jane Addams. "A Modern Lear" from THE SURVEY, Vol. 20, November 2, 1912.

Lincoln Steffens. THE SHAME OF THE CITIES (Chicago: McClure, Phillips & Co.), 1904.

William L. Riordon, editor. PLUNKITT OF TAMMANY HALL, New York, 1905.

Upton Sinclair. THE JUNGLE (New York: Doubleday, Doran & Company, Inc.), 1906.

Sinclair Lewis. Excerpted from MAIN STREET, copyright, 1920, by Harcourt Brace Jovanovich, Inc.; copyright, 1948 by Sinclair Lewis. Reprinted by permission of the Estate of Sinclair Lewis and the publishers, Harcourt Brace Jovanovich, Inc. and Jonathan Cape Ltd.

John Dos Passos. U.S.A. Harcourt, Brace, Jovanovich, 1937. Reprinted by permission.

Ruth McKenney. From INDUSTRIAL VALLEY, copyright 1939 by Ruth McKenney. Reprinted by permission of Curtis Brown, Ltd.

John Steinbeck. From THE GRAPES OF WRATH, copyright 1939, © 1967 by John Steinbeck. Reprinted by permission of The Viking Press and William Heinemann Ltd.

Henry Roth. From CALL IT SLEEP, copyright 1934 by Henry Roth. Published by Cooper Square Publishers, Inc. and Penguin Books Limited. Reprinted by permission.

Ralph Ellison. From INVISIBLE MAN, copyright 1952 by Ralph Ellison. Reprinted by permission of Random House, Inc.

Students for a Democratic Society. THE PORT HURON STATEMENT, 1962.

From RIGHTS IN CONFLICT, A Report Submitted by Daniel Walker, Director of the Chicago Study Team, to the National Commission on the Causes and Prevention of Violence. (New York: Bantam Books), 1968.

From MYSTERY TRAIN: IMAGES OF AMERICA IN ROCK 'N' ROLL MUSIC by Greil Marcus. Copyright © 1975 by Greil Marcus. Reprinted by permission of the publishers, E. P. Dutton; and Omnibus Press Ltd.

Grateful acknowledgement is given here for the illustrative material appearing in the book.

xii: Archives of the B. & O. Railroad Museum, Baltimore

16: Erneste Etienne Narjot, *Colonel J. C. Cremony Leading a Fight Against the Apaches,* Courtesy of Kennedy Galleries, Inc., New York

32: Brown Brothers

52: Harry T. Peters Collection

76: Library of Congress

90: Culver Pictures, Inc.

104: Library of Congress

122: From PLUNKITT OF TAMMANY HALL, by William L. Riordon. Permission of Alfred A. Knopf, Inc.

154: Library of Congress

190: United Press International

214: United Press International

240: Library of Congress

256: Library of Congress

300: Courtesy of the International Museum of Photography, Rochester, N.Y.

326: Courtesy of The Tuskegee Institute

346: Bernie Boston/Washington Star

368: Paul Sequeria

422: Wide World Photos, Inc.

Preface

This anthology has but a single aim: to provide selections that are genuinely worth reading for students of American history. It is not a collection of recent articles or of documents, nor does it develop some special approach. Rather, it is an offering of authentic voices from the American past, men and women who speak for themselves, who in some particular way speak for their age, and who through their writings can speak as readily to us.

The selections are sufficiently long to allow students to hear these voices in a meaningful way. The material is varied in style and genre: speeches, historical narratives, fiction, essay, memoirs and more. Some are examples of great literature, others of popular culture or folk wisdom. Some are important for the mark they made on their age; others were little noted until a later generation. A few are the writings of historians who have achieved special success in linking past and present, in allowing the past to live. Some are from the writings of great political leaders. Several are classics in journalism. While a few are literary masterpieces, many are simply authentic distillations of some piece of American experience: what it was like to live among the Indians, to be a cowboy or a slave or a ward politician or a dispossessed farmer or a Rock fan.

These writers address virtually all the major themes of American history. Margaret Leech's splendid narrative of President-elect Lincoln's stealthy entrance into Washington in the gloomy days of early 1861 offers a dramatic preface to the Civil War—the great struggle that has traditionally been viewed as the dividing line between the old republic and modern industrial America. However eroded that barrier line has become as historians push back the onset of industrialism and project forward the great antebellum issues of race relations, Indian policy, and the proportionate authority of the federal government to the states and localities, it remains vivid as a symbolic moment when American institutions withstood their ultimate test. Moreover, the modernization of government, politics, military affairs, and finance that occurred during the war remains as a tangible indicator of this acceleration toward a more modern world.

One pre-war thrust that continued at an even more rapid rate after the conflict was the westward movement. Helen Hunt Jackson looks at the primary victims of that process—the Indians. Jackson wrote just when the Indian was finally losing the capacity for military resistance and could increasingly be viewed as a victim and as a ward of the United States. Whether that produced better treatment than the old status of enemy is a painful question to debate. Few westerners bothered to debate it at all. The ranchers, the miners, the settlers, and the cowboys like Andy Adams had a job to do and Indians seemed mere impediments. They sought land and wealth, and everyone knew that those precious commodities lay to the West. This identification of wealth and opportunity—and the definition of the American character—in the availability of land to the West is as old as the nation. Thomas Jefferson believed that he had transformed his ideal of a nation of yeomen farmers into a potential reality by the Louisiana Purchase. Thus, Frederick Jackson Turner's announcement in 1893 of the end of the frontier—though somewhat premature—marked a major shift in American life. The West would rapidly fade into legend, with the cowboy its authentic hero, while American eyes reluctantly turned to the world of industry and the city, in which the American future—whether they liked it or not—appeared to dwell.

Americans of the late nineteenth and early twentieth centuries did not find the world of industrialism and urbanization a pretty sight. Much of it was ugly, but the powerful lines of factories and machines that the artist Charles Demuth loved, the skylines and teeming urban scenes that soon excited a generation of wide-eyed migrants from the farms and villages seemed at first more frightening than glamorous. A whole new aesthetic and perhaps a new American character had to develop that was more in tune with this even stranger and newer world. The millions of Americans who for over a quarter of a century read and discussed Edward Bellamy's *Looking Backward, 2000–1887* obviously wanted the wealth and the conveniences that a modern industrial society could offer, but one cannot help noticing how unwilling they were to change in order to acquire these goods. Instead they dreamed of a future world suddenly purged of the problems of competitive industrialism and of tensions between the many groups that were suddenly a part of the urban landscape. Even hard-driving and successful businessmen like George Pullman—Jane Addams' "modern Lear"—shared this vision of somehow making a few adjustments in the way industry was organized and arriving at a clean, harmonious social order. There seemed no reason at all that utopia could not be built just a little south of Chicago.

Few Americans sought utopia for very long in the nation's cities. Older visions of America had not included unassimilated immigrants, the vast growth of the Roman Catholic church, or the rise of men with strange accents to political power. Nor had they envisioned environments that seemed to encase the earth in concrete and steel, separating people from the soil, the frontier, the whole Jeffersonian world. Because this new world seemed so aberrant from all their values, writers like Upton Sinclair and Lincoln Steffens constructed anti-utopias, assuring vast audiences that things were not as bad as they seemed—they were worse. Yet in this literature of exposure, of which Steffens was such a master, there is—amid the moral indignation—an air of gaiety, something of the mood that induces people to attend freak shows. Sinclair tries to reach beneath this jolly mood of unmasking hypocracies by pushing readers to sympathize with the unfortunate victims who are his heroes. Contrary to his intent, *The Jungle* was mainly read as an exposé, not as a plea for an end to the oppression of workers.

While Americans worried about cities, few seemed capable of resisting their lure, and for some groups they clearly offered the most open field of opportunity, a virtual new frontier. The immigrants whom George Washington Plunkitt served led hard lives. Yet the opportunities for employment and for educating their children were vastly greater than in the environments they had fled. Women also found new opportunity in the city both for work and for social freedom. Carol Kennicott, the heroine of *Main Street,* finds the small town of Gopher Prairie claustrophobic and frustrating not simply because its culture suffers in comparison to the cities she has experienced, but because the demands made on women in Gopher Prairie seem so pointless and unsatisfying.

In the 1920s most Americans seemed to be coming to terms with their urban industrial world. Farmers and inhabitants of small towns fought a rearguard action, trying to accept those parts of the new culture they enjoyed—radios, autos, motion pictures, prosperity—while fending off what they disliked: big city manners, the mixing of ethnic and racial groups, changing roles of women, and the like. A fast developing aesthetic, exemplified in John Dos Passos' use of literary techniques borrowed from the new urban media, promised to create a style of dealing with the industrial world that could apply to all Americans. The industrial art form of advertising threatened—or promised (depending on how one looked at it)—to create a new unity for American culture, a role that agrarian experience had once served.

The shock of depression, however, revealed how permanently fragmented into subcultures, into groups with differing life styles, American society had become. The world of factory workers that Ruth McKenney described, the universe of hopelessly drifting

"Okies" who had lost their birthright on the land in a handful of bad years marked by drought and low prices for farm commodities, these were novel, even exotic glimpses into American life for most readers. Soon the direct voices of minorities, of subgroups that were once merely observed by outsiders, would indicate with increased precision the multiple facets of American experience. Henry Roth's extraordinary interior vision of the experience of the immigrant ghettoes as seen through the eyes of a young boy was an arresting indication of the riches that an acceptance of this fragmentation could bring to American life. Ralph Ellison's *Invisible Man,* often considered the finest post-World War II American novel, introduced thousands of Americans—and then millions as students began to pour into institutions of higher education in the 1960s—to the complex vision of American life as seen through the lense of the black experience.

In the 1960s Americans began to learn that not only were groups divided by birth, color, religion, and interest, but that cutting across these increasingly acknowledged divisions were yet other fragments. In transit through the life cycle, people experienced markedly different cultural groupings. A "youth culture" became the subject of raging debate, not just in mass media but over dining room tables and conference tables across the continent—as well as in the streets of Chicago during the now famous 1968 Democratic National Convention. Music early was one of the outward symbols of cultural division: Rock music, it seemed, was a monopoly of the young. Greil Marcus suggests some of the ways that music, the badge of the counterculture, also mediates the transition that every member of that culture must make to a broader world simply because he or she must grow older.

This book explores the many ways of being an American. In that sense its theme is the American identity, or rather the many identities that make up a diverse history and nation. It offers one kind of answer to the question asked nearly two centuries ago by Crèvecoeur: "What then is this American, this new man?" It invites students to view the experiences of these new people, these Americans, through the eyes of a few of those who saw what happened, who were there, and who had the power to tell of it.

Contents

Margaret Leech,
Arrival of a Westerner (1941) 1

Helen Hunt Jackson,
A Century of Dishonor (1881) 17

Edward Bellamy,
Looking Backward, 2000–1887 (1888) 33

Frederick Jackson Turner,
The Significance of the Frontier in American History (1893) 53

Andy Adams,
The Log of a Cowboy (1903) 77

Jane Addams,
A Modern Lear (1912) 91

Lincoln Steffens,
Philadelphia: Corrupt and Contented (1904) 105

Plunkitt of Tammany Hall (1905) 123

Upton Sinclair,
The Jungle (1906) 155

Sinclair Lewis,
Main Street (1920) 191

John Dos Passos,
U.S.A. (1937) 215

Ruth McKenney,
Industrial Valley (1939) 241

John Steinbeck,
The Grapes of Wrath (1939) 257

Henry Roth,
Call It Sleep (1934) 301

Ralph Ellison,
A Black's Education (1947) 327

Students for a Democratic Society,
The Port Huron Statement (1962) 347

Daniel Walker,
The Walker Report (1968) 369

Greil Marcus,
Elvis: Presliad (1976) 423

The unannounced arrival of President-elect Lincoln

MARGARET LEECH

Arrival of a Westerner

(1941)

Abraham Lincoln, with his mystic faith in the Union, his charity and humanity, his folk wisdom, and his identification with the former slaves, assumed a place in the American pantheon above all other heroes in our history. Northerners of the two generations after the Civil War especially made a cult of him, celebrating his birthday, naming their cities after him, and erecting statues to his honor. He became, as in the huge statue by Daniel Chester French that dominates the Lincoln Memorial in the nation's capital, larger than life, more exalted than the common man he somehow, mysteriously, represented. The martyred president became something separate from the homey philosopher and raconteur of frontier tales. What joined the two?

Lincoln the Westerner, arriving at the capital by a secret route, meeting—and being condescended to by—the mighty, seizes a part of the answer. Here (so few years before his martyrdom) was an upstart, his appearance rough, his pronunciation provincial, his worth largely untested. Faced with the threat of war, he lacked an equipped army; confronted with disunion, he had no sure following; pressed with the need to establish the power of his office, he had no reputation among the men he was supposed to command. Only the most optimistic democrat could expect him to rise to the occasion—as he rapidly did. Lincoln seemed great without preparation, one moment part of the folklife of the people, the next their transcendent leader, and last their martyr.

While preparations were being made for the inauguration of Jefferson Davis as president of the Confederate States, Abraham Lincoln was traveling eastward from Illinois. He was accompanied by his wife and three sons, and by a suite of State politicians, personal friends, relatives by marriage, secretaries and newspaper correspondents; and he also had a military escort of four Army officers appointed by the War Department. One was a friend, Major David Hunter, an honest, anti-slavery paymaster, with a dyed mustache and a dark-brown wig. Young Captain John Pope was the son of an Illinois judge, while Colonel Edwin V. Sumner was a good old white-haired cavalry officer from Massachusetts.

The militia system was represented by Colonel Elmer E. Ellsworth, the Zouave drillmaster, who was entrusted with the responsibility of passing the President-elect through the crowds at his stopping places on the route. The man on whom Mr. Lincoln placed most dependence, however, was Ward Hill Lamon, a younger lawyer who had been associated with him in practice on the circuit. Lamon, a native of Virginia, resembled the chivalry in his long hair, defiant eyes and drooping mustaches. He had brought his banjo in his baggage, and amused the party with Negro songs. Of these, *The Blue-Tailed Fly*, a buzzing ballad, was a favorite with Mr. Lincoln; and he loved to listen to many other simple tunes, both sad and comical, that Lamon sang. In addition to the banjo, Lamon carried an assortment of pistols and knives, a slingshot and brass knuckles. He was powerfully built and fearless, and he considered himself especially charged with Mr. Lincoln's safe-conduct to Washington.

It was a tour and a progress, rather than a journey. The special trains, preceded by pilot engines, ran on carefully arranged schedules between the big cities where the President-elect had appointments for speeches and receptions. Past cheering miles of people, in a confusion of bonfires, parades, salutes and handshakings, Mr. Lincoln moved to the ovation in Philadelphia. After a trip to Harrisburg on February 22, he was to proceed to Washington, where he was expected late on the following afternoon. Among the invitations with which he had been deluged, none had come from Maryland. The omission was the more conspicuous, since a slow transit through the city of Baltimore, where the cars were separately drawn by horses between the depots, was unavoidable in journeying by rail to the capital from the North.

This impending passage through a disaffected community had been a source of considerable anxiety to Mr. Lincoln's friends. The Baltimore gangs were notoriously lawless, and Maryland was boiling with secession agitation. There, as in Washington, military companies of suspect loyalty had been drilling; and threats had been heard that Mr. Lincoln would never go through Baltimore alive. The President of the Philadelphia, Wilmington and Baltimore Railroad,

Mr. Samuel M. Felton, not only felt the responsibility of conveying the President-elect across a hostile State, but he had been disturbed by reports of conspiracies to destroy railroad property. Some weeks earlier, he had sent for a trusted Chicago investigator, Allan Pinkerton, a Scottish barrelmaker who had founded one of the first private detective agencies in the United States. Pinkerton, who was also in the pay of Mr. Lincoln's Illinois advisers, placed spies in the military companies and secret societies in and about Baltimore. On receiving confirmation of the rumored plots to interrupt the railroad, Felton organized and armed some two hundred guards, whom he distributed in the guise of workmen along the line between the Susquehanna and Baltimore.

The dangers attendant on Mr. Lincoln's journey to Washington, as well as on his inauguration, had been recognized in Congress by the appointment of another committee of two, on which Congressman Washburne again represented the House, while Mr. Seward was the member for the Senate. As in the case of the committee on which Washburne served with Senator Grimes, there was close co-operation with General Scott. On February 21, Colonel Stone received a report from detectives he had placed in Baltimore that there was serious danger that Mr. Lincoln might be assassinated in passing through the city. Scott sent Stone posthaste to Seward, who agreed with the General's opinion that Mr. Lincoln should change his announced traveling schedule. To persuade him to do so, Seward dispatched his son, Frederick, to Philadelphia with a warning letter, enclosing Stone's report.

The Republicans of Washington were, in view of the ominous rumors, a stouthearted lot. They were erecting a large edifice in back of the City Hall for the inauguration ball. With eager anticipation, they were looking forward to receiving Mr. Lincoln at the depot on the afternoon of February 23, and they had prepared a quantity of banners with which to deck their wigwam. Meantime, the city was agog over the prospect of a military parade on Washington's Birthday. Early in the morning, the Avenue was cluttered with the wagons and drays of the country folk who had driven in to see the spectacle. By the market house, the City Hall and other vantage points, vendors set out tables of pigs' feet and gingerbread. Boys, with lettered placards on their breasts, offered patriotic songs for sale, and there were many flags with patriotic legends. Mr. Seward, since the New Year, had been agitating for a display of the national colors in the capital, and his efforts were rewarded on Washington's Birthday by an unusual show of red, white and blue. In the morning, the *National Intelligencer* carried the War Department's confirmation of the news for which everyone had been hoping, that the regulars would march, as well as the District militia.

At breakfast, however, General Scott had received an order countermanding the participation of the United States troops. The Virginian, John Tyler, was averse to this provocative exhibition of military force, and his protests had overwhelmed Mr. Buchanan. The militia proudly paced the Avenue, but there were no blue-clad regulars, no flying artillery nor plunging horses. Disappointment clouded the people's holiday spirits, as the rumor spread that the soldiers would not, after all, appear. The prevailing indignation was shared by Representative Daniel E. Sickles of New York, a close friend of the President. Two years earlier, Sickles had won great notoriety by shooting Mr. Philip Barton Key for trifling with his pretty wife. Key, the son of the author of "The Star-Spangled Banner," had been the District Attorney, and a popular figure in Washington society. His murder and the ensuing trial had made a tremendous sensation. Mr. Edwin M. Stanton, who conducted Dan Sickle's defense, had pleaded the unwritten law, and the verdict of acquittal had been cheered in the courtroom and received with delight by the President.

This impulsive congressman was enthusiastic for celebrating Washington's Birthday, and he rushed hotfoot to the War Office, where Secretary Holt was in conference with the President. Sickle's remonstrances induced Mr. Buchanan to change his mind, and Holt hurried off to General Scott's headquarters. The General felt a natural irritation. It was by this time midday. The officers had doffed their dress uniforms, and the soldiers had been dismissed. While a diminished force was hastily rounded up, Mr. Buchanan penned a note to ex-President Tyler, excusing himself for permitting Federal soldiers to be in evidence in the capital. In the afternoon, the people were appeased by a second parade. The artillery drill proved to be the high point of the exhibition. All were startled and amazed by the rapidity with which the guns were manned and prepared for action; and verisimilitude was lent to the martial scene by the dust of the Avenue, which floated about men and guns like the smoke of battle.

At six o'clock next morning, when the train from Philadelphia pulled into the Washington depot, the conductor might have been surprised at the sudden recovery of a sick gentleman, who on the preceding night had been quietly hustled into a berth at the end of the last car. The gentleman, in a soft, slouched hat, a muffler and a short, bobtailed overcoat, descended sprily to the platform. His tall and lanky figure would have made him an oddity in any gathering, and he had a plain, dark-skinned, melancholy face, with a stiff new crop of chin whiskers. He was closely attended by two companions, one of whom was big and heavily built, with bulges under his coat in every place where a man might carry arms; while the other was a short, bearded fellow, with a wary, peasant face. As they passed along the platform in the stream of sleepy-eyed travelers, they attracted attention from only one person in the depot, a man who had planted himself behind a pillar, and was peering out with a sharp, worried expression. As the lanky stranger passed, this man seized hold of his hand. "Abe," he cried in a loud voice, "you can't play that on me!"

"Don't strike him," the stranger hastily told his escorts. "It is Washburne." The President-elect had arrived in the capital of the United States.

The warning which Frederick Seward had carried to Philadelphia had already been sounded in a report from Detective Pinkerton of an assassination plot in Baltimore. Doubly disquieted by a second alarm, Lincoln's friends had prevailed on him to alter his published program. After his trip to Harrisburg, he had slipped secretly on the night train, accompanied only by Ward Hill Lamon and a Mr. E. J. Allen, otherwise known as Pinkerton. Frederick Seward had returned with the message that Mr. Lincoln might be early expected in Washington, and Congressman Washburne had hurried to the depot in the winter dawn. The three travelers climbed into Washburne's carriage, and drove off to Willard's.

The original plan, that Mr. Lincoln should occupy a rented house during the pre-inauguration period, had been changed on the advice of Thurlow Weed, the political manager of New York State. In a hotel, the incoming President would be accessible to the people, and Mr. Weed himself had written to Willard's to make the reservation. The best rooms in the house were, however, occupied when Mr. Lincoln made his unexpectedly early appearance, and a New York capitalist had to be hastily dislodged from the suite connected with Parlor Number 6, a large corner apartment on the second floor, overlooking the Avenue and the grounds of the Executive Mansion.

Mr. Seward was waiting at Willard's to receive the President-elect and congratulated him on his safe arrival. He was somewhat chagrined, Washburne thought, that he had not been up in time to go to the depot. At eight o'clock, however, the senator and the congressman sat down in high elation to breakfast, loading their plates with the first run of Potomac shad. Mr. Lincoln had retired to his rooms to rest. He did not share the exultation of his friends. He had yielded to the advice to change his plans, but he had not taken stock in the story that he risked assassination in Baltimore. Since his nomination, he had constantly received letters threatening his life. He believed that he was destined to suffer a violent death, had expressed the feeling that he would not return alive to Springfield; but Mr. Lincoln's apprehensions, though they may have been quickened by the menaces of his enemies or the nervous solicitude of his friends, were the shadowy alarms of premonition and anxiety, and the prospect of actual danger left him unmoved. For the rest of his life, he would regret the secret journey to Washington. It exposed him to bitter criticism from friends and enemies alike; and it seemed to many to cast reproach on a Government already sufficiently dishonored. Mr. Seward would laughingly agree with the detractors, and say that he had not believed in the Baltimore assassins, though General Scott had done so.

Mr. Lincoln breakfasted alone at nine in his parlor, and did not appear until eleven, when he left the hotel under the escort of Mr. Seward. Those solitary morning hours were the quietest he was ever to know in Washington. He would live thereafter at the mercy of the people, advancing eternally toward him in a jerking procession of faces.

The first duty of the President-elect was to pay his respects at the Executive Mansion. A special meeting of the Cabinet was in session, when the doorkeeper handed Mr. Buchanan a startling card. "Uncle Abe is downstairs!" the President cried, and hurriedly descended to the Red Room. He soon returned with the two Republicans. Mr. Lincoln was presented to the Cabinet, and paused for a few minutes' conversation before leaving to call on General Scott. One of the members, Attorney General Stanton, had a sneering contempt for Mr. Lincoln. Some years earlier, they had been associated as counsel for the defense in a famous case, a suit brought for infringement of patent rights by Cyrus McCormick, the inventor of the reaping machine. Stanton had snubbed and humiliated the backwoods lawyer, and Lincoln had not forgotten his mortification; but he had also retained a vivid impression of Edwin M. Stanton's abilities.

Mr. Lincoln was familiarly acquainted with Washington, where he had served a term as congressman from Illinois, but the capital could not return the compliment. In spite of his extraordinary figure, no one glanced a second time at the ungainly Westerner, as he walked with Mr. Seward through the streets. Rumors that he was in town caused unprecedented sales of the *Evening Star*, which was out in the early afternoon with a description of his arrival at Willard's. Many people still remained skeptical. Republicans declared that the story was a dodge to keep them from the cars; and, mounting on top of a big furniture wagon laden with their banners, they proceeded to decorate their wigwam to impress Mr. Lincoln on his way from the depot. Later, "squads of the incredulous" surged through the rain to meet the special train, and the Fourteenth Street entrance to Willard's was surrounded. The crowds were rewarded by the sight of the weary Presidential party, oppressed by the gloom of the Maryland threats and Lincoln's sudden departure. Mrs. Lincoln had become hysterical over the separation from her husband. Colonel Edwin Sumner was a very angry old soldier, thwarted in the performance of his duty; and Colonel Ellsworth had expected their train to be mobbed in Baltimore. To counteract the depression, Bob Lincoln had led the party in a rendition of "The Star-Spangled Banner," as the cars crossed the Maryland line.

Leaning on the arm of Mr. Seward, Mrs. Lincoln entered the hotel, and was received in the thronged hallway by the Messrs. Willard in person. Upstairs, the President-elect sprawled in an armchair with a beaming face, while his two spoiled boys, Willie and Tad, climbed over him. He had had a busy afternoon, for the tide of visitors had already set toward Parlor Number 6. General Scott, whom he had missed in the morning, had returned his call in full uniform, sweeping his instep with the yellow plumes of his hat as he bowed. Headed by Stephen A. Douglas, the Illinois senators and congressmen had paid their respects. Old Francis P. Blair had come in with his hatchet-faced son, Montgomery, who was hoping to be appointed Postmaster General. The Blair family, father and two sons, were a power in the Republican party. They were a fighting clan from the border slave States, Democrats who had swung into opposition to slavery. The elder Blair, formerly a famous newspaper editor and a member of Jackson's Kitchen Cabinet, was an acute politician who still wielded great influence behind the scenes. Frank, junior, former congressman, recently re-elected, was a Free-Soil leader in Missouri; while Montgomery, like his father, now lived and intrigued in Maryland. Mr. Lincoln reposed great confidence in the senior Blair, and submitted to him, as well as to his chief adviser, Mr. Seward, a copy of his inaugural address.

Soon after his family's arrival, Lincoln was informed that the delegates to the Peace Conference desired to wait on him. He appointed the hour of nine to receive them, and drove off to a seven o'clock dinner at Seward's, where the Vice-President-elect, Senator Hannibal Hamlin of Maine, was also present. The long parlor hall at Willard's was lined with people when he returned; and shaking hands on both sides, he was so interested, said the *New York Herald*, that he forgot to remove his shiny new silk hat.

Ex-President Tyler and the Honorable Salmon P. Chase of Ohio led the Peace delegates up the stairs to Parlor Number 6. Chase was as pompous as General Scott, and very nearly as antipathetic to slavery as Senator Sumner. Re-elected to the Senate after serving as governor of his State, he was the most prominent of the former Democrats in the Republican party. His rumored appointment to the Cabinet would satisfy the radicals, who were disgruntled with the conciliatory Seward. He was tall, imposing and handsome, with the noble brow of a statesman. As he stood beside Mr. Lincoln, presenting the delegates, it was Chase who looked the part of President of the United States, and Chase would have been the first to think so.

Curious and prejudiced, Easterners and men from the border slave States scrutinized the phenomenon from the prairies. The long, lean, sallow frontier lawyer was a shock to people who were unused to the Western type; and his homely phrases and mispronunciations grated on Eastern ears. It was impossible that Lincoln should have inspired confidence or admiration; but some saw shrewdness, honesty and even a natural dignity in his face. Its ugliness was partially redeemed by his eyes, though their dreamy, meditative expression did not bespeak either firmness or force. He had a pleasant, kindly smile, and was thought to be not so ill-favored and hard-looking as his pictures represented him. Chatting informally with the delegates, remembering like a good politician their claims to fame and their middle initials, Lincoln made on the whole a not unfavorable impression.

The next day was Sunday, and Mr. Lincoln attended St. John's Church with Mr. Seward. Under the same guidance he visited the Senate and the House on Monday, and also the Supreme Court; but almost his entire time during the pre-inauguration week was spent in the big, crowded parlor of the hotel suite. Willard's held an unprecedented collection of men notable in public affairs, civil, military and naval. Republican leaders were there to confer, and delegations to press their advice on the administration's policies and Cabinet appointments. The Peace Conference was winding up its session with resolutions that satisfied no one, and border slave State men came to beseech guarantees that there would be no Federal coercion. Past the new President, from early morning until late at night, streamed minor politicians, place seekers, editors, reporters and handshakers. He was still unknown to the passer-by in the street, but hundreds became familiar with his features in Parlor Number 6. Mr. Lincoln assured Mayor Berret and the Common Council of Washington, who called to tender a welcome, that he had kindly feelings toward them, and meant to treat them as neighbors. It was, he remarked, the first time since the present phase of politics that he had said anything publicly in a region where slavery existed. Again, in responding to a serenade by the Washington Republicans, Mr. Lincoln voiced his awareness of his peculiar situation in the capital city, whose population was almost entirely opposed to him in politics.

The new President had formed an inflexible determination to entertain no compromise on the extension of slavery, and to defend the Constitution, as his oath of office required. None of the multitude who, since his departure from Springfield, had casually met him or heard his speeches had been able to discern either his decision or his anxiety. In his public utterances, Mr. Lincoln had depreciated the seriousness of the crisis. His placid manner, the "jocular freedom" of his conversation, and his unceasing fund of anecdote gave the impression that he had but a shallow and provincial understanding of national affairs. Among the Republican leaders, none was more puzzled than Senator Charles Sumner. Mr. Lincoln had an amiable weakness for measuring heights with other tall men, and outraged Sumner's dignity by making the proposal to him. Sumner excused himself with the heavy pleasantry that it was a time for uniting their fronts and not their backs. The Washington Republican, Major French, who was chief marshal of the inauguration parade, declared that they all liked Old Abe, but wished "he would leave off making *little* speeches. He has not the gift of language," French went on, "though he may have of *western gab*."

With the appointment of Montgomery Blair as Postmaster General, the slate of Lincoln's Cabinet was complete. At the head of his advisers was Mr. Seward, balanced by the radical Mr. Chase, who was to be Secretary of the Treasury. Two selections had been virtually forced on Lincoln by bargains which his managers had made at the Republican convention which had nominated him. One was Caleb B. Smith of Indiana, the Secretary of the Interior, a prosaic-looking, lisping conservative. The other was Senator Simon Cameron of Pennsylvania, whom Mr. Lincoln had with much reluctance appointed Secretary of War. Cameron was the Republican leader in his own State, but his reputation for unscrupulous political practices shed no luster on the new Cabinet.

As a sop to New England, Mr. Lincoln had made Gideon Welles of Connecticut his Secretary of the Navy. He was tall and "venerably insignificant," with a flowing beard and a huge gray wig. Welles had been a newspaperman in Hartford, and did not know the stem from the stern of a ship, but he was an industrious and capable administrator. He was also very irritable, and those who undervalued him did not know that, with a pen dipped in gall, he kept a diary. In one respect, Welles was unique among the Cabinet members—he did not think himself a better man than the President.

The Attorney General, Mr. Edward Bates of Missouri, had been one of Mr. Lincoln's earliest selections. He was a former slaveholder, worthy, legalistic and reverential of the Constitution. The choice of the Marylander, Montgomery Blair, gave Lincoln two advisers from the border slave States. Blair was courageous, and had won abolitionist acclaim by acting as counsel for the slave, Dred Scott. However, while scarcely anyone could object to polite old Mr. Bates, the pinched and vindictive Montgomery had a host of enemies. He was detested by the radical wing of the Republicans, and disliked as an uncompromising and warmongering extremist by the moderates. He had plenty of secessionist relatives, and voiced his Union sympathies with challenge and defiance.

With the notable exception of sympathy with disunion, the President's advisers represented, like Mr. Chandlee's cockades, all shades of political sentiment. Four members of the Cabinet, Seward, Chase, Cameron and Bates, had been candidates for the Presidential nomination at the Republican convention, and for the first two the failure to secure it had been a rankling disappointment. It was not to be expected that these dissentient personalities should work together in harmony. Mr. Seward could foresee that it would be difficult to act as premier of the composite council. He sent in a last-minute resignation just before Mr. Lincoln's inauguration, but withdrew it in response to the President's firm request.

In spite of the pall of the national crisis, the President's party was not wanting in high spirits. Besides his oldest boy, Bob, a Harvard student of eighteen, it included three young men who had been law students in Mr. Lincoln's Springfield office, and he was on warmly affectionate terms with them all. John George Nicolay, capable, Teutonic, nearly thirty, was the private secretary. John Hay, the assistant secretary, was a clever, flippant, good-looking college graduate of twenty-two. The handsome little Zouave, Ellsworth, was not much older, and he had a magnetic boyish enthusiasm. He had worked out a plan for reforming the State militia system, and bringing it under Federal control; and he was hoping to be appointed to the chief clerkship of the War Department. Bob Lincoln had been educated at Phillips Exeter, and showed in speech and manner that he had enjoyed more advantages than his father. As a pendant to the campaign publicity for the rail splitter, Bob had been facetiously nicknamed "The Prince of Rails." Some people inevitably called him proud and affected, but he conducted himself sensibly during a prolonged ordeal of popular attention and flattery.

Nicolay thought that the bevy of ladies in the parlors made it seem like having a party every night. He was, however, occupied with the President's correspondence, while Ellsworth, though schoolgirls sighed over his black curls, was a moralist and a Spartan. John Hay and Bob Lincoln were the merry, carefree members of the party. Hay made a new friend in Henry Adams, another private secretary, who would soon be going off with his father to the Court of St. James's. In the evening, Bob sometimes tarried downstairs in the smoking room, listening to the music of the harpists and enjoying a cigar with the other men. Some disunionists, on one of these occasions, induced the musicians to play "Dixie," which Secessia had adopted as its national air; but the harpists quickly followed it with "Hail, Columbia." In Parlor Number 6, Mrs. Lincoln, attended by her sister, Mrs. Ninian Edwards, her two nieces and her cousin, Mrs. Grimsley, received a deferential throng in her stylish Springfield toilettes. The President's Kentucky wife was arrogantly pleased with her position, fancied herself of great importance in politics, and referred in company to Mr. Seward as a "dirty abolition sneak."

Every night, the new squads of militia were drilling in the open spaces of the city, but the fears of revolution had largely subsided. Many patriotic men thought that it would be ill-advised to make an ostentatious display of armed force at the inauguration. The threats to his own life, however, had convinced General Scott that the ceremony was a hazardous undertaking, and he prepared to guard the incoming President with every soldier in the city. He now had, exclusive of the marines at the Navy Yard, six hundred and fifty-three regulars at his command. He thought of Mr. Lincoln's drive from Willard's to the Capitol as a movement, and he planned to place a picked body of men, the sappers and miners from West Point, in the van. A squadron of District cavalry would ride on either side of the Presidential carriage, and infantry companies of militia would march in its rear. Squads of riflemen and a small number of United States cavalry were ordered to posts along the route. The main force of the regulars, headed by Scott in his coupé, was assigned to "flanking the movement" in F Street.

While one battery of artillery was situated near the Treasury building, two were stationed outside the north entrance to the Capitol grounds. At this latter important point, Scott himself proposed to remain during the ceremonies, and there, too, would be Major-General John E. Wool, the thin little old man who was the commander of the Department of the East.

On Saturday and Sunday, strangers, almost all men, were pouring into town in anticipation of the ceremonies on Monday. Baltimore plugs, tippling and shrieking their rallying cries, were but a noisy minority in the swelling influx of the Republicans. There were dignitaries among them—twenty-seven governors and ex-governors of States, and many former senators and congressmen—and there were also militia and civic organizations. Largest by far in number, however, were the plain men of the West—a type only recently familiar to Washington—who dodged forlornly about the city in travel-stained clothes, looking for a place to sleep. Hotel rooms were all preempted. The best accommodation to be had was a cot or a mattress in a parlor. The newcomers were not a spendthrift lot. Bonifaces noted that they were a cold-water army. Hack drivers and porters complained that they were given to walking and carrying their own carpetbags, reluctant to part with a quarter-dollar.

Sunday, with its roving crowds, did not seem like the Sabbath. In the morning, there was a rush to Fourteenth Street to see the President-elect depart for church. So many people congregated around the ladies' entrance to Willard's that police had difficulty in clearing a passage on the sidewalk. All tall men of only moderately good looks, said the tactful *Star,* were closely scanned, as they passed from the hotel. Uncle Abe, however, did not appear, and the sight-seers had to content themselves with the spectacle of the pugilist, John Morrissey, promenading in a stovepipe hat.

Willard's dined fifteen hundred on Sunday, and a thousand feasted at the National. In the evening, laborers were industriously scraping the entire width of the Avenue between the Capitol and the White House, a herculean assignment which they had been unable to finish on Saturday night. The wind whirled the thick dust into clouds, and, though there was now a water supply sufficient for the purpose, the city had no system for dampening the streets. At dusk, crowds of manifestly secular intention were walking toward the lighted Capitol, where the Senate flag was flying. Hundreds of homeless visitors slept on market stalls and lumber piles, or strolled about the streets all night. Orderlies and cavalry platoons rode through the dark. A rumor had reached Scott's headquarters that an attempt would be made to blow up the platform which had been erected at the east portico of the Capitol. A guard was placed under the floor of the stand, and at daybreak a battalion of District troops marched to form a semicircle around the foot of the steps.

The city was early astir with unaccommodated strangers, assembling to perform their toilets at the public fountains. People began to turn out for the parade. Boys screamed the morning newspapers, and there were lithographs of Uncle Abe's features, damp from the press. The sidewalks of the Avenue were filled from building line to curbstone. In the crush, Newton Leonard, aged four, with blue eyes and a full face, dressed in a plaid suit with tight knees, strayed from his parents, and was advertised for next day in the *National Intelligencer*.

In spite of bright sunshine, it was a raw, disagreeable day. Whipped by the gusty wind, the people stood waiting, while soldiers and District militia formed in line. It was not a festive gathering. The city seemed anxious and depressed. Few buildings had been decorated in honor of the inauguration. Some houses along the route had closed shutters, and many unfriendly faces frowned from balconies and windows. The story was being whispered that, if Mr. Lincoln were inducted into office in good order, a company of Virginia horsemen intended to dash across the Long Bridge and take the President captive at the Union Ball that evening.

Among the groups of spectators on the housetops, militiamen with loaded rifles moved to their posts overlooking the Avenue. It was a little after twelve when the word to present arms was passed along the line of cavalry on Fourteenth Street and infantry on the Avenue in front of Willard's. A band struck up "Hail to the Chief," and Mr. Buchanan and Mr. Lincoln emerged arm in arm from the side door of the hotel, and took their seats in an open barouche. In an hour, an Old Public Functionary would be free of a position which had covered him with ignominy and scorn. The Westerner at his side would be the man to trip over the obstacle of Fort Sumter, to guide, under the blows of hatred, an unruly country from which seven States had withdrawn. Mr. Buchanan sat in silence, as the barouche rolled toward the Capitol. His withered face was pale above his white cravat. Only four years before, he had taken this drive through cheering lanes of people, moving between two pretty floats, the Goddess of Liberty on her pedestal and a full-rigged ship, manned by sailors from the Navy Yard. Now, compact and short, the inaugural procession advanced like a military expedition, fearful of attack. There was little enthusiasm on the packed sidewalks. The spectators could scarcely see the new President through the escort of dancing cavalry. Colonel Stone, riding alongside, was digging his mount with his spurs, and he thought that he succeeded in making the militiamen's horses so uneasy that it would have been hard for even a good shot to take aim at the occupants of the carriage.

One hundred mounted marshals, with their trappings of orange, pink and blue, did their utmost to give the parade a garish air of holiday; but, after the disciplined ranks of the regulars and the sizable guard of militia, the civic procession looked straggling and insignificant. There were five hundred Washington Republicans in line, and a few delegations from the States. Thirty-four girls rode in a triumphal car, and were all later kissed by Mr. Lincoln. The *Star* made fun of the pegged boots of the New Englanders, cracking like air guns in the pauses of the Marine Band. No other startling sounds disturbed the progress on the Avenue. The rowdies had foregathered in the liquor shops. A few drunken men tried to obstruct the march of the soldiers, and one of them shouted insults at a delegation of Republicans from Virginia, and proposed three cheers for the Southern Confederacy. In the eastern park of the Capitol, a little man with red whiskers sat high in a tree and addressed the crowd with oratorical flourishes. These were, however, minor disturbances, soon silenced by the police. Chief Marshal French, after a long day on horseback, would be exultant over the perfect success of his arrangements.

The official party entered the Capitol by the north door, through a passage enclosed by a high, boarded fence, guarded by marines. While the ceremonies took place in the Senate Chamber, and Vice-President Hamlin and a few senators were sworn in, the multitude silently waited in the eastern park. They saw the spreading structure of the Capitol, with its unfinished dome surmounted by gaunt derricks braced with ropes of steel. The model of the statue of Armed Freedom, destined for its apex, stood in the grass among the littered and ruinous marbles. In every window of the stark new wings, two riflemen were posted; and Colonel Stone, looking from one of the windows, was satisfied that they perfectly flanked the steps. At last, the door opened, and the dignitaries took their places on the platform, over the heads of the fifty armed men concealed beneath it.

Silver-haired and eloquent, Mr. Lincoln's old friend, Senator Edward D. Baker of Oregon, stepped forward to introduce the new President. There was a faint ripple of cheers, as Lincoln made his way to the rickety little table provided for his address. Burdened with his gold-headed cane and glossy silk hat, he paused in embarrassment. As he laid his cane under the table, Senator Douglas smilingly reached out his hand for the hat. All the people could see Douglas, seated at the front of the platform, holding Lincoln's hat as a public profession of faith in a united country. In the background, Senator Wigfall of Texas leaned with folded arms against the Capitol doorway, watching the inaugural scene with contempt on his fierce, scarred face.

In a resonant, high-pitched voice, trained in the open-air meetings of the West, Mr. Lincoln began to speak. While his audience stood hushed in a painful silence, a tall man with a shrewd, impassive countenance detached himself from the crowd. Like one whom much familiarity backstage has robbed of interest in the play, Mr. Thurlow Weed of Albany turned his back on Mr. Lincoln, and wandered from the Capitol park. Perhaps he was too grieved to stay and see the sad-faced Westerner in the place where he had dreamed and schemed to put a subtle, smiling man. Mr. Weed was the most skillful political manager of his day, but he had failed in his fondest ambition, to manipulate the nomination of Seward by the Republican party.

As he walked north on Capitol Hill, Mr. Weed came upon two batteries of light artillery. Near one of them, General Scott drooped in splendid decay. Beside the other was General Wool, prim and perpendicular, in his high, choking collar. Like Scott, he bore in his stiffening body the scars of 1812. Mr. Weed started forward. In 1812, this cynical politician had been a drummer boy. Nearly half a century before, he had seen the two old generals, one so fat and the other so thin, as dashing, buoyant young officers. He hastened to present himself to them, and respectfully shake their hands.

Behind him, Mr. Lincoln's voice rang out, across the unenthusiastic multitude, across the sundered nation. "We are not enemies, but friends. . . . Though passion may have strained, it must not break our bonds of affection." The voice ceased. There was the noise of applause. Chief Justice Taney tottered forward, a cadaver in black silk. The old regime and the new faced each other, and a Bible lay between them, a pretty book, gilt-clasped and bound in cinnamon velvet. Mr. Lincoln solemnly swore to defend the Constitution of the United States.

There was a thundering salute from the batteries. Mr. Weed had been deeply moved by his chance encounter with the two commanders. He did not remember De Tocqueville's warning, that the army of a democracy tends to become weakened by a burden of old and unfit officers. Effulgent with that sentimentality to which the corrupt are prone, he gazed with veneration on the heroes of his boyhood; and failed to see in the antique tableau on Capitol Hill a presentation of the Union's unpreparedness for long and bloody war.

"Colonel J. C. Cremony Leading a Fight Against the Apaches"
by E. E. Narjot

HELEN HUNT JACKSON

A Century of Dishonor

(1881)

A Century of Dishonor was written to repel the public: 457 pages of a story in which, as Helen Hunt Jackson said, "neither time nor place makes any difference in the main facts," an unrelieved account of gross maltreatment of the Indians by every state in which a tribe had lived and by the federal government. Nor was Mrs. Jackson content merely to *write* of the Indians' woes. She sent a copy of her book to every member of Congress, and got herself appointed to a commission to investigate the needs of the Mission Indians of California. When the government refused to act on the commission's findings, she went back to writing, this time attacking congressional policy in a novel, Ramona, probably her best book.

Mrs. Jackson's sympathetic view of Indian life was not wholly new. She followed the trail blazed by several anthropologists, notably Henry Rowe Schoolcraft, Lewis Henry Morgan, and John Wesley Powell, who had all made important contributions to a more accurate assessment of the Indian and his culture. But A Century of Dishonor and Ramona brought these views to a public accustomed to the harsher picture of men like Theodore Roosevelt. He saw Mrs. Jackson's book as a brief addressed to "a large class of amiable but maudlin fanatics" seduced by "the high character of the author and her excellent literary work in other directions." The tradition of sentimental regard for the Indians continued unbroken after A Century of Dishonor, and even official policy, reflecting the diminution of the Indian threat, softened as the nineteenth century ended. But the Indian problem, with its background in white racism, still remained.

I

There are within the limits of the United States between two hundred and fifty and three hundred thousand Indians, exclusive of those in Alaska. The names of the different tribes and bands, as entered in the statistical tables of the Indian Office Reports, number nearly three hundred. One of the most careful estimates which has been made of their numbers and localities gives them as follows: "In Minnesota and States east of the Mississippi, about 32,500; in Nebraska, Kansas, and the Indian Territory, 70,650; in the Territories of Dakota, Montana, Wyoming, and Idaho, 65,000; in Nevada and the Territories of Colorado, New Mexico, Utah, and Arizona, 84,000; and on the Pacific slope, 48,000."

Of these, 130,000 are self-supporting on their own reservations, "receiving nothing from the Government except interest on their own moneys, or annuities granted them in consideration of the cession of their lands to the United States."*

This fact alone would seem sufficient to dispose forever of the accusation, so persistently brought against the Indian, that he will not work.

Of the remainder, 84,000 are partially supported by the Government—the interest money due them and their annuities, as provided by treaty, being inadequate to their subsistence on the reservations where they are confined. In many cases, however, these Indians furnish a large part of their support—the White River Utes, for instance, who are reported by the Indian Bureau as getting sixty-six per cent. of their living by "root-digging, hunting, and fishing;" the Squaxin band, in Washington Territory, as earning seventy-five per cent., and the Chippewas of Lake Superior as earning fifty per cent. in the same way. These facts also would seem to dispose of the accusation that the Indian will not work.

There are about 55,000 who never visit an agency, over whom the Government does not pretend to have either control or care. These 55,000 "subsist by hunting, fishing, on roots, nuts, berries, etc., and by begging and stealing;" and this also seems to dispose of the accusation that the Indian will not "work for a living." There remains a small portion, about 31,000, that are entirely subsisted by the Government.

There is not among these three hundred bands of Indians one which has not suffered cruelly at the hands either of the Government or of white settlers. The poorer, the more insignificant, the more helpless the band, the more certain the cruelty and outrage to which they have been subjected. This is especially true of the bands on the Pacific slope. These Indians found themselves of a sudden sur-

*Annual Report of Indian Commissioner for 1872.

rounded by and caught up in the great influx of gold-seeking settlers, as helpless creatures on a shore are caught up in a tidal wave. There was not time for the Government to make treaties; not even time for communities to make laws. The tale of the wrongs, the oppressions, the murders of the Pacific-slope Indians in the last thirty years would be a volume by itself, and is too monstrous to be believed.

It makes little difference, however, where one opens the record of the history of the Indians; every page and every year has its dark stain. The story of one tribe is the story of all, varied only by differences of time and place; but neither time nor place makes any difference in the main facts. Colorado is as greedy and unjust in 1880 as was Georgia in 1830, and Ohio in 1795; and the United States Government breaks promises now as deftly as then, and with an added ingenuity from long practice.

One of its strongest supports in so doing is the wide-spread sentiment among the people of dislike to the Indian, of impatience with his presence as a "barrier to civilization," and distrust of it as a possible danger. The old tales of the frontier life, with its horrors of Indian warfare, have gradually, by two or three generations' telling, produced in the average mind something like an hereditary instinct of unquestioning and unreasoning aversion which it is almost impossible to dislodge or soften.

There are hundreds of pages of unimpeachable testimony on the side of the Indian; but it goes for nothing, is set down as sentimentalism or partisanship, tossed aside and forgotten.

President after president has appointed commission after commission to inquire into and report upon Indian affairs, and to make suggestions as to the best methods of managing them. The reports are filled with eloquent statements of wrongs done to the Indians, of perfidies on the part of the Government; they counsel, as earnestly as words can, a trial of the simple and unperplexing expedients of telling truth, keeping promises, making fair bargains, dealing justly in all ways and all things. These reports are bound up with the Government's Annual Reports, and that is the end of them. It would probably be no exaggeration to say that not one American citizen out of ten thousand ever sees them or knows that they exist, and yet any one of them, circulated throughout the country, read by the right-thinking, right-feeling men and women of this land, would be of itself a "campaign document" that would initiate a revolution which would not subside until the Indians' wrongs were, so far as is now left possible, righted.

In 1869 President Grant appointed a commission of nine men, representing the influence and philanthropy of six leading States, to visit the different Indian reservations, and to "examine all matters appertaining to Indian affairs."

In the report of this commission are such paragraphs as the following: "To assert that 'the Indian will not work' is as true as it would be to say that the white man will not work.

"Why should the Indian be expected to plant corn, fence lands, build houses, or do anything but get food from day to day, when experience has taught him that the product of his labor will be seized by the white man to-morrow? The most industrious white man would become a drone under similar circumstances. Nevertheless, many of the Indians" (the commissioners might more forcibly have said 130,000 of the Indians) "are already at work, and furnish ample refutation of the assertion that 'the Indian will not work.' There is no escape from the inexorable logic of facts.

"The history of the Government connections with the Indians is a shameful record of broken treaties and unfulfilled promises. The history of the border white man's connection with the Indians is a sickening record of murder, outrage, robbery, and wrongs committed by the former, as the rule, and occasional savage outbreaks and unspeakably barbarous deeds of retaliation by the latter, as the exception.

"Taught by the Government that they had rights entitled to respect, when those rights have been assailed by the rapacity of the white man, the arm which should have been raised to protect them has ever been ready to sustain the aggressor.

"The testimony of some of the highest military officers of the United States is on record to the effect that, in our Indian wars, almost without exception, the first aggressions have been made by the white man; and the assertion is supported by every civilian of reputation who has studied the subject. In addition to the class of robbers and outlaws who find impunity in their nefarious pursuits on the frontiers, there is a large class of professedly reputable men who use every means in their power to bring on Indian wars for the sake of the profit to be realized from the presence of troops and the expenditure of Government funds in their midst. They proclaim death to the Indians at all times in words and publications, making no distinction between the innocent and the guilty. They irate the lowest class of men to the perpetration of the darkest deeds against their victims, and as judges and jurymen shield them from the justice due to their crimes. Every crime committed by a white man against an Indian is concealed or palliated. Every offence committed by an Indian against a white man is borne on the wings of the post or the telegraph to the remotest corner of the land, clothed with all the horrors which the reality or imagination can throw around it. Against such influences as these the people of the United States need to be warned."

To assume that it would be easy, or by any one sudden stroke of legislative policy possible, to undo the mischief and hurt of the long past, set the Indian policy of the country right for the future, and make the Indians at once safe and happy, is the blunder of a hasty and uninformed judgment. The notion which seems to be growing more prevalent, that simply to make all Indians at once citizens of the United States would be a sovereign and instantaneous panacea for all their ills and all the Government's perplexities, is a very inconsiderate one. To administer complete citizenship of a sudden, all round, to all Indians, barbarous and civilized alike, would be as grotesque a blunder as to dose them all round with any one medicine, irrespective of the symptoms and needs of their diseases. It would kill more than it would cure. Nevertheless, it is true, as was well stated by one of the superintendents of Indian Affairs in 1857, that, "so long as they are not citizens of the United States, their rights of property must remain insecure against invasion. The doors of the federal tribunals being barred against them while wards and dependents, they can only partially exercise the rights of free government, or give to those who make, execute, and construe the few laws they are allowed to enact, dignity sufficient to make them respectable. While they continue individually to gather the crumbs that fall from the table of the United States, idleness, improvidence, and indebtedness will be the rule, and industry, thrift, and freedom from debt the exception. The utter absence of individual title to particular lands deprives every one among them of the chief incentive to labor and exertion—the very mainspring on which the prosperity of a people depends."

All judicious plans and measures for their safety and salvation must embody provisions for their becoming citizens as fast as they are fit, and must protect them till then in every right and particular in which our laws protect other "persons" who are not citizens.

There is a disposition in a certain class of minds to be impatient with any protestation against wrong which is unaccompanied or unprepared with a quick and exact scheme of remedy. This is illogical. When pioneers in a new country find a tract of poisonous and swampy wilderness to be reclaimed, they do not withhold their hands from fire and axe till they see clearly which way roads should run, where good water will spring, and what crops will best grow on the redeemed land. They first clear the swamp. So with this poisonous and baffling part of the domain of our national affairs—let us first "clear the swamp."

However great perplexity and difficulty there may be in the details of any and every plan possible for doing at this late day anything like justice to the Indian, however hard it may be for good statesmen and good men to agree upon the things that ought to be done, there certainly is, or ought to be, no perplexity whatever, no difficulty whatever, in agreeing upon certain things that ought not to be done, and which must cease to be done before the first steps can be taken toward righting the wrongs, curing the ills, and wiping out the disgrace to us of the present condition of our Indians.

Cheating, robbing, breaking promises—these three are clearly things which must cease to be done. One more thing, also, and that is the refusal of the protection of the law to the Indian's rights of property, "of life, liberty, and the pursuit of happiness."

When these four things have ceased to be done, time, statesmanship, philanthropy, and Christianity can slowly and surely do the rest. Till these four things have ceased to be done, statesmanship and philanthropy alike must work in vain, and even Christianity can reap but small harvest.

* * *

II

[*Miss Jackson offers as evidence of Indian maltreatment by whites this letter from an army officer, stationed at Camp Grant in Arizona Territory to his commanding officer.*]

"Camp Grant, Arizona Territory, May 17th, 1871.

"DEAR COLONEL,—Thanks for your kind letter of last week. If I could see you and have a long talk, and answer all your questions, I could come nearer giving you a clear idea of the history of the Indians at this post than by any written account. Having had them constantly under my observation for nearly three months, and the care of them constantly on my mind, certain things have become so much a matter of certainty to me that I am liable to forget the amount of evidence necessary to convince even the most unprejudiced mind that has not been brought in contact with them. I will, however, try and give you a connected account, and if it proves not sufficiently full in detail, you may be sure all its positive statements will be sustained by the testimony of all competent judges who have been at this post and cognizant of the facts.

"Sometime in February a party of five old women came in under a flag of truce, with a letter from Colonel Greene, saying they were in search of a boy, the son of one of the number taken prisoner near Salt River some months before. This boy had been well cared for, and had become attached to his new mode of life, and did not wish to return. The party were kindly treated, rationed while here, and after two days went away, asking permission to return. They came in about eight days, I think, with a still larger number, with some articles for sale, to purchase manta, as they were nearly naked. Before going away they said a young chief would like to come in with a party and have a talk. This I encouraged, and in a few days he came with about twenty-five of his band. He stated in brief that he was chief of a band of about one hundred and fifty of what were originally the Aravapa Apaches; that he wanted peace; that he and his people had no home, and could make none, as they were at all times apprehensive of the approach of the cavalry. I told him he should go to the White Mountains. He said, 'That is not our country, neither are they our people. We are at peace with them, but never have mixed with them. Our fathers and their fathers before them have lived in these mountains, and have raised corn in this valley. We are taught to make mescal, our principal article of food, and in summer and winter here we have a never-failing supply. At the White Mountains there is none, and without it now we get sick. Some of our people have been in at Goodwin, and for a short time at the White Mountains; but they are not contented, and they all say, "Let us go to the Aravapa and make a final peace, and never break it."'

"I told him I had no authority to make any treaty with him, or to promise him that he would be allowed a permanent home here, but that he could bring in his band, and I would feed them, and report his wishes to the Department commander. In the mean time runners had been in from two other small bands, asking the same privileges and giving the same reasons. I made the same reply to all, and by about the 11th of March I had over three hundred here. I wrote a detailed account of the whole matter, and sent it by express to Department Head-quarters, asking for instructions, having only the general policy of the Government in such cases for my guidance. After waiting more than six weeks my letter was returned to me without comment, except calling my attention to the fact that it was not briefed properly. At first I put them in camp, about half a mile from the post, and counted them, and issued their rations every second day. The number steadily increased until it reached the number of five hundred and ten.

"Knowing, as I did, that the responsibility of the whole movement rested with me, and that, in case of any loss to the Government coming of it, I should be the sufferer, I kept them continually under my observation till I came not only to know the faces of the men, but of the women and children. They were nearly naked, and needed everything in the way of clothing. I stopped the Indians from bringing hay, that I might buy of these. I arranged a system of tickets with which to pay them and encourage them; and to be sure that they were properly treated, I personally attended to the weighing. I also made inquiries as to the kind of goods sold them, and prices. This proved a perfect success; not only the women and children engaged in the work, but the men. The amount furnished by them in about two months was nearly 300,000 pounds.

"During this time many small parties had been out with passes for a certain number of days to burn mescal. These parties were always mostly women, and I made myself sure by noting the size of the party, and from the amount of mescal brought in, that no treachery was intended. From the first I was determined to know not only all they did, but their hopes and intentions. For this purpose I spent hours each day with them in explaining to them the relations they should sustain to the Government, and their prospects for the future in case of either obedience or disobedience. I got from them in return much of their habits of thought and rules of action. I made it a point to tell them all they wished to know, and in the plainest and most positive manner. They were readily obedient, and remarkably quick of comprehension. They were happy and contented, and took every opportunity to show it. They had sent out runners to two other bands which were connected with them by intermarriages, and had received promises from them that they would come in and join them. I am confident, from all I have been able to learn, that but for this unlooked-for butchery, by this time we would have had one thousand persons, and at least two hundred and fifty able-bodied men. As their number increased and the weather grew warmer, they asked and obtained permission to move farther up the Aravapa to higher ground and plenty of water, and opposite to the ground they were proposing to plant. They were rationed every third day. Captain Stanwood arrived about the first of April, and took command of the post. He had received, while *en route,* verbal instructions from General Stoneman to recognize and feed any Indians he might find at the post as prisoners of war. After he had carefully inspected all things pertaining to their conduct and treatment, he concluded to make no changes, but had become so well satisfied of the integrity of their intentions that he left on the 24th with his whole troop for a long scout in the lower part of the Territory. The ranchmen in this vicinity were friendly and kind to them, and felt perfectly secure, and had agreed with me to employ them at a fair rate of pay to harvest their barley. The Indians seemed to have lost their characteristic anxiety to purchase ammunition, and had, in many instances, sold their best bows and arrows. I made frequent visits to their camp, and if any were absent from count, made it my business to know why.

"Such was the condition of things up to the morning of the 30th of April. They had so won on me that, from my first idea of treating them justly and honestly, as an officer of the army, I had come to feel a strong personal interest in helping to show them the way to a higher civilization. I had come to feel respect for men who, ignorant and naked, were still ashamed to lie or steal; and for women who would work cheerfully like slaves to clothe themselves and children, but, untaught, held their virtue above price. Aware of the lies industriously circulated by the puerile press of the country, I was content to know I had positive proof they were so.

"I had ceased to have any fears of their leaving here, and only dreaded for them that they might be at any time ordered to do so.

They frequently expressed anxiety to hear from the general, that they might have confidence to build for themselves better houses; but would always say, 'You know what we want, and if you can't see him you can write, and do for us what you can.' It is possible that, during this time, individuals from here had visited other bands; but that any number had ever been out to assist in any marauding expedition I know is false. On the morning of April 30th I was at breakfast at 7.30 o'clock, when a despatch was brought to me by a sergeant of Company P, 21st Infantry, from Captain Penn, commanding Camp Lowell, informing me that a large party had left Tucson on the 28th with the avowed purpose of killing all the Indians at this post. I immediately sent the two interpreters, mounted, to the Indian camp, with orders to tell the chiefs the exact state of things, and for them to bring their entire party inside the post. As I had no cavalry, and but about fifty infantry (all recruits), and no other officer, I could not leave the post to go to their defence. My messengers returned in about an hour with intelligence that they could find no living Indians.

"Their camp was burning, and the ground strewed with their dead and mutilated women and children. I immediately mounted a party of about twenty soldiers and citizens, and sent them with the post surgeon with a wagon to bring in the wounded, if any could be found. The party returned late in the afternoon, having found no wounded, and without having been able to communicate with any of the survivors. Early the next morning I took a similar party with spades and shovels, and went out and buried the dead immediately in and about the camp. I had, the day before, offered the interpreters, or any one who would do so, $100 to go to the mountains and communicate with them, and convince them that no officer or soldier of the United States Government had been concerned in the vile transaction; and, failing in this, I thought the act of caring for their dead would be an evidence to them of our sympathy, at least, and the conjecture proved correct; for while we were at the work, many of them came to the spot and indulged in expressions of grief too wild and terrible to be described.

"That evening they began to come in from all directions, singly and in small parties, so changed as hardly to be recognizable in the forty-eight hours during which they had neither eaten nor slept. Many of the men, whose families had all been killed, when I spoke to them and expressed sympathy for them, were obliged to turn away, unable to speak, and too proud to show their grief. The women whose children had been killed or stolen were convulsed with grief, and looked to me appealingly, as if I were their last hope on earth. Children, who two days before had been full of frolic, kept at a distance, expressing wondering horror.

"I did what I could: I fed them, talked to them, and listened patiently to their accounts. I sent horses to the mountains to bring in two badly wounded women, one shot through the left leg, one with an arm shattered. These were attended to, and are doing well, and will recover.

"Their camp was surrounded and attacked at daybreak. So sudden and unexpected was it, that I found a number of women shot while asleep beside their bundles of hay, which they had collected to bring in on that morning. The wounded who were unable to get away had their brains beaten out with clubs or stones, while some were shot full of arrows after having been mortally wounded by gun-shots. The bodies were all stripped. Of the number buried, one was an old man, and one was a well-grown boy; all the rest women and children. Of the whole number killed and missing—about one hundred and twenty-five—only eight were men. It has been said that the men were not there: they were all there. On the 28th we counted one hundred and twenty-eight men, a small number being absent for mescal, all of whom have since been in. I have spent a good deal of time with them since the affair, and have been astonished at their continued unshaken faith in me, and their perfectly clear understanding of their misfortune. They say, 'We know there are a great many white men and Mexicans who do not wish us to live at peace. We know that the Papagos would never have come out against us at this time unless they had been persuaded to do so.' What they do not understand is, while they are at peace and are conscious of no wrong intent, that they should be murdered.

"One of the chiefs said: 'I no longer want to live; my women and children have been killed before my face, and I have been unable to defend them. Most Indians in my place would take a knife and cut their throats; but I will live to show these people that all they have done, and all they can do, shall not make me break faith with you so long as you will stand by us and defend us, in a language we know nothing of, to a great governor we never have and never shall see.'

"About their captives they say: 'Get them back for us. Our little boys will grow up slaves, and our girls, as soon as they are large enough, will be diseased prostitutes, to get money for whoever owns them. Our women work hard, and are good women, and they and our children have no diseases. Our dead you cannot bring to life; but those that are living we gave to you, and we look to you, who can write and talk and have soldiers, to get them back.'

"I assure you it is no easy task to convince them of my zeal when they see so little being done. I have pledged my word to them that I never would rest, day or night, until they should have justice, and just now I would as soon leave the army as to be ordered away from them, or be obliged to order them away from here. But you well know the difficulties in the way. You know that parties who would engage in murder like this could and would make statements and multiply affidavits without end in their justification. I know you will use your influence on the right side. I believe, with them, this may be made either a means of making good citizens of them and their children, or of driving them out to a hopeless war of extermination. They ask to be allowed to live here in their old homes, where nature supplies nearly all their wants. They ask for a fair and impartial trial of their faith, and they ask that all their captive children may be returned to them. Is their demand unreasonable?"

This letter was written to Colonel T. G. C. Lee., U.S.A., by Lieut. Royal E. Whitman, 3d U.S. Cavalry. It is published in the Report of the Board of Indian Commissioners for 1871. There is appended to it the following affidavit of the post surgeon at Camp Grant:

"On this 16th day of September, 1871, personally appeared Conant B. Brierley, who, being duly sworn according to law, deposeth and saith: 'I am acting-assistant surgeon, U.S.A., at Camp Grant, Arizona, where I arrived April 25th, 1871, and reported to the commanding officer for duty as medical officer. Some four hundred Apache Indians were at that time held as prisoners of war by the military stationed at Camp Grant, and during the period intervening between April 25th and 30th I saw the Indians every day. They seemed very well contented, and were busily employed in bringing in hay, which they sold for manta and such little articles as they desired outside the Government ration. April 29th Chiquita and some of the other chiefs were at the post, and asked for seeds and for some hoes, stating that they had ground cleared and ready for planting. They were told that the garden-seeds had been sent for, and would be up from Tucson in a few days. They then left, and I saw nothing more of them until after the killing.

"'Sunday morning I heard a rumor that the Indians had been attacked, and learned from Lieutenant Whitman that he had sent the two interpreters to the Indian camp to warn the Indians, and bring them down where they could be protected, if possible. The interpreters returned and stated that the attack had already been made and the Indians dispersed, and that the attacking party were returning.

"'Lieutenant Whitman then ordered me to go to the Indian camp to render medical assistance, and bring down any wounded I might find. I took twelve men and a wagon, and proceeded without delay to the scene of the murder. On my arrival I found that I should have but little use for the wagon or medicine. The work had been too thoroughly done. The camp had been fired, and the dead bodies of twenty-one women and children were lying scattered over the ground; those who had been wounded in the first instance had their brains beaten out with stones. Two of the squaws had been first ravished, and then shot dead. One infant of some two months was shot twice, and one leg nearly hacked off.*** I know from my own personal observations that, during the time the Indians were in, after my arrival, they were rationed every three days, and Indians absent had to be accounted for; their faces soon became familiar to me, and I could at once tell when any strange Indian came in.

"'And I furthermore state that I have been among nearly all the tribes on the Pacific coast, and that I have never seen any Indians who showed the intelligence, honesty, and desire to learn manifested by these Indians. I came among them greatly prejudiced against them; but, after being with them, I was compelled to admit that they were honest in their intentions, and really desired peace.

"'C. B. BRIERLEY,
"'Acting Assistant Surgeon, U.S.A.'"

This is not the only instance of cruel outrage committed by white men on the Apaches. In the Report of the Board of Indian Commissioners for 1871 is the following letter from one of the Arizona pioneers, Mr. J. H. Lyman, of Northampton, Mass. Mr. Lyman spent the years of 1840–'41 among the Apaches, and thus briefly relates an occurrence which took place at a time when they were friendly and cordial to all Americans going among them:

"The Indians were then, as now, hostile to the Mexicans of Sonora, and they were constantly making raids into the State and driving off the cattle. The Mexicans feared them, and were unable to meet them man to man. At that time American trappers found the beaver very abundant about the headwaters of the Gila River, among those rich mountain valleys where the Apaches had, and still have, their secure retreats. At the time I speak of there were two companies of trappers in that region. One of the companies, about seventeen men, was under a captain named Johnson. The other company consisted of thirty men, I think. I was trapping on another head of the Gila, several miles north. The valleys were full of Apaches, but all peaceful toward the white men, both Indians and whites visiting each other's camps constantly and fearlessly, with no thought of treachery or evil. Besides the Mexicans, the only enemies of the Apaches were the Piutes and Navajoes, in the north-west. But here in their fastnesses they felt safe from all foes.

"One day Johnson concluded to go down into Sonora on a spree, as was occasionally the way with mountain-men. He there saw the Governor of Sonora, who, knowing that he had the confidence of the Indians, offered him an ounce of gold for every Apache scalp he would bring him. The bargain was struck. Johnson procured a small mountain howitzer, and then, with supplies for his party, returned to his camp. Previous to entering it he loaded his howitzer with a quantity of bullets. On approaching the valley he was met by the Indians, who joyfully welcomed him back, and proceeded at once to prepare the usual feast. While they were boiling and roasting their venison and bear meat, and were gathered in a small group around the fire laughing, and chatting in anticipation of the pleasure they expected in entertaining their guests, Johnson told those of his party who had remained behind of the offer of the governor, and with such details of temptation as easily overcame any scruples such men might have.

"As they were all armed with rifles, which were always in hand day and night, together with pistols in belt, they needed no preparation. The howitzer, which the Indians might have supposed to be a small keg of whiskey, was placed on the ground and pointed at the group of warriors, squaws, and little children round the fire, watching the roasting meal.

"While they were thus engaged, with hearts full of kindly feelings toward their white friends, Johnson gave the signal. The howitzer was discharged, sending its load of bullets scattering and tearing through the mass of miserable human beings, and nearly all who were not stricken down were shot by the rifles. A very few succeeded in escaping into the ravine, and fled over the dividing ridge into the northern valleys, where they met others of their tribe, to whom they told the horrible story.

"The Apaches at once showed that they could imitate their more civilized brothers. Immediately a band of them went in search of the other company of trappers, who, of course, were utterly unconscious of Johnson's infernal work. They were attacked, unprepared, and nearly all killed; and then the story that the Apaches were treacherous and cruel went forth into all the land, but nothing of the wrongs they had received."

Is it to be wondered at that the Apaches became one of the most hostile and dangerous tribes on the Pacific coast?

These are but four massacres out of scores, whose history, if written, would prove as clearly as do these, that, in the long contest between white men and Indians, the Indian has not always been the aggressor, and that treachery and cruelty are by no means exclusively Indian traits.

EDWARD BELLAMY

Looking Backward: 2000-1887

(1888)

The utopian tradition has deep roots in American history. The land that would become the United States began as a utopian experiment – in Massachusetts Bay, in Pennsylvania, in Georgia – and the new nation formed here was equally utopian. When a new wave of romantic reform swept Europe and America early in the nineteenth century, men like Robert Owen tried to create ideal communities as models for a future society. In the wake of the Civil War the impulse flagged until 1888 when Edward Bellamy published Looking Backward, 2000–1887. True, the passage from utopian colonies to utopian novels was something of a retreat, but nonetheless Bellamy had struck a responsive note. Within the next decade, 165 "Nationalist" clubs sprang up, and some fifty utopian novels appeared. In the twentieth century utopianism has reappeared countless times: In dozens of educational experiments, in a number of communes in the 1930s, most recently in the writings of Paul Goodman and B. F. Skinner, and in communitarian experiments of the 1960s.

Literary utopianism usually contains more a critique of what exists than a model for the future, and Bellamy's "Nationalist" program is no exception. The society of the year 2000 is culturally pure Victorian; its economy, run by an "industrial army," is but a metaphor expressing a reversal of existing capitalist arrangements; the love story threading the narrative symbolizes continuity, not change, with the hero finally marrying the granddaughter of his fiancé in the old Boston of 1887. Bellamy's subject is the evil and irrationality of late nineteenth-century capitalism. His answer is a socialism of the heart. No one pays for the transformation that Bellamy wishes. This urge toward a more humane society, achieved without coercion or any radical change in American manners or culture, expressed the deepest wishes of the reform-minded public slowly becoming aware of itself and soon to be a political power. William Allen White, the prominent progressive journalist, recalled the "tremendous thrill" of the "books from the late Eighties and early Nineties" that altered the conservative ideas he learned in his Kansas childhood. Whatever their literary merits, books that change lives remain important historical documents.

I

When, in the course of the evening the ladies retired, leaving Doctor Leete and myself alone, he sounded me as to my disposition for sleep, saying that if I felt like it my bed was ready for me; but if I was inclined to wakefulness nothing would please him better than to bear me company. "I am a late bird, myself," he said, "and, without suspicion of flattery, I may say that a companion more interesting than yourself could scarcely be imagined. It is decidedly not often that one has a chance to converse with a man of the nineteenth century."

Now I had been looking forward all the evening with some dread to the time when I should be alone, on retiring for the night. Surrounded by these most friendly strangers, stimulated and supported by their sympathetic interest, I had been able to keep my mental balance. Even then, however, in pauses of the conversation I had had glimpses, vivid as lightning flashes, of the horror of strangeness that was waiting to be faced when I could no longer command diversion. I knew I could not sleep that night, and as for lying awake and thinking, it argues no cowardice, I am sure, to confess that I was afraid of it. When, in reply to my host's question, I frankly told him this, he replied that it would be strange if I did not feel just so, but that I need have no anxiety about sleeping; whenever I wanted to go to bed, he would give me a dose which would insure me a sound night's sleep without fail. Next morning, no doubt, I would awake with the feeling of an old citizen.

"Before I acquire that," I replied, "I must know a little more about the sort of Boston I have come back to. You told me when we were upon the housetop that though a century only had elapsed since I fell asleep, it had been marked by greater changes in the conditions of humanity than many a previous millennium. With the city before me I could well believe that, but I am very curious to know what some of the changes have been. To make a beginning somewhere, for the subject is doubtless a large one, what solution, if any, have you found for the labor question? It was the Sphinx's riddle of the nineteenth century, and when I dropped out the Sphinx was threatening to devour society, because the answer was not forthcoming. It is well worth sleeping a hundred years to learn what the right answer was, if, indeed, you have found it yet."

"As no such thing as the labor question is known nowadays," replied Doctor Leete, "and there is no way in which it could arise, I suppose we may claim to have solved it. Society would indeed have fully deserved being devoured if it had failed to answer a riddle so entirely simple. In fact, to speak by the book, it was not necessary for society to solve the riddle at all. It may be said to have solved itself. The solution came as the result of a process of industrial evolution which could not have terminated otherwise. All that society had to do was to recognize and cooperate with that evolution, when its tendency had become unmistakable."

"I can only say," I answered, "that at the time I fell asleep no such evolution had been recognized."

"It was in 1887 that you fell into this sleep, I think you said."

"Yes, May 30, 1887."

My companion regarded me musingly for some moments. Then he observed, "And you tell me that even then there was no general recognition of the nature of the crisis which society was nearing? Of course, I fully credit your statement. The singular blindness of your contemporaries to the signs of the times is a phenomenon commented on by many of our historians but few facts of history are more difficult for us to realize, so obvious and unmistakable as we look back seem the indications which must also have come under your eyes, of the transformation about to come to pass. I should be interested, Mr. West, if you would give me a little more definite idea of the view which you and men of your grade of intellect took of the state and prospects of society in 1887. You must, at least, have realized that the widespread industrial and social troubles, and the underlying dissatisfaction of all classes with the inequalities of society, and the general misery of mankind, were portents of great changes of some sort."

"We did, indeed, fully realize that," I replied. "We felt that society was dragging anchor and in danger of going adrift. Whither it would drift nobody could say, but all feared the rocks."

"Nevertheless," said Doctor Leete, "the set of the current was perfectly perceptible if you had but taken pains to observe it, and it was not toward the rocks, but toward a deeper channel."

"We had a popular proverb," I replied, "that 'hindsight is better than foresight,' the force of which I shall now, no doubt, appreciate more fully than ever. All I can say is, that the prospect was such when I went into that long sleep that I should not have been surprised had I looked down from your housetop today on a heap of charred and moss-grown ruins instead of this glorious city."

Doctor Leete had listened to me with close attention and nodded thoughtfully as I finished speaking. "What you have said," he observed, "will be regarded as a most valuable vindication of Storiot, whose account of your era has been generally thought exaggerated in its picture of the gloom and confusion of men's minds. That a period of transition like that should be full of excitement and agitation was indeed to be looked for; but seeing how plain was the tendency of the forces in operation, it was natural to believe that hope rather than fear would have been the prevailing temper of the popular mind."

"You have not yet told me what was the answer to the riddle which you found," I said. "I am impatient to know by what contradiction of natural sequence the peace and prosperity which you now seem to enjoy could have been the outcome of an era like my own."

"Excuse me," replied my host, "but do you smoke?" It was not till our cigars were lighted and drawing well that he resumed. "Since you are in the humor to talk rather than to sleep, as I certainly am, perhaps I cannot do better than to try to give you enough idea of our modern industrial system to dissipate at least the impression that there is any mystery about the process of its evolution. The Bostonians of your day had the reputation of being great askers of questions, and I am going to show my descent by asking you one to begin with. What should you name as the most prominent feature of the labor troubles of your day?"

"Why, the strikes, of course," I replied.

"Exactly. But what made the strikes so formidable?"

"The great labor organizations."

"And what was the motive of these great organizations?"

"The workmen claimed they had to organize to get their rights from the big corporations," I replied.

"That is just it," said Doctor Leete. "The organization of labor and the strikes were an effect, merely, of the concentration of capital in greater masses than had ever been known before. Before this concentration began, while as yet commerce and industry were conducted by innumerable petty concerns with small capital, instead of a small number of great concerns with vast capital, the individual workman was relatively important and independent in his relations to the employer. Moreover, when a little capital or a new idea was enough to start a man in business for himself, workingmen were constantly becoming employers and there was no hard and fast line between the two classes. Labor unions were needless then, and general strikes out of the question. But when the era of small concerns with small capital was succeeded by that of the great aggregations of capital, all this was changed. The individual laborer, who had been relatively important to the small employer, was reduced to insignificance and powerlessness over against the great corporation, while at the same time the way upward to the grade of employer was closed to him. Self-defense drove him to union with his fellows.

"The records of the period show that the outcry against the concentration of capital was furious. Men believed that it threatened society with a form of tyranny more abhorrent than it had ever endured. They believed that the great corporations were preparing for them the yoke of a baser servitude than had ever been imposed on the race, servitude not to men but to soulless machines incapable of any motive but insatiable greed. Looking back, we cannot wonder at their desperation, for certainly humanity was never confronted with a fate more sordid and hideous than would have been the era of corporate tyranny which they anticipated.

"Meanwhile, without being in the smallest degree checked by the clamor against it, the absorption of business by ever larger monopolies continued. In the United States there was not, after the beginning of the last quarter of the century, any opportunity whatever for individual enterprise in any important field of industry, unless backed by a great capital. During the last decade of the century, such small businesses as still remained were fast-failing survivals of a past epoch, or mere parasites on the great corporations, or else existed in fields too small to attract the great capitalists. Small businesses, as far as they still remained, were reduced to the condition of rats and mice, living in holes and corners, and counting on evading notice for the enjoyment of existence. The railroads had gone on combining till a few great syndicates controlled every rail in the land. In manufactories, every important staple was controlled by a syndicate. These syndicates, pools, trusts, or whatever their name, fixed prices and crushed all competition except when combinations as vast as themselves arose. Then a struggle, resulting in a still greater consolidation, ensued. The great city bazaar crushed its country rivals with branch stores, and in the city itself absorbed its smaller rivals till the business of a whole quarter was concentrated under one roof, with a hundred former proprietors of shops serving as clerks. Having no business of his own to put his money in, the small capitalist, at the same time that he took service under the corporation, found no other investment for his money but its stocks and bonds, thus becoming doubly dependent upon it.

"The fact that the desperate popular opposition to the consolidation of business in a few powerful hands had no effect to check it proves that there must have been a strong economical reason for it. The small capitalists, with their innumerable petty concerns, had in fact yielded the field to the great aggregations of capital, because they belonged to a day of small things and were totally incompetent to the demands of an age of steam and telegraphs and the gigantic scale of its enterprises. To restore the former order of things, even if possible, would have involved returning to the day of stagecoaches. Oppressive and intolerable as was the regime of the great consolidations of capital, even its victims, while they cursed it, were forced to admit the prodigious increase of efficiency which had been imparted to the national industries, the vast economies effected by concentration of management and unity of organization, and to confess that since the new system had taken the place of the old the wealth of the world had increased at a rate before undreamed of. To be sure this vast increase had gone chiefly to make the rich richer, increasing the gap between them and the poor; but the fact remained that, as a means merely of producing wealth, capital had been proved efficient in proportion to its consolidation. The restoration of the old system with the subdivision of capital, if it were possible, might indeed bring back a greater equality of conditions, with more individual dignity and freedom, but it would be at the price of general poverty and the arrest of material progress.

"Was there, then, no way of commanding the services of the

mighty wealth-producing principle of consolidated capital without bowing down to a plutocracy like that of Carthage? As soon as men began to ask themselves these questions, they found the answer ready for them. The movement toward the conduct of business by larger and larger aggregations of capital, the tendency toward monopolies, which had been so desperately and vainly resisted, was recognized at last, in its true significance, as a process which only needed to complete its logical evolution to open a golden future to humanity.

"Early in the last century the evolution was completed by the final consolidation of the entire capital of the nation. The industry and commerce of the country, ceasing to be conducted by a set of irresponsible corporations and syndicates of private persons at their caprice and for their profit, were entrusted to a single syndicate representing the people, to be conducted in the common interest for the common profit. The nation, that is to say, organized as the one great business corporation in which all other corporations were absorbed; it became the one capitalist in the place of all other capitalists, the sole employer, the final monopoly in which all previous and lesser monopolies were swallowed up, a monopoly in the profits and economies of which all citizens shared. The epoch of trusts had ended in The Great Trust. In a word, the people of the United States concluded to assume the conduct of their own business, just as one hundred-odd years before they had assumed the conduct of their own government, organizing now for industrial purposes on precisely the same grounds that they had then organized for political purposes. At last, strangely late in the world's history, the obvious fact was perceived that no business is so essentially the public business as the industry and commerce on which the people's livelihood depends, and that to entrust it to private persons to be managed for private profit is a folly similar in kind, though vastly greater in magnitude, to that of surrendering the functions of political government to kings and nobles to be conducted for their personal glorification."

"Such a stupendous change as you describe," said I, "did not, of course, take place without great bloodshed and terrible convulsions."

"On the contrary," replied Doctor Leete, "there was absolutely no violence. The change had been long foreseen. Public opinion had become fully ripe for it, and the whole mass of the people was behind it. There was no more possibility of opposing it by force than by argument. On the other hand the popular sentiment toward the great corporations and those identified with them had ceased to be one of bitterness, as they came to realize their necessity as a link, a transition phase, in the evolution of the true industrial system. The most violent foes of the great private monopolies were now forced to recognize how invaluable and indispensable had been their office in educating the people up to the point of assuming control of their own business. Fifty years before, the consolidation of the industries of the country under national control would have seemed a very daring experiment to the most sanguine. But by a series of object lessons, seen and studied by all men, the great corporations had taught the people an entirely new set of ideas on this subject. They had seen for many years syndicates handling revenues greater than those of states, and directing the labors of hundreds of thousands of men with an efficiency and economy unattainable in smaller operations. It had come to be recognized as an axiom that the larger the business the simpler the principles that can be applied to it; that, as the machine is truer than the hand, so the system, which in a great concern does the work of the master's eye in a small business, turns out more accurate results. Thus it came about that, thanks to the corporations themselves, when it was proposed that the nation should assume their functions, the suggestion implied nothing which seemed impracticable even to the timid. To be sure, it was a step beyond any yet taken, a broader generalization, but the very fact that the nation would be the sole corporation in the field would, it was seen, relieve the undertaking of many difficulties with which the partial monopolies had contended."

II

Doctor Leete ceased speaking, and I remained silent, endeavoring to form some general conception of the changes in the arrangements of society implied in the tremendous revolution which he had described.

Finally I said, "The idea of such an extension of the functions of government is, to say the least, rather overwhelming."

"Extension!" he repeated. "Where is the extension?"

"In my day," I replied, "it was considered that the proper functions of government, strictly speaking, were limited to keeping the peace and defending the people against the public enemy, that is, to the military and police powers."

"And, in heaven's name, who are the public enemies?" exclaimed Doctor Leete. "Are they France, England, Germany, or hunger, cold, and nakedness? In your day governments were accustomed, on the slightest international misunderstanding, to seize upon the bodies of citizens and deliver them over by hundreds of thousands to death and mutilation, wasting their treasures the while like water; and all this oftenest for no imaginable profit to the victims. We have no wars now, and our governments no war powers, but in order to protect every citizen against hunger, cold, and nakedness, and provide for all his physical and mental needs, the function is assumed of directing his industry for a term of years. No, Mr. West, I am sure on reflection you will perceive that it was in your age, not in ours, that the extension of the functions of governments was extraordinary. Not even for the best ends would men now allow their governments such powers as were then used for the most maleficent."

"Leaving comparisons aside," I said, "the demagoguery and corruption of our public men would have been considered, in my day, insuperable objections to any assumption by government of the charge of the national industries. We should have thought that no arrangement could be worse than to entrust the politicians with control of the wealth-producing machinery of the country. Its material interests were quite too much the football of parties as it was."

"No doubt you were right," rejoined Doctor Leete, "but all that is changed now. We have no parties or politicians, and as for demagoguery and corruption, they are words having only an historical significance."

"Human nature itself must have changed very much," I said.

"Not at all," was Doctor Leete's reply, "but the conditions of human life have changed, and with them the motives of human action. The organization of society with you was such that officials were under a constant temptation to misuse their power for the private profit of themselves or others. Under such circumstances it seems almost strange that you dared entrust them with any of your affairs. Nowadays, on the contrary, society is so constituted that there is absolutely no way in which an official, however ill-disposed, could possibly make any profit for himself or any one else by a misuse of his power. Let him be as bad an official as you please, he cannot be a corrupt one. There is no motive to be. The social system no longer offers a premium on dishonesty. But these are matters which you can only understand as you come, with time, to know us better."

"But you have not yet told me how you have settled the labor problem. It is the problem of capital which we have been discussing," I said. "After the nation had assumed conduct of the mills, machinery, railroads, farms, mines, and capital in general of the country, the labor question still remained. In assuming the responsibilities of capital the nation had assumed the difficulties of the capitalist's position."

"The moment the nation assumed the responsibilities of capital those difficulties vanished," replied Doctor Leete. "The national organization of labor under one direction was the complete solution of what was, in your day and under your system, justly regarded as the insoluble labor problem. When the nation became the sole employer, all the citizens, by virtue of their citizenship, became employees, to be distributed according to the needs of industry."

"That is," I suggested, "you have simply applied the principle of universal military service, as it was understood in our day, to the labor question."

"Yes," said Doctor Leete, "that was something which followed as a matter of course as soon as the nation had become the sole capitalist. The people were already accustomed to the idea that the obligation of every citizen, not physically disabled, to contribute his military services to the defense of the nation was equal and absolute. That it was equally the duty of every citizen to contribute his quota of industrial or intellectual services to the maintenance of the nation was equally evident, though it was not until the nation became the employer of labor that citizens were able to render this sort of service with any pretense either of universality or equity. No organization of labor was possible when the employing power was divided among hundreds or thousands of individuals and corporations, between which concert of any kind was neither desired, nor indeed feasible. It constantly happened then that vast numbers who desired to labor could find no opportunity, and on the other hand, those who desired to evade a part or all of their debt could easily do so."

"Service, now, I suppose, is compulsory upon all," I suggested.

"It is rather a matter of course than of compulsion," replied Doctor Leete. "It is regarded as so absolutely natural and reasonable that the idea of its being compulsory has ceased to be thought of. He would be thought to be an incredibly contemptible person who should need compulsion in such a case. Nevertheless, to speak of service being compulsory would be a weak way to state its absolute inevitableness. Our entire social order is so wholly based upon and deduced from it that if it were conceivable that a man could escape it, he would be left with no possible way to provide for his existence. He would have excluded himself from the world, cut himself off from his kind, in a word, committed suicide."

"Is the term of service in this industrial army for life?"

"Oh, no; it both begins later and ends earlier than the average working period in your day. Your workshops were filled with children and old men, but we hold the period of youth sacred to education, and the period of maturity, when the physical forces begin to flag, equally sacred to ease and agreeable relaxation. The period of industrial service is twenty-four years, beginning at the close of the course of education at twenty-one and terminating at forty-five. After forty-five, while discharged from labor, the citizen still remains liable to special calls, in case of emergencies causing a sudden great increase in the demand for labor, till he reaches the age of fifty-five, but such calls are rarely, in fact almost never, made. The fifteenth day of October of every year is what we call Muster Day, because those who have reached the age of twenty-one are then mustered into the industrial service, and at the same time those who, after twenty-four years' service, have reached the age of forty-five are honorably mustered out. It is the great day of the year with us, whence we reckon all other events, our Olympiad, save that it is annual."

III

"It is after you have mustered your industrial army into service," I said, "that I should expect the difficulty to arise, for there its analogy with a military army must cease. Soldiers have all the same thing, and a very simple thing, to do, namely, to practice the manual of arms, to march and stand guard. But the industrial army must learn and follow two or three hundred diverse trades and avocations. What administrative talent can be equal to determine wisely what trade or business every individual in a great nation shall pursue?"

"The administration has nothing to do with determining that point."

"Who does determine it, then?" I asked.

"Every man for himself in accordance with his natural aptitude, the utmost pains being taken to enable him to find out what his natural aptitude really is. The principle on which our industrial army is organized is that a man's natural endowments, mental and physical, determine what he can work at most profitably to the nation and most satisfactorily to himself. While the obligation of service in some form is not to be evaded, voluntary election, subject only to necessary regulation, is depended on to determine the particular sort of service every man is to render. As an individual's satisfaction during his term of service depends on his having an occupation to his taste, parents and teachers watch from early years for indications of special aptitudes in children. A thorough study of the national industrial system, with the history and rudiments of all the great trades, is an essential part of our educational system. While manual training is not allowed to encroach on the general intellectual culture to which our schools are devoted, it is carried far enough to give our youth, in addition to their theoretical knowledge of the national industries, mechanical and agricultural, a certain familiarity with their tools and methods. Our schools are constantly visiting our workshops, and often are taken on long excursions to inspect particular industrial enterprises. In your day a man was not ashamed to be grossly ignorant of all trades except his own, but such ignorance would not be consistent with our idea of placing every one in a position to select intelligently the occupation for which he has most taste. Usually long before he is mustered into service a young man has found out the pursuit he wants to follow, has acquired a great deal of knowledge about it, and is waiting impatiently the time when he can enlist in its ranks."

"Surely," I said, "it can hardly be that the number of volunteers for any trade is exactly the number needed in that trade. It must be generally either under or over the demand."

"The supply of volunteers is always expected to fully equal the demand," replied Doctor Leete. "It is the business of the administration to see that this is the case. The rate of volunteering for each trade is closely watched. If there be a noticeably greater excess of volunteers over men needed in any trade, it is inferred that the trade offers greater attractions than others. On the other hand, if the number of volunteers for a trade tends to drop below the demand, it is inferred that it is thought more arduous. It is the business of the administration to seek constantly to equalize the attractions of the trades, so far as the conditions of labor in them are concerned, so that all trades shall be equally attractive to persons having natural tastes for them. This is done by making the hours of labor in different trades to differ according to their arduousness. The lighter trades, prosecuted under the most agreeable circumstances, have in this way the longest hours, while an arduous trade, such as mining, has very short hours. There is no theory, no a priori rule, by which the respective attractiveness of industries is determined. The administration, in taking burdens off one class of workers and adding them to other classes, simply follows the fluctuations of opinion among the workers themselves as indicated by the rate of volunteering. The principle is that no man's work ought to be, on the whole, harder for him than any other man's for him, the workers themselves to be the judges. There are no limits to the application of this rule. If any particular occupation is in itself so arduous or so oppressive that, in order to induce volunteers, the day's work in it had to be reduced to ten minutes, it would be done. If, even then, no man was willing to do it, it would remain undone. But of course, in point of fact, a moderate reduction in the hours of labor, or addition of other privileges, suffices to secure all needed volunteers for any occupation necessary to men. If, indeed, the unavoidable difficulties and dangers of such a necessary pursuit were so great that no inducement of compensating advantages would overcome men's repugnance to it, the administration would only need to take it out of the common order of occupations by declaring it 'extra hazardous,' and those who pursued it especially worthy of the national gratitude, to be overrun with volunteers. Our young men are very greedy of honor, and do not let slip such opportunities. Of course you will see that dependence on the purely voluntary choice of avocations involves the abolition in all of anything like unhygienic conditions or special peril to life and limb. Health and safety are conditions common to all industries. The nation does not maim and slaughter its workmen by thousands, as did the private capitalists and corporations of your day."

"When there are more who want to enter a particular trade than there is room for, how do you decide between the applicants?" I inquired.

"Preference is given to those who have acquired the most knowledge of the trade they wish to follow. No man, however, who through successive years remains persistent in his desire to show what he can do at any particular trade, is in the end denied an opportunity. Meanwhile, if a man cannot at first win entrance into the business he prefers, he has usually one or more alternative preferences, pursuits for which he has some degree of aptitude, although not the highest. Everyone, indeed, is expected to study his aptitudes so as to have not only a first choice as to occupation, but a second or third, so that if, either at the outset of his career or subsequently, owing to the progress of invention or changes in demand, he is unable to follow his first vocation, he can still find reasonably congenial employment. This principle of secondary choices as to occupation is quite important in our system. I should add, in reference to the counter-possibility of some sudden failure of volunteers in a particular trade, or some sudden necessity of an increased force, that the administration, while depending on the voluntary system for filling up the trades as a rule, holds always in reserve the power to call for special volunteers, or draft any force needed from any quarter. Generally, however, all needs of this sort can be met by details from the class of unskilled or common laborers."

"How is this class of common laborers recruited?" I asked. "Surely nobody voluntarily enters that."

"It is the grade to which all new recruits belong for the first three years of their service. It is not till after this period, during which he is assignable to do any work at the discretion of his superiors, that the young man is allowed to elect a special avocation. These three years of stringent discipline none are exempt from, and very glad our young men are to pass from this severe school into the comparative liberty of the trades. If a man were so stupid as to have no choice as to occupation, he would simply remain a common laborer; but such cases, as you may suppose, are not common."

"Having once elected and entered on a trade or occupation," I remarked, "I suppose he has to stick to it the rest of his life."

"Not necessarily," replied Doctor Leete. "While frequent and merely capricious changes of occupation are not encouraged or even permitted, every worker is allowed, of course, under certain regulations and in accordance with the exigencies of the service, to volunteer for another industry which he thinks would suit him better than his first choice. In this case his application is received just as if he were volunteering for the first time, and on the same terms. Not only this, but a worker may likewise, under suitable regulations and not too frequently, obtain a transfer to an establishment of the same industry in another part of the country which for any reason he may prefer. Under your system a discontented man could indeed leave his work at will, but he left his means of support at the same time, and took his chances as to future livelihood. We find that the number of men who wish to abandon an accustomed occupation for a new one, and old friends and associations for strange ones, is small. It is only the poorer sort of workmen who desire to change even as frequently as our regulations permit. Of course transfers or discharges, when health demands them, are always given."

"As an industrial system, I should think this might be extremely efficient," I said, "but I don't see that it makes any provision for the professional classes, the men who serve the nation with brains instead of hands. Of course you can't get along without the brain workers. How, then, are they selected from those who are to serve as farmers and mechanics? That must require a very delicate sort of sifting process, I should say."

"So it does," replied Doctor Leete. "The most delicate possible test is needed here, and so we leave the question whether a man shall be a brain or hand worker entirely to him to settle. At the end of the term of three years as a common laborer, which every man must serve, it is for him to choose, in accordance to his natural tastes, whether he will fit himself for an art or profession, or be a farmer or mechanic. If he feels that he can do better work with his brains than his muscles, he finds every facility for testing the reality of his supposed bent, of cultivating it, and, if fit, of pursuing it as his avocation. The schools of technology, of medicine, of art, of music, of histrionics, and of higher liberal learning are always open to aspirants without condition."

"Are not the schools flooded with young men whose only motive is to avoid work?"

Doctor Leete smiled a little grimly.

"No one is at all likely to enter the professional schools for the purpose of avoiding work, I assure you," he said. "They are intended for those with special aptitude for the branches they teach, and anyone without it would find it easier to do double hours at his trade than try to keep up with the classes. Of course many honestly mistake their vocation, and, finding themselves unequal to the requirements of the schools, drop out and return to the industrial service; no discredit attaches to such persons, for the public policy is to encourage all to develop suspected talents which only actual tests can prove the reality of. The professional and scientific schools of your day depended on the patronage of their pupils for support, and the practice appears to have been common of giving diplomas to unfit persons, who afterward found their way into the professions. Our schools are national institutions, and to have passed their tests is a proof of special abilities not to be questioned.

"This opportunity for a professional training," the doctor continued, "remains opens to every man till the age of thirty is reached, after which students are not received, as there would remain too brief a period before the age of discharge in which to serve the nation in their professions. In your day young men had to choose their professions very young, and therefore, in a large proportion of instances, wholly mistook their vocations. It is recognized nowadays that the natural aptitudes of some are later than those of others in developing, and therefore, while the choice of profession may be made as early as twenty-four, it remains open for six years longer."

A question which had a dozen times before been on my lips now found utterance, a question which touched upon what, in my time, had been regarded the most vital difficulty in the way of any final settlement of the industrial problem. "It is an extraordinary thing," I said, "that you should not yet have said a word about the method of adjusting wages. Since the nation is the sole employer, the government must fix the rate of wages and determine just how much everybody shall earn, from the doctors to the diggers. All I can say is, that this plan would never have worked with us, and I don't see how it can now unless human nature has changed. In my day, nobody was satisfied with his wages or salary. Even if he felt he received enough, he was sure his neighbor had too much, which was as bad. If the universal discontent on this subject, instead of being dissipated in curses and strikes directed against innumerable employers, could have been concentrated upon one, and that the government, the strongest ever devised would not have seen two pay days."

Doctor Leete laughed heartily.

"Very true, very true," he said, "a general strike would most probably have followed the first pay day, and a strike directed against a government is a revolution."

"How, then, do you avoid a revolution every pay day?" I demanded. "Has some prodigious philosopher devised a new system of calculus satisfactory to all for determining the exact and comparative value of all sorts of service, whether by brawn or brain, by hand or voice, by ear or eye? Or has human nature itself changed, so that no man looks upon his own things but 'every man on the things of his neighbor'? One or the other of these events must be the explanation."

"Neither one nor the other, however, is," was my host's laughing response. "And now, Mr. West," he continued, "you must remember that you are my patient as well as my guest, and permit me to prescribe sleep for you before we have any more conversation. It is after three o'clock."

"The prescription is, no doubt, a wise one," I said. "I only hope it can be filled."

"I will see to that," the doctor replied, and he did, for he gave me a wineglass of something or other which sent me to sleep as soon as my head touched the pillow.

* * *

[Doctor Leete said] "I don't think there has been any change in human nature . . . since your day. It is so constituted still that special incentives in the form of prizes, and advantages to be gained, are requisite to call out the best endeavors of the average man in any direction."

"But what inducement," I asked, "can a man have to put forth his best endeavors when, however much or little he accomplishes, his income remains the same? High characters may be moved by devotion to the common welfare under such a system, but does not the average man tend to rest back on his oar, reasoning that it is of no use to make a special effort, since the effort will not increase his income, nor its withholding diminish it?"

"Does it then really seem to you," answered my companion, "that human nature is insensible to any motives save fear of want and love of luxury, that you should expect security and equality of livelihood to leave them without possible incentives to effort? Your contemporaries did not really think so, though they might fancy they did. When it was a question of the grandest class of efforts, the most absolute self-devotion, they depended on quite other incentives. Not higher wages, but honor and the hope of men's gratitude, patriotism and the inspiration of duty, were the motives which they set before their soldiers when it was a question of dying for the nation, and never was there an age of the world when those motives did not call out what is best and noblest in men. And not only this, but when you come to analyze the love of money which was the general impulse to effort in your day, you find that the dread of want and desire of luxury was but one of several motives which the pursuit of money represented; the others, and with many the more influential, being desire of power, of social position, and reputation for ability and success. So you see that though we have abolished poverty and the fear of it, and inordinate luxury with the hope of it, we have not touched the greater part of the motives which underlay the love of money in former times, or any of those which prompted the supremer sorts of effort. The coarser motives, which no longer move us, have been replaced by higher motives wholly unknown to the mere wage earners of your age. Now that industry, of whatever sort, is no longer self-service, but service of the nation, patriotism, passion for humanity, impel the worker as in your day they did the soldier. The army of industry is an army, not alone by virtue of its perfect organization, but by reason also of the ardor of self-devotion which animates its members.

"But as you used to supplement the motives of patriotism with the love of glory, in order to stimulate the valor of your soldiers, so do we. Based as our industrial system is on the principle of requiring the same unit of effort from every man, that is, the best he can do, you will see that the means by which we spur the workers to do their best must be a very essential part of our scheme. With us, diligence in the national service is the sole and certain way to public repute, social distinction, and official power. The value of a man's services to society fixes his rank in it. Compared with the effort of our social arrangements in impelling men to be zealous in business, we deem the object lessons of biting poverty and wanton luxury on which you depended a device as weak and uncertain as it was barbaric. The lust of honor even in your sordid day notoriously impelled men to more desperate effort than the love of money could."

* * *

"My friends, if you would see men again the beasts of prey they seemed in the nineteenth century, all you have to do is to restore the old social and industrial system, which taught them to view their natural prey in their fellow men, and find their gain in the loss of others. No doubt it seems to you that no necessity, however dire, would have tempted you to subsist on what superior skill or strength enabled you to wrest from others equally needy. But suppose it were not merely your own life that you were responsible for. I know well that there must have been many a man among our ancestors who, if it had been merely a question of his own life, would sooner have given it up than nourished it by bread snatched from others. But this he was not permitted to do. He had dear lives dependent on him. Men loved women in those days, as now. God knows how they dared be fathers, but they had babies as sweet, no doubt, to them as ours to us, whom they must feed, clothe, educate. The gentlest creatures are fierce when they have young to provide for, and in that wolfish society the struggle for bread borrowed a peculiar desperation from the tenderest sentiments. For the sake of those dependent on him, a man might not choose, but must plunge into the foul fight—cheat, overreach, supplant, defraud, buy below worth and sell above, break down the business by which his neighbor fed his young ones, tempt men to buy what they ought not and to sell what they should not, grind his laborers, sweat his debtors, cozen his creditors. Though a man sought it carefully with tears, it was hard to find a way in which he could earn a living and provide for his family except by pressing in before some weaker rival and taking the food from his mouth. Even the ministers of religion were not exempt from this cruel necessity. While they warned their flocks against the love of money, regard for their families compelled them to keep an outlook for the pecuniary prizes of their calling. Poor fellows, theirs was indeed a trying business, preaching to men a generosity and unselfishness which they and everybody knew would, in the existing state of the world, reduce to poverty those who should practice them, laying down laws of conduct which the law of self-preservation compelled men to break. Looking on the inhuman spectacle of society, these worthy men bitterly bemoaned the depravity of human nature; as if angelic nature would not have been debauched in such a devil's school! Ah, my friends, believe me, it is not now in this happy age that humanity is proving the divinity within it. It was rather in those evil days when not even the fight for life with one another, the struggle for mere existence, in which mercy was folly, could wholly banish generosity and kindness from the earth.

"It is not hard to understand the desperation with which men and women, who under other conditions would have been full of gentleness and ruth, fought and tore each other in the scramble for gold, when we realize what it meant to miss it, what poverty was in that day. For the body it was hunger and thirst, torment by heat and frost, in sickness neglect, in health unremitting toil; for the moral nature it meant oppression, contempt, and the patient endurance of indignity, brutish associations from infancy, the loss of all the innocence of childhood, the grace of womanhood, the dignity of manhood; for the mind it meant the death of ignorance, the torpor of all those faculties which distinguish us from brutes, the reduction of life to a round of bodily functions.

"Ah, my friends, if such a fate as this were offered you and your children as the only alternative of success in the accumulation of wealth, how long do you fancy would you be in sinking to the moral level of your ancestors?

"Some two or three centuries ago an act of barbarity was committed in India, which, though the number of lives destroyed was but a few score, was attended by such peculiar horrors that its memory is likely to be perpetual. A number of English prisoners were shut up in a room containing not enough air to supply one-tenth their number. The unfortunates were gallant men, devoted comrades in service, but, as the agonies of suffocation began to take hold on them, they forgot all else, and became involved in a hideous struggle, each one for himself, and against all others, to force a way to one of the small apertures of the prison at which alone it was possible to get a breath of air. It was a struggle in which men became beasts, and the recital of its horrors by the few survivors so shocked our forefathers that for a century later we find it a stock reference in their literature as a typical illustration of the extreme possibilities of human misery, as shocking in its moral as its physical aspect. They could scarcely have anticipated that to us the Black Hole of Calcutta, with its press of maddened men tearing and trampling one another in the struggle to win a place at the breathing holes, would seem a striking type of the society of their age."

FREDERICK JACKSON TURNER

The Significance of the Frontier in American History

(1893)

Frederick Jackson Turner's celebrated essay on the frontier is perhaps the most influential single attempt to define the American identity. Despite extensive criticism of its successive formulations, the frontier hypothesis still appears to explain, at least in part, what is American about America. We did spend much of our early history looking and moving westward, and the experience did suggest ideas of economic opportunity and openness of politics and society that have not wholly left

us. Although few agree on the precise mechanisms by which this "frontier heritage" was transmitted (a subject upon which Turner himself was notoriously vague), the idea retained sufficient emotional reverberation to thrill millions of Americans when John F. Kennedy announced his "New Frontier" in 1960.

Writing in the early 1890s, Turner also recognized that his age marked the end of "the first period of American history," that by moving into the new century we were entering a new world. Perhaps the ending of the frontier line was not so significant as the imperial venture at the end of the 1890s, or the trust movement after 1897, or the huge increase in urban populations, or even than the institution of Jim Crow. But its disappearance (which was not really the closing of the frontier, since millions more acres were settled thereafter) did aptly symbolize the passing of a world based on the primacy of agriculture to a new one whose main determinants were more various and far less comfortable to behold. Turner's version of the *fin de siècle* was less pessimistic than many of his contemporaries. He sought substitutes for the openness and opportunity of an agricultural frontier, while others, who based their views on racial thinking, could not look forward to the new century with quite the same optimism.

The Significance of the Frontier in American History

In a recent bulletin of the Superintendent of the Census for 1890 appear these significant words: "Up to and including 1880 the country had a frontier of settlement, but at present the unsettled area has been so broken into by isolated bodies of settlement that there can hardly be said to be a frontier line. In the discussion of its extent, its westward movement, etc., it can not therefore, any longer have a place in the census reports." This brief official statement marks the closing of a great historic movement. Up to our own day American history has been in a large degree the history of the colonization of the Great West. The existence of an area of free land, its continuous recession, and the advance of American settlement westward, explain American development.

Behind institutions, behind constitutional forms and modifications, lie the vital forces that call these organs into life and shape them to meet changing conditions. The peculiarity of American institutions is, the fact that they have been compelled to adapt themselves to the changes of an expanding people—to the changes involved in crossing a continent, in winning a wilderness, and in developing at each area of this progress out of the primitive economic and political conditions of the frontier into the complexity of city life. Said Calhoun in 1817, "We are great, and rapidly—I was about to say fearfully—growing!" So saying, he touched the distinguishing feature of American life. All peoples show development; the germ theory of politics has been sufficiently emphasized. In the case of most nations, however, the development has occurred in a limited area; and if the nation has expanded, it has met other growing people whom it has conquered. But in the case of the United States we have a different phenomenon. Limiting our attention to the Atlantic coast, we have the familiar phenomenon of the evolution of institutions in a limited area, such as the risk of representative government; the differentiation of simple colonial governments into complex organs; the progress from primitive industrial society, without division of labor, up to manufacturing civilization. But we have in addition to this a recurrence of the process of evolution in each western area reached in the process of expansion. Thus American development has exhibited not merely advance along a single line, but a return to primitive conditions on a continually advancing frontier line, and a new development for that area. American social development has been continually beginning over again on the frontier. This perennial rebirth, this fluidity of American life, this expansion westward with its new opportunities, its continuous touch with the simplicity of primitive society, furnish the forces dominating

*The text of Turner's essay is reprinted from *Annual Report for 1893*, American Historical Association, pp. 199–227.

American character. The true point of view in the history of this nation is not the Atlantic coast, it is the great West. Even the slavery struggle, which is made so exclusive an object of attention by writers like Prof. von Holst, occupies its important place in American history because of its relation to westward expansion.

In this advance, the frontier is the outer edge of the wave—the meeting point between savagery and civilization. Much has been written about the frontier from the point of view of border warfare and the chase, but as a field for the serious study of the economist and the historian it has been neglected.

The American frontier is sharply distinguished from the European frontier—a fortified boundary line running through dense populations. The most significant thing about the American frontier is, that it lies at the hither edge of free land. In the census reports it is treated as the margin of that settlement which has a density of two or more to the square mile. The term is an elastic one, and for our purposes does not need sharp definition. We shall consider the whole frontier belt, including the Indian country and the outer margin of the "settled area" of the census reports. This paper will make no attempt to treat the subject exhaustively; its aim is simply to call attention to the frontier as a fertile field for investigation, and to suggest some of the problems which arise in connection with it.

In the settlement of America we have to observe how European life entered the continent, and how America modified and developed that life and reacted on Europe. Our early history is the study of European germs developing in an American environment. Too exclusive attention has been paid by institutional students to the Germanic origins, too little to the American factors. The frontier is the line of most rapid and effective Americanization. The wilderness masters the colonist. It finds him a European in dress, industries, tools, modes of travel, and thought. It takes him from the railroad car and puts him in the birch canoe. It strips off the garments of civilization and arrays him in the hunting shirt and the moccasin. It puts him in the log cabin of the Cherokee and Iroquois and runs an Indian palisade around him. Before long he has gone to planting Indian corn and plowing with a sharp stick; he shouts the war cry and takes the scalp in orthodox Indian fashion. In short, at the frontier the environment is at first too strong for the man. He must accept the conditions which it furnishes, or perish, and so he fits himself into the Indian clearings and follows the Indian trails. Little by little he transforms the wilderness, but the outcome is not the old Europe, not simply the development of Germanic germs, any more than the first phenomenon was a case of reversion to the Germanic mark. The fact is, that here is a new product that is American. At first, the frontier was the Atlantic coast. It was the frontier of Europe in a very real sense. Moving westward, the frontier became more and more American. As successive terminal moraines result from successive glaciations, so each frontier leaves its traces behind it, and when it becomes a settled area the region still partakes of the frontier characteristics. Thus the advance of the frontier has meant a steady movement away from the influence of Europe, a steady growth of independence on American lines. And to study this advance, the men who grew up under these conditions, and the political, economic, and social results of it, is to study the really American part of our history.

Stages of frontier advance

In the course of the seventeenth century the frontier was advanced up the Atlantic river courses, just beyond the "fall line," and the tidewater region became the settled area. In the first half of the eighteenth century another advance occurred. Traders followed the Delaware and Shawnese Indians to the Ohio as early as the end of the first quarter of the century. Governor Spotswood of Virginia made an expedition in 1714 across the Blue Ridge. The end of the first quarter of the century saw the advance of the Scotch-Irish and the Palatine Germans up the Shenandoah Valley into the western part of Virginia, and along the Piedmont region of the Carolinas. The Germans in New York pushed the frontier of settlement up the Mohawk to German Flats. In Pennsylvania the town of Bedford indicates the line of settlement. Settlements had begun on New River, a branch of the Kanawha, and on the sources of the Yadkin and French Broad. The King attempted to arrest the advance by his proclamation of 1763, forbidding settlements beyond the sources of the rivers flowing into the Atlantic; but in vain. In the period of the Revolution the frontier crossed the Alleghanies into Kentucky and Tennessee, and the upper waters of the Ohio were settled. When the first census was taken in 1790, the continuous settled area was bounded by a line which ran near the coast of Maine, and included New England except a portion of Vermont and New Hampshire, New York along the Hudson and up the Mohawk about Schenectady, eastern and southern Pennsylvania, Virginia well across the Shenandoah Valley, and the Carolinas and eastern Georgia. Beyond this region of continuous settlement were the small settled areas of Kentucky and Tennessee, and the Ohio, with the mountains intervening between them and the Atlantic area, thus giving a new and important character to the frontier. The isolation of the region increased its peculiarly American tendencies, and the need of transportation facilities to connect it with the East called out important schemes of internal improvement, which will be noted farther on. The "West," as a self-conscious section, began to evolve.

From decade to decade distinct advances of the frontier occurred. By the census of 1820 the settled area included Ohio, southern Indiana and Illinois, southeastern Missouri, and about one-half of Louisiana. This settled area had surrounded Indian areas, and the management of these tribes became an object of political concern. The frontier region of the time lay along the Great Lakes, where Astor's American Fur Company operated in the Indian trade, and beyond the Mississippi, where Indian traders extended their activity even to the Rocky Mountains; Florida also furnished frontier conditions. The Mississippi River region was the scene of typical frontier settlements.

The rising steam navigation on western waters, the opening of the Erie Canal, and the westward extension of cotton culture added five frontier states to the Union in this period. Grund, writing in 1836, declares: "It appears then that the universal disposition of Americans to emigrate to the western wilderness, in order to enlarge their dominion over inanimate nature, is the actual result of an expansive power which is inherent in them, and which by continually agitating all classes of society is constantly throwing a large portion of the whole population on the extreme confines of the State, in order to gain space for its development. Hardly is a new State or Territory formed before the same principle manifests itself again and gives rise to a further emigration; and so is it destined to go on until a physical barrier must finally obstruct its progress."

In the middle of this century the line indicated by the present eastern boundary of Indian Territory, Nebraska and Kansas marked the frontier of the Indian country. Minnesota and Wisconsin still exhibited frontier conditions, but the distinctive frontier of the period is found in California, where the gold discoveries had sent a sudden tide of adventurous miners, and in Oregon, and the settlements in Utah. As the frontier has leaped over the Alleghanies, so now it skipped the Great Plains and the Rocky Mountains; and in the same way that the advance of the frontiersmen beyond the Alleghanies had caused the rise of important questions of transportation and internal improvement, so now the settlers beyond the Rocky Mountains needed means of communication with the East, and in the furnishing of these arose the settlement of the Great Plains and the development of still another kind of frontier life. Railroads, fostered by land grants, sent an increasing tide of immigrants into the far West. The United States Army fought a series of Indian wars in Minnesota, Dakota, and the Indian Territory.

By 1880 the settled area had been pushed into northern Michigan, Wisconsin, and Minnesota, along Dakota rivers, and in the Black Hills region, and was ascending the rivers of Kansas and Nebraska. The development of mines in Colorado had drawn isolated frontier settlements into that region, and Montana and Idaho were receiving settlers. The frontier was found in these mining camps and the ranches of the Great Plains. The superintendent of the census for 1890 reports, as previously stated, that the settlements of the West lie so scattered over the region that there can no longer be said to be a frontier line.

In these successive frontiers we find natural boundary lines which have served to mark and to affect the characteristics of the frontiers, namely: The "fall line"; the Alleghany Mountains; the Mississippi; the Missouri, where its direction approximates north and south; the line of the arid lands, approximately the ninety-ninth meridian; and the Rocky Mountains. The fall line marked the frontier of the seventeenth century; the Alleghanies that of the eighteenth; the Mississippi that of the first quarter of the nineteenth; the Missouri that of the middle of this century (omitting the California movement); and the belt of the Rocky Mountains and the arid tract, the present frontier. Each was won by a series of Indian wars.

The frontier furnishes a field for comparative study of social development

At the Atlantic frontier one can study the germs of processes repeated at each successive frontier. We have the complex European life sharply precipitated by the wilderness into the simplicity of primitive conditions. The first frontier had to meet its Indian question, its question of the disposition of the public domain, of the means of intercourse with older settlements, of the extension of political organization, of religious and educational activity. And the settlement of these and similar questions for one frontier served as a guide for the next. The American student needs not to go to the "prim little townships of Sleswick" for illustrations of the law of continuity and development. For example, he may study the origin of our land policies in the colonial land policy; he may see how the system grew by adapting the statutes to the customs of the successive frontiers. He may see how the mining experience in the lead regions of Wisconsin, Illinois, and Iowa was applied to the mining laws of the Rockies, and how our Indian policy has been a series of experimentations on successive frontiers. Each tier of new States has found in the older ones material for its constitutions. Each frontier has made similar contributions to American character, as will be discussed farther on.

But with all these similarities there are essential differences, due to the place element and the time element. It is evident that the farming frontier of the Mississippi Valley presents different conditions from the mining frontier of the Rocky Mountains. The frontier reached by the Pacific Railroad, surveyed into rectangles, guarded by the United States Army, and recruited by the daily immigrant ship, moves forward at a swifter pace and in a different way than the frontier reached by the birch canoe or the pack horse. The geologist traces patiently the shores of ancient seas, maps their areas, and compares the older and the newer. It would be a work worth the historian's labors to mark these various frontiers and in detail compare one with another. Not only would there result a more adequate conception of American development and characteristics, but invaluable additions would be made to the history of society.

Loria, the Italian economist, has urged the study of colonial life as an aid in understanding the stages of European development, affirming that colonial settlement is for economic science what the mountain is for geology, bringing to light primitive stratifications. "America," he says, "has the key to the historical enigma which Europe has sought for centuries in vain, and the land which has no history reveals luminously the course of universal history." There is much truth in this. The United States lies like a huge page in the history of society. Line by line as we read this continental page from west to east we find the record of social evolution. It begins with the Indian and the hunter; it goes on to tell of the disintegration of savagery by the entrance of the trader, the pathfinder of civilization; we read the annals of the pastoral stage in ranch life; the exploitation of the soil by the raising of unrotated crops of corn and wheat in sparsely settled farming communities; the intensive culture of the denser farm settlement; and finally the manufacturing organization with city and factory system. This page is familiar to the student of census statistics, but how little of it has been used by our historians. Particularly in eastern States this page is a palimpsest. What is now a manufacturing State was in an earlier decade an area of intensive farming. Earlier yet it had been a wheat area, and still earlier the "range" had attracted the cattle herder. Thus Wisconsin, now developing manufacture, is a State with varied agricultural interests. But earlier it was given over to almost exclusive grain-raising, like North Dakota at the present time.

Each of these areas has had an influence in our economic and political history; the evolution of each into a higher stage has worked political transformations. But what constitutional historian has made any adequate attempt to interpret political facts by the light of these social areas and changes?

The Atlantic frontier was compounded of fisherman, fur-trader, miner, cattle-raiser, and farmer. Excepting the fisherman, each type of industry was on the march toward the West, impelled by an irresistible attraction. Each passed in successive waves across the continent. Stand at Cumberland Gap and watch the procession of civilization, marching single file—the buffalo following the trail to the salt springs, the Indian, the fur-trader and hunter, the cattle-raiser, the pioneer farmer—and the frontier has passed by. Stand at South Pass in the Rockies a century later and see the same procession with wider intervals between. The unequal rate of advance compels us to distinguish the frontier into the trader's frontier, the rancher's frontier, or the miner's frontier, and the farmer's frontier. When the mines and the cow pens were still near the fall line the traders' pack trains were tinkling across the Alleghanies, and the French on the Great Lakes were fortifying their posts, alarmed by the British trader's birch canoe. When the trappers scaled the Rockies, the farmer was still near the mouth of the Missouri.

The Indian trader's frontier

Why was it that the Indian trader passed so rapidly across the continent? What effects followed from the trader's frontier? The trade was coeval with American discovery. The Norsemen, Vespuccius, Verrazani, Hudson, John Smith, all trafficked for furs. The Plymouth pilgrims settled in Indian cornfields, and their first return cargo was of beaver and lumber. The records of the various New England colonies show how steadily exploration was carried into the wilderness by this trade. What is true for New England is, as would be expected, even plainer for the rest of the colonies. All along the coast from Maine to Georgia the Indian trade opened up the river courses. Steadily the trader passed westward, utilizing the older lines of French trade. The Ohio, the Great Lakes, the Mississippi, the Missouri, and the Platte, the lines of western advance, were ascended by traders. They found the passes in the Rocky Mountains and guided Lewis and Clark, Fremont, and Bidwell. The explanation of the rapidity of this advance is connected with the effects of the trader on the Indian. The trading post left the unarmed tribes at the mercy of those that had purchased fire-arms—a truth which the Iroquois Indians wrote in blood, and so the remote and unvisited tribes gave eager welcome to the trader. "The savages," wrote La Salle, "take better care of us French than of their own children; from us only can they get guns and goods." This accounts for the trader's power and the rapidity of his advance. Thus the disintegrating forces of civilization entered the wilderness. Every river valley and Indian trail became a fissure in Indian society, and so that society became honeycombed. Long before the pioneer farmer appeared on the scene, primitive Indian life had passed away. The farmers met Indians armed with guns. The trading frontier, while steadily undermining Indian power by making the tribes ultimately dependent on the whites, yet, through its sale of guns, gave to the Indians increased power of resistance to the farming frontier. French colonization was dominated by its trading frontier; English colonization by its farming frontier. There was an antagonism between the two frontiers as between the two nations. Said Duquesne to the Iroquois, "Are you ignorant of the difference between the king of England and the king of France? Go see the forts that our king has established and you will see that you can still hunt under their very walls. They have been placed for your advantage in places which you frequent. The English, on the contrary, are no sooner in possession of a place than the game is driven away. The forest falls before them as they advance, and the soil is laid bare so that you can scarce find the wherewithal to erect a shelter for the night."

And yet, in spite of this opposition of the interests of the trader and the farmer, the Indian trade pioneered the way for civilization. The buffalo trail became the Indian trail, and this became the trader's "trace"; the trails widened into roads, and the roads into turnpikes, and these in turn were transformed into railroads. The same origin can be shown for the railroads of the South, the far West, and the Dominion of Canada. The trading posts reached by these trails were on the sites of Indian villages which had been placed in positions suggested by nature; and these trading posts, situated so as to command the water systems of the country, have grown into such cities as Albany, Pittsburgh, Detroit, Chicago, St. Louis, Council Bluffs, and Kansas City. Thus civilization in America has followed the arteries made by geology, pouring an ever richer tide through them, until at last the slender paths of aboriginal intercourse have been broadened and interwoven into the complex mazes of modern commercial lines; the wilderness has been interpenetrated by lines of civilization growing ever more numerous. It is like the steady growth of a complex nervous system for the originally simple, inert continent. If one would understand why we are to-day one nation, rather than a collection of isolated states, he must study this economic and social consolidation of the country. In this progress from savage conditions lie topics for the evolutionist.

The effect of the Indian frontier as a consolidating agent in our history is important. From the close of the seventeenth century various intercolonial congresses have been called to treat with Indians and establish common measures of defense. Particularism was strongest in colonies with no Indian frontier. This frontier stretched along the western border like a cord of union. The Indian was a common danger, demanding united action. Most celebrated of these conferences was the Albany congress of 1754, called to treat with the Six Nations, and to consider plans of union. Even a cursory reading of the plan proposed by the congress reveals the importance of the frontier. The powers of the general council and the officers were, chiefly, the determination of peace and war with the Indians, the regulation of Indian trade, the purchase of Indian lands, and the creation and government of new settlements as a security against the Indians. It is evident that the unifying tendencies of the Revolutionary period were facilitated by the previous cooperation in the regulation of the frontier. In this connection may be mentioned the importance of the frontier, from that day to this, as a military training school, keeping alive the power of resistance to aggression, and developing the stalwart and rugged qualities of the frontiersman.

The rancher's frontier

It would not be possible in the limits of this paper to trace the other frontiers across the continent. Travelers of the eighteenth century found the "cowpens" among the canebrakes and peavine pastures of the South, and the "cow drivers" took their droves to Charleston, Philadelphia, and New York. Travelers at the close of the War of 1812 met droves of more than a thousand cattle and swine from the interior of Ohio going to Pennsylvania to fatten for the Philadelphia market. The ranges of the Great Plains, with ranch and cowboy and nomadic life, are things of yesterday and of to-day. The experience of the Carolina cowpens guided the ranchers of Texas. One element favoring the rapid extension of the rancher's frontier is the fact that in a remote country lacking transportation facilities the product must be in small bulk, or must be able to transport itself, and the cattle raiser could easily drive his product to market. The effect of these great ranches on the subsequent agrarian history of the localities in which they existed should be studied.

The farmer's frontier

The maps of the census reports show an uneven advance of the farmer's frontier, with tongues of settlement pushed forward and with indentations of wilderness. In part this is due to Indian resistance, in part to the location of river valleys and passes, in part to the unequal force of the centers of frontier attraction. Among the important centers of attraction may be mentioned the following: fertile and favorably situated soils, salt springs, mines, and army posts.

Army posts

The frontier army post, serving to protect the settlers from the Indians, has also acted as a wedge to open the Indian country, and has been a nucleus for settlement. In this connection mention should also be made of the Government military and exploring expeditions in determining the lines of settlement. But all the more important expeditions were greatly indebted to the earliest pathmakers, the Indian guides, the traders and trappers, and the French voyageurs, who were inevitable parts of governmental expeditions from the days of Lewis and Clark. Each expedition was an epitome of the previous factors in western advance.

Salt springs

In an interesting monograph, Victor Hehn has traced the effect of salt upon early European development, and has pointed out how it affected the lines of settlement and the form of administration. A similar study might be made for the salt springs of the United States. The early settlers were tied to the coast by the need of salt, without which they could not preserve their meats or live in comfort. Writing in 1752, Bishop Spangenburg says of a colony for which he was seeking lands in North Carolina, "They will require salt & other necessaries which they can neither manufacture nor raise. Either they must go to Charleston, which is 300 miles distant . . . Or else they must go to Boling's Point in V^{a} on a branch of the James & is also 300 miles from here . . . Or else they must go down the Roanoke—I know not how many miles—where salt is brought up from the Cape Fear." This may serve as a typical illustration. An annual pilgrimage to the coast for salt thus became essential. Taking flocks or furs and ginseng root, the early settlers sent their pack trains after seeding time each year to the coast. This proved to be an important educational influence, since it was almost the only way in which the pioneer learned what was going on in the East. But when discovery was made of the salt springs of the Kanawha, and the Holston, and Kentucky, and central New York, the West began to be freed from dependence on the coast. It was in part the effect of finding these salt springs that enabled settlement to cross the mountains.

From the time the mountains rose between the pioneer and the seaboard, a new order of Americanism arose. The West and the East began to get out of touch of each other. The settlements from the sea to the mountains kept connection with the rear and had a certain solidarity. But the overmountain men grew more and more independent. The East took a narrow view of American advance, and nearly lost these men. Kentucky and Tennessee history bears abundant witness to the truth of this statement. The East began to try to hedge and limit westward expansion. Though Webster could declare that there were no Alleghanies in his politics, yet in politics in general they were a very solid factor.

Land

The exploitation of the beasts took hunter and trader to the west, the exploitation of the grasses took the rancher west, and the exploitation of the virgin soil of the river valleys and prairies attracted the farmer. Good soils have been the most continuous attraction to the farmer's frontier. The land hunger of the Virginians drew them down the rivers into Carolina, in early colonial days; the search for soils took the Massachusetts men to Pennsylvania and to New York. As the eastern lands were taken up migration flowed across them to the west. Daniel Boone, the great backwoodsman, who combined the occupations of hunter, trader, cattle raiser, farmer, and surveyor—learning, probably from the traders, of the fertility of the lands on the upper Yadkin, where the traders were wont to rest as they took their way to the Indians, left his Pennsylvania home with his father, and passed down the Great Valley road to that stream. Learning from a trader whose posts were on the Red River in Kentucky of its game and rich pastures, he pioneered the way for the farmers to that region. Thence he passed to the frontier of Missouri, where his settlement was long a landmark on the frontier. Here again he helped to open the way for civilization, finding salt licks, and trails, and land. His son was among the earliest trappers in the passes of the Rocky Mountains, and his party are said to have been the first to camp on the present site of

Denver. His grandson, Col. A. J. Boone, of Colorado, was a power among the Indians of the Rocky Mountains, and was appointed an agent by the Government. Kit Carson's mother was a Boone. Thus this family epitomizes the backwoodsman's advance across the continent.

The farmer's advance came in a distinct series of waves. In Peck's New Guide to the West, published in Boston in 1837, occurs this suggestive passage:

> *Generally, in all the western settlements, three classes, like the waves of the ocean, have rolled one after the other. First comes the pioneer, who depends for the subsistence of his family chiefly upon the natural growth of vegetation, called the "range," and the proceeds of hunting. His implements of agriculture are rude, chiefly of his own make, and his efforts directed mainly to a crop of corn and a "truck patch." The last is a rude garden for growing cabbage, beans, corn for roasting ears, cucumbers, and potatoes. A log cabin and, occasionally, a stable and corn-crib, and a field of a dozen acres, the timber girdled or "deadened," and fenced, are enough for his occupancy. It is quite immaterial whether he ever becomes the owner of the soil. He is the occupant for the time being, pays no rent, and feels as independent as the "lord of the manor." With a horse, cow, and one or two breeders of swine, he strikes into the woods with his family, and becomes the founder of a new county, or perhaps state. He builds his cabin, gathers around him a few other families of similar tastes and habits, and occupies till the range is somewhat subdued, and hunting a little precarious, or, which is more frequently the case, till the neighbors crowd around, roads, bridges, and fields annoy him, and he lacks elbow room. The preemption law enables him to dispose of his cabin and cornfield to the next class of emigrants; and, to employ his own figures, he "breaks for the high timber," "clears out for the New Purchase," or migrates to Arkansas or Texas, to work the same process over.*
>
> *The next class of emigrants purchase the lands, add field to field, clear out the roads, throw rough bridges over the streams, put up hewn log houses with glass windows and brick or stone chimneys, occasionally plant orchards, build mills, schoolhouses, court-houses, etc., and exhibit the picture and forms of plain frugal, civilized life.*
>
> *Another wave rolls on. The men of capital and enterprise come. The settler is ready to sell out and take the advantage of the rise in property, push farther into the interior and become, himself, a man of capital and enterprise in turn. The small village rises to a spacious town or city; substantial edifices of brick, extensive fields, orchards, gardens, colleges, and churches are seen. Broadcloths, silks, leghorns, crapes, and all the refinements, luxuries, elegancies, frivolities, and fashions are in vogue. Thus wave after wave is rolling westward; the real Eldorado is still farther on.*
>
> *A portion of the two first classes remain stationary amidst the general movement, improve their habits and condition, and rise in the scale of society.*

The writer has traveled much amongst the first class, the real pioneers. He has lived many years in connection with the second grade; and now the third wave is sweeping over large districts of Indiana, Illinois, and Missouri. Migration has become almost a habit in the West. Hundreds of men can be found, not over 50 years of age, who have settled for the fourth, fifth, or sixth time on a new spot. To sell out and remove only a few hundred miles makes up a portion of the variety of backwoods life and manners.

Omitting those of the pioneer farmers who move from the love of adventure, the advance of the more steady farmer is easy to understand. Obviously the immigrant was attracted by the cheap lands of the frontier, and even the native farmer felt their influence strongly. Year by year the farmers who lived on soil whose returns were diminished by unrotated crops were offered the virgin soil of the frontier at nominal prices. Their growing families demanded more lands, and these were dear. The competition of the unexhausted, cheap, and easily tilled prairie lands compelled the farmer either to go west and continue the exhaustion of the soil on a new frontier, or to adopt intensive culture. Thus the census of 1890 shows, in the Northwest, many counties in which there is an absolute or a relative decrease of population. These States have been sending farmers to advance the frontier on the plains, and have themselves begun to turn to intensive farming and to manufacture. A decade before this, Ohio had shown the same transition stage. Thus the demand for land and the love of wilderness freedom drew the frontier ever onward.

Having now roughly outlined the various kinds of frontiers, and their modes of advance, chiefly from the point of view of the frontier itself, we may next inquire what were the influences on the East and on the Old World. A rapid enumeration of some of the more noteworthy effects is all that I have time for.

Composite nationality

First, we note that the frontier promoted the formation of a composite nationality for the American people. The coast was preponderantly English, but the later tides of continental immigration flowed across to the free lands. This was the case from the early colonial days. The Scotch-Irish and the Palatine Germans, or "Pennsylvania Dutch," furnished the dominant element in the stock of the colonial frontier. With these peoples were also the freed indented servants, or redemptioners, who at the expiration of their time of service passed to the frontier. Governor Spottswood of Virginia writed in 1717, "The inhabitants of our frontiers are composed generally of such as have been transported hither as servants, and, being out of their time, settle themselves where land is to be taken up and that will produce the necessarys of life with little labour." Very generally these redemptioners were of non-English stock. In the crucible of the frontier the immigrants were Americanized, liberated, and fused into a mixed race, English in neither nationality nor characteristics. The process has gone on from the early days to our own. Burke and other writers in the middle of the eighteenth century believed that Pennsylvania was "threatened with the danger of being wholly foreign in language, manners, and perhaps even inclinations." The German and Scotch-Irish elements in the frontier of the South were only less great. In the middle of the present century the German element in Wisconsin was already so considerable that leading publicists looked to the creation of a German state out of the commonwealth by concentrating their colonization. Such examples teach us to beware of misinterpreting the fact that there is a common English speech in America into a belief that the stock is also English.

Industrial independence

In another way the advance of the frontier decreased our dependence on England. The coast, particularly of the South, lacked diversified industries, and was dependent on England for the bulk of its supplies. In the South there was even a dependence on the Northern colonies for articles of food. Governor Glenn, of South Carolina, writes in the middle of the eighteenth century: "Our trade with New York and Philadelphia was of this sort, draining us of all the little money and bills we could gather from other places for their bread, flour, beer, hams, bacon, and other things of their produce, all which, except beer, our new townships begin to supply us with, which are settled with very industrious and thriving Germans. This no doubt diminishes the number of shipping and the appearance of our trade, but it is far from being a detriment to us." Before long the frontier created a demand for merchants. As it retreated from the coast it became less and less possible for England to bring her supplies directly to the consumer's wharfs, and carry away staple crops, and staple crops began to give way to diversified agriculture for a time. The effect of this phase of the frontier action upon the northern section is perceived when we realize how the advance of the frontier aroused seaboard cities like Boston, New York, and Baltimore, to engage in rivalry for what Washington called "the extensive and valuable trade of a rising empire."

Effects on national legislation

The legislation which most developed the powers of the National Government, and played the largest part in its activity, was conditioned on the frontier. Writers have discussed the subjects of tariff, land, and internal improvement, as subsidiary to the slavery question. But when American history comes to be rightly viewed it will be seen that the slavery question is an incident. In the period from the end of the first half of the present century to the close of the civil war slavery rose to primary, but far from exclusive, importance. But this does not justify Dr. von Holst (to take an example) in treating our constitutional history in its formative period down to 1828 in a single volume, giving six volumes chiefly to the history of slavery from 1828 to 1861, under the title "Constitutional History of the United States." The growth of nationalism and the evolution of American political institutions were dependent on the advance of the frontier. Even so recent a writer as Rhodes, in his "History of the United States since the Compromise of 1850," has treated the legislation called out by the western advance as incidental to the slavery struggle.

This is a wrong perspective. The pioneer needed the goods of the coast, and so the grand series of internal improvement and railroad legislation began, with potent nationalizing effects. Over internal improvements occurred great debates, in which grave constitutional questions were discussed. Sectional groupings appear in the votes, profoundly significant for the historian. Loose construction increased as the nation marched westward. But the West was not content with bringing the farm to the factory. Under the lead of Clay—"Harry of the West"—protective tariffs were passed, with the cry of bringing the factory to the farm. The disposition of the public lands was a third important subject of national legislation influenced by the frontier.

The public domain

The public domain has been a force of profound importance in the nationalization and development of the Government. The effects of the struggle of the landed and the landless States, and of the ordinance of 1787, need no discussion. Administratively the frontier called out some of the highest and most vitalizing activities of the General Government. The purchase of Louisiana was perhaps the constitutional turning point in the history of the Republic, inasmuch as it afforded both a new area for national legislation and the occasion of the downfall of the policy of strict construction. But the purchase of Louisiana was called out by frontier needs and demands. As frontier States accrued to the Union the national power grew. In a speech on the dedication of the Calhoun monument Mr. Lamar explained: "In 1789 the States were the creators of the Federal Government; in 1861 the Federal Government was the creator of a large majority of the States."

When we consider the public domain from the point of view of the sale and disposal of the public lands we are again brought face to face with the frontier. The policy of the United States in dealing with its lands is in sharp contrast with the European system of scientific administration. Efforts to make this domain a source of revenue, and to withhold it from emigrants in order that settlement might be compact, were in vain. The jealousy and the fears of the East were powerless in the face of the demands of the frontiersmen. John Quincy Adams was obliged to confess: "My own system of administration, which was to make the national domain the inexhaustible fund for progressive and unceasing internal improvement, has failed." The reason is obvious; a system of administration was not what the West demanded; it wanted land. Adams states the situation as follows: "The slaveholders of the South have bought the cooperation of the western country by the bribe of the western lands, abandoning to the new Western States their own proportion of the public property and aiding them in the design of grasping all the lands into their own hands." Thomas H. Benton was the author of this system, which he brought forward as a substitute for the American system of Mr. Clay, and to supplant him as the leading statesman than like that of the tide-water portion of the South, which later came to spread its industrial type throughout the South.

The Middle region, entered by New York harbor, was an open door to all Europe. The tide-water part of the South represented typical Englishmen, modified by a warm climate and servile labor, and living in baronial fashion on great plantations; New England stood for a special English movement—Puritanism. The Middle region was less English than the other sections. It had a wide mixture of nationalities, a varied society, the mixed town and county system of local government, a varied economic life, many religious sects. In short, it was a region mediating between New England and the South, and the East and the West. It represented that composite nationality which the contemporary United States exhibits, that juxtaposition of non-English groups, occupying a valley or a little settlement, and presenting reflections of the map of Europe in their variety. It was typical of the modern United States. It was least sectional, not only because it lay between North and South, but also because with no barriers to shut out its frontiers from its settled region, and with a system of connecting waterways, the Middle region mediated between East and West as well as between North and South. Thus it became the typically American region. Even the New Englander, who was shut out from the frontier by the Middle region, tarrying in New York or Pennsylvania on his westward march, lost the acuteness of his sectionalism on the way.

The spread of cotton culture into the interior of the South finally broke down the contrast between the "tide-water" region and the rest of the State, and based Southern interests on slavery. Before this process revealed its results the western portion of the South, which was akin to Pennsylvania in stock, society, and industry, showed tendencies to fall away from the faith of the fathers into internal improvement legislation and nationalism. In the Virginia convention of 1829–30, called to revise the constitution, Mr. Leigh, of Chesterfield, one of the tide-water counties, declared:

One of the main causes of discontent which led to this convention, that which had the strongest influence in overcoming our veneration for the work of our fathers, which taught us to contemn the sentiments of Henry and Mason and Pendleton, which weaned us from our reverence for the constituted authorities of the State, was an overweening passion for internal improvement. I say this with perfect knowledge, for it has been avowed to me by gentlemen from the West over and over again. And let me tell the gentleman from Albemarle (Mr. Gordon) that it has been another principal object of those who set this ball of revolution in motion, to overturn the doctrine of State rights, of which Virginia has been the very pillar, and to remove the barrier she has interposed to the interference of the Federal Government in that same work of internal improvement, by so reorganizing the legislature that Virginia, too, may be hitched to the Federal car.

It was this nationalizing tendency of the West that transformed the democracy of Jefferson into the national republicanism of Monroe and the democracy of Andrew Jackson. The West of the War of 1812, the West of Clay, and Benton, and Harrison, and Andrew Jackson, shut off by the Middle States and the mountains from the coast sections, had a solidarity of its own with national tendencies. On the tide of the Father of Waters, North and South met and mingled into a nation. Interstate migration went steadily on—a process of cross-fertilization of ideas and institutions. The fierce struggle of the sections over slavery on the western frontier does not diminish the truth of this statement; it proves the truth of it. Slavery was a sectional trait that would not down, but in the West it could not remain sectional. It was the greatest of frontiersmen who declared: "I believe this Government can not endure permanently half slave and half free. It will become all of one thing or all of the other." Nothing works for nationalism like intercourse within the nation. Mobility of population is death to localism, and the western frontier worked irresistibly in unsettling population. The effects reached back from the frontier and affected profoundly the Atlantic coast and even the Old World.

Growth of democracy

But the most important effect of the frontier has been in the promotion of democracy here and in Europe. As has been indicated, the frontier is productive of individualism. Complex society is precipitated by the wilderness into a kind of primitive organization based on the family. The tendency is anti-social. It produces antipathy to control, and particularly to any direct control. The tax gatherer is viewed as a representative of oppression. Professor Osgood, in an able article, has pointed out that the frontier conditions prevalent in the colonies are important factors in the explanation of the American Revolution, where individual liberty was sometimes confused with absence of all effective government. The same conditions aid in explaining the difficulty of instituting a strong government in the period of the confederacy. The frontier individualism has from the beginning promoted democracy.

The frontier States that came into the Union in the first quarter of a century of its existence came in with democratic suffrage provisions, and had reactive effects of the highest importance upon the older States whose peoples were being attracted there. An extension of the franchise became essential. It was *western* New York that forced an extension of suffrage in the constitutional convention of that State in 1821; and it was *western* Virginia that compelled the tide-water region to put a more liberal suffrage provision in the constitution framed in 1830, and to give to the frontier region a more nearly proportionate representation with the tide-water aristocracy. The rise of democracy as an effective force in the nation came in with western preponderance under Jackson and William Henry Harrison, and it meant the triumph of the frontier—with all of its good and with all of its evil elements. An interesting illustration of the tone of frontier democracy in 1830 comes from the same debates in the Virginia convention already referred to. A representative from western Virginia declared:

> *But, sir, it is not the increase of population in the West which this gentleman ought to fear. It is the energy which the mountain breeze and western habits impart to those emigrants. They are regenerated, politically I mean, sir. They soon become* working politicians; *and the difference, sir, between a* talking *and a* working *politician is immense. The Old Dominion has long been celebrated for producing great orators; the ablest metaphysicians in policy; men that can split hairs in all abstruse questions of political economy. But at home, or when they return from Congress, they have negroes to fan them asleep. But a Pennsylvania, a New York, an Ohio, or a western Virginia statesman, though far inferior in logic, metaphysics, and rhetoric to an old Virginia statesman, has this advantage, that when he returns home he takes off his coat and takes hold of the plow. This gives him bone and muscle, sir, and preserves his republican principles pure and uncontaminated.*

So long as free land exists, the opportunity for a competency exists, and economic power secures political power. But the democracy born of free land, strong in selfishness and individualism, intolerant of administrative experience and education, and pressing individual liberty beyond its proper bounds, has its dangers as well as its benefits. Individualism in America has allowed a laxity in regard to governmental affairs which has rendered possible the spoils system and all the manifest evils that follow from the lack of a highly developed civic spirit. In this connection may be noted also the influence of frontier conditions in permitting lax business honor, inflated paper currency and wild-cat banking. The colonial and revolutionary frontier was the region whence emanated many of the worst forms of an evil currency. The West in the War of 1812 repeated the phenomenon on the frontier of that day, while the speculation and the wild-cat banking of the period of the crisis of 1837 occurred on the new frontier belt of the next tier of States. Thus each one of the periods of lax financial integrity coincides with periods when a new set of frontier communities had arisen, and coincides in area with these successive frontiers, for the most part. The recent Populist agitation is a case in point. Many a State that now declines any connection with the tenets of the Populists, itself adhered to such ideas in an earlier stage of the development of the State. A primitive society can hardly be expected to show the intelligent appreciation of the complexity of business interests in a developed society. The continual recurrence of these areas of paper-money agitation is another evidence that the frontier can be isolated and studied as a factor in American history of the highest importance.

Attempts to check and regulate the frontier

The East has always feared the result of an unregulated advance of the frontier, and has tried to check and guide it. The English authorities would have checked settlement at the headwaters of the Atlantic tributaries and allowed the "savages to enjoy their deserts in quiet lest the peltry trade should decrease." This called out Burke's splendid protest:

> *If you stopped your grants, what would be the consequence? The people would occupy without grants. They have already so occupied in many places. You can not station garrisons in every part of these deserts. If you drive the people from one place, they will carry on their annual tillage and remove with their flocks and herds to another. Many of the people in the back settlements are already little attached to particular situations. Already they have topped the Appalachian mountains. From thence they behold before them an immense plain, one vast, rich, level meadow; a square of five hundred miles. Over this they would wander without a possibility of restraint; they would change their manners with their habits of life; would soon forget a government by which they were disowned; would become hordes of English Tartars; and, pouring down upon your unfortified frontiers a fierce and irresistible cavalry, become masters of your governors and your counselors, your collectors and comptrollers, and of all the slaves that adhered to them. Such would, and in no long time must, be the effect of attempting to forbid as a crime and to suppress as an evil the command and blessing of Providence, "Increase and multiply." Such would be the happy result of an endeavor to keep as a lair of wild beasts that earth which God, by an express charter, has given to the children of men.*

But the English Government was not alone in its desire to limit the advance of the frontier and guide its destinies. Tide-water Virginia and South Carolina gerrymandered those colonies to insure the dominance of the coast in their legislatures. Washington desired to settle a State at a time in the Northwest; Jefferson would reserve from settlement the territory of his Louisiana purchase north of the thirty-second parallel, in order to offer it to the Indians in exchange for their settlements east of the Mississippi. "When we shall be full on this side," he writes, "we may lay off a range of States on the western bank from the head to the mouth, and so range after range, advancing compactly as we multiply." Madison went so far as to argue to the French minister that the United States had no interest in seeing population extend itself on the right bank of the Mississippi, but should rather fear it. When the Oregon question was under debate, in 1824, Smyth, of Virginia, would draw an unchangeable line for the limits of the United States at the outer limit of two tiers of States beyond the Mississippi, complaining that the seaboard States were being drained of the flower of their population by the bringing of too much land into market. Even Thomas Benton, the man of widest views of the destiny of the West, at this stage of his career declared that along the ridge of the Rocky mountains "the western limits of the Republic should be drawn, and the statue of the fabled god Terminus should be raised upon its highest peak, never to be thrown down." But the attempts to limit the boundaries, to restrict land sales and settlement, and to deprive the West of its share of political power were all in vain. Steadily the frontier of settlement advanced and carried with it individualism, democracy, and nationalism, and powerfully affected the East and the Old World.

Missionary activity

The most effective efforts of the East to regulate the frontier came through its educational and religious activity, exerted by interstate migration and by organized societies. Speaking in 1835, Dr. Lyman Beecher declared: "It is equally plain that the religious and political destiny of our nation is to be decided in the West," and he pointed out that the population of the West "is assembled from all the States of the Union and from all the nations of Europe, and is rushing in like the waters of the flood, demanding for its moral preservation the immediate and universal action of those institutions which discipline the mind and arm the conscience and the heart. And so various are the opinions and habits, and so recent and imperfect is the acquaintance, and so sparse are the settlements of the West, that no homogeneous public sentiment can be formed to legislate immediately into being the requisite institutions. And yet they are all needed immediately in their utmost perfection and power. A nation is being 'born in a day.' . . . But what will become of the West if her prosperity rushes up to such a majesty of power, while those great institutions linger which are necessary to form the mind and the conscience and the heart of that vast world? It must not be permitted. . . . Let no man at the East quiet himself and dream of liberty, whatever may become of the West. . . . Her destiny is our destiny."

With the appeal to the conscience of New England, he adds appeals to her fears lest other religious sects anticipate her own. The New England preacher and school-teacher left their mark on the West. The dread of Western emancipation from New England's political and economic control was paralleled by her fears lest the West cut loose from her religion. Commenting in 1850 on reports that settlement was rapidly extending northward in Wisconsin, the editor of the Home Missionary writes: "We scarcely know whether to rejoice or mourn over this extension of our settlements. While we sympathize in whatever tends to increase the physical resources and prosperity of our country, we can not forget that with all these dispersions into remote and still remoter corners of the land the supply of the means of grace is becoming relatively less and less." Acting in accordance with such ideas, home missions were established and Western colleges were erected. As seaboard cities like Philadelphia, New York, and Baltimore strove for the mastery of Western trade, so the various denominations strove for the possession of the West. Thus an intellectual stream from New England sources fertilized the West. Other sections sent their missionaries; but the real struggle was between sects. The contest for power and the expansive tendency furnished to the various sects by the existence of a moving frontier must have had important results on the character of religious organization in the United States. The multiplication of rival churches in the little frontier towns had deep and lasting social effects. The religious aspects of the frontier make a chapter in our history which needs study.

Intellectual traits

From the conditions of frontier life came intellectual traits of profound importance. The works of travelers along each frontier from colonial days onward describe certain common traits, and these traits have, while softening down, still persisted as survivals in the place of their origin, even when a higher social organization succeeded. The result is that to the frontier the American intellect owes its striking characteristics. That coarseness and strength combined with acuteness and inquisitiveness; that practical, inventive turn of mind, quick to find expedients; that masterful grasp of material things, lacking in the artistic but powerful to effect great ends; that restless, nervous energy; that dominant individualism, working for good and for evil, and withal that buoyancy and exuberance which comes with freedom—these are traits of the frontier, or traits called out elsewhere because of the existence of the frontier. Since the days when the fleet of Columbus sailed into the waters of the New World, America has been another name for opportunity, and the people of the United States have taken their tone from the incessant expansion which has not only been open but has even been forced upon them. He would be a rash prophet who should assert that the expansive character of American life has now entirely ceased. Movement has been its dominant fact, and, unless this training has no effect upon a people, the American energy will continually demand a wider field for its exercise. But never again will such gifts of free land offer themselves. For a moment, at the frontier, the bonds of custom are broken and unrestraint is triumphant. There is not *tabula rasa*. The stubborn American environment is there with its imperious summons to accept its conditions; the inherited ways of doing things are also there; and yet, in spite of environment, and in spite of custom, each frontier did indeed furnish a new field of opportunity, a gate of escape from the bondage of the past; and freshness, and confidence, and scorn of older society, impatience of its restraints and its ideas, and indifference to its lessons, have accompanied the frontier. What the Mediterranean Sea was to the Greeks, breaking the bond of custom, offering new experiences, calling out new institutions and activities, that, and more, the ever retreating frontier has been to the United States directly, and to the nations of Europe more remotely. And now, four centuries from the discovery of America, at the end of a hundred years of life under the Constitution, the frontier has gone, and with its going has closed the first period of American history.

A cowboy in front of his dugout

ANDY ADAMS

The Log of a Cowboy

(1903)

Andy Adams was born in Indiana just before the Civil War, went west in 1882, and for the next eight years took part in the last drives which moved cattle over the trails from Texas to the rail heads in Kansas. The Log of a Cowboy, the first of seven books, appeared in 1903, the year after Owen Wister's best-selling novel The Virginian. For years thereafter, men who had experienced the life of the cowboy venerated Adams' book, but most of the public still preferred Wister's famous novel. It wasn't until the 1920s that academic experts on the West began to trumpet Adams' work as the best picture of the cattle drives we will ever have.

The Log of a Cowboy is a novel, although it has no real plot, no character development, and little drama more breathtaking than the account below of a cattle crossing. Walter Prescott Webb, a prominent historian of the West, noted that Adams wrote his stories so true to life that many people believed them to be history. His is the most remarkable fiction we have on the West because it is so realistic. Adams' version of the cowboy life is the workaday one – a tough, lonely, grubby job which few men took from choice. About one quarter of the men who drove over 10,000,000 animals north were black. The dashing, violent, and romantic cowboys of Wister's novel became the ten-gallon movie heroes who another Western historian, J. Frank Dobie, described as "cowboys without any cows." It is a long way from Slaughter's bridge to the wide open spaces of Ken Maynard and the cigarette commercials. Just as Americans loved the pastoral life and hated farm work enough to move to the city, so they seemed to preserve the image of the Wild West as a haven from urban life.

Slaughter's Bridge

Herds bound for points beyond the Yellowstone, in Montana, always considered Dodge as the halfway landmark on the trail, though we had hardly covered half the distance to the destination of our Circle Dots. But with Dodge in our rear, all felt that the backbone of the drive was broken, and it was only the middle of June. In order to divide the night work more equitably, for the remainder of the trip the first and fourth guards changed, the second and third remaining as they were. We had begun to feel the scarcity of wood for cooking purposes some time past, and while crossing the plains of western Kansas, we were frequently forced to resort to the old bed grounds of a year or two previous for cattle chips. These chips were a poor substitute, and we swung a cowskin under the reach of the wagon, so that when we encountered wood on creeks and rivers we could lay in a supply. Whenever our wagon was in the rear, the riders on either side of the herd were always on the skirmish for fuel, which they left alongside the wagon track, and our cook was sure to stow it away underneath on the cowskin.

In spite of any effort on our part, the length of the days made long drives the rule. The cattle could be depended on to leave the bed ground at dawn, and before the outfit could breakfast, secure mounts, and overtake the herd, they would often have grazed forward two or three miles. Often we never threw them on the trail at all, yet when it came time to bed them at night, we had covered twenty miles. They were long, monotonous days; for we were always sixteen to eighteen hours in the saddle, while in emergencies we got the benefit of the limit. We frequently saw mirages, though we were never led astray by shady groves of timber or tempting lakes of water, but always kept within a mile or two of the trail. The evening of the third day after Forrest left us, he returned as we were bedding down the cattle at dusk, and on being assured that no officers had followed us, resumed his place with the herd. He had not even reached the Solomon River, but had stopped with a herd of Millet's on Big Boggy. This creek he reported as bottomless, and the Millet herd as having lost between forty and fifty head of cattle in attempting to force it at the regular crossing the day before his arrival. They had scouted the creek both up and down since without finding a safe crossing. It seemed that there had been unusually heavy June rains through that section, which accounted for Boggy being in its dangerous condition. Millet's foreman had not considered it necessary to test such an insignificant stream until he got a couple of hundred head of cattle floundering in the mire. They had saved the greater portion of the mired cattle, but quite a number were trampled to death by the others, and now the regular crossing was not approachable for the stench of dead cattle. Flood knew the stream, and so did a number of our outfit, but none of them had any idea that it could get into such an impassable condition as Forrest reported.

The next morning Flood started to the east and Priest to the west to look out a crossing, for we were then within half a day's drive of the creek. Big Boggy paralleled the Solomon River in our front, the two not being more than five miles apart. The confluence was far below in some settlements, and we must keep to the westward of all immigration, on account of the growing crops in the fertile valley of the Solomon. On the westward, had a favorable crossing been found, we would almost have had to turn our herd backward, for we were already within the half circle which this creek described in our front. So after the two men left us, we allowed the herd to graze forward, keeping several miles to the westward of the trail in order to get the benefit of the best grazing. Our herd, when left to itself, would graze from a mile to a mile and a half an hour, and by the middle of the forenoon the timber on Big Boggy and the Solomon beyond was sighted. On reaching this last divide, some one sighted a herd about five or six miles to the eastward and nearly parallel with us. As they were three or four miles beyond the trail, we could easily see that they were grazing along like ourselves, and Forrest was appealed to know if it was the Millet herd. He said not, and pointed out to the northeast about the location of the Millet cattle, probably five miles in advance of the stranger on our right. When we overtook our wagon at noon, McCann, who had never left the trail, reported having seen the herd. They looked to him like heavy beef cattle, and had two yoke of oxen to their chuck wagon, which served further to proclaim them as strangers.

Neither Priest nor Flood returned during the noon hour, and when the herd refused to lie down and rest longer, we grazed them forward till the fringe of timber which grew along the stream loomed up not a mile distant in our front. From the course we were traveling, we would strike the creek several miles above the regular crossing, and as Forrest reported that Millet was holding below the old crossing on a small rivulet, all we could do was to hold our wagon in the rear, and await the return of our men out on scout for a ford. Priest was the first to return, with word that he had ridden the creek out for twenty-five miles and had found no crossing that would be safe for a mud turtle. On hearing this, we left two men with the herd, and the rest of the outfit took the wagon, went on to Boggy, and made camp. It was a deceptive-looking stream, not over fifty or sixty feet wide. In places the current barely moved, shallowing and deepening, from a few inches in places to several feet in others, with an occasional pool that would swim a horse. We probed it with poles until we were satisfied that we were up against a proposition different from anything we had yet encountered. While we were discussing the situation, a stranger rode up on a fine roan horse, and inquired for our foreman. Forrest informed him that our boss was away looking for a crossing, but we were expecting his return at any time; and invited the stranger to dismount. He did so, and threw himself down in the shade of our wagon. He was a small, boyish-looking fellow, of sandy complexion, not much, if any, over twenty years old, and smiled continuously.

"My name is Pete Slaughter," said he, by way of introduction, "and I've got a herd of twenty-eight hundred beef steers, beyond the trail and a few miles back. I've been riding since daybreak down the creek, and I'm prepared to state that the chance of crossing is as good right here as anywhere. I wanted to see your foreman, and if he'll help, we'll bridge her. I've been down to see this other outfit, but they ridicule the idea, though I think they'll come around all right. I borrowed their axe, and to-morrow morning you'll see me with my outfit cutting timber to bridge Big Boggy. That's right, boys; it's the only thing to do. The trouble is I've only got eight men all told. I don't aim to travel over eight or ten miles a day, so I don't need a big outfit. You say your foreman's name is Flood? Well, if he don't return before I go, some of you tell him that he's wasting good time looking for a ford, for there ain't none."

In the conversation which followed, we learned that Slaughter was driving for his brother Lum, a widely known cowman and drover, whom we had seen in Dodge. He had started with the grass from north Texas, and by the time he reached the Platte, many of his herd would be fit to ship to market, and what were not would be in good demand as feeders in the corn belt of eastern Nebraska. He asked if we had seen his herd during the morning, and on hearing we had, got up and asked McCann to let him see our axe. This he gave a critical examination, before he mounted his horse to go, and on leaving said, —

"If your foreman don't want to help build a bridge, I want to borrow that axe of yours. But you fellows talk to him. If any of you boys has ever been over on the Chisholm trail, you will remember the bridge on Rush Creek, south of the Washita River. I built that bridge in a day with an outfit of ten men. Why, shucks! if these outfits would pull together, we could cross to-morrow evening. Lots of these old foremen don't like to listen to a cub like me, but, holy snakes! I've been over the trail oftener than any of them. Why, when I wasn't big enough to make a hand with the herd,—only ten years old,—in the days when we drove to Abilene, they used to send me in the lead with an old cylinder gun to shoot at the buffalo and scare them off the trail. And I've made the trip every year since. So you tell Flood when he comes in, that Pete Slaughter was here, and that he's going to build a bridge, and would like to have him and his outfit help."

Had it not been for his youth and perpetual smile, we might have taken young Slaughter more seriously, for both Quince Forrest and The Rebel remembered the bridge on Rush Creek over on the Chisholm. Still there was an air of confident assurance in the young fellow; and the fact that he was the trusted foreman of Lum Slaughter, in charge of a valuable herd of cattle, carried weight with those who knew that drover. The most unwelcome thought in the project was that it required the swinging of an axe to fell trees and to cut them into the necessary lengths, and, as I have said before, the Texan never took kindly to manual labor. But Priest looked favorably on the suggestion, and so enlisted my support, and even pointed out a spot where timber was most abundant as a suitable place to build the bridge.

"Hell's fire," said Joe Stallings, with infinite contempt, "there's thousands of places to build a bridge, and the timber's there, but the idea is to cut it." And his sentiments found a hearty approval in the majority of the outfit.

Flood returned late that evening, having ridden as far down the creek as the first settlement. The Rebel, somewhat antagonized by the attitude of the majority, reported the visit and message left for him by young Slaughter. Our foreman knew him by general reputation amongst trail bosses, and when Priest vouched for him as the builder of the Rush Creek bridge on the Chisholm trail, Flood said, "Why, I crossed my herd four years ago on that Rush Creek bridge within a week after it was built, and wondered who it could be that had the nerve to undertake that task. Rush isn't over half as wide a bayou as Boggy, but she's a true little sister to this miry slough. So he's going to build a bridge anyhow, is he?"

The next morning young Slaughter was at our camp before sunrise, and never once mentioning his business or waiting for the formality of an invitation, proceeded to pour out a tin cup of coffee and otherwise provide himself with a substantial breakfast. There was something amusing in the audacity of the fellow which all of us liked, though he was fifteen years the junior of our foreman. McCann pointed out Flood to him, and taking his well-loaded plate, he went over and sat down by our foreman, and while he ate talked rapidly, to enlist our outfit in the building of the bridge. During breakfast, the outfit listened to the two bosses as they discussed the feasibility of the project,—Slaughter enthusiastic, Flood reserved, and asking all sorts of questions as to the mode of procedure. Young Pete met every question with promptness, and assured our foreman that the building of bridges was his long suit. After breakfast, the two foremen rode off down the creek together, and within half an hour Slaughter's wagon and *remuda* pulled up within sight of the regular crossing, and shortly afterwards our foreman returned, and ordered our wagon to pull down to a clump of cottonwoods which grew about half a mile below our camp. Two men were detailed to look after our herd during the day, and the remainder of us returned with our foreman to the site selected for the bridge. On our arrival three axes were swinging against as many cottonwoods, and there was no doubt in any one's mind that we were going to be under a new foreman for that day at least. Slaughter had a big negro cook who swung an axe in a manner which bespoke him a job for the day, and McCann was instructed to provide dinner for the extra outfit.

The site chosen for the bridge was a miry bottom over which oozed three or four inches of water, where the width of the stream was about sixty feet, with solid banks on either side. To get a good foundation was the most important matter, but the brush from the trees would supply the material for that; and within an hour, brush began to arrive, dragged from the pommels of saddles, and was piled into the stream. About this time a call went out for a volunteer who could drive oxen, for the darky was too good an axeman to be recalled. As I had driven oxen as a boy, I was going to offer my services, when Joe Stallings eagerly volunteered in order to avoid using an axe. Slaughter had some extra chain, and our four mules were pressed into service as an extra team in snaking logs. As McCann was to provide for the inner man, the mule team fell to me; and putting my saddle on the nigh wheeler, I rode jauntily past Mr. Stallings as he trudged alongside his two yoke of oxen.

About ten o'clock in the morning, George Jacklin, the foreman of the Millet herd, rode up with several of his men, and seeing the bridge taking shape, turned in and assisted in dragging brush for the foundation. By the time all hands knocked off for dinner, we had a foundation of brush twenty feet wide and four feet high, to say nothing about what had sunk in the mire. The logs were cut about fourteen feet long, and old Joe and I had snaked them up as fast as the axemen could get them ready. Jacklin returned to his wagon for dinner and a change of horses, though Slaughter, with plenty of assurance, had invited him to eat with us, and when he declined had remarked, with no less confidence, "Well, then, you'll be back right after dinner. And say, bring all the men you can spare; and if you've got any gunny sacks or old tarpaulins, bring them; and by all means don't forget your spade."

Pete Slaughter was a harsh master, considering he was working volunteer labor; but then we all felt a common interest in the bridge, for if Slaughter's beeves could cross, ours could, and so could Millet's. All the men dragging brush changed horses during dinner, for there was to be no pause in piling in a good foundation as long as the material was at hand. Jacklin and his outfit returned, ten strong, and with thirty men at work, the bridge grew. They began laying the logs on the brush after dinner, and the work of sodding the bridge went forward at the same time. The bridge stood about two feet above the water in the creek, but when near the middle of the stream was reached, the foundation gave way, and for an hour ten horses were kept busy dragging brush to fill that sink hole until it would bear the weight of the logs. We had used all the acceptable timber on our side of the stream for half a mile either way, and yet there were not enough logs to complete the bridge. When we lacked only some ten or twelve logs, Slaughter had the boys sod a narrow strip across the remaining brush, and the horsemen led their mounts across to the farther side. Then the axemen crossed, felled the nearest trees, and the last logs were dragged up from the pommels of our saddles.

It now only remained to sod over and dirt the bridge thoroughly. With only three spades the work was slow, but we cut sod with axes, and after several hours' work had it finished. The two yoke of oxen were driven across and back for a test, and the bridge stood it nobly. Slaughter then brought up his *remuda,* and while the work of dirting the bridge was still going on, crossed and recrossed his band of saddle horses twenty times. When the bridge looked completed to every one else, young Pete advised laying stringers across on either side; so a number of small trees were felled and guard rails strung across the ends of the logs and staked. Then more dirt was carried in on tarpaulins and in gunny sacks, and every chink and crevice filled with sod and dirt. It was now getting rather late in the afternoon, but during the finishing touches, young Slaughter had dispatched his outfit to bring up his herd; and at the same time Flood had sent a number of our outfit to bring up our cattle. Now Slaughter and the rest of us took the oxen, which we had unyoked, and went out about a quarter of a mile to meet his herd coming up. Turning the oxen in the lead, young Pete took one point and Flood the other, and pointed in the lead cattle for the bridge. On reaching it the cattle hesitated for a moment, and it looked as though they were going to balk, but finally one of the oxen took the lead, and they began to cross in almost Indian file. They were big four and five year old beeves, and too many of them on the bridge at one time might have sunk it, but Slaughter rode back down the line of cattle and called to the men to hold them back.

"Don't crowd the cattle," he shouted. "Give them all the time they want. We're in no hurry now; there's lots of time."

They were a full half hour in crossing, the chain of cattle taking the bridge never for a moment being broken. Once all were over, his men rode to the lead and turned the herd up Boggy, in order to have it well out of the way of ours, which were then looming up in sight. Slaughter asked Flood if he wanted the oxen; and as our cattle had never seen a bridge in their lives, the foreman decided to use them; so we brought them back and met the herd, now strung out nearly a mile. Our cattle were naturally wild, but we turned the oxen in the lead, and the two bosses again taking the points, moved the herd up to the bridge. The oxen were again slow to lead out in crossing, and several hundred head of cattle had congested in front of the new bridge, making us all rather nervous, when a big white ox led off, his mate following, and the herd began timidly to follow. Our cattle required careful handling, and not a word was spoken as we nursed them forward, or rode through them to scatter large bunches. A number of times we cut the train of cattle off entirely, as they were congesting at the bridge entrance, and, in crossing, shied and crowded so that several were forced off the bridge into the mire. Our herd crossed in considerably less time than did Slaughter's beeves, but we had five head to pull out; this, however, was considered nothing, as they were light, and the mire was as thin as soup. Our wagon and saddle horses crossed while we were pulling out the bogged cattle, and about half the outfit, taking the herd, drifted them forward towards the Solomon. Since Millet intended crossing that evening, herds were likely to be too thick for safety at night. The sun was hardly an hour high when the last herd came up to cross. The oxen were put in the lead, as with ours, and all four of the oxen took the bridge, but when the cattle reached the bridge, they made a decided balk and refused to follow the oxen. Not a hoof of the herd would even set foot on the bridge. The oxen were brought back several times, but in spite of all coaxing and nursing, and our best endeavors and devices, they would not risk it. We worked with them until dusk, when all three of the foremen decided it was useless to try longer, but both Slaughter and Flood promised to bring back part of their outfits in the morning and make another effort.

McCann's camp-fire piloted us to our wagon, at least three miles from the bridge, for he had laid in a good supply of wood during the day; and on our arrival our night horses were tied up, and everything made ready for the night. The next morning we started the herd, but Flood took four of us with him and went back to Big Boggy. The Millet herd was nearly two miles back from the bridge, where we found Slaughter at Jacklin's wagon; and several more of his men were, we learned, coming over with the oxen at about ten o'clock. That hour was considered soon enough by the bosses, as the heat of the day would be on the herd by that time, which would make them lazy. When the oxen arrived at the bridge, we rode out twenty strong and lined the cattle up for another trial. They had grazed until they were full and sleepy, but the memory of some of them was too vivid of the hours they had spent in the slimy ooze of Big Boggy once on a time, and they began milling on sight of the stream. We took them back and brought them up a second time with the same results. We then brought them around in a circle a mile in diameter, and as the rear end of the herd was passing, we turned the last hundred, and throwing the oxen into their lead, started them for the bridge; but they too sulked and would have none of it. It was now high noon, so we turned the herd and allowed them to graze back while we went to dinner. Millet's foreman was rather discouraged with the outlook, but Slaughter said they must be crossed if he had to lay over a week and help. After dinner, Jacklin asked us if we wanted a change of horses, and as we could see a twenty mile ride ahead of us in overtaking our herd, Flood accepted.

When all was ready to start, Slaughter made a suggestion. "Let's go out," he said, "and bring them up slowly in a solid body, and when we get them opposite the bridge, round them in gradually as if we were going to bed them down. I'll take a long lariat to my white wheeler, and when they have quieted down perfectly, I'll lead old Blanco through them and across the bridge, and possibly they'll follow. There's no use crowding them, for that only excites them, and if you ever start them milling, the jig's up. They're nice, gentle cattle, but they've been balked once and they haven't forgotten it."

What we needed right then was a leader, for we were all ready to catch at a straw, and Slaughter's suggestion was welcome, for he had established himself in our good graces until we preferred him to either of the other foremen as a leader. Riding out to the herd, which were lying down, we roused and started them back towards Boggy. While drifting them back, we covered a front a quarter of a mile in width, and as we neared the bridge we gave them perfect freedom. Slaughter had caught out his white ox, and we gradually worked them into a body, covering perhaps ten acres, in front of the bridge. Several small bunches attempted to mill, but some of us rode in and split them up, and after about half an hour's wait, they quieted down. Then Slaughter rode in whistling and leading his white ox at the end of a thirty-five foot lariat, and as he rode through them they were so logy that he had to quirt them out of the way. When he came to the bridge, he stopped the white wheeler until everything had quieted down; then he led old Blanco on again, but giving him all the time he needed and stopping every few feet. We held our breath, as one or two of the herd started to follow him, but they shied and turned back, and our hopes of the moment were crushed. Slaughter detained the ox on the bridge for several minutes, but seeing it was useless, he dismounted and drove him back into the herd. Again and again he tried the same ruse, but it was of no avail. Then we threw the herd back about half a mile, and on Flood's suggestion cut off possibly two hundred head, a bunch which with our numbers we ought to handle readily in spite of their will, and by putting their *remuda* of over a hundred saddle horses in the immediate lead, made the experiment of forcing them. We took the saddle horses down and crossed and recrossed the bridge several times with them, and as the cattle came up turned the horses into the lead and headed for the bridge. With a cordon of twenty riders around them, no animal could turn back, and the horses crossed the bridge on a trot, but the cattle turned tail and positively refused to have anything to do with it. We held them like a block in a vise, so compactly that they could not even mill, but they would not cross the bridge. When it became evident that it was a fruitless effort, Jacklin, usually a very quiet man, gave vent to a fit of profanity which would have put the army in Flanders to shame. Slaughter, somewhat to our amusement, reproved him: "Don't fret, man; this is nothing,—I balked a herd once in crossing a railroad track, and after trying for two days to cross them, had to drive ten miles and put them under a culvert. You want to cultivate patience, young fellow, when you're handling dumb brutes."

If Slaughter's darky cook had been thereabouts then, and suggested a means of getting that herd to take the bridge, his suggestion would have been welcomed, for the bosses were at their wits' ends. Jacklin swore that he would bed that herd at the entrance, and hold them there until they starved to death or crossed, before he would let an animal turn back. But cooler heads were present, and The Rebel mentioned a certain adage, to the effect that when a bird or a girl, he didn't know which, could sing and wouldn't, she or it ought to be made to sing. He suggested that we hold the four oxen on the bridge, cut off fifteen head of cattle, and give them such a running start, they wouldn't know which end their heads were on when they reached the bridge. Millet's foreman approved of the idea, for he was nursing his wrath. The four oxen were accordingly cut out, and Slaughter and one of his men, taking them, started for the bridge with instructions to hold them on the middle. The rest of us took about a dozen head of light cattle, brought them within a hundred yards of the bridge, then with a yell started them on a run from which they could not turn back. They struck the entrance squarely, and we had our first cattle on the bridge. Two men held the entrance, and we brought up another bunch in the same manner, which filled the bridge. Now, we thought, if the herd could be brought up slowly, and this bridgeful let off in their lead, they might follow. To june a herd of cattle across in this manner would have been shameful, and the foreman of the herd knew it as well as any one present; but no one protested, so we left men to hold the entrance securely and went back after the herd. When we got them within a quarter of a mile of the creek, we cut off about two hundred head of the leaders and brought them around to the rear, for amongst these leaders were certain to be the ones which had been bogged, and we wanted to have new leaders in this trial. Slaughter was on the farther end of the bridge, and could be depended on to let the oxen lead off at the opportune moment. We brought them up cautiously, and when the herd came within a few rods of the creek the cattle on the bridge lowed to their mates in the herd, and Slaughter, considering the time favorable, opened out and allowed them to leave the bridge on the farther side. As soon as the cattle started leaving on the farther side, we dropped back, and the leaders of the herd to the number of a dozen, after smelling the fresh dirt and seeing the others crossing, walked cautiously up on the bridge. It was a moment of extreme anxiety. None of us spoke a word, but the cattle crowding off the bridge at the farther end set it vibrating. That was enough: they turned as if panic-stricken and rushed back to the body of the herd. I was almost afraid to look at Jacklin. He could scarcely speak, but he rode over to me, ashen with rage, and kept repeating, "Well, wouldn't that beat hell!"

Slaughter rode back across the bridge, and the men came up and gathered around Jacklin. We seemed to have run the full length of our rope. No one even had a suggestion to offer, and if any one had had, it needed to be a plausible one to find approval, for hope seemed to have vanished. While discussing the situation, a one-eyed, pox-marked fellow belonging to Slaughter's outfit galloped up from the rear, and said almost breathlessly, "Say, fellows, I see a cow and calf in the herd. Let's rope the calf, and the cow is sure to follow. Get the rope around the calf's neck, and when it chokes him, he's liable to bellow, and that will call the steers. And if you never let up on the choking till you get on the other side of the bridge, I think it'll work. Let's try it, anyhow."

We all approved, for we knew that next to the smell of blood, nothing will stir range cattle like the bellowing of a calf. At the mere suggestion, Jacklin's men scattered into the herd, and within a few minutes we had a rope round the neck of the calf. As the roper came through the herd leading the calf, the frantic mother followed, with a train of excited steers at her heels. And as the calf was dragged bellowing across the bridge, it was followed by excited, struggling steers who never knew whether they were walking on a bridge or on *terra firma*. The excitement spread through the herd, and they thickened around the entrance until it was necessary to hold them back, and only let enough pass to keep the chain unbroken.

They were nearly a half hour in crossing, for it was fully as large a herd as ours; and when the last animal had crossed, Pete Slaughter stood up in his stirrups and led the long yell. The sun went down that day on nobody's wrath, for Jacklin was so tickled that he offered to kill the fattest beef in his herd if we would stay overnight with him. All three of the herds were now over, but had not this herd balked on us the evening before, over nine thousand cattle would have crossed Slaughter's bridge the day it was built.

It was now late in the evening, and as we had to wait some little time to get our own horses, we stayed for supper. It was dark before we set out to overtake the herd, but the trail was plain, and letting our horses take their own time, we jollied along until after midnight. We might have missed the camp, but, by the merest chance, Priest sighted our camp-fire a mile off the trail, though it had burned to embers. On reaching camp, we changed saddles to our night horses, and, calling Officer, were ready for our watch. We were expecting the men on guard to call us any minute, and while Priest was explaining to Officer the trouble we had had in crossing the Millet herd, I dozed off to sleep there as I sat by the rekindled embers. In that minute's sleep my mind wandered in a dream to my home on the San Antonio River, but the next moment I was aroused to the demands of the hour by The Rebel shaking me and saying,—

"Wake up, Tom, and take a new hold. They're calling us on guard. If you expect to follow the trail, son, you must learn to do your sleeping in the winter."

Federal troops guarding a train in the midst of the Pullman strike, Chicago, 1894

JANE ADDAMS

"A Modern Lear"

(1912)

The Pullman strike of 1894 was, by every measure, an important event in the evolution of industrial America. President Grover Cleveland's act of sending troops to Illinois over the protest of Governor John Peter Altgeld initiated presidential intervention in labor-management disputes, transforming theoretically private quarrels into the public issues that, in fact, they were. This conservative President inadvertently served to strip the veil from the laissez-faire industrial universe in which he believed. The strike leader Eugene V. Debs (see pp. 222–224 reference in Dos Passos) entered the contest reluctantly, drawn beyond his men's resources. He left the strike—and the jail term he served in its wake—on his way to leadership of American socialism. He would march beyond private negotiation and the sporadic tests of strength that remained the dominant pattern in American labor history.

But what of the third man in this drama, George M. Pullman? Having cut wages in response to business depression, he seemed the unmoved mover, endlessly announcing that "there is nothing to arbitrate" with his striking workers. Was he merely a smug, self-righteous, troglodytic businessman? Jane Addams probes the mind of this strange man who attempted to build a private utopia for his workers. She recognizes a genuine moral code now rendered obsolete, but yet to be replaced by a new one better suited to industrial conditions. It would be precisely the task of the liberalism that Miss Addams represented to search for a common ground that would meet the workers' rising aspirations for control of their own lives and fortunes without doing violence to the creative role that men—businessmen and philanthropists both—like Pullman had played. No one has defined the issues any more clearly than Jane Addams.

Those of us who lived in Chicago during the summer of 1894 were confronted by a drama which epitomized and, at the same time, challenged the code of social ethics under which we live, for a quick series of unusual events had dispelled the good nature which in happier times envelops the ugliness of the industrial situation. It sometimes seems as if the shocking experiences of that summer, the barbaric instinct to kill, roused on both sides, the sharp division into class lines, with the resultant distrust and bitterness, can only be endured if we learn from it all a great ethical lesson. To endure is all we can hope for. It is impossible to justify such a course of rage and riot in a civilized community to whom the methods of conciliation and control were open. Every public-spirited citizen in Chicago during that summer felt the stress and perplexity of the situation and asked himself, "How far am I responsible for this social disorder? What can be done to prevent such outrageous manifestations of ill-will?"

If the responsibility of tolerance lies with those of the widest vision, it behooves us to consider this great social disaster, not alone in its legal aspect nor in its sociological bearings, but from those deep human motives, which, after all, determine events.

During the discussions which followed the Pullman strike, the defenders of the situation were broadly divided between the people pleading for individual benevolence and those insisting upon social righteousness; between those who held that the philanthropy of the president of the Pullman company had been most ungratefully received and those who maintained that the situation was the inevitable outcome of the social consciousness developing among working people.

In the midst of these discussions the writer found her mind dwelling upon a comparison which modified and softened all her judgments. Her attention was caught by the similarity of ingratitude suffered by an indulgent employer and an indulgent parent. King Lear came often to her mind. We have all shared the family relationship and our code of ethics concerning it is somewhat settled. We also bear a part in the industrial relationship, but our ethics concerning that are still uncertain. A comparative study of these two relationships presents an advantage, in that it enables us to consider the situation from the known experience toward the unknown. The minds of all of us reach back to our early struggles, as we emerged from the state of self-willed childhood to a recognition of the family claim.

We have all had glimpses of what it might be to blaspheme against family ties; to ignore the elemental claim they make upon us, but on the whole we have recognized them, and it does not occur to us to throw them over. The industrial claim is so difficult; the ties are so intangible that we are constantly ignoring them and shirking the duties which they impose. It will probably be easier to treat of the tragedy of the Pullman strike as if it were already long past when we compare it to the family tragedy of Lear which has already become historic to our minds and which we discuss without personal feeling.

Historically considered, the relation of Lear to his children was archaic and barbaric, holding in it merely the beginnings of a family life, since developed. We may in later years learn to look back upon the industrial relationships in which we are now placed as quite as incomprehensible and selfish, quite as barbaric and undeveloped, as was the family relationship between Lear and his daughters. We may then take the relationship of this unusually generous employer at Pullman to his own townful of employes as at least a fair one, because so exceptionally liberal in many of its aspects. King Lear doubtless held the same notion of a father's duty that was held by the other fathers of his time; but he alone was a king and had kingdoms to bestow upon his children. He was unique, therefore, in the magnitude of his indulgence, and in the magnitude of the disaster which followed it. The sense of duty held by the president of the Pullman company doubtless represents the ideal in the minds of the best of the present employers as to their obligations toward their employes, but he projected this ideal more magnificently than the others. He alone gave his men so model a town, such perfect surroundings. The magnitude of his indulgence and failure corresponded and we are forced to challenge the ideal itself: the same deal which, more or less clearly defined, is floating in the minds of all philanthropic employers.

This older tragedy implied mal-adjustment between individuals; the forces of the tragedy were personal and passionate. This modern tragedy in its inception is a mal-adjustment between two large bodies of men, an employing company and a mass of employes. It deals not with personal relationships, but with industrial relationships.

Owing, however, to the unusual part played in it by the will of one man, we find that it closely approaches Lear in motif. The relation of the British King to his family is very like the relation of the president of the Pullman company to his town; the denouement of a daughter's break with her father suggests the break of the employes with their benefactor. If we call one an example of the domestic tragedy, the other of the industrial tragedy, it is possible to make them illuminate each other.

It is easy to discover striking points of similarity in the tragedies of the royal father and the philanthropic president of the Pullman company. The like quality of ingratitude they both suffered is at once apparent. It may be said that the ingratitude which Lear received was poignant and bitter to him in proportion as he recalled the extraordinary benefits he had heaped upon his daughters, and that he found his fate harder to bear because he had so far exceeded the measure of a father's duty, as he himself says. What, then, would be the bitterness of a man who had heaped extraordinary benefits upon those toward whom he had no duty recognized by common consent; who had not only exceeded the righteousness of the employer, but who had worked out original and striking methods for lavishing goodness and generosity? More than that, the president had been almost persecuted for this goodness by the more utilitarian members of his company and had at one time imperilled his business reputation for the sake of the benefactions to his town, and he had thus reached the height of sacrifice for it. This model town embodied not only his hopes and ambitions, but stood for the peculiar effort which a man makes for that which is misunderstood.

It is easy to see that although the heart of Lear was cut by ingratitude and by misfortune, it was cut deepest of all by the public pity of his people, in that they should remember him no longer as a king and benefactor, but as a defeated man who had blundered through oversoftness. So the heart of the Chicago man was cut by the unparalleled publicity which brought him to the minds of thousands as a type of oppression and injustice, and to many others as an example of the evil of an irregulated sympathy for the "lower classes." He who had been dined and feted throughout Europe as the creator of a model town, as the friend and benefactor of workingmen, was now execrated by workingmen throughout the entire country. He had not only been good to those who were now basely ungrateful to him, but he felt himself deserted by the admiration of his people.

In shops such as those at Pullman, indeed, in all manufacturing affairs since the industrial revolution, industry is organized into a vast social operation. The shops are managed, however, not for the development of the workman thus socialized, but for the interests of the company owning the capital. The divergence between the social form and the individual aim becomes greater as the employes are more highly socialized and dependent, just as the clash in a family is more vital in proportion to the development and closeness of the family tie. The president of the Pullman company went further than the usual employer does. He socialized not only the factory but the form in which his workmen were living. He built and, in a great measure, regulated an entire town. This again might have worked out into a successful associated effort, if he had had in view the sole good of the inhabitants thus socialized, if he had called upon them for self-expression and had made the town a growth and manifestation of their wants and needs. But, unfortunately, the end to be obtained became ultimately commercial and not social, having in view the payment to the company of at least 4 per cent on the money invested, so that with this rigid requirement there could be no adaptation of rent to wages, much less to needs. The rents became statical and the wages competitive, shifting inevitably with the demands of trade. The president assumed that he himself knew the needs of his men, and so far from wishing them to express their needs he denied to them the simple rights of trade organization, which would have been, of course, the merest preliminary to an attempt at associated expression. If we may take the dictatorial relation of Lear to Cordelia as a typical and most dramatic example of the distinctively family tragedy, one will asserting its authority through all the entanglement of wounded affection, and insisting upon its selfish ends at all costs, may we not consider the absolute authority of this employer over his town as a typical and dramatic example of the industrial tragedy? One will directing the energies of many others, without regard to their desires, and having in view in the last analysis only commercial results?

It shocks our ideal of family life that a man should fail to know his daughter's heart because she awkwardly expressed her love, that he should refuse to comfort and advise her through all difference of opinion and clashing of will. That a man should be so absorbed in his own indignation as to fail to apprehend his child's thought; that he should lose his affection in his anger, is really no more unnatural than that the man who spent a million of dollars on a swamp to make it sanitary for his employes, should refuse to speak to them for ten minutes, whether they were in the right or wrong; or that a man who had given them his time and thought for twenty years should withdraw from them his guidance when he believed them misled by ill-advisers and wandering in a mental fog; or that he should grow hard and angry when they needed tenderness and help.

Lear ignored the common ancestry of Cordelia and himself. He forgot her royal inheritance of magnanimity, and also the power of obstinacy which he shared with her. So long had he thought of himself as the noble and indulgent father that he had lost the faculty by which he might perceive himself in the wrong. Even when his spirit was broken by the storm he declared himself more sinned against than sinning. He could believe any amount of kindness and goodness of himself, but could imagine no fidelity on the part of Cordelia unless she gave him the sign he demanded.

The president of the Pullman company doubtless began to build his town from an honest desire to give his employes the best surroundings. As it developed it became a source of pride and an exponent of power, that he cared most for when it gave him a glow of benevolence. Gradually, what the outside world thought of it became of importance to him and he ceased to measure its usefulness by the standard of the men's needs. The theater was complete in equipment and beautiful in design, but too costly for a troupe who depended upon the patronage of mechanics, as the church was too expensive to be rented continuously. We can imagine the founder of the town slowly darkening his glints of memory and forgetting the common stock of experience which he held with his men. He cultivated the great and noble impulses of the benefactor, until the power of attaining a simple human relationship with his employes, that of frank equality with them, was gone from him. He, too, lost the faculty of affectionate interpretation, and demanded a sign. He and his employes had no mutual interest in a common cause.

Was not the grotesque situation of the royal father and the philanthropic employer to perform so many good deeds that they lost the power of recognizing good in beneficiaries? Were not both so absorbed in carrying out a personal plan of improvement that they failed to catch the great moral lesson which their times offered them? This is the crucial point of the tragedies and may be further elucidated.

Lear had doubtless swung a bauble before Cordelia's baby eyes that he might have the pleasure of seeing the little pink and tender hands stretched for it. A few years later he had given jewels to the young princess, and felt an exquisite pleasure when she stood before him, delighted with her gaud and grateful to her father. He demanded the same kind of response for his gift of the kingdom, but the gratitude must be larger and more carefully expressed, as befitted such a gift. At the opening of the drama he sat upon his throne ready for this enjoyment, but instead of delight and gratitude he found the first dawn of character. His daughter made the awkward attempt of an untrained soul to be honest, to be scrupulous in the expressions of its feelings. It was new to him that his child should be moved by a principle outside of himself, which even his imagination could not follow; that she had caught the notion of an existence so vast that her relationship as a daughter was but part of it.

Perhaps her suitors, the King of France or the Duke of Burgundy, had first hinted to the young Cordelia that there was a fuller life beyond the seas. Certain it is that someone had shaken her from the quiet measure of her insular existence and that she had at last felt the thrill of the world's life. She was transformed by a dignity which recast her speech and made it self-contained, as is becoming a citizen of the world. She found herself in the sweep of a notion of justice so large that the immediate loss of a kingdom seemed of little consequence to her. Even an act which might be construed as disrespect to her father was justified in her eyes because she was vainly striving to fill out this larger conception of duty.

The test which comes sooner or later to many parents had come to Lear, to maintain the tenderness of the relation between father and child, after that relation had become one between adults; to be contented with the responses which this adult made to the family claim, while, at the same time, she felt the tug upon her emotions and faculties of the larger life, the life which surrounds and completes the individual and family life, and which shares and widens her attention. He was not sufficiently wise to see that only that child can fulfill the family claim in its sweetness and strength who also fulfills the larger claim, that the adjustment of the lesser and larger implies no conflict. The mind of Lear was not big enough for this test. He failed to see anything but the personal slight involved; the ingratitude alone reached him. It was impossible for him to calmly watch his child developing beyond the strength of his own mind and sympathy.

Without pressing the analogy too hard may we not compare the indulgent relation of this employer to his town to the relation which existed between Lear and Cordelia? He fostered his employes for many years, gave them sanitary houses and beautiful parks, but in their extreme need, when they were struggling with the most difficult question which the times could present to them, when, if ever, they required the assistance of a trained mind and a comprehensive outlook, he lost his touch and had nothing wherewith to help them. He did not see the situation. He had been ignorant of their gropings toward justice. His conception of goodness for them had been cleanliness, decency of living, and above all, thrift and temperance. He had provided them means for all this; had gone further, and given them opportunities for enjoyment and comradeship. But he suddenly found his town in the sweep of a world-wide moral impulse. A movement had been going on about him and through the souls of his workingmen of which he had been unconscious. He had only heard of this movement by rumor. The men who consorted with him at his club and in his business had spoken but little of it, and when they had discussed it had contemptuously called it the "Labor Movement," headed by deadbeats and agitators. Of the force and power of this movement, of all the vitality within it, of that conception of duty which induces men to go without food and to see their wives and children suffer for the sake of securing better wages for fellow-workmen whom they have never seen, this president had dreamed absolutely nothing. But his town had at last become swept into this larger movement, so that the giving up of comfortable homes, of beautiful surroundings, seemed as naught to the men within its grasp.

Outside the ken of this philanthropist, the proletariat had learned to say in many languages that "the injury of one is the concern of all." Their watchwords were brotherhood, sacrifice, the subordination of individual and trade interests to the good of the working class; and their persistent strivings were toward the ultimate freedom of that class from the conditions under which they now labor.

Compared to these watchwords the old ones which the philanthropic employer had given his town were negative and inadequate.

When this movement finally swept in his own town, or, to speak more fairly, when in their distress and perplexity his own employes appealed to the organized manifestation of this movement, they were quite sure that simply because they were workmen in distress they would not be deserted by it. This loyalty on the part of a widely ramified and well organized union toward the workmen in a "scab shop," who had contributed nothing to its cause, was certainly a manifestation of moral power.

That the movement was ill-directed, that it was ill-timed and disastrous in results, that it stirred up and became confused in the minds of the public with the elements of riot and bloodshed, can never touch the fact that it started from an unselfish impulse.

In none of his utterances or correspondence did the president of the company for an instant recognize this touch of nobility, although one would imagine that he would gladly point out this bit of virtue, in what he must have considered the moral ruin about him. He stood throughout pleading for the individual virtues, those which had distinguished the model workman of his youth, those which had enabled him and so many of his contemporaries to rise in life, when "rising in life" was urged upon every promising boy as the goal of his efforts. Of the new code of ethics he had caught absolutely nothing. The morals he had taught his men did not fail them in their hour of confusion. They were self-controlled and destroyed no property. They were sober and exhibited no drunkenness, even though obliged to hold their meetings in the saloon hall of a neighboring town. They repaid their employer in kind, but he had given them no rule for the higher fellowship and life of association into which they were plunged.

The virtues of one generation are not sufficient for the next, any more than the accumulations of knowledge possessed by one age are adequate to the needs of another.

Of the virtues received from our fathers we can afford to lose none. We accept as a precious trust those principles and precepts which the race has worked out for its highest safeguard and protection. But merely to preserve those is not enough. A task is laid upon each generation to enlarge their application, to ennoble their conception, and, above all, to apply and adapt them to the peculiar problems presented to it for solution.

The president of this company desired that his employes should possess the individual and family virtues, but did nothing to cherish in them those social virtues which his own age demanded. He rather substituted for that sense of responsibility to the community, a feeling of gratitude to himself, who had provided them with public buildings, and had laid out for them a simulacrum of public life.

Is it strange that when the genuine feeling of the age struck his town this belated and almost feudal virtue of personal gratitude fell before it?

Day after day during that horrible suspense, when the wires constantly reported the same message, "The president of the company holds that there is nothing to arbitrate," one longed to find out what was in the mind of this man, to unfold his ultimate motive. One concludes that he must have been sustained by the consciousness of being in the right. Only that could have held him against the great desire for fair play which swept over the country. Only the training which an arbitrary will receives by years of consulting first its own personal and commercial ends could have made it strong enough to withstand the demands for social adjustment. He felt himself right from the *commercial* standpoint, and could not see the situation from the *social* standpoint. For years he had gradually accustomed himself to the thought that his motive was beyond reproach; that his attitude to his town was always righteous and philanthropic. Habit held him persistent in this view of the case through all the changing conditions.

The diffused and subtle notion of dignity held by the modern philanthropist bears a curious analogy to the personal barbaric notion of dignity held by Lear. The man who persistently paced the seashore, while the interior of his country was racked with a strife which he alone might have arbitrated, lived out within himself the tragedy of King Lear. The shock of disaster upon egotism is apt to produce self-pity. It is possible that his self-pity and loneliness may have been so great and absorbing as to completely shut out from his mind a compunction of derelict duty. He may have been unconscious that men were charging him with a shirking of the issue.

Lack of perception is the besetting danger of the egoist, from whatever cause his egoism arises and envelopes him. But, doubtless, philanthropists are more exposed to this danger than any other class of people within the community. Partly because their efforts are overestimated, as no standard of attainment has yet been established, and partly because they are the exponents of a large amount of altruistic feeling with which the community has become equipped and which has not yet found adequate expression, they are therefore easily idealized.

Long ago Hawthorne called our attention to the fact that "philanthropy ruins, or is fearfully apt to ruin, the heart, the rich juices of which God never meant should be pressed violently out, and distilled into alcoholic liquor by an unnatural process; but it should render life sweet, bland and gently beneficent."

One might add to this observation that the muscles of this same heart may be stretched and strained until they lose the rhythm of the common heart-beat of the rest of the world.

Modern philanthropists need to remind themselves of the old definition of greatness: that it consists in the possession of the largest share of the common human qualities and experiences, not in the acquirements of peculiarities and excessive virtues. Popular opinion calls him the greatest of Americans who gathered to himself the largest amount of American experience, and who never forgot when he was in Washington how the "crackers" in Kentucky and the pioneers of Illinois thought and felt, striving to retain their thoughts and feelings, and to embody only the mighty will of the "common people." The danger of professionally attaining to the power of the righteous man, of yielding to the ambition "for doing good," compared to which the ambitions for political position, learning, or wealth are vulgar and commonplace, ramifies throughout our modern life, and is a constant and settled danger in philanthropy.

In so far as philanthropists are cut off from the influence of the *Zeit-Geist,* from the code of ethics which rule the body of men, from the great moral life springing from our common experiences, so long as they are "good to people," rather than "with them," they are bound to accomplish a large amount of harm. They are outside of the influence of that great faith which perennially springs up in the hearts of the people, and re-creates the world.

In spite of the danger of overloading the tragedies with moral reflections, a point ought to be made on the other side. It is the weakness in the relation of the employes to the employer, the fatal lack of generosity in the attitude of workmen toward the company under whose exactions they feel themselves wronged.

In reading the tragedy of King Lear, Cordelia does not escape our censure. Her first words are cold, and we are shocked by her lack of tenderness. Why should she ignore her father's need for indulgence, and be so unwilling to give him what he so obviously craved? We see in the old king "the overmastering desire of being beloved, which is selfish, and yet characteristic of the selfishness of a loving and kindly nature alone." His eagerness produces in us a strange pity for him, and we are impatient that his youngest and best-beloved child cannot feel this, even in the midst of her search for truth and her newly acquired sense of a higher duty. It seems to us a narrow conception that would break thus abruptly with the past, and would assume that her father had no part in her new life. We want to remind her that "pity, memory and faithfulness are natural ties," and surely as much to be prized as is the development of her own soul. We do not admire the Cordelia "who loves according to her bond" as we later admire the same Cordelia who comes back from France that she may include in her happiness and freer life the father whom she had deserted through her self-absorption. She is aroused to her affection through her pity, but when the floodgates are once open she acknowledges all. It sometimes seems as if only hardship and sorrow could arouse our tenderness, whether in our personal or social relations; that the king, the prosperous man, was the last to receive the justice which can come only through affectionate interpretation. We feel less pity for Lear on his throne than in the storm, although he is the same man, bound up in the same self-righteousness, and exhibiting the same lack of self-control.

As the vision of the life of Europe caught the sight and quickened the pulses of Cordelia, so a vision of the wider life has caught the sight of workingmen. After the vision has once been seen it is impossible to do aught but to press toward its fulfillment. We have all seen it. We are all practically agreed that the social passion of the age is directed toward the emancipation of the wage-worker; that a great accumulation of moral force is overmastering men and making for this emancipation as in another time it has made for the emancipation of the slave; that nothing will satisfy the aroused conscience of men short of the complete participation of the working classes in the spiritual, intellectual and material inheritance of the human race. But just as Cordelia failed to include her father in the scope of her salvation and selfishly took it for herself alone, so workingmen in the dawn of the vision are inclined to claim it for themselves, putting out of their thoughts the old relationships; and just as surely as Cordelia's conscience developed in the new life and later drove her back to her father, where she perished, drawn into the cruelty and wrath which had now become objective and tragic, so the emancipation of working people will have to be inclusive of the employer from the first or it will encounter many failures, cruelties and reactions. It will result not in the position of the repentant Cordelia but in that of King Lear's two older daughters.

If the workingmen's narrow conception of emancipation was fully acted upon, they would hold much the same relationship to their expropriated employer that the two elder daughters held to their abdicated father. When the kingdom was given to them they received it as altogether their own, and were dominated by a sense of possession; "it is ours not yours" was never absent from their consciousness. When Lear ruled the kingdom he had never been without this sense of possession, although he expressed it in indulgence and condescending kindness. His older daughters expressed it in cruelty, but the motive of father and children was not unlike. They did not wish to be reminded by the state and retinue of the old King that he had been the former possessor. Finally, his mere presence alone reminded them too much of that and they banished him from the palace. That a newly acquired sense of possession should result in the barbaric, the incredible scenes of bitterness and murder, which were King Lear's portion, is not without a reminder of the barbaric scenes in our political and industrial relationships, when the sense of possession, to obtain and to hold, is aroused on both sides. The scenes in Paris during the political revolution or the more familiar scenes at the mouths of the mines and the terminals of railways occur to all of us.

The doctrine of emancipation preached to the wage-workers alone runs an awful risk of being accepted for what it offers them, for the sake of the fleshpots, rather than for the human affection and social justice which it involves. This doctrine must be strong enough in its fusing power to touch those who think they lose, as well as those who think they gain. Only thus can it become the doctrine of a universal movement.

The new claim on the part of the toiling multitude, the new sense of responsibility on the part of the well-to-do, arise in reality from the same source. They are in fact the same "social compunction," and, in spite of their widely varying manifestations, logically converge into the same movement. Mazzini once preached, "the consent of men and your own conscience are two wings given you whereby you may rise to God." It is so easy for the good and powerful to think that they can rise by following the dictates of conscience by pursuing their own ideals, leaving those ideals unconnected with the consent of their fellow-men. The president of the Pullman company thought out within his own mind a beautiful town. He had power with which to build this town, but he did not appeal to nor obtain the consent of the men who were living in it. The most unambitious reform, recognizing the necessity for this consent, makes for slow but sane and strenuous progress, while the most ambitious of social plans and experiments, ignoring this, is prone to the failure of the model town of Pullman.

The man who insists upon consent, who moves with the people, is bound to consult the feasible right as well as the absolute right. He is often obliged to attain only Mr. Lincoln's "best possible," and often have the sickening sense of compromising with his best convictions. He has to move along with those whom he rules toward a goal that neither he nor they see very clearly till they come to it. He has to discover what people really want, and then "provide the channels in which the growing moral force of their lives shall flow." What he does attain, however, is not the result of his individual striving, as a solitary mountain climber beyond the sight of the valley multitude, but it is underpinned and upheld by the sentiments and aspirations of many others. Progress has been slower perpendicularly, but incomparably greater because lateral.

He has not taught his contemporaries to climb mountains, but he has persuaded the villagers to move up a few feet higher. It is doubtful if personal ambition, whatever may have been its commercial results, has ever been of any value as a motive power in social reform. But whatever it may have done in the past, it is certainly too archaic to accomplish anything now. Our thoughts, at least for this generation, cannot be too much directed from mutual relationships and responsibilities. They will be warped, unless we look all men in the face, as if a community of interests lay between, unless we hold the mind open, to take strength and cheer from a hundred connections.

To touch to vibrating response the noble fibre in each man, to pull these many fibres, fragile, impalpable and constantly breaking, as they are, into one impulse, to develop that mere impulse through its feeble and tentative stages into action, is no easy task, but lateral progress is impossible without it.

If only a few families of the English speaking race had profited by the dramatic failure of Lear, much heart-breaking and domestic friction might have been spared. Is it too much to hope that some of us will carefully consider this modern tragedy, if perchance it may contain a warning for the troublous times in which we live? By considering the dramatic failure of the liberal employer's plans for his employes we may possibly be spared useless industrial tragedies in the uncertain future which lies ahead of us.

View of Market Street, Philadelphia, 1904

LINCOLN STEFFENS

Philadelphia: Corrupt and Contented

(1904)

In Pilgrim's Progress, the seventeenth-century Puritan parable, the "man with the muck rake" is so busy looking down that he misses the heaven above him. President Theodore Roosevelt applied this image to the journalists who made a specialty of criticizing American institutions in the early years of the twentieth century. Like so many names leveled in opprobrium—Yankee, Rebel, Know-Nothing—this one not only stuck but also became a badge of honor. Lincoln Steffens' prose fairly breathes pride in knowing how bad things *really* were, a pride he and his fellow muckrakers shared with a huge audience of middle-class Americans. For about a decade this audience could not read enough about what was wrong with their governments, corporations, labor unions, cities, and morals.

Steffens' The Shame of the Cities was perhaps the most influential single piece of muckraking, stirring reform movements in nearly every city it discussed—even Philadelphia. In some ways it was typical of the movement, mixing a realistic description of events with the kind of moral righteousness that the public cherished. But Steffens did not share the faith of many of his compatriots that exposure would of itself force change. Reform, he correctly if cynically stated, was revolt, not government. Steffens feared that expressions of moral indignation would merely lead to flurries of activity, easing only people's consciences, not their social problems. He was beginning a long road that led from student of reform to patron of revolution.

Progressivism, the spirit of middle-class and optimistic reform that marked the first decades of the twentieth century, lived and died with its journalism. The progressive vision of reality was essentially journalistic. It tended to see the world as a headline expressing a moral point atop a story giving the seamy details that justified indignation. This reflected an incomplete realism that dominated American letters throughout the period. Reality to progressives was dirty and hidden: the backroom deal, the respectable man's secret vice, the blow in the dark. Yet few progressives would move the distance that Steffens finally did and apply such realism to the moral pretensions of a public feasting on tales of other people's greed. The progressives wanted to apply absolute moral standards to a world in which everything was relative. When the effort failed, as it had to, many people were left—despite all the good that resulted from a generation's efforts—with the sense that no standards at all remained. The modern world was indeed upon us.

Other American cities, no matter how bad their own condition may be, all point with scorn to Philadelphia as worse—"the worst-governed city in the country." St. Louis, Minneapolis, Pittsburg submit with some patience to the jibes of any other community; the most friendly suggestion from Philadelphia is rejected with contempt. The Philadelphians are "supine," "asleep"; hopelessly ring-ruled, they are "complacent." "Politically benighted," Philadelphia is supposed to have no light to throw upon a state of things that is almost universal.

This is not fair. Philadelphia is, indeed, corrupt; but it is not without significance. Every city and town in the country can learn something from the typical political experience of this great representative city. New York is excused for many of its ills because it is the metropolis, Chicago because of its forced development; Philadelphia is our "third largest" city and its growth has been gradual and natural. Immigration has been blamed for our municipal conditions; Philadelphia, with 47 per cent. of its population native-born of native-born parents, is the most American of our greater cities. It is "good," too, and intelligent. I don't know just how to measure the intelligence of a community, but a Pennsylvania college professor who declared to me his belief in education for the masses as a way out of political corruption, himself justified the "rake-off" of preferred contractors on public works on the ground of a "fair business profit." Another plea we have made is that we are too busy to attend to public business, and we have promised, when we come to wealth and leisure, to do better. Philadelphia has long enjoyed great and widely distributed prosperity; it is the city of homes; there is a dwelling house for every five persons,—men, women, and children,—of the population; and the people give one a sense of more leisure and repose than any community I ever dwelt in. Some Philadelphians account for their political state on the ground of their ease and comfort. There is another class of optimists whose hope is in an "aristocracy" that is to come by and by; Philadelphia is surer that it has a "real aristocracy" than any other place in the world, but its aristocrats, with few exceptions, are in the ring, with it, or of no political use. Then we hear that we are a young people and that when we are older and "have traditions," like some of the old countries, we also will be honest. Philadelphia is one of the oldest of our cities and treasures for us scenes and relics of some of the noblest traditions of "our fair land." Yet I was told how once, "for a joke," a party of boodlers counted out the "divvy" of their graft in unison with the ancient chime of Independence Hall.

Philadelphia is representative. This very "joke," told, as it was, with a laugh, is typical. All our municipal governments are more or less bad, and all our people are optimists. Philadelphia is simply the most corrupt and the most contented. Minneapolis has cleaned up, Pittsburg has tried to, New York fights every other election, Chicago fights all the time. Even St. Louis has begun to stir (since the elections are over), and at the worst was only shameless. Philadelphia is proud; good people there defend corruption and boast of their machine. My college professor, with his philosophic view of "rake-offs," is one Philadelphia type. Another is the man, who, driven to bay with his local pride, says: "At least you must admit that our machine is the best you have ever seen."

Disgraceful? Other cities say so. But I say that if Philadelphia is a disgrace, it is a disgrace not to itself alone, nor to Pennsylvania, but to the United States and to American character. For this great city, so highly representative in other respects, is not behind in political experience, but ahead, with New York. Philadelphia is a city that has had its reforms. Having passed through all the typical stages of corruption, Philadelphia reached the period of miscellaneous loot with a boss for chief thief, under James McManes and the Gas Ring 'way back in the late sixties and seventies. This is the Tweed stage of corruption from which St. Louis, for example, is just emerging. Philadelphia, in two inspiring popular revolts, attacked the Gas Ring, broke it, and in 1885 achieved that dream of American cities—a good charter. The present condition of Philadelphia, therefore, is not that which precedes, but that which follows reform, and in this distinction lies its startling general significance. What has happened since the Bullitt Law or charter went into effect in Philadelphia may happen in any American city "after reform is over."

For reform with us is usually revolt, not government, and is soon over. Our people do not seek, they avoid self-rule, and "reforms" are spasmodic efforts to punish bad rulers and get somebody that will give us good government or something that will make it. A self-acting form of government is an ancient superstition. We are an inventive people, and we all think that we shall devise some day a legal machine that will turn out good government automatically. The Philadelphians have treasured this belief longer than the rest of us and have tried it more often. Throughout their history they have sought this wonderful charter and they thought they had it when they got the Bullitt Law, which concentrates in the mayor ample power, executive and political, and complete responsibility. Moreover, it calls for very little thought and action on the part of the people. All they expected to have to do when the Bullitt Law went into effect was to elect as mayor a good business man, who, with his probity and common sense, would give them that good business administration which is the ideal of many reformers.

The Bullitt Law went into effect in 1887. A committee of twelve—four men from the Union League, four from business organizations, and four from the bosses—picked out the first man to run under it on the Republican ticket, Edwin H. Fitler, an able, upright business man, and he was elected. Strange to say, his administration was satisfactory to the citizens, who speak well of it to this day, and to the politicians also; Boss McManes (the ring was broken, not the boss) took to the next national convention from Philadelphia a delegation solid for Fitler for President of the United States. It was a farce, but it pleased Mr. Fitler, so Matthew S. Quay, the State boss, let him have a complimentary vote on the first ballot. The politicians "fooled" Mr. Fitler, and they "fooled" also the next business mayor, Edwin S. Stuart, likewise a most estimable gentleman. Under these two administrations the foundation was laid for the present government of Philadelphia, the corruption to which Philadelphians seemed so reconciled, and the machine which is "at least the best you have ever seen."

The Philadelphia machine isn't the best. It isn't sound, and I doubt if it would stand in New York or Chicago. The enduring strength of the typical American political machine is that it is a natural growth—a sucker, but deep-rooted in the people. The New Yorkers vote for Tammany Hall. The Philadelphians do not vote; they are disfranchised, and their disfranchisement is one anchor of the foundation of the Philadelphia organization.

This is no figure of speech. The honest citizens of Philadelphia have no more rights at the polls than the negroes down South. Nor do they fight very hard for this basic privilege. You can arouse their Republican ire by talking about the black Republican votes lost in the Southern States by white Democratic intimidation, but if you remind the average Philadelphian that he is in the same position, he will look startled, then say, "That's so, that's literally true, only I never thought of it in just that way." And it is literally true.

The machine controls the whole process of voting, and practices fraud at every stage. The assessor's list is the voting list, and the assessor is the machine's man. "The assessor of a division kept a disorderly house; he padded his lists with fraudulent names registered from his house; two of these names were used by election officers. . . . The constable of the division kept a disreputable house; a policeman was assessed as living there. . . . The election was held in the disorderly house maintained by the assessor. . . . The man named as judge had a criminal charge for a life offense pending against him. . . . Two hundred and fifty-two votes were returned in a division that had less than one hundred legal votes within its boundaries." These extracts from a report of the Municipal League suggest the election methods. The asssessor pads the list with the names of dead dogs, children, and non-existent persons. One newspaper printed the picture of a dog, another that of a little four-year-old negro boy, down on such a list. A ring orator in a speech resenting sneers at his ward as "low down" reminded his hearers that that was the ward of Independence Hall, and naming over signers of the Declaration of Independence, he closed his highest flight of eloquence with the statement that "these men, the fathers of American liberty, voted down here once. And," he added, with a catching grin, "they vote here yet." Rudolph Blankenburg, a persistent fighter for the right and the use of the right to vote (and, by the way, an immigrant), sent out just before one election a registered letter to each voter on the rolls of a certain selected division. Sixty-three per cent. were returned marked "not at," "removed," "deceased," etc. From one four-story house where forty-four voters were addressed, eighteen letters came back undelivered; from another of forty-eight voters, came back forty-one letters; from another sixty-one out of sixty-two; from another, forty-four out of forty-seven. Six houses in one division were assessed at one hundred and seventy-two voters, more than the votes cast in the previous election in any one of two hundred entire divisions.

The repeating is done boldly, for the machine controls the election officers, often choosing them from among the fraudulent names; and when no one appears to serve, assigning the heeler ready for the expected vacancy. The police are forbidden by law to stand within thirty feet of the polls, but they are at the box and they are there to see that the machine's orders are obeyed and that repeaters whom they help to furnish are permitted to vote without "intimidation" on the names they, the police, have supplied. The editor of an anti-machine paper who was looking about for himself once told me that a ward leader who knew him well asked him into a polling place. "I'll show you how it's done," he said, and he had the repeaters go round and round voting again and again on the names handed them on slips. "But," as the editor said, "that isn't the way it's done." The repeaters go from one polling place to another, voting on slips, and on their return rounds change coats, hats, etc. The business proceeds with very few hitches; there is more jesting than fighting. Violence in the past has had its effect; and is not often necessary nowadays, but if it is needed the police are there to apply it. Several citizens told me that they had seen the police help to beat citizens or elections officers who were trying to do their duty, then arrest the victim; and Mr. Clinton Rogers Woodruff, the executive counsel of the Municipal League, has published a booklet of such cases. But an official statement of the case is at hand in an announcement by John Weaver, the new machine mayor of Philadelphia, that he is going to keep the police out of politics and away from the polls. "I shall see," he added, "that every voter enjoys the full right of suffrage and that ballots may be placed in the ballot box without fear of intimidation."

But many Philadelphians do not try to vote. They leave everything to the machine, and the machine casts their ballots for them. It is estimated that 150,000 voters did not go to the polls at the last election. Yet the machine rolled up a majority of 130,000 for Weaver, with a fraudulent vote estimated all the way from forty to eighty thousand, and this in a campaign so machine-made that it was called "no contest." Francis Fisher Kane, the Democrat, got 32,000 votes out of some 204,000. "What is the use of voting?" these stay-at-homes ask. A friend of mine told me he was on the lists in the three wards in which he had successively dwelt. He votes personally in none, but the leader of his present ward tells him how he has been voted. Mr. J. C. Reynolds, the proprietor of the St. James Hotel, went to the polls at eleven o'clock last election day, only to be told that he had been voted. He asked how many others from his house had voted. An election officer took up a list, checked off twelve names, two down twice, and handed it to him. When Mr. Reynolds got home he learned that one of these had voted, the others had been voted. Another man said he rarely attempted to vote, but when he did, the officers let him, even though his name had already been voted on; and then the negro repeaters would ask if his "brother was coming 'round to-day." They were going to vote him, as they vote all good-natured citizens who stay away. "When this kind of man turns out," said a leader to me, "we simply have two repeaters extra—one to balance him and one more to the good." If necessary, after all this, the machine counts the vote "right," and there is little use appealing to the courts, since they have held, except in one case, that the ballot box is secret and cannot be opened. The only legal remedy lies in the purging of the assessor's lists, and when the Municipal League had this done in 1899, they reported that there was "wholesale voting on the very names stricken off."

Deprived of self-government, the Philadelphians haven't even self-governing machine government. They have their own boss, but he and his machine are subject to the State ring, and take their orders from the State boss, Matthew S. Quay, who is the proprietor of Pennsylvania and the real ruler of Philadelphia, just as William Penn, the Great Proprietor, was. Philadelphians, especially the local bosses, dislike this description of their government, and they point for refutation to their charter. But this very Bullitt Law was passed by Quay, and he put it through the Legislature, not for reform reasons, but at the instance of David H. Lane, his Philadelphia lieutenant, as a check upon the power of Boss McManes. Later, when McManes proved hopelessly insubordinate, Quay decided to have done with him forever. He chose David Martin for boss, and from his seat in the United States Senate, Penn's successor raised up his man and set him over the people. Croker, who rose by his own strength to the head of Tammany Hall, has tried twice to appoint a successor; no one else could, and he failed. The boss of Tammany Hall is a growth. So Croker has attempted to appoint district leaders and failed; a Tammany district leader is a growth. Boss Martin, picked up and set down from above, was accepted by Philadelphia and the Philadelphia machine, and he removed old ward leaders and appointed new ones. Some leaders in Philadelphia own their wards, of course, but Martin and, after him, Durham have sent men into a ward to lead it, and they have led it.

The Philadelphia organization is upside down. It has its root in the air, or, rather, like the banyan tree, it sends its roots from the center out both up and down and all around, and there lies its peculiar strength. For when I said it was dependent and not sound, I did not mean that it was weak. It is dependent as a municipal machine, but the organization that rules Philadelphia is, as we have seen, not a mere municipal machine, but a city, State, and national organization. The people of Philadelphia are Republicans in a Republican city in a Republican State in a Republican nation, and they are bound ring on ring on ring. The President of the United States and his patronage; the National Cabinet and their patronage; the Congress and the patronage of the Senators and the Congressmen from Pennsylvania; the Governor of the State and the State Legislature with their powers and patronage; and all that the mayor and city councils have of power and patronage—all these bear down upon Philadelphia to keep it in the control of Quay's boss and his little ring. This is the ideal of party organization, and, possibly, is the end toward which our democratic republic is tending. If it is, the end is absolutism. Nothing but a revolution could overthrow this oligarchy, and there is its danger. With no outlet at the polls for public feeling, the machine cannot be taught anything it does not know except at the cost of annihilation.

But the Philadelphia machine-leaders know their business. As I said in "Tweed Days in St. Louis," the politicians will learn, if the people won't, from exposure and reform. The Pennsylvania bosses learned the "uses of reform"; we have seen Quay applying it to discipline McManes, and he since has turned reformer himself, to punish local bosses. The bosses have learned also the danger of combination between citizens and the Democrats. To prevent this, Quay and his friends have spread sedulously the doctrine of "reform within the party," and, from the Committee of One Hundred on, the reformers have stuck pretty faithfully to this principle. But lest the citizens should commit such a sin against their party, Martin formed a permanent combination of the Democratic with the Republican organization, using to that end a goodly share of the Federal and county patronage. Thus the people of Philadelphia were "fixed" so that they couldn't vote if they wanted to, and if they should want to, they couldn't vote for a Democrat, except of Republican or independent choosing. In other words, having taken away their ballot, the bosses took away also the choice of parties.

But the greatest lesson learned and applied was that of conciliation and "good government." The people must not want to vote or rebel against the ring. This ring, like any other, was formed for the exploitation of the city for private profit, and the cementing force is the "cohesive power of public plunder." But McManes and Tweed had proved that miscellaneous larceny was dangerous, and why should a lot of cheap politicians get so much and the people nothing at all? The people had been taught to expect but little from their rulers: good water, good light, clean streets well paved, fair transportation, the decent repression of vice, public order and public safety, and no scandalous or open corruption, would more than satisfy them. It would be good business and good politics to give them these things. Like Chris Magee, who studied out the problem with him, Martin took away from the rank and file of the party and from the ward leaders and office holders the privilege of theft, and he formed companies and groups to handle the legitimate public business of the city. It was all graft, but it was to be all lawful, and, in the main, it was. Public franchises, public works, and public contracts were the principal branches of the business, and Martin adopted the dual boss idea, which we have seen worked out by Magee and Flinn in Pittsburg. In Philadelphia it was Martin and Porter, and just as Flinn had a firm, Booth & Flinn, Ltd., so Porter was Filbert and Porter.

Filbert and Porter got all the public contracts they could handle, and the rest went to other contractors friendly to them and to the ring. Sometimes the preferred contractor was the lowest bidder, but he did not have to be. The law allowed awards to be the "lowest and best," and the courts held that this gave the officials discretion. But since public criticism was to be considered, the ring, to keep up appearances, resorted to many tricks. One was to have fake bids made above the favorite. Another was to have the favorite bid high, but set an impossible time limit; the department of the city councils could extend the time afterwards. Still another was to arrange for specifications which would make outsiders bid high, then either openly alter the plans or let the ring firm perform work not up to requirements.

Many of Martin's deals and jobs were scandals, but they were safe; they were in the direction of public service; and the great mass of the business was done quietly. Moreover, the public was getting something for its money,—not full value, but a good percentage. In other words, there was a limit to the "rake-off," and some insiders have told me that it had been laid down as a principle with the ring that the people should have in value (that is, in work or benefit, including a fair profit) ninety-five cents out of every dollar. In some of the deals I have investigated, the "rake-off" over and above profit was as high as twenty-five per cent. Still, even at this, there was "a limit," and the public was getting, as one of the leaders told me, "a run for its money." Cynical as it all sounds, this view is taken by many Philadelphians almost if not quite as intelligent as my college professor.

But there was another element in the policy of conciliation which is a potent factor in the contentment of Philadelphia, and I regard it as the key to that "apathy" which has made the community notorious. We have seen how Quay had with him the Federal resources and those of the State, and the State ring, and we have seen how Martin, having the city, mayor, and councils, won over the Democratic city leaders. Here they had under pay in office at least 15,000 men and women. But each of these 15,000 persons was selected for office because he could deliver votes, either by organizations, by parties, or by families. These must represent pretty near a majority of the city's voters. But this is by no means the end of the ring's reach. In the State ring are the great corporations, the Standard Oil Company, Cramp's Shipyard, and the steel companies, with the Pennsylvania Railroad at their head, and all the local transportation and other public utility companies following after. They get franchises, privileges, exemptions, etc.; they have helped finance Quay through deals: the Pennsylvania paid Martin, Quay said once, a large yearly salary; the Cramps get contracts to build United States ships, and for years have been begging for a subsidy on home-made ships. The officers, directors, and stockholders of these companies, with their friends, their bankers, and their employees, are of the organization. Better still, one of the local bosses of Philadelphia told me he could always give a worker a job with these companies, just as he could in a city department, or in the mint, or post-office. Then there are the bankers who enjoy, or may some day enjoy, public deposits; those that profit on loans to finance political financial deals; the promoting capitalists who share with the bosses on franchises; and the brokers who deal in ring securities and speculation on ring tips. Through the exchange the ring financiers reach the investing public, which is a large and influential body. The traction companies, which bought their way from beginning to end by corruption, which have always been in the ring, and whose financiers have usually shared in other big ring deals, adopted early the policy of bribing the people with "small blocks of stock." Dr. Frederick Speirs, in his "The Street Railway System of Philadelphia," came upon transactions which "indicate clearly that it is the policy of the Union Company to get the securities into the hands of a large number of small holders, the plain inference being that a wide distribution of securities will fortify the company against possible attacks by the public." In 1895 he found a director saying: "Our critics have engaged the Academy of Music, and are to call an assemblage of people opposed to the street railways as now managed. It would take eight Academies of Music to hold the stockholders of the Union Traction Company."

But we are not yet through. Quay has made a specialty all his life of reformers, and he and his local bosses have won over so many that the list of former reformers is very, very long. Martin drove down his roots through race and religion, too. Philadelphia was one of the hot-beds of "knownothingism." Martin recognized the Catholic, and the Irish-Irish, and so drew off into the Republican party the great natural supply of the Democrats; and his successors have given high places to representative Jews. "Surely this isn't corruption!" No, and neither is that corruption which makes the heads of great educational and charity institutions "go along," as they say in Pennsylvania, in order to get appropriations for their institutions from the State and land from the city. They know what is going on, but they do not join reform movements. The provost of the University of Pennsylvania declined to join in a revolt because, he said, it might impair his usefulness to the University. And so it is with others, and with clergymen who have favorite charities; with Sabbath associations and City Beautiful clubs; with lawyers who want briefs; with real estate dealers who like to know in advance about public improvements, and real estate owners who appreciate light assessments; with shopkeepers who don't want to be bothered with strict inspections.

If there is no other hold for the ring on a man there always is the protective tariff. "I don't care," said a manufacturer. "What if they do plunder and rob us, it can't hurt me unless they raise the tax rates, and even that won't ruin me. Our party keeps up the tariff. If they should reduce that, my business would be ruined."

Such, then, are the ramifications of this machine, such is its strength. No wonder Martin could break his own rules, as he did, and commit excesses. Philadelphia is not merely corrupt, it is corrupted. Martin's doom was proclaimed not in Philadelphia, but in the United States Senate, and his offense was none of this business of his, but his failure to nominate as successor to Mayor Stuart the man, Boise Penrose, whom Matt Quay chose for that place. Martin had consented, but at the last moment he ordered the nomination of Charles F. Warwick instead. The day that happened Mr. Quay arose on the floor of the Senate and, in a speech so irrelevant to the measure under consideration that nobody out of Pennsylvania understood it, said that there was in his town a man who had given as his reason for not doing what he had promised to do, the excuse that he was "under a heavy salary from a great corporation (the Pennsylvania Railroad) and was compelled to do what the corporation wished him to do. And," added Senator Quay, "men in such a position with high power for good or evil ought . . . to go about . . . with the dollar mark of the corporation on their foreheads." Quay named as the new boss Israel W. Durham, a ward leader under Martin.

Martin having the city through Mayor Warwick fought Quay in the State, with Chris Magee for an ally, but Quay beat them both there, and then prepared to beat them in their own cities. His cry was Reform, and he soon had the people shouting for it.

Quay responded with a Legislative committee to investigate abuses in the cities, but this so-called "Lexow" was called off before it amounted to much more than a momentary embarrassment to Martin. Martin's friends, on the other hand, caught Quay and nearly sent him to prison. The People's Bank, James McManes, president, failed. The cashier, John S. Hopkins, had been speculating and letting Quay and other politicians have bank funds without collateral for stock gambling. In return Quay and the State Treasurer left heavy State deposits with the bank. Hopkins lost his nerve and shot himself. McManes happened to call in friends of Martin to advise him, and these suggested a Martin man for receiver. They found among the items money lent to Quay without security, except the State funds, and telegrams asking Hopkins to buy "1000 Met" (Metropolitan) and promising in return to "shake the plum tree." Quay, his son, Richard R., and Benjamin J. Haywood, the State Treasurer, were indicted for conspiracy, and every effort was made to have the trial precede the next election for the Legislature which was to elect a successor to Quay in the United States Senate; but Quay got stays and postponements in the hopes that a more friendly District Attorney could be put in that office. Martin secured the election of Peter F. Rothermel, who was eager to try the case, and Quay had to depend on other resources. The trial came in due course, and failed; Judge Biddle ruled out the essential evidence on the ground that it was excluded by the statute of limitation. Rothermel went on with the trial, but it was hopeless; Quay was acquitted and the other cases were abandoned.

Popular feeling was excited by this exposure of Quay, but there was no action till the factional fighting suggested a use for it. Quay had refused the second United States Senatorship to John Wanamaker, and Wanamaker led through the State and in Philadelphia a fight against the boss, which has never ceased. It took the form of a reform campaign, and Quay's methods were made plain, but the boss beat Wanamaker at every point, had Penrose made Senator, and through Penrose and Durham was gradually getting possession of Philadelphia. The final triumph came with the election of Samuel H. Ashbridge as mayor.

"Stars-and-Stripes Sam," as Ashbridge is sometimes called, was a speech-maker and a "joiner." That is to say, he made a practice of going to lodges, associations, brotherhoods, Sunday-schools, and all sorts of public and private meetings, joining some, but making at all speeches patriotic and sentimental. He was very popular. Under the Bullitt Law, as I have said, all that is necessary to a good administration and complete, though temporary reform, is a good mayor. The politicians feel that they must nominate a man in whom the people as well as themselves have faith. They had had faith in Warwick, both the ring and the people, and Warwick had found it impossible to satisfy two such masters. Now they put their faith in Ashbridge, and so did Durham, and so did Martin. All interests accepted him, therefore, and all watched him with hope and more or less assurance; none more than the good people. And, indeed, no man could have promised more or better public service than Ashbridge. The result, however, was distracting.

Mr. Ashbridge "threw down" Martin, and he recognized Quay's man, "Is" Durham, as the political boss. Durham is a high type of boss, candid, but of few words; generous, but businesslike; complete master of himself, and a genius at organization. For Pennsylvania politics he is a conservative leader, and there would have been no excesses under him, as there have been few "rows." But Mr. Durham has not been the master of the Philadelphia situation. He bowed to Quay, and he could not hold Ashbridge. Philadelphians say that if it should come to a fight, Durham could beat Quay in Philadelphia, but it doesn't come to a fight. Another thing Philadelphians say is that he "keeps his word," yet he broke it (with notice) when Quay asked him to stand for Pennypacker for Governor. As I said before, however, Philadelphia is so constituted that it apparently cannot have self-government, not even its own boss, so that the allegiance paid to Quay is comprehensible. But the submission of the boss to the mayor was extraordinary, and it seemed to some sagacious politicians dangerous.

For Mr. Ashbridge broke through all the principles of moderate grafting developed by Martin. Durham formed his ring—taking in James P. McNichol as co-ruler and preferred contractor; John M. Mack as promoter and financier; and he widened the inside circle to include more individuals. But while he was more liberal toward his leaders, and not inclined "to grab off everything for himself," as one leader told me, he maintained the principle of concentration and strict control as good politics and good business. So, too, he adopted Martin's programme of public improvements, the filtration, boulevards, etc., and he added to it. When Ashbridge was well settled in office, these schemes were all started, and the mayor pushed them with a will. According to the "Philadelphia Plan," the mayor should not be in the ring. He should be an ambitious man, and his reward promotion, not riches. If he is "out for the stuff," he is likely to be hurried by the fretful thought that his term is limited to four years, and since he cannot succeed himself as mayor, his interest in the future of the machine is less than that of a boss, who goes on forever.

When he was nominated, Ashbridge had debts of record amounting to some $40,000. Before he was elected these were satisfied. Soon after he took office he declared himself to former Postmaster Thomas L. Hicks. Here is Mr. Hicks's account of the incident:

"At one of the early interviews I had with the mayor in his office, he said to me: 'Tom, I have been elected mayor of Philadelphia. I have four years to serve. I have no further ambitions. I want no other office when I am out of this one, and I shall get out of this office all there is in it for Samuel H. Ashbridge.'

"I remarked that this was a very foolish thing to say. 'Think how that could be construed,' I said.

"'I don't care anything about that,' he declared. 'I mean to get out of this office everything there is in it for Samuel H. Ashbridge.'"

When he retired from office last April, he became the president of a bank, and was reputed to be rich. Here is the summary published by the Municipal League at the close of his labors:

"The four years of the Ashbridge administration have passed into history, leaving behind them a scar on the fame and reputation of our city which will be a long time healing. Never before, and let us hope never again, will there be such brazen defiance of public opinion, such flagrant disregard of public interest, such abuse of powers and responsibilities for private ends. These are not generalizations, but each statement can be abundantly proved by numerous instances."

These "numerous instances" are notorious in Philadelphia; some of them were reported all over the country. One of them was the attempted intimidation of John Wanamaker. Thomas B. Wanamaker, John Wanamaker's son, bought the *North American*, a newspaper which had been, and still is, exposing the abuses and corruption of the political ring. Abraham L. English, Mr. Ashbridge's Director of the Department of Public Safety, called on Mr. John Wanamaker, said he had been having him watched, and was finally in a position to demand that the newspaper stop the attacks. The merchant exposed the whole thing, and a committee appointed to investigate reported that: "Mr. English has practically admitted that he attempted to intimidate a reputable citizen and unlawfully threatened him in an effort to silence criticism of a public newspaper; that from the mayor's refusal to order an investigation of the conduct of Mr. English on the request of a town meeting of representative citizens, the community is justified in regarding him as aiding and abetting Mr. English in the corrupt act committed, and that the mayor is therefore to be equally censured by the community."

The other "instances of brazen abuse of power" were the increase of protected vice—the importation from New York of the "white slavery system of prostitution," the growth of "speak-easies," and the spread of gambling and of policy-playing until it took in the school children. This last the *North American* exposed, but in vain till it named police officers who had refused when asked to interfere. Then a judge summoned the editors and reporters of the paper, the mayor, Director English, school children, and police officers to appear before him. The mayor's personal attorney spoke for the police during the inquiry, and it looked black for the newspaper till the children began to tell their stories. When the hearing was over the judge said:

"The evidence shows conclusively that our public school system in this city is in danger of being corrupted at its fountain; that in one of the schools over a hundred and fifty children were buyers of policy, as were also a large number of scholars in other schools. It was first discovered about eighteen months ago, and for about one year has been in full operation." The police officers were not punished, however.

That corruption had reached the public schools and was spreading rapidly through the system, was discovered by the exposure and conviction of three school directors of the twenty-eighth ward. It was known before that teachers and principals, like any other office holders, had to have a "pull" and pay assessments for election expenses. "Voluntary contributions" was the term used, but over the notices in blue pencil was written "2 per cent.," and teachers who asked directors and ward bosses what to do, were advised that they would "better pay." Those that sent less than the amount suggested, got receipts: "Check received; shall we hold for balance or enter on account?" But the exposure in the twenty-eighth ward brought it home to the parents of the children that the teachers were not chosen for fitness, but for political reasons, and that the political reasons had become cash.

Miss Rena A. Haydock testified as follows: "I went to see Mr. Travis, who was a friend of mine, in reference to getting a teacher's certificate. He advised me to see all of the directors, especially Mr. Brown. They told me that it would be necessary for me to pay $120 to get the place. They told me of one girl who had offered $250, and her application had been rejected. That was before they broached the subject of money to me. I said that I didn't have $120 to pay, and they replied that it was customary for teachers to pay $40 a month out of their first three months' salary. The salary was $47. They told me they didn't want the money for themselves, but that it was necessary to buy the other faction. Finally I agreed to the proposition, and they told me that I must be careful not to mention it to anybody or it would injure my reputation. I went with my brother to pay the money to Mr. Johnson. He held out a hat, and when my brother handed the money to him he took it behind the hat."

* * *

Ashbridgeism put Philadelphia and the Philadelphia machine to a test which candid ring leaders did not think it would stand. What did the Philadelphians do? Nothing. They have their reformers: they have men like Francis B. Reeves, who fought with every straight reform movement from the days of the Committee of One Hundred; they have men like Rudolph Blankenburg, who have fought with every reform that promised any kind of relief; there are the Municipal League, with an organization by wards, the Citizens' Municipal League, the Allied Reform League, and the Law and Order Society; there are young men and veterans; there are disappointed politicians and ambitious men who are not advanced fast enough by the machine. There is discontent in a good many hearts, and some men are ashamed. But "the people" won't follow. One would think the Philadelphians would follow any leader; what should they care whether he is pure white or only gray? But they do care. "The people" seem to prefer to be ruled by a known thief than an ambitious reformer. They will make you convict their Tweeds, McManeses, Butlers, and Shepherds, and even then they may forgive them and talk of monuments to their precious memory, but they take delight in the defeat of John Wanamaker because they suspect that he is a hypocrite and wants to go to the United States Senate.

All the stout-hearted reformers had made a campaign to re-elect Rothermel, the District Attorney who had dared to try Quay. Surely there was an official to support! But no, Quay was against him. The reformers used money, some $250,000, I believe,—fighting the devil with fire,—but the machine used more money, $700,000, from the teachers, "speak-easies," office holders, bankers, and corporations. The machine handled the ballots. Rothermel was beaten by John Weaver. There have been other campaigns, before and since, led by the Municipal League, which is managed with political sense, but each successive defeat was by a larger majority for the machine.

There is no check upon this machine excepting the chance of a mistake, the imminent fear of treachery, and the remote danger of revolt. To meet this last, the machine, as a State organization, has set about throttling public criticism. Ashbridge found that blackmail was ineffective. Durham, Quay, and Governor Pennypacker have passed a libel law which meant to muzzle the press. The Governor was actuated apparently only by his sufferings from cartoons and comments during his campaign; the Philadelphia ring has boodling plans ahead which exposure might make exasperating to the people. The Philadelphia *Press*, the leading Republican organ in the State, puts it right: "The Governor wanted it [the law] in the hope of escaping from the unescapable cartoon. The gang wanted it in hope of muzzling the opposition to jobs. . . . The act is distinctly designed to gag the press in the interest of the plunderers and against the interest of the people."

Disfranchised, without a choice of parties; denied, so the Municipal League declares, the ancient right of petition; and now to lose "free speech,"—is there no hope for Philadelphia? Yes, the Philadelphians have a very present hope. It is in their new mayor, John Weaver. There is nothing in his record to inspire faith in an outsider. He speaks himself of two notorious "miscarriages of justice" during his term as District Attorney; he was the nominee of the ring; and the ring men have confidence in him. But so have the people, and Mr. Weaver makes fair promises. So did Ashbridge. There is this difference, however: Mr. Weaver has made a good start. He compromised with the machine on his appointments, but he declared against the protection of vice, for free voting, and he stopped some "wholesale grabs" or "maces" that appeared in the Legislature, just before he took office.

One was a bill to enable (ring) companies to "appropriate, take, and use all water within this commonwealth and belonging either to public or to private persons as it may require for its private purposes." This was a scheme to sell out the water-works of Philadelphia, and all other such plants in the State. Another bill was to open the way to a seizure of the light and power of the city and of the State. Martin and Warwick "leased" the city gas works. Durham and his crowd wanted a whack at it. "It shall be lawful," the bill read, "for any city, town, or borough owning any gas works or electric light plant for supplying light, heat, and power, to sell, lease, or otherwise dispose of the same to individuals or corporations, and in order to obtain the best possible returns therefor, such municipal body may . . . vest in the lessees or purchasers the exclusive right, both as against such municipal corporations and against any and all other persons and corporations, to supply gas or electricity. . . ." As in St. Louis, the public property of the city is to be sold off. These schemes are to go through later, I am told, but on Mr. Weaver's declarations that he would not "stand for them," they were laid over.

It looks as if the Philadelphians were right about Mr. Weaver, but what if they are? Think of a city putting its whole faith in one man, in the *hope* that John Weaver, an Englishman by birth, will *give* them good government! And why should he do that? Why should he serve the people and not the ring? The ring can make or break him; the people of Philadelphia can neither reward nor punish him. For even if he restores to them their ballots and proves himself a good mayor, he cannot succeed himself; the good charter forbids more than one term.

George Washington Plunkitt on his rostrum, the New York County Court House Bootblack Stand

Plunkitt of Tammany Hall

(1905)

George Washington Plunkitt's reflections on his political experience, recorded and perhaps embroidered upon by newspaperman William L. Riordon, made a most unusual book in 1905. Beneath the facade of comedy lay a view of previous American politics more accurate than almost anything written by the ostensibly serious political journalists and scholars. The main thrust of American thinking in the progressive era was against Plunkitt's faith in the dominance of political parties. Various reforms—civil service; the initiative, referendum, and recall; the city manager and commission forms of municipal government; the strengthening of mayors against town councils or boards of aldermen; and especially the direct primary—all aimed to break the hold of party over political life. To some extent these stratagems succeeded. Party, competing with the rising mass media and commercial entertainment, went into a steep decline from its nineteenth-century importance as a force dominating public opinion. Insurgency became a national fad, and the "independent" vote grew. Yet party still remained the most important single determinant of voting.

Against this background, Plunkitt's view of the need for party to retain the patriotism and brighten the prospects of his poor voters takes on added meaning. He points both to the role that machine politics served—rendering aid to the poor and inducting them into the life of the citizen—and the causes of its decline: the shrinking respect for machine leaders by the organs of opinion, and a growing intolerance for "honest graft," the oil that kept the machine in motion. Graft was defensible in public debate only by coating it with humor and giving it an extra-political interest through a neat evocation of the life of lower-class immigrant New York. Ironically, the villain of the piece, "The" McManus, goes marching on: his descendants still control the district, artfully mixing the traditional methods so well outlined by their old enemy Plunkitt with the modern demands for social services and reform that the machines did not know how to meet.

A Tribute to Plunkitt by the Leader of Tammany Hall

Senator Plunkitt is a straight organization man. He believes in party government; he does not indulge in cant and hypocrisy and he is never afraid to say exactly what he thinks. He is a believer in thorough political organization and all-the-year-around work, and he holds to the doctrine that, in making appointments to office, party workers should be preferred if they are fitted to perform the duties of the office. Plunkitt is one of the veteran leaders of the organization; he has always been faithful and reliable, and he has performed valuable services for Tammany Hall.

CHARLES F. MURPHY

Honest Graft and Dishonest Graft

Everybody is talkin' these days about Tammany men growin' rich on graft, but nobody thinks of drawin' the distinction between honest graft and dishonest graft. There's all the difference in the world between the two. Yes, many of our men have grown rich in politics. I have myself. I've made a big fortune out of the game, and I'm gettin' richer every day, but I've not gone in for dishonest graft—blackmailin' gamblers, saloonkeepers, disorderly people, etc.—and neither has any of the men who have made big fortunes in politics.

There's an honest graft, and I'm an example of how it works. I might sum up the whole thing by sayin': "I seen my opportunities and I took 'em."

Just let me explain by examples. My party's in power in the city, and it's goin' to undertake a lot of public improvements. Well, I'm tipped off, say, that they're going to lay out a new park at a certain place.

I see my opportunity and I take it. I go to that place and I buy up all the land I can in the neighborhood. Then the board of this or that makes its plan public, and there is a rush to get my land, which nobody cared particular for before.

Ain't it perfectly honest to charge a good price and make a profit on my investment and foresight? Of course, it is. Well, that's honest graft.

Or supposin' it's a new bridge they're goin' to build. I get tipped off and I buy as much property as I can that has to be taken for approaches. I sell at my own price later on and drop some more money in the bank.

Wouldn't you? It's just like lookin' ahead in Wall Street or in the coffee or cotton market. It's honest graft, and I'm lookin' for it every day in the year. I will tell you frankly that I've got a good lot of it, too.

I'll tell you of one case. They were goin' to fix up a big park, no matter where. I got on to it, and went lookin' about for land in that neighborhood.

I could get nothin' at a bargain but a big piece of swamp, but I took it fast enough and held on to it. What turned out was just what I counted on. They couldn't make the park complete without Plunkitt's swamp, and they had to pay a good price for it. Anything dishonest in that?

Up in the watershed I made some money, too. I bought up several bits of land there some years ago and made a pretty good guess that they would be bought up for water purposes later by the city.

Somehow, I always guessed about right, and shouldn't I enjoy the profit of my foresight? It was rather amusin' when the condemnation commissioners came along and found piece after piece of the land in the name of George Plunkitt of the Fifteenth Assembly District, New York City. They wondered how I knew just what to buy. The answer is—I seen my opportunity and I took it. I haven't confined myself to land; anything that pays is in my line.

For instance, the city is repavin' a street and has several hundred thousand old granite blocks to sell. I am on hand to buy, and I know just what they are worth.

How? Never mind that. I had a sort of monopoly of this business for a while, but once a newspaper tried to do me. It got some outside men to come over from Brooklyn and New Jersey to bid against me.

Was I done? Not much. I went to each of the men and said: "How many of these 250,000 stones do you want?" One said 20,000, and another wanted 15,000, and other wanted 10,000. I said: "All right, let me bid for the lot, and I'll give each of you all you want for nothin'."

They agreed, of course. Then the auctioneer yelled: "How much am I bid for these 250,000 fine pavin' stones?"

"Two dollars and fifty cents," says I.

"Two dollars and fifty cents!" screamed the auctioneer. "Oh, that's a joke! Give me a real bid."

He found the bid was real enough. My rivals stood silent. I got the lot for $2.50 and gave them their share. That's how the attempt to do Plunkitt ended, and that's how all such attempts end.

I've told you how I got rich by honest graft. Now, let me tell you that most politicians who are accused of robbin' the city get rich the same way.

They didn't steal a dollar from the city treasury. They just seen their opportunities and took them. That is why, when a reform administration comes in and spends a half million dollars in tryin' to find the public robberies they talked about in the campaign, they don't find them.

The books are always all right. The money in the city treasury is all right. Everything is all right. All they can show is that the Tammany heads of departments looked after their friends, within the law, and gave them what opportunities they could to make honest graft. Now, let me tell you that's never goin' to hurt Tammany with the people. Every good man looks after his friends, and any man who doesn't isn't likely to be popular. If I have a good thing to hand out in private life, I give it to a friend. Why shouldn't I do the same in public life?

Another kind of honest graft. Tammany has raised a good many salaries. There was an awful howl by the reformers, but don't you know that Tammany gains ten votes for every one it lost by salary raisin'?

The Wall Street banker thinks it shameful to raise a department clerk's salary from $1500 to $1800 a year, but every man who draws a salary himself says: "That's all right. I wish it was me." And he feels very much like votin' the Tammany ticket on election day, just out of sympathy.

Tammany was beat in 1901 because the people were deceived into believin' that it worked dishonest graft. They didn't draw a distinction between dishonest and honest graft, but they saw that some Tammany men grew rich, and supposed they had been robbin' the city treasury or levyin' blackmail on disorderly houses, or workin' in with the gamblers and lawbreakers.

As a matter of policy, if nothing else, why should the Tammany leaders go into such dirty business, when there is so much honest graft lyin' around when they are in power? Did you ever consider that?

Now, in conclusion, I want to say that I don't own a dishonest dollar. If my worst enemy was given the job of writin' my epitaph when I'm gone, he couldn't do more than write:

"George W. Plunkitt. He Seen His Opportunities, and He Took 'Em."

How to Become a Statesman

There's thousands of young men in this city who will go to the polls for the first time next November. Among them will be many who have watched the careers of successful men in politics, and who are longin' to make names and fortunes for themselves at the same game. It is to these youths that I want to give advice. First, let me say that I am in a position to give what the courts call expert testimony on the subject. I don't think you can easily find a better example than I am of success in politics. After forty years' experience at the game I am—well, I'm George Washington Plunkitt. Everybody knows what figure I cut in the greatest organization on earth, and if you hear people say that I've laid away a million or so since I was a butcher's boy in

Washington Market, don't come to me for an indignant denial. I'm pretty comfortable, thank you.

Now, havin' qualified as an expert, as the lawyers say, I am goin' to give advice free to the young men who are goin' to cast their first votes, and who are lookin' forward to political glory and lots of cash. Some young men think they can learn how to be successful in politics from books, and they cram their heads with all sorts of college rot. They couldn't make a bigger mistake. Now, understand me, I ain't sayin' nothin' against colleges. I guess they'll have to exist as long as there's bookworms, and I suppose they do some good in a certain way, but they don't count in politics. In fact, a young man who has gone through the college course is handicapped at the outset. He may succeed in politics, but the chances are 100 to 1 against him.

Another mistake: some young men think that the best way to prepare for the political game is to practice speakin' and becomin' orators. That's all wrong. We've got some orators in Tammany Hall, but they're chiefly ornamental. You never heard of Charlie Murphy delivering a speech, did you? Or Richard Croker, or John Kelly, or any other man who has been a real power in the organization? Look at the thirty-six district leaders of Tammany Hall today. How many of them travel on their tongues? Maybe one or two, and they don't count when business is doin' at Tammany Hall. The men who rule have practiced keepin' their tongues still, not exercisin' them. So you want to drop the orator idea unless you mean to go into politics just to perform the skyrocket act.

Now, I've told you what not to do; I guess I can explain best what to do to succeed in politics by tellin' you what I did. After goin' through the apprenticeship of the business while I was a boy by workin' around the district headquarters and hustlin' about the polls on election day, I set out when I cast my first vote to win fame and money in New York City politics. Did I offer my services to the district leader as a stump-speaker? Not much. The woods are always full of speakers. Did I get up a book on municipal government and show it to the leader? I wasn't such a fool. What I did was to get some marketable goods before goin' to the leaders. What do I mean by marketable goods? Let me tell you: I had a cousin, a young man who didn't take any particular interest in politics. I went to him and said: "Tommy, I'm goin' to be a politician, and I want to get a followin'; can I count on you?" He said: "Sure, George." That's how I started in business. I got a marketable commodity—one vote. Then I went to the district leader and told him I could command two votes on election day, Tommy's and my own. He smiled on me and told me to go ahead. If I had offered him a speech or a bookful of learnin', he would have said, "Oh, forget it!"

That was beginnin' business in a small way, wasn't it? But that is the only way to become a real lastin' statesman. I soon branched out. Two young men in the flat next to mine were school friends. I went to them, just as I went to Tommy, and they agreed to stand by me. Then I had a followin' of three voters and I began to get a bit chesty. Whenever I dropped into district headquarters, everybody shook hands with me, and the leader one day honored me by lightin' a match for my cigar. And so it went on like a snowball rollin' down a hill. I worked the flat-house that I lived in from the basement to the top floor, and I got about a dozen young men to follow me. Then I tackled the next house and so on down the block and around the corner. Before long I had sixty men back of me, and formed the George Washington Plunkitt Association.

What did the district leader say then when I called at headquarters? I didn't have to call at headquarters. He came after me and said: "George, what do you want? If you don't see what you want, ask for it. Wouldn't you like to have a job or two in the departments for your friends?" I said: "I'll think it over; I haven't yet decided what the George Washington Plunkitt Association will do in the next campaign." You ought to have seen how I was courted and petted then by the leaders of the rival organizations. I had marketable goods and there was bids for them from all sides, and I was a risin' man in politics. As time went on, and my association grew, I thought I would like to go to the Assembly. I just had to hint at what I wanted, and three different organizations offered me the nomination. Afterwards, I went to the Board of Aldermen, then to the State Senate, then became leader of the district, and so on up and up till I became a statesman.

That is the way and the only way to make a lastin' success in politics. If you are goin' to cast your first vote next November and want to go into politics, do as I did. Get a followin', if it's only one man, and then go to the district leader and say: "I want to join the organization. I've got one man who'll follow me through thick and thin." The leader won't laugh at your one-man followin'. He'll shake your hand warmly, offer to propose you for membership in his club, take you down to the corner for a drink and ask you to call again. But go to him and say: "I took first prize at college in Aristotle; I can recite all Shakespeare forwards and backwards; there ain't nothin' in science that ain't as familiar to me as blockades on the elevated roads and I'm the real thing in the way of silver-tongued orators." What will he answer? He'll probably say: "I guess you are not to blame for your misfortunes, but we have no use for you here."

The Curse of Civil Service Reform

This civil service law is the biggest fraud of the age. It is the curse of the nation. There can't be no real patriotism while it lasts. How are you goin' to interest our young men in their country if you have no offices to give them when they work for their party? Just look at things in this city today. There are ten thousand good offices, but we can't get at more than a few hundred of them. How are we goin' to provide for the thousands of men who worked for the Tammany ticket? It can't be done. These men were full of patriotism a short time ago. They expected to be servin' their city, but when we tell them that we can't place them, do you think their patriotism is goin' to last? Not much. They say: "What's the use of workin' for your country anyhow? There's nothin' in the game." And what can they do? I don't know, but I'll tell you what I do know. I know more than one young man in past years who worked for the ticket and was just overflowin' with patriotism, but when he was knocked out by the civil service humbug he got to hate his country and became an Anarchist.

This ain't no exaggeration. I have good reason for sayin' that most of the Anarchists in this city today are men who ran up against civil service examinations. Isn't it enough to make a man sour on his country when he wants to serve it and won't be allowed unless he answers a lot of fool questions about the number of cubic inches of water in the Atlantic and the quality of sand in the Sahara desert? There was once a bright young man in my district who tackled one of these examinations. The next I heard of him he had settled down in Herr Most's saloon smokin' and drinkin' beer and talkin' socialism all day. Before that time he had never drank anything but whisky. I knew what was comin' when a young Irishman drops whisky and takes to beer and long pipes in a German saloon. That young man is today one of the wildest Anarchists in town. And just to think! He might be a patriot but for that cussed civil service.

Say, did you hear about that Civil Service Reform Association kickin' because the tax commissioners want to put their fifty-five deputies on the exempt list, and fire the outfit left to them by Low? That's civil service for you. Just think! Fifty-five Republicans and mugwumps holdin' $3000 and $4000 and $5000 jobs in the tax department when 1555 good Tammany men are ready and willin' to take their places! It's an outrage! What did the people mean when they voted for Tammany? What is representative government, anyhow? Is it all a fake that this is a government of the people, by the people and for the people? If it isn't a fake, then why isn't the people's voice obeyed and Tammany men put in all the offices?

When the people elected Tammany, they knew just what they were doin'. We didn't put up any false pretenses. We didn't go in for humbug civil service and all that rot. We stood as we have always stood, for rewardin' the men that won the victory. They call that the spoils system. All right; Tammany is for the spoils system, and when we go in we fire every anti-Tammany man from office that can be fired under the law. It's an elastic sort of law and you can bet it will be stretched to the limit. Of course the Republican State Civil Service Board will stand in the way of our local Civil Service Commission all it can; but say!—suppose we carry the State sometime, won't we fire the upstate Board all right? Or we'll make it work in harmony with the local board, and that means that Tammany will get everything in sight. I know that the civil service humbug is stuck into the constitution, too, but, as Tim Campbell said: "What's the constitution among friends?"

Say, the people's voice is smothered by the cursed civil service law; it is the root of all evil in our government. You hear of this thing or that thing goin' wrong in the nation, the State or the city. Look down beneath the surface and you can trace everything wrong to civil service. I have studied the subject and I know. The civil service humbug is underminin' our institutions and if a halt ain't called soon this great republic will tumble down like a Park Avenue house when they were buildin' the subway, and on its ruins will rise another Russian government.

This is an awful serious proposition. Free silver and the tariff and imperialism and the Panama Canal are triflin' issues when compared to it. We could worry along without any of these things, but civil service is sappin' the foundation of the whole shootin' match. Let me argue it out for you. I ain't up on sillygisms, but I can give you some arguments that nobody can answer.

First, this great and glorious country was built up by political parties; second, parties can't hold together if their workers don't get the offices when they win; third, if the parties go to pieces, the government they built up must go to pieces, too; fourth, then there'll be h——— to pay.

Could anything be clearer than that? Say, honest now; can you answer that argument? Of course you won't deny that the government was built up by the great parties. That's history, and you can't go back of the returns. As to my second proposition, you can't deny that either. When parties can't get offices, they'll bust. They ain't far from the bustin' point now, with all this civil service business keepin' most of the good things from them. How are you goin' to keep up patriotism if this thing goes on? You can't do it. Let me tell you that patriotism has been dying out fast for the last twenty years. Before then when a party won, its workers got everything in sight. That was somethin' to make a man patriotic. Now, when a party wins and its men come forward and ask for their rewards, the reply is, "Nothin' doin', unless you can answer a list of questions about Egyptian mummies and how many years it will take for a bird to wear out a mass of iron as big as the earth by steppin' on it once in a century?"

I have studied politics and men for forty-five years, and I see how things are driftin'. Sad indeed is the change that has come over the young men, even in my district, where I try to keep up the fire of patriotism by gettin' a lot of jobs for my constituents, whether Tammany is in or out. The boys and men don't get excited any more when they see a United States flag or hear "The Star-Spangled Banner."

They don't care no more for firecrackers on the Fourth of July. And why should they? What is there in it for them? They know that no matter how hard they work for their country in a campaign, the jobs will go to fellows who can tell about the mummies and the bird steppin' on the iron. Are you surprised then that the young men of the country are beginnin' to look coldly on the flag and don't care to put up a nickel for firecrackers?

Say, let me tell of one case. After the battle of San Juan Hill, the Americans found a dead man with a light complexion, red hair and blue eyes. They could see he wasn't a Spaniard, although he had on a Spanish uniform. Several officers looked him over, and then a private of the Seventy-first Regiment saw him and yelled, "Good Lord, that's Flaherty." That man grew up in my district, and he was once the most patriotic American boy on the West Side. He couldn't see a flag without yellin' himself hoarse.

Now, how did he come to be lying dead with a Spanish uniform on? I found out all about it, and I'll vouch for the story. Well, in the municipal campaign of 1897, that young man, chockful of patriotism, worked day and night for the Tammany ticket. Tammany won, and the young man determined to devote his life to the service of the city. He picked out a place that would suit him, and sent in his application to the head of department. He got a reply that he must take a civil service examination to get the place. He didn't know what these examinations were, so he went, all lighthearted, to the Civil Service Board. He read the questions about the mummies, the bird on the iron, and all the other fool questions—and he left that office an enemy of the country that he had loved so well. The mummies and the bird blasted his patriotism. He went to Cuba, enlisted in the Spanish army at the breakin' out of the war, and died fightin' his country.

That is but one victim of the infamous civil service. If that young man had not run up against the civil examination, but had been allowed to serve his country as he wished, he would be in a good office today, drawin' a good salary. Ah, how many young men have had their patriotism blasted in the same way!

Now, what is goin' to happen when civil service crushes out patriotism? Only one thing can happen: the republic will go to pieces. Then a czar or a sultan will turn up, which brings me to the fourthly of my argument—that is, there will be h——— to pay. And that ain't no lie.

Reformers Only Mornin' Glories

College professors and philosophers who go up in a balloon to think are always discussin' the question: "Why Reform Administrations

Never Succeed Themselves!" The reason is plain to anybody who has learned the a, b, c of politics.

I can't tell just how many of these movements I've seen started in New York during my forty years in politics, but I can tell you how many have lasted more than a few years—none. There have been reform committees of fifty, of sixty, of seventy, of one hundred and all sorts of numbers that started out to do up the regular political organizations. They were mornin' glories—looked lovely in the mornin' and withered up in a short time, while the regular machines went on flourishin' forever, like fine old oaks. Say, that's the first poetry I ever worked off. Ain't it great?

Just look back a few years. You remember the People's Municipal League that nominated Frank Scott for mayor in 1890? Do you remember the reformers that got up that league? Have you ever heard of them since? I haven't. Scott himself survived because he had always been a first-rate politician, but you'd have to look in the newspaper almanacs of 1891 to find out who made up the People's Municipal League. Oh, yes! I remember one name: Ollie Teall; dear, pretty Ollie and his big dog. They're about all that's left of the League.

Now take the reform movement of 1894. A lot of good politicians joined in that—the Republicans, the State Democrats, the Stecklerites and the O'Brienites, and they gave us a lickin', but the real reform part of the affair, the Committee of Seventy that started the thing goin', what's become of those reformers? What's become of Charles Stewart Smith? Where's Bangs? Do you ever hear of Cornell, the iron man, in politics now? Could a search party find R. W. G. Welling? Have you seen the name of Fulton McMahon or McMahon Fulton—I ain't sure which—in the papers lately? Or Preble Tucker? Or—but it's no use to go through the list of the reformers who said they sounded in the death knell of Tammany in 1894. They're gone for good, and Tammany's pretty well, thank you. They did the talkin' and posin', and the politicians in the movement got all the plums. It's always the case.

The Citizens' Union has lasted a little bit longer than the reform crowd that went before them, but that's because they learned a thing or two from us. They learned how to put up a pretty good bluff—and bluff counts a lot in politics. With only a few thousand members, they had the nerve to run the whole Fusion movement, make the Republicans and other organizations come to their headquarters to select a ticket and dictate what every candidate must do or not do. I love nerve, and I've had a sort of respect for the Citizens' Union lately, but the Union can't last. Its people haven't been trained to politics, and whenever Tammany calls their bluff they lay right down. You'll never hear of the Union again after a year or two.

And, by the way, what's become of the good government clubs, the political nurseries of a few years ago? Do you ever hear of Good Government Club D and P and Q and Z any more? What's become of the infants who were to grow up and show us how to govern the city? I know what's become of the nursery that was started in my district. You can find pretty much the whole outfit over in my headquarters, Washington Hall.

The fact is that a reformer can't last in politics. He can make a show for a while, but he always comes down like a rocket. Politics is as much a regular business as the grocery or the dry-goods or the drug business. You've got to be trained up to it or you're sure to fail. Suppose a man who knew nothing about the grocery trade suddenly went into the business and tried to conduct it according to his own ideas. Wouldn't he make a mess of it? He might make a splurge for a while, as long as his money lasted, but his store would soon be empty. It's just the same with a reformer. He hasn't been brought up in the difficult business of politics and he makes a mess of it every time.

I've been studyin' the political game for forty-five years, and I don't know it all yet. I'm learnin' somethin' all the time. How, then, can you expect what they call "business men" to turn into politics all at once and make a success of it? It is just as if I went up to Columbia University and started to teach Greek. They usually last about as long in politics as I would last at Columbia.

You can't begin too early in politics if you want to succeed at the game. I began several years before I could vote, and so did every successful leader in Tammany Hall. When I was twelve years old I made myself useful around the district headquarters and did work at all the polls on election day. Later on, I hustled about gettin' out voters who had jags on or who were too lazy to come to the polls. There's a hundred ways that boys can help, and they get an experience that's the first real step in statesmanship. Show me a boy that hustles for the organization on election day, and I'll show you a comin' statesman.

That's the a, b, c of politics. It ain't easy work to get up to y and z. You have to give nearly all your time and attention to it. Of course, you may have some business or occupation on the side, but the great business of your life must be politics if you want to succeed in it. A few years ago Tammany tried to mix politics and business in equal quantities, by havin' two leaders for each district, a politician and a business man. They wouldn't mix. They were like oil and water. The politician looked after the politics of his district; the business man looked after his grocery store or his milk route, and whenever he appeared at an executive meeting, it was only to make trouble. The whole scheme turned out to be a farce and was abandoned mighty quick.

Do you understand now, why it is that a reformer goes down and out in the first or second round, while a politician answers to the gong every time? It is because the one has gone into the fight without trainin', while the other trains all the time and knows every fine point of the game.

* * *

To Hold Your District: Study Human Nature and Act Accordin'

There's only one way to hold a district: you must study human nature and act accordin'. You can't study human nature in books. Books is a hindrance more than anything else. If you have been to college, so much the worse for you. You'll have to unlearn all you learned before you can get right down to human nature, and unlearnin' takes a lot of time. Some men can never forget what they learned at college. Such men may get to be district leaders by a fluke, but they never last.

To learn real human nature you have to go among the people, see them and be seen. I know every man, woman, and child in the Fifteenth District, except them that's been born this summer—and I know some of them, too. I know what they like and what they don't like, what they are strong at and what they are weak in, and I reach them by approachin' at the right side.

For instance, here's how I gather in the young men. I hear of a young feller that's proud of his voice, thinks that he can sing fine. I ask him to come around to Washington Hall and join our Glee Club. He comes and sings, and he's a follower of Plunkitt for life. Another young feller gains a reputation as a baseball player in a vacant lot. I bring him into our baseball club. That fixes him. You'll find him workin' for my ticket at the polls next election day. Then there's the feller that likes rowin' on the river, the young feller that makes a name as a waltzer on his block, the young feller that's handy with his dukes—I rope them all in by givin' them opportunities to show themselves off. I don't trouble them with political arguments. I just study human nature and act accordin'.

But you may say this game won't work with the high-toned fellers, the fellers that go through college and then join the Citizens' Union. Of course it wouldn't work. I have a special treatment for them. I ain't like the patent medicine man that gives the same medicine for all diseases. The Citizens' Union kind of a young man! I love him! He's the daintiest morsel of the lot, and he don't often escape me.

Before telling you how I catch him, let me mention that before the election last year, the Citizens' Union said they had four hundred or five hundred enrolled voters in my district. They had a lovely headquarters, too, beautiful roll-top desks and the cutest rugs in the world. If I was accused of havin' contributed to fix up the nest for them, I wouldn't deny it under oath. What do I mean by that? Never mind. You can guess from the sequel, if you're sharp.

Well, election day came. The Citizens' Union's candidate for Senator, who ran against me, just polled five votes in the district, while I polled something more than 14,000 votes. What became of the 400 or 500 Citizens' Union enrolled voters in my district? Some people guessed that many of them were good Plunkitt men all along and worked with the Cits just to bring them into the Plunkitt camp by election day. You can guess that way, too, if you want to. I never contradict stories about me, especially in hot weather. I just call your attention to the fact that on last election day 395 Citizens' Union enrolled voters in my district were missin' and unaccounted for.

I tell you frankly, though, how I have captured some of the Citizens' Union's young men. I have a plan that never fails. I watch the City Record to see when there's civil service examinations for good things. Then I take my young Cit in hand, tell him all about the good thing and get him worked up till he goes and takes an examination. I don't bother about him any more. It's a cinch that he comes back to me in a few days and asks to join Tammany Hall. Come over to Washington Hall some night and I'll show you a list of names on our rolls marked "C.S." which means, "bucked up against civil service."

As to the older voters, I reach them, too. No, I don't send them campaign literature. That's rot. People can get all the political stuff they want to read—and a good deal more, too—in the papers. Who reads speeches, nowadays, anyhow? It's bad enough to listen to them. You ain't goin' to gain any votes by stuffin' the letter boxes with campaign documents. Like as not you'll lose votes, for there's nothin' a man hates more than to hear the letter carrier ring his bell and go to the letter box expectin' to find a letter he was lookin' for, and find only a lot of printed politics. I met a man this very mornin' who told me he voted the Democratic State ticket last year just because the Republicans kept crammin' his letter box with campaign documents.

What tells in holdin' your grip on your district is to go right down among the poor families and help them in the different ways they need help. I've got a regular system for this. If there's a fire in Ninth, Tenth, or Eleventh Avenue, for example, any hour of the day or night, I'm usually there with some of my election district captains as soon as the fire engines. If a family is burned out I don't ask whether they are Republicans or Democrats, and I don't refer them to the Charity Organization Society, which would investigate their case in a month or two and decide they were worthy of help about the time they are dead from starvation. I just get quarters for them, buy clothes for them if their clothes were burned up, and fix them up till they get things runnin' again. It's philanthropy, but it's politics, too—mighty good politics. Who can tell how many votes one of these fires bring me? The poor are the most grateful people in the world, and, let me tell you, they have more friends in their neighborhoods than the rich have in theirs.

If there's a family in my district in want I know it before the charitable societies do, and me and my men are first on the ground. I have a special corps to look up such cases. The consequence is that the poor look up to George W. Plunkitt as a father, come to him in trouble—and don't forget him on election day.

Another thing, I can always get a job for a deservin' man. I make it a point to keep on the track of jobs, and it seldom happens that I don't have a few up my sleeve ready for use. I know every big employer in the district and in the whole city, for that matter, and they ain't in the habit of sayin' no to me when I ask them for a job.

And the children—the little roses of the district! Do I forget them? Oh, no! They know me, every one of them, and they know that a sight of Uncle George and candy means the same thing. Some of them are the best kind of vote-getters. I'll tell you a case. Last year a little Eleventh Avenue rosebud, whose father is a Republican, caught hold of his whiskers on election day and said she wouldn't let go till he'd promise to vote for me. And she didn't.

On The Shame of the Cities

I've been readin' a book by Lincoln Steffens on *The Shame of the Cities*. Steffens means well but, like all reformers, he don't know how to make distinctions. He can't see no difference between honest graft and dishonest graft and, consequent, he gets things all mixed up. There's the biggest kind of a difference between political looters and politicians who make a fortune out of politics by keepin' their eyes wide open. The looter goes in for himself alone without considerin' his organization or his city. The politician looks after his own interests, the organization's interests, and the city's interests all at the same time. See the distinction? For instance, I ain't no looter. The looter hogs it. I never hogged. I made my pile in politics, but, at the same time, I served the organization and got more big improvements for New York City than any other livin' man. And I never monkeyed with the penal code.

The difference between a looter and a practical politician is the difference between the Philadelphia Republican gang and Tammany Hall. Steffens seems to think they're both about the same; but he's all wrong. The Philadelphia crowd runs up against the penal code. Tammany don't. The Philadelphians ain't satisfied with robbin' the bank of all its gold and paper money. They stay to pick up the nickels and pennies and the cop comes and nabs them. Tammany ain't no such fool. Why, I remember, about fifteen or twenty years ago, a

Republican superintendent of the Philadelphia almshouse stole the zinc roof off the buildin' and sold it for junk. That was carryin' things to excess. There's a limit to everything, and the Philadelphia Republicans go beyond the limit. It seems like they can't be cool and moderate like real politicians. It ain't fair, therefore, to class Tammany men with the Philadelphia gang. Any man who undertakes to write political books should never for a moment lose sight of the distinction between honest graft and dishonest graft, which I explained in full in another talk. If he puts all kinds of graft on the same level, he'll make the fatal mistake that Steffens made and spoil his book.

A big city like New York or Philadelphia or Chicago might be compared to a sort of Garden of Eden, from a political point of view. It's an orchard full of beautiful apple trees. One of them has got a big sign on it, marked: "Penal Code Tree—Poison." The other trees have lots of apples on them for all. Yet the fools go to the Penal Code Tree. Why? For the reason, I guess, that a cranky child refuses to eat good food and chews up a box of matches with relish. I never had any temptation to touch the Penal Code Tree. The other apples are good enough for me, and O Lord! how many of them there are in a big city!

Steffens made one good point in his book. He said he found that Philadelphia, ruled almost entirely by Americans, was more corrupt than New York, where the Irish do almost all the governin'. I could have told him that before he did any investigatin' if he had come to me. The Irish was born to rule, and they're the honestest people in the world. Show me the Irishman who would steal a roof off an almshouse! He don't exist. Of course, if an Irishman had the political pull and the roof was much worn, he might get the city authorities to put on a new one and get the contract for it himself, and buy the old roof at a bargain—but that's honest graft. It's goin' about the thing like a gentleman, and there's more money in it than in tearin' down an old roof and cartin' it to the junkman's—more money and no penal code.

One reason why the Irishman is more honest in politics than many Sons of the Revolution is that he is grateful to the country and the city that gave him protection and prosperity when he was driven by oppression from the Emerald Isle. Say, that sentence is fine, ain't it? I'm goin' to get some literary feller to work it over into poetry for next St. Patrick's Day dinner.

Yes, the Irishman is grateful. His one thought is to serve the city which gave him a home. He has this thought even before he lands in New York, for his friends here often have a good place in one of the city departments picked out for him while he is still in the old country. Is it any wonder that he has a tender spot in his heart for old New York when he is on its salary list the mornin' after he lands?

Now, a few words on the general subject of the so-called shame of cities. I don't believe that the government of our cities is any worse, in proportion to opportunities, than it was fifty years ago. I'll explain what I mean by "in proportion to opportunities." A half a century ago, our cities were small and poor. There wasn't many temptations lyin' around for politicians. There was hardly anything to steal, and hardly any opportunities for even honest graft. A city could count its money every night before goin' to bed, and if three cents was missin', all the fire bells would be rung. What credit was there in bein' honest under them circumstances? It makes me tired to hear of old codgers back in the thirties or forties boastin' that they retired from politics without a dollar except what they earned in their profession or business. If they lived today, with all the existin' opportunities, they would be just the same as twentieth-century politicians. There ain't any more honest people in the world just now than the convicts in Sing Sing. Not one of them steals anything. Why? Because they can't. See the application?

Understand, I ain't defendin' politicians of today who steal. The politician who steals is worse than a thief. He is a fool. With the grand opportunities all around for the man with a political pull, there's no excuse for stealin' a cent. The point I want to make is that if there is some stealin' in politics, it don't mean that the politicians of 1905 are, as a class, worse than them of 1835. It just means that the old-timers had nothin' to steal, while the politicians now are surrounded by all kinds of temptations and some of them naturally—the fool ones—buck up against the penal code.

Ingratitude in Politics

There's no crime so mean as ingratitude in politics, but every great statesman from the beginnin' of the world has been up against it. Caesar had his Brutus; that king of Shakespeare's—Leary, I think you call him—had his own daughters go back on him; Platt had his Odell, and I've got my "The" McManus. It's a real proof that a man is great when he meets with political ingratitude. Great men have a tender, trustin' nature. So have I, outside of the contractin' and real estate business. In politics I have trusted men who have told me they were my friends, and if traitors have turned up in my camp—well, I only had the same experience as Caesar, Leary, and the others. About my Brutus. McManus, you know, has seven brothers and they call him "The" because he is the boss of the lot, and to distinguish him from all other McManuses. For several years he was a political bushwhacker. In campaigns he was sometimes on the fence, sometimes on both sides of the fence, and sometimes under the fence. Nobody knew where to find him at any particular time, and nobody trusted him—that is, nobody but me. I thought there was some good in him after all and that, if I took him in hand, I could make a man of him yet.

I did take him in hand, a few years ago. My friends told me it would be the Brutus-Leary business all over again, but I didn't believe them.

I put my trust in "The." I nominated him for the Assembly, and he was elected. A year afterwards, when I was runnin' for re-election as Senator, I nominated him for the Assembly again on the ticket with me. What do you think happened? We both carried the Fifteenth Assembly District, but he ran away ahead of me. Just think! Ahead of me in my own district! I was just dazed. When I began to recover, my election district captains came to me and said that McManus had sold me out with the idea of knockin' me out of the Senatorship, and then tryin' to capture the leadership of the district. I couldn't believe it. My trustin' nature couldn't imagine such treachery.

I sent for McManus and said, with my voice tremblin' with emotions: "They say you have done me dirt, 'The.' It can't be true. Tell me it ain't true."

"The" almost wept as he said he was innocent.

"Never have I done you dirt, George," he declared. "Wicked traitors have tried to do you. I don't know just who they are yet, but I'm on their trail, and I'll find them or abjure the name of 'The' McManus. I'm goin' out right now to find them."

Well, "The" kept his word as far as goin' out and findin' the traitors was concerned. He found them all right—and put himself at their head. Oh, no! He didn't have to go far to look for them. He's got them gathered in his clubrooms now, and he's doin' his best to take the leadership from the man that made him. So you see that Caesar and Leary and me's in the same boat, only I'll come out on top while Caesar and Leary went under.

Now let me tell you that the ingrate in politics never flourishes long. I can give you lots of examples. Look at the men who done up Roscoe Conkling when he resigned from the United States Senate and went to Albany to ask for re-election! What's become of them? Passed from view like a movin' picture. Who took Conkling's place in the Senate? Twenty dollars even that you can't remember his name without looking in the almanac. And poor old Platt! He's down and out now and Odell is in the saddle, but that don't mean that he'll always be in the saddle. His enemies are workin' hard all the time to do him, and I wouldn't be a bit surprised if he went out before the next State campaign.

The politicians who make a lastin' success in politics are the men who are always loyal to their friends, even up to the gate of State prison, if necessary; men who keep their promises and never lie. Richard Croker used to say that tellin' the truth and stickin' to his friends was the political leader's stock in trade. Nobody ever said anything truer, and nobody lived up to it better than Croker. That is why he remained leader of Tammany Hall as long as he wanted to. Every man in the organization trusted him. Sometimes he made mistakes that hurt in campaigns, but they were always on the side of servin' his friends.

It's the same with Charles F. Murphy. He has always stood by his friends even when it looked like he would be downed for doin' so. Remember how he stuck to McClellan in 1903 when all the Brooklyn leaders were against him, and it seemed as if Tammany was in for a grand smash-up! It's men like Croker and Murphy that stay leaders as long as they live; not men like Brutus and McManus.

Now I want to tell you why political traitors, in New York City especially, are punished quick. It's because the Irish are in a majority. The Irish, above all people in the world, hates a traitor. You can't hold them back when a traitor of any kind is in sight and, rememberin' old Ireland, they take particular delight in doin' up a political traitor. Most of the voters in my district are Irish or of Irish descent; they've spotted "The" McManus, and when they get a chance at him at the polls next time, they won't do a thing to him.

The question has been asked: Is a politician ever justified in goin' back on his district leader? I answer: "No; as long as the leader hustles around and gets all the jobs possible for his constituents." When the voters elect a man leader, they make a sort of a contract with him. They say, although it ain't written out: "We've put you here to look out for our interests. You want to see that this district gets all the jobs that's comin' to it. Be faithful to us, and we'll be faithful to you."

The district leader promises and that makes a solemn contract. If he lives up to it, spends most of his time chasin' after places in the departments, picks up jobs from railroads and contractors for his followers, and shows himself in all ways a true statesman, then his followers are bound in honor to uphold him, just as they're bound to uphold the Constitution of the United States. But if he only looks after his own interests or shows no talent for scenting out jobs or ain't got the nerve to demand and get his share of the good things that are goin', his followers may be absolved from their allegiance and they may up and swat him without bein' put down as political ingrates.

Reciprocity in Patronage

Whenever Tammany is whipped at the polls, the people set to predictin' that the organization is goin' to smash. They say we can't get along without the offices and that the district leaders are goin' to desert wholesale. That was what was said after the throwdowns in 1894 and 1901. But it didn't happen, did it? Not one big Tammany man deserted, and today the organization is stronger than ever.

How was that? It was because Tammany has more than one string to its bow.

I acknowledge that you can't keep an organization together without patronage. Men ain't in politics for nothin'. They want to get somethin' out of it.

But there is more than one kind of patronage. We lost the public kind, or a greater part of it, in 1901, but Tammany has an immense private patronage that keeps things goin' when it gets a setback at the polls.

Take me, for instance. When Low came in, some of my men lost public jobs, but I fixed them all right. I don't know how many jobs I got for them on the surface and elevated railroads—several hundred.

I placed a lot more on public works done by contractors, and no Tammany man goes hungry in my district. Plunkitt's O.K. on an application for a job is never turned down, for they all know that Plunkitt and Tammany don't stay out long. See!

Let me tell you, too, that I got jobs from Republicans in office—Federal and otherwise. When Tammany's on top I do good turns for the Republicans. When they're on top they don't forget me.

Me and the Republicans are enemies just one day in the year—election day. Then we fight tooth and nail. The rest of the time it's live and let live with us.

On election day I try to pile up as big a majority as I can against George Wanmaker, the Republican leader of the Fifteenth. Any other day George and I are the best of friends. I can go to him and say: "George, I want you to place this friend of mine." He says: "All right, Senator." Or vice versa.

You see, we differ on tariffs and currencies and all them things, but we agree on the main proposition that when a man works in politics, he should get something out of it.

The politicians have got to stand together this way or there wouldn't be any political parties in a short time. Civil service would gobble up everything, politicians would be on the bum, the republic would fall and soon there would be the cry of "Vevey le roi!"

The very thought of this civil service monster makes my blood boil. I have said a lot about it already, but another instance of its awful work just occurs to me.

Let me tell you a sad but true story. Last Wednesday a line of carriages wound into Cavalry Cemetery. I was in one of them. It was the funeral of a young man from my district—a bright boy that I had great hopes of.

When he went to school, he was the most patriotic boy in the district. Nobody could sing "The Star-Spangled Banner" like him, nobody was as fond of waving a flag, and nobody shot off as many firecrackers on the Fourth of July. And when he grew up he made up his mind to serve his country in one of the city departments. There was no way of gettin' there without passin' a civil service examination. Well, he went down to the civil service office and tackled the fool questions. I saw him next day—it was Memorial Day, and soldiers were marchin' and flags flyin' and people cheerin'.

Where was my young man? Standin' on the corner, scowlin' at the whole show. When I asked him why he was so quiet, he laughed in a wild sort of way and said: "What rot all this is!"

Just then a band came along playing "Liberty." He laughed wild again and said: "Liberty? Rats!"

I don't guess I need to make a long story of it.

From the time that young man left the civil service office he lost all patriotism. He didn't care no more for his country. He went to the dogs.

He ain't the only one. There's a gravestone over some bright young man's head for every one of them infernal civil service examinations. They are underminin' the manhood of the nation and makin' the Declaration of Independence a farce. We need a new Declaration of Independence—independence of the whole fool civil service business.

I mention all this now to show why it is that the politicians of two big parties help each other along, and why Tammany men are tolerably happy when not in power in the city. When we win I won't let any deservin' Republican in my neighborhood suffer from hunger or thirst, although, of course, I look out for my own people first.

Now, I've never gone in for nonpartisan business, but I do think that all the leaders of the two parties should get together and make an open, nonpartisan fight against civil service, their common enemy. They could keep up their quarrels about imperialism and free silver and high tariff. They don't count for much alongside of civil service, which strikes right at the root of the government.

The time is fast coming when civil service or the politicians will have to go. And it will be here sooner than they expect if the politicians don't unite, drop all them minor issues for a while and make a stand against the civil service flood that's sweepin' over the country like them floods out West.

* * *

Tammany's Patriotism

Tammany's the most patriotic organization on earth, notwithstandin' the fact that the civil service law is sappin' the foundations of patriotism all over the country. Nobody pays any attention to the Fourth of July any longer except Tammany and the small boy. When the Fourth comes, the reformers, with Revolutionary names parted in the middle, run off to Newport or the Adirondacks to get out of the way of the noise and everything that reminds them of the glorious day. How different it is with Tammany! The very constitution of the Tammany Society requires that we must assemble at the wigwam on the Fourth, regardless of the weather, and listen to the readin' of the Declaration of Independence and patriotic speeches.

You ought to attend one of these meetin's. They're a liberal education in patriotism. The great hall upstairs is filled with five thousand people, suffocatin' from heat and smoke. Every man Jack of these five thousand knows that down in the basement there's a hundred cases of champagne and two hundred kegs of beer ready to flow when the signal is given. Yet that crowd stick to their seats without turnin' a hair while, for four solid hours, the Declaration of Independence is read, long-winded orators speak, and the glee club sings itself hoarse.

Talk about heroism in the battlefield! That comes and passes away in a moment. You ain't got time to be anything but heroic. But just think of five thousand men sittin' in the hottest place on earth for four long hours, with parched lips and gnawin' stomachs, and knowin' all the time that the delights of the oasis in the desert were only two flights downstairs! Ah, that is the highest kind of patriotism, the patriotism of long sufferin' and endurance. What man wouldn't rather face a cannon for a minute or two than thirst for four hours, with champagne and beer almost under his nose?

And then see how they applaud and yell when patriotic things are said! As soon as the man on the platform starts off with "when, in the course of human events," word goes around that it's the Declaration of Independence, and a mighty roar goes up. The Declaration ain't a very short document and the crowd has heard it on every Fourth but they give it just as fine a send-off as if it was brand-new and awful excitin'. Then the "long talkers" get in their work, that is two or three orators who are good for an hour each. Heat never has any effect on these men. They use every minute of their time. Sometimes human nature gets the better of a man in the audience and he begins to nod, but he always wakes up with a hurrah for the Declaration of Independence.

The greatest hero of the occasion is the Grand Sachem of the Tammany Society who presides. He and the rest of us Sachems come on the stage wearin' stovepipe hats, accordin' to the constitution, but we can shed ours right off, while the Grand Sachem is required to wear his hat all through the celebration. Have you any idea what that means? Four hours under a big silk hat in a hall where the heat registers 110 and the smoke 250! And the Grand Sachem is expected to look pleasant all the time and say nice things when introducin' the speakers! Often his hand goes to his hat, unconscious-like, then he catches himself up in time and looks around like a man who is in the tenth story of a burnin' buildin' seekin' a way to escape. I believe that Fourth-of-July silk hat shortened the life of one of our Grand Sachems, the late Supreme Court Justice Smyth, and I know that one of our Sachems refused the office of Grand Sachem because he couldn't get up sufficient patriotism to perform this four-hour hat act. You see, there's degrees of patriotism just as there's degrees in everything else.

You don't hear of the Citizens' Union people holdin' Fourth-of-July celebrations under a five-pound silk hat, or any other way, do you? The Cits take the Fourth like a dog I had when I was a boy. That dog knew as much as some Cits and he acted just like them about the glorious day. Exactly forty-eight hours before each Fourth of July, the dog left our house on a run and hid himself in the Bronx woods. The day after the Fourth he turned up at home as regular as clockwork. He must have known what a dog is up against on the Fourth. Anyhow, he kept out of the way. The name-parted-in-the-middle aristocrats act in just the same way. They don't want to be annoyed with firecrackers and the Declaration of Independence, and when they see the Fourth comin' they hustle off to the woods like my dog.

Tammany don't only show its patriotism at Fourth-of-July celebrations. It's always on deck when the country needs its services. After the Spanish-American War broke out, John J. Scannell, the Tammany leader of the Twenty-fifth District, wrote to Governor Black offerin' to raise a Tammany regiment to go to the front. If you want proof, go to Tammany Hall and see the beautiful set of engrossed resolutions about this regiment. It's true that the Governor didn't accept the offer, but it showed Tammany's patriotism. Some enemies of the organization have said that the offer to raise the regiment was made after the Governor let it be known that no more volunteers were wanted, but that's the talk of envious slanderers.

Now, a word about Tammany's love for the American flag. Did you ever see Tammany Hall decorated for a celebration? It's just a mass of flags. They even take down the window shades and put flags in place of them. There's flags everywhere except on the floors. We don't care for expense where the American flag is concerned, especially after we have won an election. In 1904 we originated the custom of givin' a small flag to each man as he entered Tammany Hall for the Fourth-of-July celebration. It took like wildfire. The men waved their flags whenever they cheered and the sight made me feel so patriotic that I forgot all about civil service for a while. And the good work of the flags didn't stop there. The men carried them home and gave them to the children, and the kids got patriotic, too. Of course, it all cost a pretty penny, but what of that? We had won at the polls the precedin' November, had the offices and could afford to make an extra investment in patriotism.

* * *

Bosses Preserve the Nation

When I retired from the Senate, I thought I would take a good, long rest, such a rest as a man needs who has held office for about forty years, and has held four different offices in one year and drawn salaries from three of them at the same time. Drawin' so many salaries is rather fatiguin', you know, and, as I said, I started out for a rest; but when I seen how things were goin' in New York State, and how a great big black shadow hung over us, I said to myself: "No rest for you, George. Your work ain't done. You country still needs you and you mustn't lay down yet."

What was the great big black shadow? It was the primary election law, amended so as to knock out what are called the party bosses by lettin' in everybody at the primaries and givin' control over them to state officials. Oh, yes, that is a good way to do up the so-called bosses, but have you ever thought what would become of the country if the bosses were put out of business, and their places were taken by a lot of cart-tail orators and college graduates? It would mean chaos. It would be just like takin' a lot of dry-goods clerks and settin' them to run express trains on the New York Central Railroad. It makes my heart bleed to think of it. Ignorant people are always talkin' against party bosses, but just wait till the bosses are gone! Then, and not until then, will they get the right sort of epitaphs, as Patrick Henry or Robert Emmet said.

Look at the bosses of Tammany Hall in the last twenty years. What magnificent men! To them New York City owes pretty much all it is today. John Kelly, Richard Croker, and Charles F. Murphy—what names in American history compares with them, except Washington and Lincoln? They built up the grand Tammany organization, and the organization built up New York. Suppose the city had to depend for the last twenty years on irresponsible concerns like the Citizens' Union, where would it be now? You can make a pretty good guess if you recall the Strong and Low administrations when there was no boss, and the heads of departments were at odds all the time with each other, and the Mayor was at odds with the lot of them. They spent so much time in arguin' and makin' grandstand play, that the interests of the city were forgotten. Another administration of that kind would put New York back a quarter of a century.

Then see how beautiful a Tammany city government runs, with a so-called boss directin' the whole shootin' match! The machinery moves so noiseless that you wouldn't think there was any. If there's any differences of opinion, the Tammany leader settles them quietly, and his orders go every time. How nice it is for the people to feel that they can get up in the mornin' without bein' afraid of seein' in the papers that the Commissioner of Water Supply has sandbagged the Dock Commissioner, and that the Mayor and heads of the departments have been taken to the police court as witnesses! That's no joke. I remember that, under Strong, some commissioners came very near sandbaggin' one another.

Of course, the newspapers like the reform administration. Why? Because these administrations, with their daily rows, furnish as racy news as prizefights or divorce cases. Tammany don't care to get in the papers. It goes right along attendin' to business quietly and only wants to be let alone. That's one reason why the papers are against us.

Some papers complain that the bosses get rich while devotin' their lives to the interests of the city. What of it? If opportunities for turnin' an honest dollar comes their way, why shouldn't they take advantage of them, just as I have done? As I said, in another talk, there is honest graft and dishonest graft. The bosses go in for the former. There is so much of it in this big town that they would be fools to go in for dishonest graft.

Now, the primary election law threatens to do away with the boss and make the city government a menagerie. That's why I can't take the rest I counted on. I'm goin' to propose a bill for the next session of the legislature repealin' this dangerous law, and leavin' the primaries entirely to the organizations themselves, as they used to be. Then will return the good old times, when our district leaders could have nice comfortable primary elections at some place selected by themselves and let in only men that they approved of as good Democrats. Who is a better judge of the Democracy of a man who offers his vote than the leader of the district? Who is better equipped to keep out undesirable voters?

The men who put through the primary law are the same crowd that stand for the civil service blight and they have the same objects in view—the destruction of governments by party, the downfall of the constitution and hell generally.

* * *

A Parting Word on the Future of the Democratic Party in America

The Democratic party of the nation ain't dead, though it's been givin' a lifelike imitation of a corpse for several years. It can't die while it's got Tammany for its backbone. The trouble is that the party's been chasin' after theories and stayin' up nights readin' books instead of studyin' human nature and actin' accordin', as I've advised in tellin' how to hold your district. In two Presidential campaigns, the leaders talked themselves red in the face about silver bein' the best money and gold bein' no good, and they tried to prove it out of books. Do you think the people cared for all that guff? No. They heartily indorsed what Richard Croker said at the Hoffman House one day in 1900. "What's the use of discussin' what's the best kind of money?" said Croker. "I'm in favor of all kinds of money—the more the better." See how a real Tammany statesman can settle in twenty-five words a problem that monopolized two campaigns!

Then imperialism. The Democratic party spent all its breath on that in the last national campaign. Its position was all right, sure, but you can't get people excited about the Philippines. They've got too much at home to interest them; they're too busy makin' a livin' to bother about the niggers in the Pacific. The party's got to drop all them put-you-to-sleep issues and come out in 1908 for somethin' that will wake the people up; somethin' that will make it worth while to work for the party.

There's just one issue that would set this country on fire. The Democratic party should say in the first plank of its platform: "We hereby declare, in national convention assembled, that the paramount issue now, always and forever, is the abolition of the iniquitous and villainous civil service laws which are destroyin' all patriotism, ruinin' the country and takin' away good jobs from them that earn them. We pledge ourselves, if our ticket is elected, to repeal those laws at once and put every civil service reformer in jail."

Just imagine the wild enthusiasm of the party, if that plank was adopted, and the rush of Republicans to join us in restorin' our country to what it was before this college professor's nightmare, called civil service reform, got hold of it! Of course, it would be all right to work in the platform some stuff about the tariff and sound money and the Philippines, as no platform seems to be complete without them, but they wouldn't count. The people would read only the first plank and then hanker for election day to come to put the Democratic party in office.

I see a vision. I see the civil service monster lyin' flat on the ground. I see the Democratic party standin' over it with foot on its neck and wearin' the crown of victory. I see Thomas Jefferson lookin' out from a cloud and sayin': "Give him another sockdologer; finish him." And I see millions of men wavin' their hats and singin' "Glory Hallelujah!"

Strenuous Life of the Tammany District Leader

NOTE: *This chapter is based on extracts from Plunkitt's Diary and on my daily observation of the work of the district leader.*—W.L.R.

The life of the Tammany district leader is strenuous. To his work is due the wonderful recuperative power of the organization.

One year it goes down in defeat and the prediction is made that it will never again raise its head. The district leader, undaunted by defeat, collects his scattered forces, organizes them as only Tammany knows how to organize, and in a little while the organization is as strong as ever.

No other politician in New York or elsewhere is exactly like the Tammany district leader or works as he does. As a rule, he has no business or occupation other than politics. He plays politics every day and night in the year, and his headquarters bears the inscription, "Never closed."

Everybody in the district knows him. Everybody knows where to find him, and nearly everybody goes to him for assistance of one sort or another, especially the poor of the tenements.

He is always obliging. He will go to the police courts to put in a good word for the "drunks and disorderlies" or pay their fines, if a good word is not effective. He will attend christenings, weddings, and funerals. He will feed the hungry and help bury the dead.

A philanthropist? Not at all. He is playing politics all the time.

Brought up in Tammany Hall, he has learned how to reach the hearts of the great mass of voters. He does not bother about reaching their heads. It is his belief that arguments and campaign literature have never gained votes.

He seeks direct contact with the people, does them good turns when he can, and relies on their not forgetting him on election day. His heart is always in his work, too, for his subsistence depends on its results.

If he holds his district and Tammany is in power, he is amply rewarded by a good office and the opportunities that go with it. What these opportunities are has been shown by the quick rise to wealth of so many Tammany district leaders. With the examples before him of Richard Croker, once leader of the Twentieth District; John F. Carroll, formerly leader of the Twenty-ninth; Timothy ("Dry Dollar") Sullivan, late leader of the Sixth, and many others, he can always look forward to riches and ease while he is going through the drudgery of his daily routine.

This is a record of a day's work by Plunkitt:

2 A.M.: Aroused from sleep by the ringing of his doorbell; went to the door and found a bartender, who asked him to go to the police station and bail out a saloon-keeper who had been arrested for violating the excise law. Furnished bail and returned to bed at three o'clock.

6 A.M.: Awakened by fire engines passing his house. Hastened to the scene of the fire, according to the custom of the Tammany district leaders, to give assistance to the fire sufferers, if needed. Met several of his election district captains who are always under orders to look out for fires, which are considered great vote-getters. Found several tenants who had been burned out, took them to a hotel, supplied them with clothes, fed them, and arranged temporary quarters for them until they could rent and furnish new apartments.

8:30 A.M.: Went to the police court to look after his constituents. Found six "drunks." Secured the discharge of four by a timely word with the judge, and paid the fines of two.

9 A.M.: Appeared in the Municipal District Court. Directed one of his district captains to act as counsel for a widow against whom dispossess proceedings had been instituted and obtained an extension of

time. Paid the rent of a poor family about to be dispossessed and gave them a dollar for food.

11 A.M.: At home again. Found four men waiting for him. One had been discharged by the Metropolitan Railway Company for neglect of duty, and wanted the district leader to fix things. Another wanted a job on the road. The third sought a place on the Subway and the fourth, a plumber, was looking for work with the Consolidated Gas Company. The district leader spent nearly three hours fixing things for the four men, and succeeded in each case.

3 P.M.: Attended the funeral of an Italian as far as the ferry. Hurried back to make his appearance at the funeral of a Hebrew constituent. Went conspicuously to the front both in the Catholic church and the synagogue, and later attended the Hebrew confirmation ceremonies in the synagogue.

7 P.M.: Went to district headquarters and presided over a meeting of election district captains. Each captain submitted a list of all the voters in his district, reported on their attitude toward Tammany, suggested who might be won over and how they could be won, told who were in need, and who were in trouble of any kind and the best way to reach them. District leader took notes and gave orders.

8 P.M.: Went to a church fair. Took chances on everything, bought ice cream for the young girls and the children. Kissed the little ones, flattered their mothers and took their fathers out for something down at the corner.

9 P.M.: At the clubhouse again. Spent $10 on tickets for a church excursion and promised a subscription for a new church bell. Bought tickets for a baseball game to be played by two nines from his district. Listened to the complaints of a dozen pushcart peddlers who said they were persecuted by the police and assured them he would go to Police Headquarters in the morning and see about it.

10:30 P.M.: Attended a Hebrew wedding reception and dance. Had previously sent a handsome wedding present to the bride.

12 P.M.: In bed.

That is the actual record of one day in the life of Plunkitt. He does some of the same things every day, but his life is not so monotonous as to be wearisome.

Sometimes the work of a district leader is exciting, especially if he happens to have a rival who intends to make a contest for the leadership at the primaries. In that case, he is even more alert, tries to reach the fires before his rival, sends out runners to look for "drunks and disorderlies" at the police stations, and keeps a very close watch on the obituary columns of the newspapers.

A few years ago there was a bitter contest for the Tammany leadership of the Ninth District between John C. Sheehan and Frank J. Goodwin. Both had had long experience in Tammany politics and both understood every move of the game.

Every morning their agents went to their respective headquarters before seven o'clock and read through the death notices in all the morning papers. If they found that anybody in the district had died, they rushed to the homes of their principals with the information and then there was a race to the house of the deceased to offer condolences, and, if the family were poor, something more substantial.

On the day of the funeral there was another contest. Each faction tried to surpass the other in the number and appearance of the carriages it sent to the funeral, and more than once they almost came to blows at the church or in the cemetery.

On one occasion the Goodwinites played a trick on their adversaries which has since been imitated in other districts. A well-known liquor dealer who had a considerable following died, and both Sheehan and Goodwin were eager to become his political heir by making a big showing at the funeral.

Goodwin managed to catch the enemy napping. He went to all the livery stables in the district, hired all the carriages for the day, and gave orders to two hundred of his men to be on hand as mourners.

Sheenan had never had any trouble about getting all the carriages that he wanted, so he let the matter go until the night before the funeral. Then he found that he could not hire a carriage in the district.

He called his district committee together in a hurry and explained the situation to them. He could get all the vehicles he needed in the adjoining district, he said, but if he did that, Goodwin would rouse the voters of the Ninth by declaring that he (Sheehan) had patronized foreign industries.

Finally, it was decided that there was nothing to do but to go over to Sixth Avenue and Broadway for carriages. Sheehan made a fine turnout at the funeral, but the deceased was hardly in his grave before Goodwin raised the cry of "Protection to home industries," and denounced his rival for patronizing livery-stable keepers outside of his district. The cry had its effect in the primary campaign. At all events, Goodwin was elected leader.

A recent contest for the leadership of the Second District illustrated further the strenuous work of the Tammany district leaders. The contestants were Patrick Divver, who had managed the district for years, and Thomas F. Foley.

Both were particularly anxious to secure the large Italian vote. They not only attended all the Italian christenings and funerals, but also kept a close lookout for the marriages in order to be on hand with wedding presents.

At first, each had his own reporter in the Italian quarter to keep track of the marriages. Later, Foley conceived a better plan. He hired a man to stay all day at the City Hall marriage bureau, where most Italian couples go through the civil ceremony, and telephone to him at his saloon when anything was doing at the bureau.

Foley had a number of presents ready for use and, whenever he received a telephone message from his man, he hastened to the City

Hall with a ring or a watch or a piece of silver and handed it to the bride with his congratulations. As a consequence, when Divver got the news and went to the home of the couple with his present, he always found that Foley had been ahead of him. Toward the end of the campaign, Divver also stationed a man at the marriage bureau and then there were daily foot races and fights between the two heelers.

Sometimes the rivals came into conflict at the deathbed. One night a poor Italian peddler died in Roosevelt Street. The news reached Divver and Foley about the same time, and as they knew the family of the man was destitute, each went to an undertaker and brought him to the Roosevelt Street tenement.

The rivals and the undertakers met at the house and an altercation ensued. After much discussion the Divver undertaker was selected. Foley had more carriages at the funeral, however, and he further impressed the Italian voters by paying the widow's rent for a month, and sending her half a ton of coal and a barrel of flour.

The rivals were put on their mettle toward the end of the campaign by the wedding of a daughter of one of the original Cohens of the Baxter Street region. The Hebrew vote in the district is nearly as large as the Italian vote, and Divver and Foley set out to capture the Cohens and their friends.

They stayed up nights thinking what they would give the bride. Neither knew how much the other was prepared to spend on a wedding present, or what form it would take; so spies were employed by both sides to keep watch on the jewelry stores, and the jewelers of the district were bribed by each side to impart the desired information.

At last Foley heard that Divver had purchased a set of silver knives, forks and spoons. He at once bought a duplicate set and added a silver tea service. When the presents were displayed at the home of the bride, Divver was not in a pleasant mood and he charged his jeweler with treachery. It may be added that Foley won at the primaries.

One of the fixed duties of a Tammany district leader is to give two outings every summer, one for the men of his district and the other for the women and children, and a beefsteak dinner and a ball every winter. The scene of the outings is, usually, one of the groves along the Sound.

The ambition of the district leader on these occasions is to demonstrate that his men have broken all records in the matter of eating and drinking. He gives out the exact number of pounds of beef, poultry, butter, etc., that they have consumed and professes to know how many potatoes and ears of corn have been served.

According to his figures, the average eating record of each man at the outing is about ten pounds of beef, two or three chickens, a pound of butter, a half peck of potatoes, and two dozen ears of corn. The drinking records, as given out, are still more phenomenal. For some reason, not yet explained, the district leader thinks that his popularity will be greatly increased if he can show that his followers can eat and drink more than the followers of any other district leader.

The same idea governs the beefsteak dinners in the winter. It matters not what sort of steak is served or how it is cooked; the district leader considers only the question of quantity, and when he excels all others in this particular, he feels, somehow, that he is a bigger man and deserves more patronage than his associates in the Tammany Executive Committee.

As to the balls, they are the events of the winter in the extreme East Side and West Side society. Mamie and Maggie and Jennie prepare for them months in advance, and their young men save up for the occasion just as they save for the summer trips to Coney Island.

The district leader is in his glory at the opening of the ball. He leads the cotillion with the prettiest woman present—his wife, if he has one, permitting—and spends almost the whole night shaking hands with his constituents. The ball costs him a pretty penny, but he has found that the investment pays.

By these means the Tammany district leader reaches out into the homes of his district, keeps watch not only on the men, but also on the women and children; knows their needs, their likes and dislikes, their troubles and their hopes, and places himself in a position to use his knowledge for the benefit of his organization and himself. Is it any wonder that scandals do not permanently disable Tammany and that it speedily recovers from what seems to be crushing defeat?

Scalding hogs preparatory to scraping, Swift and Company packinghouse, Chicago

UPTON SINCLAIR

The Jungle

(1906)

The publication of Upton Sinclair's The Jungle was one of the major events of the Progressive Era. Written as a plea for socialism, a gasping public received the book as an exposé not of the economic system, but of sanitary conditions in the packinghouses. Sinclair said that he had taken aim at America's heart and instead hit their stomachs. Somehow the empty stomach of the immigrant worker Jurgis mattered less than their own, filled with packinghouse wastes that possibly came mixed with their dinner.

Sinclair was a dedicated if unconventional non-Marxist socialist. In addition to The Jungle he wrote over 70 books, many of them also exposés. In 1935 he almost became governor of California on a promise of ending poverty through socialism. Although his writing improved with the years—he won a Pulitzer Prize in 1943—none of his works ever had the extra-literary impact of The Jungle. With President Theodore Roosevelt's pressure the book helped persuade Congress to enact the first national pure food, drug, and meat inspection acts.

I

The people of Chicago saw the government inspectors in Packingtown, and they all took that to mean that they were protected from diseased meat; they did not understand that these hundred and sixty-three inspectors had been appointed at the request of the packers, and that they were paid by the United States government to certify that all the diseased meat was kept in the state. They had no authority beyond that; for the inspection of meat to be sold in the city and state the whole force in Packingtown consisted of three henchmen of the local political machine!* And shortly afterward one of these, a physician, made the discovery that the carcasses of steers which had been condemned as tubercular by the government inspectors, and which therefore contained ptomaines, which are deadly poisons, were left upon an open platform and carted away to be sold in the city; and so he insisted that these carcasses be treated with an injection of kerosene—and was ordered to resign the same week! So indignant were the packers that they went farther, and compelled the mayor to abolish the whole bureau of inspection; so that since then there has not been even a pretence of any interference with the graft. There was said to be two thousand dollars a week hush-money from the tubercular steers alone; and as much again from the hogs which had died of cholera on the trains, and which you might see any day being loaded into box-cars and hauled away to a place called Globe, in Indiana, where they made a fancy grade of lard.

Jurgis heard of these things little by little, in the gossip of those who were obliged to perpetrate them. It seemed as if every time you met a person from a new department, you heard of new swindles and new crimes. There was, for instance, a Lithuanian who was a cattle-butcher for the plant where Marija had worked, which killed meat for canning only; and to hear this man describe the animals which came to his place would have been worth while for a Dante or a Zola. It seemed that they must have agencies all over the country, to hunt out old and crippled and diseased cattle to be canned. There were cattle which had been fed on "whiskey-malt," the refuse of the breweries, and had become what the men called "steerly"—which means covered with boils. It was a nasty job killing these, for when you

*"Rules and Regulations for the Inspection of Live Stock and their Products." United States Department of Agriculture, Bureau of Animal Industries, Order No. 125:—

Section 1. Proprietors of slaughterhouses, canning, salting, packing, or rendering establishments engaged in the slaughtering of cattle, sheep, or swine, or the packing of any of their products, *the carcasses or products of which are to become subjects of interstate or foreign commerce,* shall make application to the Secretary of Agriculture for inspection of said animals and their products. . . .

Section 15. Such rejected or condemned animals shall at once be removed by the owners from the pens containing animals which have been inspected and found to be free from disease and fit for human food, and *shall be disposed of in accordance with the laws, ordinances, and regulations of the state and municipality in which said rejected or condemned animals are located. . . .*

Section 25. A microscopic examination for trichinæ shall be made of all swine products exported to countries requiring such examination. *No microscopic examination will be made of hogs slaughtered for interstate trade, but this examination shall be confined to those intended for the export trade.*

plunged your knife into them they would burst and splash foul-smelling stuff into your face; and when a man's sleeves were smeared with blood, and his hands steeped in it, how was he ever to wipe his face, or to clear his eyes so that he could see? It was stuff such as this that made the "embalmed beef" that had killed several times as many United States soldiers as all the bullets of the Spaniards; only the army beef, besides, was not fresh canned, it was old stuff that had been lying for years in the cellars.

Then one Sunday evening, Jurgis sat puffing his pipe by the kitchen stove, and talking with an old fellow whom Jonas had introduced, and who worked in the canningrooms at Durham's; and so Jurgis learned a few things about the great and only Durham canned goods, which had become a national institution. They were regular alchemists at Durham's; they advertised a mushroom-catsup, and the men who made it did not know what a mushroom looked like. They advertised "potted chicken,"—and it was like the boarding-house soup of the comic papers, through which a chicken had walked with rubbers on. Perhaps they had a secret process for making chickens chemically—who knows? said Jurgis's friend; the things that went into the mixture were tripe, and the fat of pork, and beef suet, and hearts of beef, and finally the waste ends of veal, when they had any. They put these up in several grades, and sold them at several prices; but the contents of the cans all came out of the same hopper. And then there was "potted game" and "potted grouse," "potted ham," and "devilled ham"—de-vyled, as the men called it. "De-vyled" ham was made out of the waste ends of smoked beef that were too small to be sliced by the machines; and also tripe, dyed with chemicals so that it would not show white; and trimmings of hams and corned beef; and potatoes, skins and all; and finally the hard cartilaginous gullets of beef, after the tongues had been cut out. All this ingenious mixture was ground up and flavored with spices to make it taste like something. Anybody who could invent a new imitation had been sure of a fortune from old Durham, said Jurgis's informant; but it was hard to think of anything new in a place where so many sharp wits had been at work for so long; where men welcomed tuberculosis in the cattle they were feeding, because it made them fatten more quickly; and where they bought up all the old rancid butter left over in the grocery-stores of a continent, and "oxidized" it by a forced-air process, to take away the odor, rechurned it with skim-milk, and sold it in bricks in the cities! Up to a year or two ago it had been the custom to kill horses in the yards—ostensibly for fertilizer; but after long agitation the newspapers had been able to make the public realize that the horses were being canned. Now it was against the law to kill horses in Packingtown, and the law was really complied with—for the present, at any rate. Any day, however, one might see sharp-horned and shaggy-haired creatures running with the sheep—and yet what a job you would have to get the public to believe that a good part of what it buys for lamb and mutton is really goat's flesh!

There was another interesting set of statistics that a person might have gathered in Packingtown—those of the various afflictions of the workers. When Jurgis had first inspected the packing-plants with Szedvilas, he had marvelled while he listened to the tale of all the things that were made out of the carcasses of animals, and of all the lesser industries that were maintained there; now he found that each one of these lesser industries was a separate little inferno, in its way as horrible as the killing-beds, the source and fountain of them all. The workers in each of them had their own peculiar diseases. And the wandering visitor might be sceptical about all the swindles, but he could not be sceptical about these, for the worker bore the evidence of them about on his own person—generally he had only to hold out his hand.

There were the men in the pickle-rooms, for instance, where old Antanas had gotten his death; scarce a one of these that had not some spot of horror on his person. Let a man so much as scrape his finger pushing a truck in the pickle-rooms, and he might have a sore that would put him out of the world; all the joints in his fingers might be eaten by the acid, one by one. Of the butchers and floorsmen, the beef-boners and trimmers, and all those who used knives, you could scarcely find a person who had the use of his thumb; time and time again the base of it had been slashed, till it was a mere lump of flesh against which the man pressed the knife to hold it. The hands of these men would be criss-crossed with cuts, until you could no longer pretend to count them or to trace them. They would have no nails,—they had worn them off pulling hides; their knuckles were swollen so that their fingers spread out like a fan. There were men who worked in the cooking-rooms, in the midst of steam and sickening odors, by artificial light; in these rooms the germs of tuberculosis might live for two years, but the supply was renewed every hour. There were the beef-luggers, who carried two-hundred-pound quarters into the refrigerator-cars; a fearful kind of work, that began at four o'clock in the morning, and that wore out the most powerful men in a few years. There were those who worked in the chilling-rooms, and whose special disease was rheumatism; the time-limit that a man could work in the chilling-rooms was said to be five years. There were the wool-pluckers, whose hands went to pieces even sooner than the hands of the pickle-men; for the pelts of the sheep had to be painted with acid to loosen the wool, and then the pluckers had to pull out this wool with their bare hands, till the acid had eaten their fingers off. There were those who made the tins for the canned-meat; and their hands, too, were a maze of cuts, and each cut represented a chance for blood-poisoning. Some worked at the stamping-machines, and it was very seldom that one could work long there at the pace that was set, and not give out and forget himself, and have a part of his hand chopped off. There were the "hoisters," as they were called, whose task it was to press the lever which lifted the dead cattle off the floor. They ran along upon a rafter, peering down through the damp and the steam; and as old Durham's architects had not built the killing-room for the convenience of the hoisters, at every few feet they would have to stoop under a beam, say four feet above the one they ran on; which got them into the habit of stooping, so that in a few years they would be walking like chimpanzees. Worst of any, however, were the fertilizer-men, and those who served in the cooking-rooms. These people could not be shown to the visitor,—for the odor of a fertilizer-man would scare any ordinary visitor at a hundred yards, and as for the other men, who worked in tank-rooms full of steam, and in some of which there were open vats near the level of the floor, their peculiar trouble was that they fell into the vats; and when they were fished out, there was never enough of them left to be worth exhibiting,—sometimes they would be overlooked for days, till all but the bones of them had gone out to the world as Durham's Pure Leaf Lard!

* * *

It was only when the whole ham was spoiled that it came into the department of Elzbieta. Cut up by the two-thousand-revolutions-a-minute flyers, and mixed with half a ton of other meat, no odor that ever was in a ham could make any difference. There was never the least attention paid to what was cut up for sausage; there would come all the way back from Europe old sausage that had been rejected, and that was mouldy and white—it would be dosed with borax and glycerine, and dumped into the hoppers, and made over again for home consumption. There would be meat that had tumbled out on the floor, in the dirt and sawdust, where the workers had tramped and spit uncounted billions of consumption germs. There would be meat stored in great piles in rooms; and the water from leaky roofs would drip over it, and thousands of rats would race about on it. It was too dark in these storage places to see well, but a man could run his hand over these piles of meat and sweep off handfuls of the dried dung of rats. These rats were nuisances, and the packers would put poisoned bread out for them; they would die, and then rats, bread, and meat would go into the hoppers together. This is no fairy story and no joke; the meat would be shovelled into carts, and the man who did the shovelling would not trouble to lift out a rat even when he saw one—there were things that went into the sausage in comparison with which a poisoned rat was a tidbit. There was no place for the men to wash their hands before they ate their dinner, and so they made a practice of washing them in the water that was to be ladled into the sausage. There were the butt-ends of smoked meat, and the scraps of corned beef, and all the odds and ends of the waste of the plants, that would be dumped into old barrels in the cellar and left there. Under the system of rigid economy which the packers enforced, there were some jobs that it only paid to do once in a long time, and among these was the cleaning out of the waste-barrels. Every spring they did it; and in the barrels would be dirt and rust and old nails and stale water—and cart load after cart load of it would be taken up and dumped into the hoppers with fresh meat, and sent out to the public's breakfast. Some of it they would make into "smoked" sausage—but as the smoking took time, and was therefore expensive, they would call upon their chemistry department, and preserve it with borax and color it with gelatine to make it brown. All of their sausage came out of the same bowl, but when they came to wrap it they would stamp some of it "special," and for this they would charge two cents more a pound.

Such were the new surroundings in which Elzbieta was placed, and such was the work she was compelled to do. It was stupefying, brutalizing work; it left her no time to think, no strength for anything. She was part of the machine she tended, and every faculty that was not needed for the machine was doomed to be crushed out of existence. There was only one mercy about the cruel grind—that it gave her the gift of insensibility. Little by little she sank into a torpor—she fell silent. She would meet Jurgis and Ona in the evening, and the three would walk home together, often without saying a word. Ona, too, was falling into a habit of silence—Ona, who had once gone about singing like a bird. She was sick and miserable, and often she would barely have strength enough to drag herself home. And there they would eat what they had to eat, and afterwards, because there was only their misery to talk of, they would crawl into bed and fall into a stupor and never stir until it was time to get up again, and dress by candle-light, and go back to the machines. They were so numbed that they did not even suffer much from hunger, now; only the children continued to fret when the food ran short.

Yet the soul of Ona was not dead—the souls of none of them were dead, but only sleeping; and now and then they would waken, and these were cruel times. The gates of memory would roll open—old joys would stretch out their arms to them, old hopes and dreams would call to them, and they would stir beneath the burden that lay upon them, and feel its forever immeasurable weight. They could not even cry out beneath it; but anguish would seize them, more dreadful than the agony of death. It was a thing scarcely to be spoken—a thing never spoken by all the world, that will not know its own defeat.

They were beaten; they had lost the game, they were swept aside. It was not less tragic because it was so sordid, because that it had to do with wages and grocery bills and rents. They had dreamed of freedom; of a chance to look about them and learn something; to be decent and clean, to see their child grow up to be strong. And now it was all gone—it would never be! They had played the game and they had lost. Six years more of toil they had to face before they could expect the least respite, the cessation of the payments upon the house; and how cruelly certain it was that they could never stand six years of such a life as they were living! They were lost, they were going down—and there was no deliverance for them, no hope; for all the help it gave them the vast city in which they lived might have been an ocean waste, a wilderness, a desert, a tomb. So often this mood would come to Ona, in the night-time, when something wakened her; she would lie, afraid of the beating of her own heart, fronting the blood-red eyes of the old primeval terror of life. Once she cried aloud, and woke Jurgis, who was tired and cross. After that she learned to weep silently—their moods so seldom came together now! It was as if their hopes were buried in separate graves.

Jurgis, being a man, had troubles of his own. There was another spectre following him. He had never spoken of it, nor would he allow any one else to speak of it—he had never acknowledged its existence to himself. Yet the battle with it took all the manhood that he had—and once or twice, alas, a little more. Jurgis had discovered drink.

He was working in the steaming pit of hell; day after day, week after week—until now there was not an organ of his body that did its work without pain, until the sound of ocean breakers echoed in his head day and night, and the buildings swayed and danced before him as he went down the street. And from all the unending horror of this there was a respite, a deliverance—he could drink! He could forget the pain, he could slip off the burden; he would see clearly again, he would be master of his brain, of his thoughts, of his will. His dead self would stir in him, and he would find himself laughing and cracking jokes with his companions—he would be a man again, and master of his life.

It was not an easy thing for Jurgis to take more than two or three drinks. With the first drink he could eat a meal, and he could persuade himself that that was economy; with the second he could eat another meal—but there would come a time when he could eat no more, and then to pay for a drink was an unthinkable extravagance, a defiance of the age-long instincts of his hunger-haunted class. One day, however, he took the plunge, and drank up all that he had in his pockets, and went home half "piped," as the men phrase it. He was happier than he had been in a year; and yet, because he knew that the happiness would not last, he was savage, too—with those who would wreck it, and with the world, and with his life; and then again, beneath this, he was sick with the shame of himself. Afterward, when he saw the despair of his family, and reckoned up the money he had spent, the tears came into his eyes, and he began the long battle with the spectre.

It was a battle that had no end, that never could have one. But Jurgis did not realize that very clearly; he was not given much time for reflection. He simply knew that he was always fighting. Steeped in misery and despair as he was, merely to walk down the street was to be put upon the rack. There was surely a saloon on the corner—perhaps on all four corners, and some in the middle of the block as well; and each one stretched out a hand to him—each one had a personality of its own, allurements unlike any other. Going and coming—before sunrise and after dark—there was warmth and a glow of light, and the steam of hot food, and perhaps music, or a friendly face, and a word of good cheer. Jurgis developed a fondness for having Ona on his arm whenever he went out on the street, and he would hold her tightly, and walk fast. It was pitiful to have Ona know of this—it drove him wild to think of it; the thing was not fair, for Ona had never tasted drink, and so could not understand. Sometimes, in desperate hours, he would find himself wishing that she might learn what it was, so that he need not be ashamed in her presence. They might drink together, and escape from the horror—escape for a while, come what would.

So there came a time when nearly all the conscious life of Jurgis consisted of a struggle with the craving for liquor. He would have ugly moods, when he hated Ona and the whole family, because they stood in his way. He was a fool to have married; he had tied himself down, had made himself a slave. It was all because he was a married man that he was compelled to stay in the yards; if it had not been for that he might have gone off like Jonas, and to hell with the packers. There were few single men in the fertilizer-mill—and those few were working only for a chance to escape. Meantime, too, they had something to think about while they worked,—they had the memory of the last time they had been drunk, and the hope of the time when they would be drunk again. As for Jurgis, he was expected to bring home every penny; he could not even go with the men at noontime—he was supposed to sit down and eat his dinner on a pile of fertilizer dust.

This was not always his mood, of course; he still loved his family. But just now was a time of trial. Poor little Antanas, for instance—who had never failed to win him with a smile—little Antanas was not smiling just now, being a mass of fiery red pimples. He had had all the diseases that babies are heir to, in quick succession, scarlet fever, mumps, and whooping-cough in the first year, and now he was down with the measles. There was no one to attend him but Kotrina; there was no doctor to help him, because they were too poor, and children did not die of the measles—at least not often. Now and then Kotrina would find time to sob over his woes, but for the greater part of the time he had to be left alone, barricaded upon the bed. The floor was full of draughts, and if he caught cold he would die. At night he was tied down, lest he should kick the covers off him, while the family lay in their stupor of exhaustion. He would lie and scream for hours, almost in convulsions; and then, when he was worn out, he would lie whimpering and wailing in his torment. He was burning up with fever, and his eyes were running sores; in the daytime he was a thing uncanny and impish to behold, a plaster of pimples and sweat, a great purple lump of misery.

Yet all this was not really as cruel as it sounds, for, sick as he was, little Antanas was the least unfortunate member of that family. He was quite able to bear his sufferings—it was as if he had all these complaints to show what a prodigy of health he was. He was the child of his parents' youth and joy; he grew up like the conjurer's rose bush, and all the world was his oyster. In general, he toddled around the kitchen all day with a lean and hungry look—the portion of the family's allowance that fell to him was not enough, and he was unrestrainable in his demand for more. Antanas was but little over a year old, and already no one but his father could manage him.

It seemed as if he had taken all of his mother's strength—had left nothing for those that might come after him. Ona was with child again now, and it was a dreadful thing to contemplate; even Jurgis, dumb and despairing as he was, could not but understand that yet other agonies were on the way, and shudder at the thought of them.

For Ona was visibly going to pieces. In the first place she was developing a cough, like the one that had killed old Dede Antanas. She had had a trace of it ever since that fatal morning when the greedy street-car corporation had turned her out into the rain; but now it was beginning to grow serious, and to wake her up at night. Even worse than that was the fearful nervousness from which she suffered; she would have frightful headaches and fits of aimless weeping; and sometimes she would come home at night shuddering and moaning, and would fling herself down upon the bed and burst into tears. Several times she was quite beside herself and hysterical; and then Jurgis would go half mad with fright. Elzbieta would explain to him that it could not be helped, that a woman was subject to such things when she was pregnant; but he was hardly to be persuaded, and would beg and plead to know what had happened. She had never been like this before, he would argue—it was monstrous and unthinkable. It was the life she had to live, the accursed work she had to do, that was killing her by inches. She was not fitted for it—no woman was fitted for it, no woman ought to be allowed to do such work; if the world could not keep them alive any other way it ought to kill them at once and be done with it. They ought not to marry, to have children; no workingman ought to marry—if he, Jurgis, had known what a woman was like, he would have had his eyes torn out first. So he would carry on, becoming half hysterical himself, which was an unbearable thing to see in a big man; Ona would pull herself together and fling herself into his arms, begging him to stop, to be still, that she would be better, it would be all right. So she would lie and sob out her grief upon his shoulder, while he gazed at her, as helpless as a wounded animal, the target of unseen enemies.

II

The beginning of these perplexing things was in the summer; and each time Ona would promise him with terror in her voice that it would not happen again—but in vain. Each crisis would leave Jurgis more and more frightened, more disposed to distrust Elzbieta's consolations, and to believe that there was some terrible thing about all this that he was not allowed to know. Once or twice in these outbreaks he caught Ona's eye, and it seemed to him like the eye of a hunted animal; there were broken phrases of anguish and despair now and then, amid her frantic weeping. It was only because he was so numb and beaten himself that Jurgis did not worry more about this. But he never thought of it, except when he was dragged to it—he lived like a dumb beast of burden, knowing only the moment in which he was.

The winter was coming on again, more menacing and cruel than ever. It was October, and the holiday rush had begun. It was necessary for the packing-machines to grind till late at night to provide food that would be eaten at Christmas breakfasts; and Marija and Elzbieta and Ona, as part of the machine, began working fifteen or sixteen hours a day. There was no choice about this—whatever work there was to be done they had to do, if they wished to keep their places; besides that, it added another pittance to their incomes, so they staggered on with the awful load. They would start work every morning at seven, and eat their dinners at noon, and then work until ten or eleven at night without another mouthful of food. Jurgis wanted to wait for them, to help them home at night, but they would not think of this; the fertilizer-mill was not running overtime, and there was no place for him to wait save in a saloon. Each would stagger out into the darkness, and make her way to the corner, where they met; or if the others had already gone, would get into a car, and begin a painful struggle to keep awake. When they got home they were always too tired either to eat or to undress; they would crawl into bed with their shoes on, and lie like logs. If they should fail, they would certainly be lost; if they held out, they might have enough coal for the winter.

A day or two before Thanksgiving Day there came a snow-storm. It began in the afternoon, and by evening two inches had fallen. Jurgis tried to wait for the women, but went into a saloon to get warm, and took two drinks, and came out and ran home to escape from the demon; there he lay down to wait for them, and instantly fell asleep. When he opened his eyes again he was in the midst of a nightmare, and found Elzbieta shaking him and crying out. At first he could not realize what she was saying—Ona had not come home. What time was it, he asked. It was morning—time to be up. Ona had not been home that night! And it was bitter cold, and a foot of snow on the ground.

Jurgis sat up with a start. Marija was crying with fright and the children were wailing in sympathy—little Stanislovas in addition, because the terror of the snow was upon him. Jurgis had nothing to put on but his shoes and his coat, and in half a minute he was out of the door. Then, however, he realized that there was no need of haste, that he had no idea where to go. It was still dark as midnight, and the thick snowflakes were sifting down—everything was so silent that he could hear the rustle of them as they fell. In the few seconds that he stood there hesitating he was covered white.

He set off at a run for the yards, stopping by the way to inquire in the saloons that were open. Ona might have been overcome on the way; or else she might have met with an accident in the machines. When he got to the place where she worked he inquired of one of the watchmen—there had not been any accident, so far as the man had heard. At the time-office, which he found already open, the clerk told him that Ona's check had been turned in the night before, showing that she had left her work.

After that there was nothing for him to do but wait, pacing back and forth in the snow, meantime, to keep from freezing. Already the yards were full of activity; cattle were being unloaded from the cars in the distance, and across the way the "beef-luggers" were toiling in the darkness, carrying two-hundred-pound quarters of bullocks into the refrigerator-cars. Before the first streaks of daylight there came the crowding throngs of workingmen, shivering, and swinging their dinner pails as they hurried by. Jurgis took up his stand by the time-office window, where alone there was light enough for him to see; the snow fell so thick that it was only by peering closely that he could make sure that Ona did not pass him.

Seven o'clock came, the hour when the great packing-machine began to move. Jurgis ought to have been at his place in the fertilizer-mill; but instead he was waiting, in an agony of fear, for Ona. It was fifteen minutes after the hour when he saw a form emerge from the snow-mist, and sprang toward it with a cry. It was she, running swiftly; as she saw him, she staggered forward, and half fell into his outstretched arms.

"What has been the matter?" he cried, anxiously. "Where have you been?"

It was several seconds before she could get breath to answer him. "I couldn't get home," she exclaimed. "The snow—the cars had stopped."

"But where were you then?" he demanded.

"I had to go home with a friend," she panted—"with Jadvyga."

Jurgis drew a deep breath; but then he noticed that she was sobbing and trembling—as if in one of those nervous crises that he dreaded so. "But what's the matter?" he cried. "What has happened?"

"Oh, Jurgis, I was so frightened!" she said, clinging to him wildly. "I have been so worried!"

They were near the time-station window, and people were staring at them. Jurgis led her away. "How do you mean?" he asked, in perplexity.

"I was afraid—I was just afraid!" sobbed Ona. "I knew you wouldn't know where I was, and I didn't know what you might do. I tried to get home, but I was so tired. Oh, Jurgis, Jurgis!"

He was so glad to get her back that he could not think clearly about anything else. It did not seem strange to him that she should be so very much upset; all her fright and incoherent protestations did not matter since he had her back. He let her cry away her fears; and then, because it was nearly eight o'clock, and they would lose another hour if they delayed, he left her at the packinghouse door, with her ghastly white face and her haunted eyes of terror.

There was another brief interval. Christmas was almost come; and because the snow still held, and the searching cold, morning after morning Jurgis half carried his wife to her post, staggering with her through the darkness; until at last, one night, came the end.

It lacked but three days of the holidays. About midnight Marija and Elzbieta came home, exclaiming in alarm when they found that Ona had not come. The two had agreed to meet her; and, after waiting, had gone to the room where she worked, only to find that the ham-wrapping girls had quit work an hour before, and left. There was no snow that night, nor was it especially cold; and still Ona had not come! Something more serious must be wrong this time.

They aroused Jurgis, and he sat up and listened crossly to the story. She must have gone home again with Jadvyga, he said; Jadvyga lived only two blocks from the yards, and perhaps she had been tired. Nothing could have happened to her—and even if there had, there was nothing could be done about it until morning. Jurgis turned over in his bed, and was snoring again before the two had closed the door.

In the morning, however, he was up and out nearly an hour before the usual time. Jadvyga Marcinkus lived on the other side of the yards, beyond Halsted Street, with her mother and sisters, in a single basement room—for Mikolas had recently lost one hand from blood-poisoning, and their marriage had been put off forever. The door of the room was in the rear, reached by a narrow court, and Jurgis saw a light in the window and heard something frying as he passed; he knocked, half expecting that Ona would answer.

Instead there was one of Jadvyga's little sisters, who gazed at him through a crack in the door. "Where's Ona?" he demanded; and the child looked at him in perplexity. "Ona?" she said.

"Yes," said Jurgis, "isn't she here?"

"No," said the child, and Jurgis gave a start. A moment later came Jadvyga, peering over the child's head. When she saw who it was, she slid around out of sight, for she was not quite dressed. Jurgis must excuse her, she began, her mother was very ill——

"Ona isn't here?" Jurgis demanded, too alarmed to wait for her to finish.

"Why, no," said Jadvyga. "What made you think she would be here? Had she said she was coming?"

"No," he answered. "But she hasn't come home—and I thought she would be here the same as before."

"As before?" echoed Jadvyga, in perplexity.

"The time she spent the night here," said Jurgis.

"There must be some mistake," she answered, quickly. "Ona has never spent the night here."

He was only half able to realize her words. "Why—why—" he exclaimed. "Two weeks ago, Jadvyga! She told me so—the night it snowed, and she could not get home."

"There must be some mistake," declared the girl, again; "she didn't come here."

He steadied himself by the door-sill; and Jadvyga in her anxiety—for she was fond of Ona—opened the door wide, holding her jacket across her throat. "Are you sure you didn't misunderstand her?" she cried. "She must have meant somewhere else. She——"

"She said here," insisted Jurgis. "She told me all about you, and how you were, and what you said. Are you sure? You haven't forgotten? You weren't away?"

"No, no!" she exclaimed—and then came a peevish voice—"Jadvyga, you are giving the baby a cold. . Shut the door!" Jurgis stood for a half a minute more, stammering his perplexity through an eighth of an inch of crack; and then, as there was really nothing more to be said, he excused himself and went away.

He walked on half dazed, without knowing where he went. Ona had deceived him! She had lied to him! And what could it mean—where had she been? Where was she now? He could hardly grasp the thing—much less try to solve it; but a hundred wild surmises came to him, a sense of impending calamity overwhelmed him.

Because there was nothing else to do, he went back to the time-office to watch again. He waited until nearly an hour after seven, and then went to the room where Ona worked to make inquiries of Ona's "forelady." The "forelady," he found, had not yet come; all the lines of cars that came from down-town were stalled—there had been an accident in the power-house, and no cars had been running since last night. Meantime, however, the ham-wrappers were working away, with some one else in charge of them. The girl who answered Jurgis was busy, and as she talked she looked to see if she were being watched. Then a man came up, wheeling a truck; he knew Jurgis for Ona's husband, and was curious about the mystery.

"Maybe the cars had something to do with it," he suggested—"maybe she had gone down-town."

"No " said Jurgis, "she never went down-town."

"Perhaps not," said the man.

Jurgis thought he saw him exchange a swift glance with the girl as he spoke, and he demanded quickly, "What do you know about it?"

But the man had seen that the boss was watching him; he started on again, pushing his truck. "I don't know anything about it," he said, over his shoulder. "How should I know where your wife goes?"

Then Jurgis went out again, and paced up and down before the building. All the morning he stayed there, with no thought of his work. About noon he went to the police station to make inquiries, and then came back again for another anxious vigil. Finally, toward the middle of the afternoon, he set out for home once more.

He was walking out Ashland Avenue. The street-cars had begun running again, and several passed him, packed to the steps with people. The sight of them set Jurgis to thinking again of the man's sarcastic remark; and half involuntarily he found himself watching the cars—with the result that he gave a sudden startled exclamation, and stopped short in his tracks.

Then he broke into a run. For a whole block he tore after the car, only a little ways behind. That rusty black hat with the drooping red flower, it might not be Ona's, but there was very little likelihood of it. He would know for certain very soon, for she would get out two blocks ahead. He slowed down, and let the car go on.

She got out; and as soon as she was out of sight on the side street Jurgis broke into a run. Suspicion was rife in him now, and he was not ashamed to shadow her; he saw her turn the corner near their home, and then he ran again, and saw her as she went up the porch-steps of the house. After that he turned back, and for five minutes paced up and down, his hands clenched tightly and his lips set, his mind in a turmoil. Then he went home and entered.

As he opened the door, he saw Elzbieta, who had also been looking for Ona, and had come home again. She was now on tiptoe, and had a finger on her lips. Jurgis waited until she was close to him.

"Don't make any noise," she whispered, hurriedly.

"What's the matter?" he asked.

"Ona is asleep," she panted. "She's been very ill. I'm afraid her mind's been wandering, Jurgis. She was lost on the street all night, and I've only just succeeded in getting her quiet."

"When did she come in?" he asked.

"Soon after you left this morning," said Elzbieta.

"And has she been out since?"

"No, of course not. She's so weak, Jurgis, she——"

And he set his teeth hard together. "You are lying to me," he said.

Elzbieta started, and turned pale. "Why!" she gasped. "What do you mean?"

But Jurgis did not answer. He pushed her aside, and strode to the bedroom door and opened it.

Ona was sitting on the bed. She turned a startled look upon him as he entered. He closed the door in Elzbieta's face, and went toward his wife. "Where have you been?" he demanded.

She had her hands clasped tightly in her lap, and he saw that her face was as white as paper, and drawn with pain. She gasped once or twice as she tried to answer him, and then began, speaking low, and swiftly, "Jurgis, I—I think I have been out of my mind. I started to come last night, and I could not find the way. I walked—I walked all night, I think, and—and I only got home—this morning."

"You needed a rest," he said, in a hard tone. "Why did you go out again?"

He was looking her fairly in the face, and he could read the sudden fear and wild uncertainty that leaped into her eyes. "I—I had to go to—to the store," she gasped, almost in a whisper, "I had to go——"

"You are lying to me," said Jurgis.

Then he clenched his hands and took a step toward her. "Why do you lie to me?" he cried, fiercely. "What are you doing that you have to lie to me?"

"Jurgis!" she exclaimed, starting up in fright. "Oh, Jurgis, how can you?"

"You have lied to me, I say!" he cried. "You told me you had been to Jadvyga's house that other night, and you hadn't. You had been where you were last night—somewheres down-town, for I saw you get off the car. Where were you?"

It was as if he had struck a knife into her. She seemed to go all to pieces. For half a second she stood, reeling and swaying, staring at him with horror in her eyes; then, with a cry of anguish, she tottered forward, stretching out her arms to him.

But he stepped aside, deliberately, and let her fall. She caught herself at the side of the bed, and then sank down, burying her face in her hands and bursting into frantic weeping.

There came one of those hysterical crises that had so often dismayed him. Ona sobbed and wept, her fear and anguish building themselves up into long climaxes. Furious gusts of emotion would come sweeping over her, shaking her as the tempest shakes the trees upon the hills; all her frame would quiver and throb with them—it was as if some dreadful thing rose up within her and took possession of her, torturing her, tearing her. This thing had been wont to set Jurgis quite beside himself; but now he stood with his lips set tightly and his hands clenched—she might weep till she killed herself, but she should not move him this time—not an inch, not an inch. Because the sounds she made set his blood to running cold and his lips to quivering in spite of himself, he was glad of the diversion when Teta Elzbieta, pale with fright, opened the door and rushed in; yet he turned upon her with an oath. "Go out!" he cried, "go out!" And then, as she stood hesitating, about to speak, he seized her by the arm, and half flung her from the room, slamming the door and barring it with a table. Then he turned again and faced Ona, crying—"Now, answer me!"

Yet she did not hear him—she was still in the grip of the fiend. Jurgis could see her outstretched hands, shaking and twitching, roaming here and there over the bed at will, like living things; he could see convulsive shudderings start in her body and run through her limbs. She was sobbing and choking—it was as if there were too many sounds for one throat, they came chasing each other, like waves upon the sea. Then her voice would begin to rise into screams, louder and louder until it broke in wild, horrible peals of laughter. Jurgis bore it until he could bear it no longer, and then he sprang at her, seizing her by the shoulders and shaking her, shouting into her ear: "Stop it, I say! Stop it!"

She looked up at him, out of her agony; then she fell forward at his feet. She caught them in her hands, in spite of his efforts to step aside, and with her face upon the floor lay writhing. It made a choking in Jurgis's throat to hear her, and he cried again, more savagely than before: "Stop it, I say!"

This time she heeded him, and caught her breath and lay silent, save for the gasping sobs that wrenched all her frame. For a long minute she lay there, perfectly motionless, until a cold fear seized her husband, thinking that she was dying. Suddenly, however, he heard her voice, faintly: "Jurgis! Jurgis!"

"What is it?" he said.

He had to bend down to her, she was so weak. She was pleading with him, in broken phrases, painfully uttered: "Have faith in me! Believe me!"

"Believe what?" he cried.

"Believe that I—that I know best—that I love you! And do not ask me—what you did. Oh, Jurgis, please, please! It is for the best—it is——"

He started to speak again, but she rushed on frantically, heading him off. "If you will only do it! If you will only—only believe me! It wasn't my fault—I couldn't help it—it will be all right—it is nothing—it is no harm. Oh, Jurgis—please, please!"

She had hold of him, and was trying to raise herself to look at him; he could feel the palsied shaking of her hands and the heaving of the bosom she pressed against him. She managed to catch one of his hands and gripped it convulsively, drawing it to her face, and bathing it in her tears. "Oh, believe me, believe me!" she wailed again; and he shouted in fury, "I will not!"

But still she clung to him, wailing aloud in her despair: "Oh, Jurgis, think what you are doing! It will ruin us—it will ruin us! Oh, no, you must not do it! No, don't, don't do it. You must not do it! It will drive me mad—it will kill me—no, no, Jurgis, I am crazy—it is nothing. You do not really need to know. We can be happy—we can love each other just the same. Oh, please, please, believe me!"

Her words fairly drove him wild. He tore his hands loose, and flung her off. "Answer me," he cried. "God damn it, I say—answer me!"

She sank down upon the floor, beginning to cry again. It was like listening to the moan of a damned soul, and Jurgis could not stand it. He smote his fist upon the table by his side, and shouted again at her, "Answer me!"

She began to scream aloud, her voice like the voice of some wild beast: "Ah! Ah! I can't! I can't do it!"

"Why can't you do it?" he shouted.

"I don't know how!"

He sprang and caught her by the arm, lifting her up, and glaring into her face. "Tell me where you were last night!" he panted. "Quick, out with it!"

Then she began to whisper, one word at a time: "I—was in—a house—down-town——"

"What house? What do you mean?"

She tried to hide her eyes away, but he held her. "Miss Henderson's house," she gasped.

He did not understand at first. "Miss Henderson's house," he echoed. And then suddenly, as in an explosion, the horrible truth burst over him, and he reeled and staggered back with a scream. He caught himself against the wall, and put his hand to his forehead, staring about him, and whispering, "Jesus! Jesus!"

An instant later he leaped at her, as she lay grovelling at his feet. He seized her by the throat. "Tell me!" he gasped, hoarsely. "Quick! Who took you to that place?"

She tried to get away, making him furious; he thought it was fear, or the pain of his clutch—he did not understand that it was the agony of her shame. Still she answered him, "Connor."

"Connor," he gasped. "Who is Connor?"

"The boss," she answered. "The man——"

He tightened his grip, in his frenzy, and only when he saw her eyes closing did he realize that he was choking her. Then he relaxed his fingers, and crouched, waiting, until she opened her lids again. His breath beat hot into her face.

"Tell me," he whispered, at last, "tell me about it."

She lay perfectly motionless, and he had to hold his breath to catch her words. "I did not want—to do it," she said; "I tried—I tried not to do it. I only did it—to save us. It was our only chance."

Again, for a space, there was no sound but his panting. Ona's eyes closed and when she spoke again she did not open them. "He told me—he would have me turned off. He told me he would—we would all of us lose our places. We could never get anything to do—here—again. He—he meant it—he would have ruined us."

Jurgis's arms were shaking so that he could scarcely hold himself up, and lurched forward now and then as he listened. "When—when did this begin?" he gasped.

"At the very first," she said. She spoke as if in a trance. "It was all—it was their plot—Miss Henderson's plot. She hated me. And he—he wanted me. He used to speak to me—out on the platform. Then he began to—to make love to me. He offered me money. He begged me—he said he loved me. Then he threatened me. He knew all about us, he knew we would starve. He knew your boss—he knew Marija's. He would hound us to death, he said—then he said if I would—if I—we would all of us be sure of work—always. Then one day he caught hold of me—he would not let go—he—he——"

"Where was this?"

"In the hallway—at night—after every one had gone. I could not help it. I thought of you—of the baby—of mother and the children. I was afraid of him—afraid to cry out."

A moment ago her face had been ashen gray, now it was scarlet. She was beginning to breathe hard again. Jurgis made not a sound.

"That was two months ago. Then he wanted me to come—to that house. He wanted me to stay there. He said all of us—that we would not have to work. He made me come there—in the evenings. I told you—you thought I was at the factory. Then—one night it snowed, and I couldn't get back. And last night—the cars were stopped. It was such a little thing—to ruin us all. I tried to walk, but I couldn't. I didn't want you to know. It would have—it would have been all right. We could have gone on—just the same—you need never have known about it. He was getting tired of me—he would have let me alone soon. I am going to have a baby—I am getting ugly. He told me that—twice, he told me, last night. He kicked me—last night—too. And now you will kill him—you—you will kill him—and we shall die."

All this she had said without a quiver; she lay still as death, not an eyelid moving. And Jurgis, too, said not a word. He lifted himself by the bed, and stood up. He did not stop for another glance at her, but went to the door and opened it. He did not see Elzbieta, crouching terrified in the corner. He went out, hatless, leaving the street door open behind him. The instant his feet were on the sidewalk he broke into a run.

He ran like one possessed, blindly, furiously, looking neither to the right nor left. He was on Ashland Avenue before exhaustion compelled him to slow down, and then, noticing a car, he made a dart for it and drew himself aboard. His eyes were wild and his hair flying, and he was breathing hoarsely, like a wounded bull; but the people on the car did not notice this particularly—perhaps it seemed natural to them that a man who smelt as Jurgis smelt should exhibit an aspect to correspond. They began to give way before him as usual. The conductor took his nickel gingerly, with the tips of his fingers, and then left him with the platform to himself. Jurgis did not even notice it—his thoughts were far away. Within his soul it was like a roaring furnace; he stood waiting, waiting, crouching as if for a spring.

He had some of his breath back when the car came to the entrance of the yards, and so he leaped off and started again, racing at full speed. People turned and stared at him, but he saw no one—there was the factory, and he bounded through the doorway and down the corridor. He knew the room where Ona worked, and he knew Connor, the boss of the loading-gang outside. He looked for the man as he sprang into the room.

The truckmen were hard at work, loading the freshly packed boxes and barrels upon the cars. Jurgis shot one swift glance up and down the platform—the man was not on it. But then suddenly he heard a voice in the corridor, and started for it with a bound. In an instant more he fronted the boss.

He was a big, red-faced Irishman, coarse-featured, and smelling of liquor. He saw Jurgis as he crossed the threshold, and turned white. He hesitated one second, as if meaning to run; and in the next his assailant was upon him. He put up his hands to protect his face, but Jurgis, lunging with all the power of his arm and body, struck him fairly between the eyes and knocked him backward. The next moment he was on top of him, burying his fingers in his throat.

To Jurgis this man's whole presence reeked of the crime he had committed; the touch of his body was madness to him—it set every nerve of him a-tremble, it aroused all the demon in his soul. It had worked its will upon Ona, this great beast—and now he had it, he had it! It was his turn now! Things swam blood before him, and he screamed aloud in his fury, lifting his victim and smashing his head upon the floor.

The place, of course, was in an uproar; women fainting and shrieking, and men rushing in. Jurgis was so bent upon his task that he knew nothing of this, and scarcely realized that people were trying to interfere with him; it was only when half a dozen men had seized him by the legs and shoulders and were pulling at him, that he understood that he was losing his prey. In a flash he had bent down and sunk his teeth into the man's cheek; and when they tore him away he was dripping with blood, and little ribbons of skin were hanging in his mouth.

They got him down upon the floor, clinging to him by his arms and legs, and still they could hardly hold him. He fought like a tiger, writhing and twisting, half flinging them off, and starting toward his unconscious enemy. But yet others rushed in, until there was a little mountain of twisted limbs and bodies, heaving and tossing, and working its way about the room. In the end, by their sheer weight, they choked the breath out of him, and then they carried him to the company police-station, where he lay still until they had summoned a patrol wagon to take him away.

III

When Jurgis got up again he went quietly enough. He was exhausted and half dazed, and besides he saw the blue uniforms of the policemen. He drove in a patrol wagon with half a dozen of them watching him; keeping as far away as possible, however, on account of the fertilizer. Then he stood before the sergeant's desk and gave his name and address, and saw a charge of assault and battery entered against him. On his way to his cell a burly policeman cursed him because he started down the wrong corridor, and then added a kick when he was not quick enough; nevertheless, Jurgis did not even lift his eyes—he had lived two years and a half in Packingtown, and he knew what the police were. It was as much as a man's very life was worth to anger them, here in their inmost lair; like as not a dozen would pile on to him at once, and pound his face into a pulp. It would be nothing unusual if he got his skull cracked in the mêlée—in which case they would report that he had been drunk and had fallen down, and there would be no one to know the difference or to care.

So a barred door clanged upon Jurgis and he sat down upon a bench and buried his face in his hands. He was alone; he had the afternoon and all of the night to himself.

At first he was like a wild beast that has glutted itself; he was in a dull stupor of satisfaction. He had done up the scoundrel pretty well—not as well as he would have if they had given him a minute more, but pretty well, all the same; the ends of his fingers were still tingling from their contact with the fellow's throat. But then, little by little, as his strength came back and his senses cleared, he began to see beyond his momentary gratification; that he had nearly killed the boss would not help Ona—not the horrors that she had borne, nor the memory that would haunt her all her days. It would not help to feed her and her child; she would certainly lose her place, while he—what was to happen to him God only knew.

Half the night he paced the floor, wrestling with this nightmare; and when he was exhausted he lay down, trying to sleep, but finding instead, for the first time in his life, that his brain was too much for him. In the cell next to him was a drunken wife-beater and in the one beyond a yelling maniac. At midnight they opened the stationhouse to the homeless wanderers who were crowded about the door, shivering in the winter blast, and they thronged into the corridor outside of the cells. Some of them stretched themselves out on the bare stone floor and fell to snoring; others sat up, laughing and talking, cursing and quarrelling. The air was fetid with their breath, yet in spite of this some of them smelt Jurgis and called down the torments of hell upon him, while he lay in a far corner of his cell, counting the throbbings of the blood in his forehead.

They had brought him his supper, which was "duffers and dope"—being hunks of dry bread on a tin plate, and coffee, called "dope" because it was drugged to keep the prisoners quiet. Jurgis had not known this, or he would have swallowed the stuff in desperation; as it was, every nerve of him was a-quiver with shame and rage. Toward morning the place fell silent, and he got up and began to pace his cell; and then within the soul of him there rose up a fiend, red-eyed and cruel, and tore out the strings of his heart.

It was not for himself that he suffered—what did a man who worked in Durham's fertilizer-mill care about anything that the world might do to him! What was any tyranny of prison compared with the tyranny of the past, of the thing that had happened and could not be recalled, of the memory that could never be effaced! The horror of it drove him mad; he stretched out his arms to heaven, crying out for deliverance from it—and there was no deliverance, there was no power even in heaven that could undo the past. It was a ghost that would not down; it followed him, it seized upon him and beat him to the ground. Ah, if only he could have foreseen it—but then, he would have foreseen it, if he had not been a fool! He smote his hands upon his forehead, cursing himself because he had ever allowed Ona to work where she had, because he had not stood between her and a fate which every one knew to be so common. He should have taken her away, even if it were to lie down and die of starvation in the gutters of Chicago's streets! And now—oh, it could not be true; it was too monstrous, too horrible.

It was a thing that could not be faced; a new shuddering seized him every time he tried to think of it. No, there was no bearing the load of it, there was no living under it. There would be none for her—he knew that he might pardon her, might plead with her on his knees, but she would never look him in the face again, she would never be his wife again. The shame of it would kill her—there could be no other deliverance, and it was best that she should die.

This was simple and clear, and yet, with cruel inconsistency, whenever he escaped from this nightmare it was to suffer and cry out at the vision of Ona starving. They had put him in jail, and they would keep him here a long time, years maybe. And Ona would surely not go to work again, broken and crushed as she was. And Elzbieta and Marija, too, might lose their places—if that hellfiend Connor chose to set to work to ruin them, they would all be turned out. And even if he did not, they could not live—even if the boys left school again, they could surely not pay all the bills without him and Ona. They had only a few dollars now—they had just paid the rent of the house a week ago, and that after it was two weeks over-due. So it would be due again in a week! They would have no money to pay it then—and they would lose the house, after all their long, heart-breaking struggle. Three times now the agent had warned him that he would not tolerate another delay. Perhaps it was very base of Jurgis to be thinking about the house when he had the other unspeakable thing to fill his mind; yet, how much he had suffered for this house, how much they had all of them suffered! It was their one hope of respite, as long as they lived; they had put all their money into it—and they were working-people, poor people, whose money was their strength, the very substance of them, body and soul, the thing by which they lived and for lack of which they died.

And they would lose it all; they would be turned out into the streets, and have to hide in some icy garret, and live or die as best they could! Jurgis had all the night—and all of many more nights—to think about this, and he saw the thing in its details; he lived it all, as if he were there. They would sell their furniture, and then run into debt at the stores, and then be refused credit; they would borrow a little from the Szedvilases, whose delicatessen store was tottering on the brink of ruin; the neighbors would come and help them a little—poor, sick Jadvyga would bring a few spare pennies, as she always did when people were starving, and Tamoszius Kusleika would bring them the proceeds of a night's fiddling. So they would struggle to hang on until he got out of jail—or would they know that he was in jail, would they be able to find out anything about him? Would they be allowed to see him—or was it to be part of his punishment to be kept in ignorance about their fate?

His mind would hang upon the worst possibilities; he saw Ona ill and tortured, Marija out of her place, little Stanislovas unable to get to work for the snow, the whole family turned out on the street. God Almighty! would they actually let them lie down in the street and die? Would there be no help even then—would they wander about in the snow till they froze? Jurgis had never seen any dead bodies in the streets, but he had seen people evicted and disappear, no one knew where; and though the city had a relief-bureau, though there was a charity organization society in the stockyards district, in all his life there he had never heard of either of them. They did not advertise their activities, having more calls than they could attend to without that.

—So on until morning. Then he had another ride in the patrol wagon, along with the drunken wife-beater and the maniac, several "plain drunks" and "saloon fighters," a burglar, and two men who had been arrested for stealing meat from the packing-houses. Along with them he was driven into a large, white-walled room, stale-smelling and crowded. In front, upon a raised platform behind a rail, sat a stout, florid-faced personage, with a nose broken out in purple blotches.

Our friend realized vaguely that he was about to be tried. He wondered what for—whether or not his victim might be dead, and if so, what they would do with him. Hang him, perhaps, or beat him to death—nothing would have surprised Jurgis, who knew little of the laws. Yet he had picked up gossip enough to have it occur to him that the loud-voiced man upon the bench might be the notorious Justice Callahan, about whom the people of Packingtown spoke with bated breath.

"Pat" Callahan—"Growler" Pat, as he had been known before he ascended the bench—had begun life as a butcher-boy and a bruiser of local reputation; he had gone into politics almost as soon as he had learned to talk, and had held two offices at once before he was old enough to vote. If Scully was the thumb, Pat Callahan was the first finger of the unseen hand whereby the packers held down the people of the district. No politician in Chicago ranked higher in their confidence; he had been at it a long time—had been the business agent in the city council of old Durham, the self-made merchant, way back in the early days, when the whole city of Chicago had been up at auction. "Growler" Pat had given up holding city offices very early in his career—caring only for party power, and giving the rest of his time to superintending his dives and brothels. Of late years, however, since his children were growing up, he had begun to value respectability, and had had himself made a magistrate; a position for which he was admirably fitted, because of his strong conservatism and his contempt for "foreigners."

Jurgis sat gazing about the room for an hour or two; he was in hopes that some one of the family would come, but in this he was disappointed. Finally, he was led before the bar, and a lawyer for the company appeared against him. Connor was under the doctor's care, the lawyer explained briefly, and if his Honor would hold the prisoner for a week— "Three hundred dollars," said his Honor, promptly.

Jurgis was staring from the judge to the lawyer in perplexity. "Have you any one to go on your bond?" demanded the judge, and then a clerk who stood at Jurgis's elbow explained to him what this meant. The latter shook his head, and before he realized what had happened the policemen were leading him away again. They took him to a room where other prisoners were waiting, and here he stayed until court adjourned, when he had another long and bitterly cold ride in a patrol wagon to the county jail, which is on the north side of the city, and nine or ten miles from the stockyards.

Here they searched Jurgis, leaving him only his money, which consisted of fifteen cents. Then they led him to a room and told him to strip for a bath; after which he had to walk down a long gallery, past the grated cell-doors of the inmates of the jail. This was a great event to the latter—the daily review of the new arrivals, all stark naked, and many and diverting were the comments. Jurgis was required to stay in the bath longer than any one, in the vain hope of getting out of him a few of his phosphates and acids. The prisoners roomed two in a cell, but that day there was one left over, and he was the one.

The cells were in tiers, opening upon galleries. His cell was about five feet by seven in size, with a stone floor and a heavy wooden bench built into it. There was no window—the only light came from windows near the roof at one end of the court outside. There were two bunks, one above the other, each with a straw mattress and a pair of gray blankets—the latter stiff as boards with filth, and alive with fleas, bed-bugs, and lice. When Jurgis lifted up the mattress he discovered beneath it a layer of scurrying roaches, almost as badly frightened as himself.

Here they brought him more "duffers and dope," with the addition of a bowl of soup. Many of the prisoners had their meals brought in from a restaurant, but Jurgis had no money for that. Some had books to read and cards to play, with candles to burn by night, but Jurgis was all alone in darkness and silence. He could not sleep again; there was the same maddening procession of thoughts that lashed him like whips upon his naked back. When night fell he was pacing up and down his cell like a wild beast that breaks its teeth upon the bars of its cage. Now and then in his frenzy he would fling himself against the walls of the place, beating his hands upon them. They cut him and bruised him—they were cold and merciless as the men who had built them.

In the distance there was a church-tower bell that tolled the hours one by one. When it came to midnight Jurgis was lying upon the floor with his head in his arms, listening. Instead of falling silent at the end, the bell broke into a sudden clangor. Jurgis raised his head; what could that mean—a fire? God! suppose there were to be a fire in this jail! But then he made out a melody in the ringing; there were chimes. And they seemed to waken the city—all around, far and near, there were bells, ringing wild music; for fully a minute Jurgis lay lost in wonder, before, all at once, the meaning of it broke over him—that this was Christmas Eve!

Christmas Eve—he had forgotten it entirely! There was a breaking of flood-gates, a whirl of new memories and new griefs rushing into his mind. In far Lithuania they had celebrated Christmas; and it came to him as if it had been yesterday—himself a little child, with his lost brother and his dead father in the cabin in the deep black forest, where the snow fell all day and all night and buried them from the world. It was too far off for Santa Claus in Lithuania, but it was not too far for peace and good will to men, for the wonder-bearing vision of the Christ-child. And even in Packingtown they had not forgotten it—some gleam of it had never failed to break their darkness. Last Christmas Eve and all Christmas Day Jurgis had toiled on the killing-beds, and Ona at wrapping hams, and still they had found strength enough to take the children for a walk upon the avenue, to see the store windows all decorated with Christmas trees and ablaze with electric lights. In one window there would be live geese, in another marvels in sugar—pink and white canes big enough for ogres, and cakes with cherubs upon them; in a third there would be rows of fat yellow turkeys, decorated with rosettes, and rabbits and squirrels hanging; in a fourth would be a fairy-land of toys—lovely dolls with pink dresses, and woolly sheep and drums and soldier hats. Nor did they have to go without their share of all this, either. The last time they had had a big basket with them and all their Christmas marketing to do—a roast of pork and a cabbage and some rye-bread, and a pair of mittens for Ona, and a rubber doll that squeaked, and a little green cornucopia full of candy to be hung from the gas jet and gazed at by half a dozen pairs of longing eyes.

Even half a year of the sausage-machines and the fertilizer-mill had not been able to kill the thought of Christmas in them; there was a choking in Jurgis's throat as he recalled that the very night Ona had not come home Teta Elzbieta had taken him aside and shown him an old valentine that she had picked up in a paper store for three cents—dingy and shop-worn, but with bright colors, and figures of angels and doves. She had wiped all the specks off this, and was going to set it on the mantel, where the children could see it. Great sobs shook Jurgis at this memory—they would spend their Christmas in misery and despair, with him in prison and Ona ill and their home in desolation. Ah, it was too cruel! Why at least had they not left him alone—why, after they had shut him in jail, must they be ringing Christmas chimes in his ears!

But no, their bells were not ringing for him—their Christmas was not meant for him, they were simply not counting him at all. He was of no consequence—he was flung aside, like a bit of trash, the carcass of some animal. It was horrible, horrible! His wife might be dying, his baby might be starving, his whole family might be perishing in the cold—and all the while they were ringing their Christmas chimes! And the bitter mockery of it—all this was punishment for him! They put him in a place where the snow could not beat in, where the cold could not eat through his bones; they brought him food and drink—why, in the name of heaven, if they must punish him, did they not put his family in jail and leave him outside—why could they find no better way to punish him than to leave three weak women and six helpless children to starve and freeze?

That was their law, that was their justice! Jurgis stood upright, trembling with passion, his hands clenched and his arms upraised, his whole soul ablaze with hatred and defiance. Ten thousand curses upon them and their law! Their justice—it was a lie, it was a lie, a hideous, brutal lie, a thing too black and hateful for any world but a world of nightmares. It was a sham and a loathsome mockery. There was no justice, there was no right, anywhere in it—it was only force, it was tyranny, the will and the power, reckless and unrestrained!

They had ground him beneath their heel, they had devoured all his substance; they had murdered his old father, they had broken and wrecked his wife, they had crushed and cowed his whole family; and now they were through with him, they had no further use for him—and because he had interfered with them, had gotten in their way, this was what they had done to him! They had put him behind bars, as if he had been a wild beast, a thing without sense or reason, without rights, without affections, without feelings. Nay, they would not even have treated a beast as they had treated him! Would any man in his senses have trapped a wild thing in its lair, and left its young behind to die?

These midnight hours were fateful ones to Jurgis; in them was the beginning of his rebellion, of his outlawry and his unbelief. He had no wit to trace back the social crime to its far sources—he could not say that it was the thing men have called "the system" that was crushing him to the earth; that it was the packers, his masters, who had bought up the law of the land, and had dealt out their brutal will to him from the seat of justice. He only knew that he was wronged, and that the world had wronged him; that the law, that society, with all its powers, had declared itself his foe. And every hour his soul grew blacker, every hour he dreamed new dreams of vengeance, of defiance, of raging, frenzied hate.

"The vilest deeds, like poison weeds,
Bloom well in prison air;
It is only what is good in Man
That wastes and withers there;
Pale Anguish keeps the heavy gate,
And the Warder is Despair."

So wrote a poet, to whom the world had dealt its justice—

"I know not whether Laws be right,
Or whether Laws be wrong;
All that we know who lie in gaol
Is that the wall is strong.
And they do well to hide their hell,
For in it things are done
That Son of God nor son of Man
Ever should look upon!"

IV

At seven o'clock the next morning Jurgis was let out to get water to wash his cell—a duty which he performed faithfully, but which most of the prisoners were accustomed to shirk, until their cells became so filthy that the guards interposed. Then he had more "duffers and dope," and afterward was allowed three hours for exercise, in a long, cement-walled court roofed with glass. Here were all the inmates of the jail crowded together. At one side of the court was a place for visitors, cut off by two heavy wire screens, a foot apart, so that nothing could be passed in to the prisoners; here Jurgis watched anxiously, but there came no one to see him.

Soon after he went back to his cell, a keeper opened the door to let in another prisoner. He was a dapper young fellow, with a light brown mustache and blue eyes, and a graceful figure. He nodded to Jurgis, and then, as the keeper closed the door upon him, began gazing critically about him.

"Well, pal," he said, as his glance encountered Jurgis again, "good morning."

"Good morning," said Jurgis.

"A rum go for Christmas, eh?" added the other.

Jurgis nodded.

The new-comer went to the bunks and inspected the blankets; he lifted up the mattress, and then dropped it with an exclamation. "My God!" he said, "that's the worst yet."

He glanced at Jurgis again. "Looks as if it hadn't been slept in last night. Couldn't stand it, eh?"

"I didn't want to sleep last night," said Jurgis.

"When did you come in?"

"Yesterday."

The other had another look round, and then wrinkled up his nose. "There's the devil of a stink in here," he said, suddenly. "What is it?"

"It's me," said Jurgis.

"You?"

"Yes, me."

"Didn't they make you wash?"

"Yes, but this don't wash."

"What is it?"

"Fertilizer."

"Fertilizer! The deuce! What are you?"

"I work in the stockyards—at least I did until the other day. It's in my clothes."

"That's a new one on me," said the new-comer. "I thought I'd been up against 'em all. What are you in for?"

"I hit my boss."

"Oh—that's it. What did he do?"

"He—he treated me mean."

"I see. You're what's called an honest working-man!"

"What are you?" Jurgis asked.

"I?" The other laughed. "They say I'm a cracksman," he said.

"What's that?" asked Jurgis.

"Safes, and such things," answered the other.

"Oh," said Jurgis, wonderingly, and stared at the speaker in awe. "You mean you break into them—you—you—"

"Yes," laughed the other, "that's what they say."

He did not look to be over twenty-two or three, though, as Jurgis found afterward, he was thirty. He spoke like a man of education, like what the world calls a "gentleman."

"Is that what you're here for?" Jurgis inquired.

"No," was the answer. "I'm here for disorderly conduct. They were mad because they couldn't get any evidence."

"What's your name?" the young fellow continued after a pause. "My name's Duane—Jack Duane. I've more than a dozen, but that's my company one." He seated himself on the floor with his back to the wall and his legs crossed, and went on talking easily; he soon put Jurgis on a friendly footing—he was evidently a man of the world, used to getting on, and not too proud to hold conversation with a mere laboring man. He drew Jurgis out, and heard all about his life—all but the one unmentionable thing; and then he told stories about his own life. He was a great one for stories, not always of the choicest. Being sent to jail had apparently not disturbed his cheerfulness; he had "done time" twice before, it seemed, and he took it all with a frolic welcome. What with women and wine and the excitement of his vocation, a man could afford to rest now and then.

Naturally, the aspect of prison life was changed for Jurgis by the arrival of a cell-mate. He could not turn his face to the wall and sulk, he had to speak when he was spoken to; nor could he help being interested in the conversation of Duane—the first educated man with whom he had ever talked. How could he help listening with wonder while the other told of midnight ventures and perilous escapes, of feastings and orgies, of fortunes squandered in a night? The young fellow had an amused contempt for Jurgis, as a sort of working mule; he, too, had felt the world's injustice, but instead of bearing it patiently, he had struck back, and struck hard. He was striking all the time—there was war between him and society. He was a genial freebooter, living off the enemy, without fear or shame. He was not always victorious, but then defeat did not mean annihilation, and need not break his spirit.

Withal he was a good-hearted fellow—too much so, it appeared. His story came out, not in the first day, nor the second, but in the long hours that dragged by, in which they had nothing to do but talk, and nothing to talk of but themselves. Jack Duane was from the East; he was a college-bred man—had been studying electrical engineering. Then his father had met with misfortune in business and killed himself; and there had been his mother and a younger brother and sister. Also, there was an invention of Duane's; Jurgis could not understand it clearly, but it had to do with telegraphing, and it was a very important thing—there were fortunes in it, millions upon millions of dollars. And Duane had been robbed of it by a great company, and got tangled up in lawsuits and lost all his money. Then somebody had given him a tip on a horse-race, and he had tried to retrieve his fortune with another person's money, and had to run away, and all the rest had come from that. The other asked him what had led him to safe-breaking—to Jurgis a wild and appalling occupation to think about. A man he had met, his cell-mate had replied—one thing leads to another. Didn't he ever wonder about his family, Jurgis asked. Sometimes, the other answered, but not often—he didn't allow it. Thinking about it would make it no better. This wasn't a world in which a man had any business with a family; sooner or later Jurgis would find that out also, and give up the fight and shift for himself.

Jurgis was so transparently what he pretended to be that his cell-mate was as open with him as a child; it was pleasant to tell him adventures, he was so full of wonder and admiration, he was so new to the ways of the country. Duane did not even bother to keep back names and places—he told all his triumphs and his failures, his loves and his griefs. Also he introduced Jurgis to many of the other prisoners, nearly half of whom he knew by name. The crowd had already given Jurgis a name—they called him "the stinker." This was cruel, but they meant no harm by it, and he took it with a good-natured grin.

Our friend had caught now and then a whiff from the sewers over which he lived, but this was the first time that he had ever been splashed by their filth. This jail was a Noah's ark of the city's crime—there were murderers, "hold-up men" and burglars, embezzlers, counterfeiters and forgers, bigamists, "shoplifters," "confidence-men," petty thieves and pickpockets, gamblers and procurers, brawlers, beggars, tramps and drunkards; they were black and white, old and young, Americans and natives of every nation under the sun. There were hardened criminals and innocent men too poor to give bail; old men, and boys literally not yet in their teens. They were the drainage of the great festering ulcer of society; they were hideous to look upon, sickening to talk to. All life had turned to rottenness and stench in them—love was a beastliness, joy was a snare, and God was an imprecation. They strolled here and there about the courtyard, and Jurgis listened to them. He was ignorant and they were wise; they had been everywhere and tried everything. They could tell the whole hateful story of it, set forth the inner soul of a city in which justice and honor, women's bodies and men's souls, were for sale in the market-place, and human beings writhed and fought and fell upon each other like wolves in a pit; in which lusts were raging fires, and men were fuel, and humanity was festering and stewing and wallowing in its own corruption. Into this wild-beast tangle these men had been born without their consent, they had taken part in it because they could not help it; that they were in jail was no disgrace to them, for the game had never been fair, the dice were loaded. They were swindlers and thieves of pennies and dimes, and they had been trapped and put out of the way by the swindlers and thieves of millions of dollars.

To most of this Jurgis tried not to listen. They frightened him with their savage mockery; and all the while his heart was far away, where his loved ones were calling. Now and then in the midst of it his thoughts would take flight; and then the tears would come into his eyes—and he would be called back by the jeering laughter of his companions.

He spent a week in this company, and during all that time he had no word from his home. He paid one of his fifteen cents for a postal card, and his companion wrote a note to the family, telling them where he was and when he would be tried. There came no answer to it, however, and at last, the day before New Year's, Jurgis bade goodby to Jack Duane. The latter gave him his address, or rather the address of his mistress, and made Jurgis promise to look him up. "Maybe I could help you out of a hole some day," he said, and added that he was sorry to have him go. Jurgis rode in the patrol wagon back to Justice Callahan's court for trial.

One of the first things he made out as he entered the room was Teta Elzbieta and little Kotrina, looking pale and frightened, seated far in the rear. His heart began to pound, but he did not dare to try to signal to them, and neither did Elzbieta. He took his seat in the prisoners' pen and sat gazing at them in helpless agony. He saw that Ona was not with them, and was full of foreboding as to what that might mean. He spent half an hour brooding over this—and then suddenly he straightened up and the blood rushed into his face. A man had come in—Jurgis could not see his features for the bandages that swathed him, but he knew the burly figure. It was Connor! A trembling seized him, and his limbs bent as if for a spring. Then suddenly he felt a hand on his collar, and heard a voice behind him: "Sit down, you son of a ——!"

He subsided, but he never took his eyes off his enemy. The fellow was still alive, which was a disappointment, in one way; and yet it was pleasant to see him, all in penitential plasters. He and the company lawyer, who was with him, came and took seats within the judge's railing; and a minute later the clerk called Jurgis's name, and the policeman jerked him to his feet and led him before the bar, gripping him tightly by the arm, lest he should spring upon the boss.

Jurgis listened while the man entered the witness chair, took the oath, and told his story. The wife of the prisoner had been employed in a department near him, and had been discharged for impudence to him. Half an hour later he had been violently attacked, knocked down, and almost choked to death. He had brought witnesses—

"They will probably not be necessary," observed the judge, and he turned to Jurgis. "You admit assaulting the plaintiff?" he asked.

"Him?" inquired Jurgis, pointing at the boss.

"Yes," said the judge.

"I hit him, sir," said Jurgis.

"Say 'your Honor,'" said the officer, pinching his arm hard.

"Your Honor," said Jurgis, obediently.

"You tried to choke him?"

"Yes, sir, your Honor."

"Ever been arrested before?"

"No, sir, your Honor."

"What have you to say for yourself?"

Jurgis hesitated. What had he to say? In two years and a half he had learned to speak English for practical purposes, but these had never included the statement that some one had intimidated and seduced his wife. He tried once or twice, stammering and balking, to the annoyance of the judge, who was gasping from the odor of fertilizer. Finally, the prisoner made it understood that his vocabulary was inadequate, and there stepped up a dapper young man with waxed mustaches, bidding him speak in any language he knew.

Jurgis began; supposing that he would be given time, he explained how the boss had taken advantage of his wife's position to make advances to her and had threatened her with the loss of her place. When the interpreter had translated this, the judge, whose calendar was crowded, and whose automobile was ordered for a certain hour, interrupted with the remark: "Oh, I see. Well, if he made love to your wife, why didn't she complain to the superintendent or leave the place?"

Jurgis hesitated, somewhat taken aback; he began to explain that they were very poor—that work was hard to get—

"I see," said Justice Callahan; "so instead you thought you would knock him down." He turned to the plaintiff, inquiring, "Is there any truth in this story, Mr. Connor?"

"Not a particle, your Honor," said the boss. "It is very unpleasant—they tell some such tale every time you have to discharge a woman—"

"Yes, I know," said the judge. "I hear it often enough. The fellow seems to have handled you pretty roughly. Thirty days and costs. Next case."

Jurgis had been listening in perplexity. It was only when the policeman who had him by the arm turned and started to lead him away that he realized that sentence had been passed. He gazed round him wildly. "Thirty days!" he panted—and then he whirled upon the judge. "What will my family do?" he cried, frantically. "I have a wife and baby, sir, and they have no money—my God, they will starve to death!"

"You would have done well to think about them before you committed the assault," said the judge, dryly, as he turned to look at the next prisoner.

Jurgis would have spoken again, but the policeman had seized him by the collar and was twisting it, and a second policeman was making for him with evidently hostile intentions. So he let them lead him away.

* * *

So Jurgis went out to the stockyards again, and was introduced to the political lord of the district, the boss of Chicago's mayor. It was Scully who owned the brickyards and the dump and the ice pond—though Jurgis did not know it. It was Scully who was to blame for the unpaved street in which Jurgis's child had been drowned; it was Scully who had put into office the magistrate who had first sent Jurgis to jail; it was Scully who was principal stockholder in the company which had sold him the ramshackle tenement, and then robbed him of it. But Jurgis knew none of these things—any more than he knew that Scully was but a tool and puppet of the packers. To him Scully was a mighty power, the "biggest" man he had ever met.

He was a little, dried-up Irishman, whose hands shook. He had a brief talk with his visitor, watching him with his rat-like eyes, and making up his mind about him; and then he gave him a note to Mr. Harmon, one of the head managers of Durham's:—

"The bearer, Jurgis Rudkus, is a particular friend of mine, and I would like you to find him a good place, for important reasons. He was once indiscreet, but you will perhaps be so good as to overlook that."

Mr. Harmon looked up inquiringly when he read this. "What does he mean by 'indiscreet'?" he asked.

"I was blacklisted, sir," said Jurgis.

At which the other frowned. "Blacklisted?" he said. "How do you mean?"

And Jurgis turned red with embarrassment. He had forgotten that a blacklist did not exist. "I—that is—I had difficulty in getting a place," he stammered.

"What was the matter?"

"I got into a quarrel with a foreman—not my own boss, sir—and struck him."

"I see," said the other, and meditated for a few moments. "What do you wish to do?" he asked.

"Anything, sir," said Jurgis—"only I had a broken arm this winter, and so I have to be careful."

"How would it suit you to be a night-watchman?"

"That wouldn't do, sir. I have to be among the men at night."

"I see—politics. Well, would it suit you to trim hogs?"

"Yes, sir," said Jurgis.

And Mr. Harmon called a time-keeper and said, "Take this man to Pat Murphy and tell him to find room for him somehow."

And so Jurgis marched into the hog-killing room, a place where, in the days gone by, he had come begging for a job. Now he walked jauntily, and smiled to himself, seeing the frown that came to the boss's face as the time-keeper said, "Mr. Harmon says to put this man on." It would overcrowd his department and spoil the record he was trying to make—but he said not a word except "All right."

And so Jurgis became a working-man once more; and straightway he sought out his old friends, and joined the union, and began to "root" for "Scotty" Doyle. Doyle had done him a good turn once, he explained, and was really a bully chap; Doyle was a working-man himself, and would represent the working-men—why did they want to vote for a millionnaire "sheeny," and what the hell had Mike Scully ever done for them that they should back his candidates all the time? And meantime Scully had given Jurgis a note to the Republican leader of the ward, and he had gone there and met the crowd he was to work with. Already they had hired a big hall, with some of the brewer's money, and every night Jurgis brought in a dozen new members of the "Doyle Republican Association." Pretty soon they had a grand opening night; and there was a brass band, which marched through the streets, and fireworks and bombs and red lights in front of the hall; and there was an enormous crowd, with two overflow meetings—so that the pale and trembling candidate had to recite three times over the little speech which one of Scully's henchmen had written, and which he had been a month learning by heart. Best of all, the famous and eloquent Senator Spareshanks, presidential candidate, rode out in an automobile to discuss the sacred privileges of American citizenship, and protection and prosperity for the American working-man. His inspiriting address was quoted to the extent of half a column in all the morning newspapers, which also said that it could be stated upon excellent authority that the unexpected popularity developed by Doyle, the Republican candidate for alderman, was giving great anxiety to Mr. Scully, the chairman of the Democratic City Committee.

The chairman was still more worried when the monster torchlight procession came off, with the members of the Doyle Republican Association all in red capes and hats, and free beer for every voter in the ward—the best beer ever given away in a political campaign, as the whole electorate testified. During this parade, and at innumerable cart-tail meetings as well, Jurgis labored tirelessly. He did not make any speeches—there were lawyers and other experts for that—but he helped to manage things: distributing notices and posting placards and bringing out the crowds; and when the show was on he attended to the fireworks and the beer. Thus in the course of the campaign he handled many hundreds of dollars of the Hebrew brewer's money, administering it with naïve and touching fidelity. Toward the end, however, he learned that he was regarded with hatred by the rest of the "boys," because he compelled them either to make a poorer showing than he or to do without their share of the pie. After that Jurgis did his best to please them, and to make up for the time he had lost before he discovered the extra bung-holes of the campaign-barrel.

He pleased Mike Scully, also. On election morning he was out at four o'clock, "getting out the vote"; he had a two-horse carriage to ride in, and he went from house to house for his friends, and escorted them in triumph to the polls. He voted half a dozen times himself, and voted some of his friends as often; he brought bunch after bunch of the newest foreigners—Lithuanians, Poles, Bohemians, Slovaks—and when he had put them through the mill he turned them over to another man to take to the next polling-place. When Jurgis first set out, the captain of the precinct gave him a hundred dollars, and three times in the course of the day he came for another hundred, and not more than twenty-five out of each lot got stuck in his own pocket. The balance all went for actual votes, and on a day of Democratic land-slides they elected "Scotty" Doyle, the ex-ten-pin setter, by nearly a thousand plurality—and beginning at five o'clock in the afternoon, and ending at three the next morning, Jurgis treated himself to a most unholy and horrible "jag." Nearly everyone else in Packingtown did the same, however, for there was universal exultation over this triumph of popular government, this crushing defeat of an arrogant plutocrat by the power of the common people.

RIPON WISCONSIN
BIRTHPLACE REPUBLICAN PARTY
DIAMOND JUBILEE CELEBRATION
JUNE 8
HOTEL

SINCLAIR LEWIS

Main Street

(1920)

Main Street, a story about a young woman in rebellion against the arid cultural life of a small town, is also a text in women's liberation. Carol Kennicott senses the new possibilities for educated women in the emerging urban-industrial society. Yet, finding no secure foothold in this world, she is pulled back into the older feminine universe of marriage and family. Surrendering the opportunities the city presents for work and culture, she fiercely maintains her touchingly unsteady hold over the new ideas she has but half understood. Carol longs to be a "modern" woman, discussing perhaps the dancing of Isadora Duncan or the plays of Eugene O'Neill or the "modern art" of the Armory Show. Yet the town to which marriage brings her lay but a scratch away from the rude and boisterous frontier.

Carol, her mind perpetually in a shining future, struggles with the present.

Sinclair Lewis, blessed with a phonographic as well as a photographic memory, seems able to recapture the speech patterns of the rural 1920s as well as the visual atmosphere of the small town. Sometimes he falls into burlesque, beginning each sentence with "hey" or "golly," and ending it with an exclamation point. But he sat endlessly in Pullman car smokers and hotel convention lobbies studying his subjects. There is a ring of authenticity in Lewis as well as a tendency toward overstatement. He is satiric as only someone in love with his subject can be: his feeling for the daily life of a mid-American small town is a balance to Carol's sense of imprisonment. Both heroes of the novel – Carol Kennicott and Gopher Prairie – stick hard in our vision of the American past.

When Carol had walked for thirty-two minutes she had completely covered the town, east and west, north and south; and she stood at the corner of Main Street and Washington Avenue and despaired.

Main Street with its two-story brick shops, its story-and-a-half wooden residences, its muddy expanse from concrete walk to walk, its huddle of Fords and lumber-wagons, was too small to absorb her. The broad, straight, unenticing gashes of the streets let in the grasping prairie on every side. She realized the vastness and the emptiness of the land. The skeleton iron windmill on the farm a few blocks away, at the north end of Main Street, was like the ribs of a dead cow. She thought of the coming of the Northern winter, when the unprotected houses would crouch together in terror of storms galloping out of that wild waste. They were so small and weak, the little brown houses. They were shelters for sparrows, not homes for warm laughing people.

She told herself that down the street the leaves were a splendor. The maples were orange; the oaks a solid tint of raspberry. And the lawns had been nursed with love. But the thought would not hold. At best the trees resembled a thinned woodlot. There was no park to rest the eyes. And since not Gopher Prairie but Wakamin was the county-seat, there was no court-house with its grounds.

She glanced through the fly-specked windows of the most pretentious building in sight, the one place which welcomed strangers and determined their opinion of the charm and luxury of Gopher Prairie—the Minniemashie House. It was a tall lean shabby structure, three stories of yellow-streaked wood, the corners covered with sanded pine slabs purporting to symbolize stone. In the hotel office she could see a stretch of bare unclean floor, a line of rickety chairs with brass cuspidors between, a writing-desk with advertisements in mother-of-pearl letters upon the glass-covered back. The dining-room beyond was a jungle of stained table-cloths and catsup bottles.

She looked no more at the Minniemashie House.

A man in cuffless shirt-sleeves with pink arm-garters, wearing a linen collar but no tie, yawned his way from Dyer's Drug Store across to the hotel. He leaned against the wall, scratched a while, sighed, and in a bored way gossiped with a man tilted back in a chair. A lumber-wagon, its long green box filled with large spools of barbed-wire fencing, creaked down the block. A Ford, in reverse, sounded as though it were shaking to pieces, then recovered and rattled away. In the Greek candy-store was the whine of a peanut-roaster, and the oily smell of nuts.

There was no other sound nor sign of life.

She wanted to run, fleeing from the encroaching prairie, demanding the security of a great city. Her dreams of creating a beautiful town were ludicrous. Oozing out from every drab wall, she felt a forbidding spirit which she could never conquer.

She trailed down the street on one side, back on the other, glancing into the cross streets. It was a private Seeing Main Street tour. She was within ten minutes beholding not only the heart of a place called Gopher Prairie, but ten thousand towns from Albany to San Diego:

Dyer's Drug Store, a corner building of regular and unreal blocks of artificial stone. Inside the store, a greasy marble soda-fountain with an electric lamp of red and green and curdled-yellow mosaic shade. Pawed-over heaps of toothbrushes and combs and packages of shaving-soap. Shelves of soap-cartons, teething-rings, garden-seeds, and patent medicines in yellow packages—nostrums for consumption, for "women's diseases"—notorious mixtures of opium and alcohol, in the very shop to which her husband sent patients for the filling of prescriptions.

From a second-story window the sign "W. P. Kennicott, Phys. & Surgeon," gilt on black sand.

A small wooden motion-picture theater called "The Rosebud Movie Palace." Lithographs announcing a film called "Fatty in Love."

Howland & Gould's Grocery. In the display window, black, overripe bananas and lettuce on which a cat was sleeping. Shelves lined with red crêpe paper which was now faded and torn and concentrically spotted. Flat against the wall of the second story the signs of lodges—the Knights of Pythias, the Maccabees, the Woodmen, the Masons.

Dahl & Oleson's Meat Market—a reek of blood.

A jewelry shop with tinny-looking wrist-watches for women. In front of it, at the curb, a huge wooden clock which did not go.

A fly-buzzing saloon with a brilliant gold and enamel whisky sign across the front. Other saloons down the block. From them a stink of stale beer, and thick voices bellowing pidgin German or trolling out dirty songs—vice gone feeble and unenterprising and dull—the delicacy of a mining-camp minus its vigor. In front of the saloons, farmwives sitting on the seats of wagons, waiting for their husbands to become drunk and ready to start home.

A tobacco shop called "The Smoke House," filled with young men shaking dice for cigarettes. Racks of magazines, and pictures of coy fat prostitutes in striped bathing-suits.

A clothing store with a display of "ox-blood-shade Oxfords with bull-dog toes." Suits which looked worn and glossless while they were still new, flabbily draped on dummies like corpses with painted cheeks.

The Bon Ton Store—Haydock & Simons'—the largest shop in town. The first-story front of clear glass, the plates cleverly bound at the edges with brass. The second story of pleasant tapestry brick. One window of excellent clothes for men, interspersed with collars of floral piqué which showed mauve daisies on a saffron ground. Newness and an obvious notion of neatness and service. Haydock & Simons. Haydock. She had met a Haydock at the station; Harry Haydock; an active person of thirty-five. He seemed great to her, now, and very like a saint. His shop was clean!

Axel Egge's General Store, frequented by Scandinavian farmers. In the shallow dark window-space heaps of sleazy sateens, badly woven galateas, canvas shoes designed for women with bulging ankles, steel and red glass buttons upon cards with broken edges, a cottony blanket, a granite-ware frying-pan reposing on a sun-faded crêpe blouse.

Sam Clark's Hardware Store. An air of frankly metallic enterprise. Guns and churns and barrels of nails and beautiful shiny butcher knives.

Chester Dashaway's House Furnishing Emporium. A vista of heavy oak rockers with leather seats, asleep in a dismal row.

Billy's Lunch. Thick handleless cups on the wet oilcloth-covered counter. An odor of onions and the smoke of hot lard. In the doorway a young man audibly sucking a toothpick.

The warehouse of the buyer of cream and potatoes. The sour smell of a dairy.

The Ford Garage and the Buick Garage, competent one-story brick and cement buildings opposite each other. Old and new cars on grease-blackened concrete floors. Tire advertisements. The roaring of a tested motor; a racket which beat at the nerves. Surly young men in khaki union-overalls. The most energetic and vital places in town.

A large warehouse for agricultural implements. An impressive barricade of green and gold wheels, of shafts and sulky seats, belonging to machinery of which Carol knew nothing—potato-planters, manure-spreaders, silage-cutters, disk-harrows, breaking-plows.

A feed store, its windows opaque with the dust of bran, a patent medicine advertisement painted on its roof.

Ye Art Shoppe, Prop. Mrs. Mary Ellen Wilks, Christian Science Library open daily free. A touching fumble at beauty. A one-room shanty of boards recently covered with rough stucco. A show-window delicately rich in error: vases starting out to imitate tree-trunks but running off into blobs of gilt—an aluminum ash-tray labeled "Greetings from Gopher Prairie"—a Christian Science magazine—a stamped sofa-cushion portraying a large ribbon tied to a small poppy, the correct skeins of embroidery-silk lying on the pillow. Inside the shop, a glimpse of bad carbon prints of bad and famous pictures, shelves of phonograph records and camera films, wooden toys, and in the midst an anxious small woman sitting in a padded rocking chair.

A barber shop and pool room. A man in shirt sleeves, presumably Del Snafflin the proprietor, shaving a man who had a large Adam's apple.

Nat Hicks's Tailor Shop, on a side street off Main. A one-story building. A fashion-plate showing human pitchforks in garments which looked as hard as steel plate.

On another side street a raw red-brick Catholic Church with a varnished yellow door.

The post-office—merely a partition of glass and brass shutting off the rear of a mildewed room which must once have been a shop. A tilted writing-shelf against a wall rubbed black and scattered with official notices and army recruiting-posters.

The damp, yellow-brick schoolbuilding in its cindery grounds.

The State Bank, stucco masking wood.

The Farmers' National Bank. An Ionic temple of marble. Pure, exquisite, solitary. A brass plate with "Ezra Stowbody, Pres't."

A score of similar shops and establishments.

Behind them and mixed with them, the houses, meek cottages or large, comfortable, soundly uninteresting symbols of prosperity.

In all the town not one building save the Ionic bank which gave pleasure to Carol's eyes; not a dozen buildings which suggested that, in the fifty years of Gopher Prairie's existence, the citizens had realized that it was either desirable or possible to make this, their common home, amusing or attractive.

It was not only the unsparing unapologetic ugliness and the rigid straightness which overwhelmed her. It was the planlessness, the flimsy temporariness of the buildings, their faded unpleasant colors. The street was cluttered with electric-light poles, telephone poles, gasoline pumps for motor cars, boxes of goods. Each man had built with the most valiant disregard of all the others. Between a large new "block" of two-story brick shops on one side, and the fire-brick Overland garage on the other side, was a one-story cottage turned into a millinery shop. The white temple of the Farmers' Bank was elbowed back by a grocery of glaring yellow brick. One store-building had a patchy galvanized iron cornice; the building beside it was crowned with battlements and pyramids of brick capped with blocks of red sandstone.

She escaped from Main Street, fled home.

She wouldn't have cared, she insisted, if the people had been comely. She had noted a young man loafing before a shop, one unwashed hand holding the cord of an awning; a middle-aged man who had a way of staring at women as though he had been married too long and too prosaically; an old farmer, solid, wholesome, but not clean—his face like a potato fresh from the earth. None of them had shaved for three days.

"If they can't build shrines, out here on the prairie, surely there's nothing to prevent their buying safety-razors!" she raged.

She fought herself: "I must be wrong. People do live here. It *can't* be as ugly as—as I know it is! I must be wrong. But I can't do it. I can't go through with it."

She came home too seriously worried for hysteria; and when she found Kennicott waiting for her, and exulting, "Have a walk? Well, like the town? Great lawns and trees, eh?" she was able to say, with a self-protective maturity new to her, "It's very interesting."

* * *

The recently built house of Sam Clark, in which was given the party to welcome Carol, was one of the largest in Gopher Prairie. It had a clean sweep of clapboards, a solid squareness, a small tower, and a large screened porch. Inside, it was as shiny, as hard, and as cheerful as a new oak upright piano.

Carol looked imploringly at Sam Clark as he rolled to the door and shouted, "Welcome, little lady! The keys of the city are yourn!"

Beyond him, in the hallway and the living-room, sitting in a vast prim circle as though they were attending a funeral, she saw the guests. They were *waiting* so! They were waiting for her! The determination to be all one pretty flowerlet of appreciation leaked away. She begged of Sam, "I don't dare face them! They expect so much. They'll swallow me in one mouthful—glump!—like that!"

"Why, sister, they're going to love you—same as I would if I didn't think the doc here would beat me up!"

"B-but——I don't dare! Faces to the right of me, faces in front of me, volley and wonder!"

She sounded hysterical to herself; she fancied that to Sam Clark she sounded insane. But he chuckled, "Now you just cuddle under Sam's wing, and if anybody rubbers at you too long, I'll shoo 'em off. Here we go! Watch my smoke—Sam'l, the ladies' delight and the bridegrooms' terror!"

His arm about her, he led her in and bawled, "Ladies and worser halves, the bride! We won't introduce her round yet, because she'll never get your bum names straight anyway. Now bust up this star-chamber!"

They tittered politely, but they did not move from the social security of their circle, and they did not cease staring.

Carol had given creative energy to dressing for the event. Her hair was demure, low on her forehead with a parting and a coiled braid. Now she wished that she had piled it high. Her frock was an ingénue slip of lawn, with a wide gold sash and a low square neck, which gave a suggestion of throat and molded shoulders. But as they looked her over she was certain that it was all wrong. She wished alternately that she had worn a spinsterish high-necked dress, and that she had dared to shock them with a violent brick-red scarf which she had bought in Chicago.

She was led about the circle. Her voice mechanically produced safe remarks:

"Oh, I'm sure I'm going to like it here ever so much," and "Yes, we did have the best time in Colorado—mountains," and "Yes, I lived in St. Paul several years. Euclid P. Tinker? No, I don't *remember* meeting him, but I'm pretty sure I've heard of him."

Kennicott took her aside and whispered, "Now I'll introduce you to them, one at a time."

"Tell me about them first."

"Well, the nice-looking couple over there are Harry Haydock and his wife, Juanita. Harry's dad owns most of the Bon Ton, but it's Harry who runs it and gives it the pep. He's a hustler. Next to him is

Dave Dyer the druggist—you met him this afternoon—mighty good duck-shot. The tall husk beyond him is Jack Elder—Jackson Elder—owns the planing-mill, and the Minniemashie House, and quite a share in the Farmers' National Bank. Him and his wife are good sports—him and Sam and I go hunting together a lot. The old cheese there is Luke Dawson, the richest man in town. Next to him is Nat Hicks, the tailor."

"Really? A tailor?"

"Sure. Why not? Maybe we're slow, but we are democratic. I go hunting with Nat same as I do with Jack Elder."

"I'm glad. I've never met a tailor socially. It must be charming to meet one and not have to think about what you owe him. And do you——Would you go hunting with your barber, too?"

"No but——No use running this democracy thing into the ground. Besides, I've known Nat for years, and besides, he's a mighty good shot and——That's the way it is, see? Next to Nat is Chet Dashaway. Great fellow for chinning. He'll talk your arm off, about religion or politics or books or anything."

Carol gazed with a polite approximation to interest at Mr. Dashaway, a tan person with a wide mouth. "Oh, I know! He's the furniture-store man!" She was much pleased with herself.

"Yump, and he's the undertaker. You'll like him. Come shake hands with him."

"Oh no, no! He doesn't—he doesn't do the embalming and all that—himself? I couldn't shake hands with an undertaker!"

"Why not? You'd be proud to shake hands with a great surgeon, just after he'd been carving up people's bellies."

She sought to regain her afternoon's calm of maturity. "Yes. You're right. I want—oh, my dear, do you know how much I want to like the people you like? I want to see people as they are."

"Well, don't forget to see people as other folks see them as they are! They have the stuff. Did you know that Percy Bresnahan came from here? Born and brought up here!"

"Bresnahan?"

"Yes—you know—president of the Velvet Motor Company of Boston, Mass.—make the Velvet Twelve—biggest automobile factory in New England."

"I think I've heard of him."

"Sure you have. Why, he's a millionaire several times over! Well, Perce comes back here for the black-bass fishing almost every summer, and he says if he could get away from business, he'd rather live here than in Boston or New York or any of those places. *He* doesn't mind Chet's undertaking."

"Please! I'll—I'll like everybody! I'll be the community sunbeam!"

He led her to the Dawsons.

Luke Dawson, lender of money on mortgages, owner of Northern cut-over land, was a hesitant man in unpressed soft gray clothes, with bulging eyes in a milky face. His wife had bleached cheeks, bleached hair, bleached voice, and a bleached manner. She wore her expensive green frock, with its passementeried bosom, bead tassels, and gaps between the buttons down the back, as though she had bought it second-hand and was afraid of meeting the former owner. They were shy. It was "Professor" George Edwin Mott, superintendent of schools, a Chinese mandarin turned brown, who held Carol's hand and made her welcome.

When the Dawsons and Mr. Mott had stated that they were "pleased to meet her," there seemed to be nothing else to say, but the conversation went on automatically.

"Do you like Gopher Prairie?" whimpered Mrs. Dawson.

"Oh, I'm sure I'm going to be ever so happy."

"There's so many nice people." Mrs. Dawson looked to Mr. Mott for social and intellectual aid. He lectured:

"There's a fine class of people. I don't like some of these retired farmers who come here to spend their last days—especially the Germans. They hate to pay school-taxes. They hate to spend a cent. But the rest are a fine class of people. Did you know that Percy Bresnahan came from here? Used to go to school right at the old building!"

"I heard he did."

"Yes. He's a prince. He and I went fishing together, last time he was here."

The Dawsons and Mr. Mott teetered upon weary feet, and smiled at Carol with crystallized expressions. She went on:

"Tell me, Mr. Mott: Have you ever tried any experiments with any of the new educational systems? The modern kindergarten methods or the Gary system?"

"Oh. Those. Most of these would-be reformers are simply notoriety-seekers. I believe in manual training, but Latin and mathematics always will be the backbone of sound Americanism, no matter what these faddists advocate—heaven knows what they do want—knitting, I suppose, and classes in wiggling the ears!"

The Dawsons smiled their appreciation of listening to a savant. Carol waited till Kennicott should rescue her. The rest of the party waited for the miracle of being amused.

Harry and Juanita Haydock, Rita Simons and Dr. Terry Gould—the young smart set of Gopher Prairie. She was led to them. Juanita Haydock flung at her in a high, cackling, friendly voice:

"Well, this is *so* nice to have you here. We'll have some good parties—dances and everything. You'll have to join the Jolly Seventeen. We play bridge and we have a supper once a month. You play, of course?"

"N-no, I don't."

"Really? In St. Paul?"

"I've always been such a book-worm."

"We'll have to teach you. Bridge is half the fun of life." Juanita had become patronizing and she glanced disrespectfully at Carol's golden sash, which she had previously admired.

Harry Haydock said politely, "How do you think you're going to like the old burg?"

"I'm sure I shall like it tremendously."

"Best people on earth here. Great hustlers, too. Course I've had lots of chances to go live in Minneapolis, but we like it here. Real he-town. Did you know that Percy Bresnahan came from here?"

Carol perceived that she had been weakened in the biological struggle by disclosing her lack of bridge. Roused to nervous desire to regain her position she turned on Dr. Terry Gould, the young and pool-playing competitor of her husband. Her eyes coquetted with him while she gushed:

"I'll learn bridge. But what I really love most is the outdoors. Can't we all get up a boating party, and fish, or whatever you do, and have a picnic supper afterwards?"

"Now you're talking!" Dr. Gould affirmed. He looked rather too obviously at the cream-smooth slope of her shoulder. "Like fishing? Fishing is my middle name. I'll teach you bridge. Like cards at all?"

"I used to be rather good at bezique."

She knew that bezique was a game of cards—or a game of something else. Roulette, possibly. But her lie was a triumph. Juanita's handsome, high-colored, horsey face showed doubt. Harry stroked his nose and said humbly, "Bezique? Used to be great gambling game, wasn't it?"

While others drifted to her group, Carol snatched up the conversation. She laughed and was frivolous and rather brittle. She could not distinguish their eyes. They were a blurry theater-audience before which she self-consciously enacted the comedy of being the Clever Little Bride of Doc Kennicott:

"These-here celebrated Open Spaces, that's what I'm going out for. I'll never read anything but the sporting-page again. Will converted me on our Colorado trip. There were so many mousey tourists who were afraid to get out of the motor 'bus that I decided to be Annie Oakley, the Wild Western Wampire, and I bought oh! a vociferous skirt which revealed my perfectly nice ankles to the Presbyterian glare of all the Ioway schoolma'ams, and I leaped from peak to peak like the nimble chamoys, and——You may think that Herr Doctor Kennicott is a Nimrod, but you ought to have seen me daring him to strip to his B. V. D.'s and go swimming in an icy mountain brook."

She knew that they were thinking of becoming shocked, but Juanita Haydock was admiring, at least. She swaggered on:

"I'm sure I'm going to ruin Will as a respectable practitioner——Is he a good doctor, Dr. Gould?"

Kennicott's rival gasped at this insult to professional ethics, and he took an appreciable second before he recovered his social manner. "I'll tell you, Mrs. Kennicott." He smiled at Kennicott, to imply that whatever he might say in the stress of being witty was not to count against him in the commercio-medical warfare. "There's some people in town that say the doc is a fair to middlin' diagnostician and prescription-writer, but let me whisper this to you—but for heaven's sake don't tell him I said so—don't you ever go to him for anything more serious than a pendectomy of the left ear or a strabismus of the cardiograph."

No one save Kennicott knew exactly what this meant, but they laughed, and Sam Clark's party assumed a glittering lemon-yellow color of brocade panels and champagne and tulle and crystal chandeliers and sporting duchesses. Carol saw that George Edwin Mott and the blanched Mr. and Mrs. Dawson were not yet hypnotized. They looked as though they wondered whether they ought to look as though they disapproved. She concentrated on them:

"But I know whom I wouldn't have dared to go to Colorado with! Mr. Dawson there! I'm sure he's a regular heartbreaker. When we were introduced he held my hand and squeezed it frightfully."

"Haw! Haw! Haw!" The entire company applauded. Mr. Dawson was beatified. He had been called many things—loan-shark, skinflint, tightwad, pussyfoot—but he had never before been called a flirt.

"He is wicked, isn't he, Mrs. Dawson? Don't you have to lock him up?"

"Oh no, but maybe I better," attempted Mrs. Dawson, a tint on her pallid face.

For fifteen minutes Carol kept it up. She asserted that she was going to stage a musical comedy, that she preferred café parfait to beefsteak, that she hoped Dr. Kennicott would never lose his ability to make love to charming women, and that she had a pair of gold stockings. They gaped for more. But she could not keep it up. She retired to a chair behind Sam Clark's bulk. The smile-wrinkles solemnly flattened out in the faces of all the other collaborators in having a party, and again they stood about hoping but not expecting to be amused.

Carol listened. She discovered that conversation did not exist in Gopher Prairie. Even at this affair, which brought out the young smart set, the hunting squire set, the respectable intellectual set, and the solid financial set, they sat up with gaiety as with a corpse.

Juanita Haydock talked a good deal in her rattling voice but it was invariably of personalities: the rumor that Raymie Wutherspoon was going to send for a pair of patent leather shoes with gray buttoned tops; the rheumatism of Champ Perry; the state of Guy Pollock's grippe; and the dementia of Jim Howland in painting his fence salmon-pink.

Sam Clark had been talking to Carol about motor cars, but he felt his duties as host. While he droned, his brows popped up and down. He interrupted himself, "Must stir 'em up." He worried at his wife,

"Don't you think I better stir 'em up?" He shouldered into the center of the room, and cried:

"Let's have some stunts, folks."

"Yes, let's!" shrieked Juanita Haydock.

"Say, Dave, give us that stunt about the Norwegian catching a hen."

"You bet; that's a slick stunt; do that, Dave!" cheered Chet Dashaway.

Mr. Dave Dyer obliged.

All the guests moved their lips in anticipation of being called on for their own stunts.

"Ella, come on and recite 'Old Sweetheart of Mine,' for us," demanded Sam.

Miss Ella Stowbody, the spinster daughter of the Ionic bank, scratched her dry palms and blushed. "Oh, you don't want to hear that old thing again."

"Sure we do! You bet!" asserted Sam.

"My voice is in terrible shape tonight."

"Tut! Come on!"

Sam loudly explained to Carol, "Ella is our shark at elocuting. She's had professional training. She studied singing and oratory and dramatic art and shorthand for a year, in Milwaukee."

Miss Stowbody was reciting. As encore to "An Old Sweetheart of Mine," she gave a peculiarly optimistic poem regarding the value of smiles.

There were four other stunts: one Jewish, one Irish, one juvenile, and Nat Hicks's parody of Mark Antony's funeral oration.

During the winter Carol was to hear Dave Dyer's hen-catching impersonation seven times, "An Old Sweetheart of Mine" nine times, the Jewish story and the funeral oration twice; but now she was ardent and, because she did so want to be happy and simple-hearted, she was as disappointed as the others when the stunts were finished, and the party instantly sank back into coma.

They gave up trying to be festive; they began to talk naturally, as they did at their shops and homes.

The men and women divided, as they had been tending to do all evening. Carol was deserted by the men, left to a group of matrons who steadily pattered of children, sickness, and cooks—their own shop-talk. She was piqued. She remembered visions of herself as a smart married woman in a drawing-room, fencing with clever men. Her dejection was relieved by speculation as to what the men were discussing, in the corner between the piano and the phonograph. Did they rise from these housewifely personalities to a larger world of abstractions and affairs?

She made her best curtsy to Mrs. Dawson; she twittered, "I won't have my husband leaving me so soon! I'm going over and pull the wretch's ears." She rose with a *jeune fille* bow. She was self-absorbed and self-approving because she had attained that quality of sentimentality. She proudly dipped across the room and, to the interest and commendation of all beholders, sat on the arm of Kennicott's chair.

He was gossiping with Sam Clark, Luke Dawson, Jackson Elder of the planing-mill, Chet Dashaway, Dave Dyer, Harry Haydock, and Ezra Stowbody, president of the Ionic bank.

Ezra Stowbody was a troglodyte. He had come to Gopher Prairie in 1865. He was a distinguished bird of prey—swooping thin nose, turtle mouth, thick brows, port-wine cheeks, floss of white hair, contemptuous eyes. He was not happy in the social changes of thirty years. Three decades ago, Dr. Westlake, Julius Flickerbaugh the lawyer, Merriman Peedy the Congregational pastor and himself had been the arbiters. That was as it should be; the fine arts—medicine, law, religion, and finance—recognized as aristocratic; four Yankees democratically chatting with but ruling the Ohioans and Illini and Swedes and Germans who had ventured to follow them. But Westlake was old, almost retired; Julius Flickerbaugh had lost much of his practice to livelier attorneys; Reverend (not The Reverend) Peedy was dead; and nobody was impressed in this rotten age of automobiles by the "spanking grays" which Ezra still drove. The town was as heterogeneous as Chicago. Norwegians and Germans owned stores. The social leaders were common merchants. Selling nails was considered as sacred as banking. These upstarts—the Clarks, the Haydocks—had no dignity. They were sound and conservative in politics, but they talked about motor cars and pump-guns and heaven only knew what new-fangled fads. Mr. Stowbody felt out of place with them. But his brick house with the mansard roof was still the largest residence in town, and he held his position as squire by occasionally appearing among the younger men and reminding them by a wintry eye that without the banker none of them could carry on their vulgar businesses.

As Carol defied decency by sitting down with the men, Mr. Stowbody was piping to Mr. Dawson, "Say, Luke, when was't Biggins first settled in Winnebago Township? Wa'n't it in 1879?"

"Why no 'twa'n't!" Mr. Dawson was indignant. "He come out from Vermont in 1867—no, wait, in 1868, it must have been—and took a claim on the Rum River, quite a ways above Anoka."

"He did not!" roared Mr. Stowbody. "He settled first in Blue Earth County, him and his father!"

("What's the point at issue?" Carol whispered to Kennicott.

("Whether this old duck Biggins had an English setter or a Llewellyn. They've been arguing it all evening!")

Dave Dyer interrupted to give tidings, "D' tell you that Clara Biggins was in town couple days ago? She bought a hot-water bottle—expensive one, too—two dollars and thirty cents!"

"Yaaaaaah!" snarled Mr. Stowbody. "Course. She's just like her grandad was. Never save a cent. Two dollars and twenty—thirty, was it?—two dollars and thirty cents for a hot-water bottle! Brick wrapped up in a flannel petticoat just as good, anyway!"

"How's Ella's tonsils, Mr. Stowbody?" yawned Chet Dashaway.

While Mr. Stowbody gave a somatic and psychic study of them, Carol reflected, "Are they really so terribly interested in Ella's tonsils, or even in Ella's esophagus? I wonder if I could get them away from personalities? Let's risk damnation and try."

"There hasn't been much labor trouble around here, has there, Mr. Stowbody?" she asked innocently.

"No, ma'am, thank God, we've been free from that, except maybe with hired girls and farm-hands. Trouble enough with these foreign farmers; if you don't watch these Swedes they turn socialist or populist or some fool thing on you in a minute. Of course, if they have loans you can make 'em listen to reason. I just have 'em come into the bank for a talk, and tell 'em a few things. I don't mind their being democrats, so much, but I won't stand having socialists around. But thank God, we ain't got the labor trouble they have in these cities. Even Jack Elder here gets along pretty well, in the planing-mill, don't you, Jack?"

"Yep. Sure. Don't need so many skilled workmen in my place, and it's a lot of these cranky, wage-hogging, half-baked skilled mechanics that start trouble—reading a lot of this anarchist literature and union papers and all."

"Do you approve of union labor?" Carol inquired of Mr. Elder.

"Me? I should say not! It's like this: I don't mind dealing with my men if they think they've got any grievances—though Lord knows what's come over workmen, nowadays—don't appreciate a good job. But still, if they come to me honestly, as man to man, I'll talk things over with them. But I'm not going to have any outsider, any of these walking delegates, or whatever fancy names they call themselves now—bunch of rich grafters, living on the ignorant workmen! Not going to have any of those fellows butting in and telling *me* how to run *my* business!"

Mr. Elder was growing more excited, more belligerent and patriotic. "I stand for freedom and constitutional rights. If any man don't like my shop, he can get up and git. Same way, if I don't like him, he gits. And that's all there is to it. I simply can't understand all these complications and hoop-te-doodles and government reports and wage-scales and God knows what all that these fellows are balling up the labor situation with, when it's all perfectly simple. They like what I pay 'em, or they get out. That's all there is to it!"

"What do you think of profit-sharing?" Carol ventured.

Mr. Elder thundered his answer, while the others nodded, solemnly and in tune, like a shop-window of flexible toys, comic mandarins and judges and ducks and clowns, set quivering by a breeze from the open door:

"All this profit-sharing and welfare work and insurance and old-age pension is simply poppycock. Enfeebles a workman's independence—and wastes a lot of honest profit. The half-baked thinker that isn't dry behind the ears yet, and these suffragettes and God knows what all buttinskis there are that are trying to tell a business man how to run his business, and some of those college professors are just about as bad, the whole kit and bilin' of 'em are nothing in God's world but socialism in disguise! And it's my bounden duty as a producer to resist every attack on the integrity of American industry to the last ditch. Yes—SIR!"

Mr. Elder wiped his brow.

Dave Dyer added, "Sure! You bet! What they ought to do is simply to hang every one of these agitators, and that would settle the whole thing right off. Don't you think so, doc?"

"You bet," agreed Kennicott.

The conversation was at last relieved of the plague of Carol's intrusions and they settled down to the question of whether the justice of the peace had sent that hobo drunk to jail for ten days or twelve. It was a matter not readily determined. Then Dave Dyer communicated his carefree adventures on the gipsy trail:

"Yep. I get good time out of the flivver. 'Bout a week ago I motored down to New Wurttemberg. That's forty-three——No, let's see: It's seventeen miles to Belldale, and 'bout six and three-quarters, call it seven, to Torgenquist, and it's a good nineteen miles from there to New Wurttemberg—seventeen and seven and nineteen, that makes, uh, let me see: seventeen and seven 's twenty-four, plus nineteen, well say plus twenty, that makes forty-four, well anyway, say about forty-three or four miles from here to New Wurttemberg. We got started about seven-fifteen, prob'ly seven-twenty, because I had to stop and fill the radiator, and we ran along, just keeping up a good steady gait——"

Mr. Dyer did finally, for reasons and purposes admitted and justified, attain to New Wurttemberg.

Once—only once—the presence of the alien Carol was recognized. Chet Dashaway leaned over and said asthmatically, "Say, uh, have you been reading this serial 'Two Out' in *Tingling Tales?* Corking yarn! Gosh, the fellow that wrote it certainly can sling baseball slang!"

The others tried to look literary. Harry Haydock offered, "Juanita is a great hand for reading high-class stuff, like 'Mid the Magnolias' by this Sara Hetwiggin Butts, and 'Riders of Ranch Reckless.' Books. But me," he glanced about importantly, as one convinced that no other hero had ever been in so strange a plight, "I'm so darn busy I don't have much time to read."

"I never read anything I can't check against," said Sam Clark.

Thus ended the literary portion of the conversation, and for seven minutes Jackson Elder outlined reasons for believing that the pike-fishing was better on the west shore of Lake Minniemashie than on the east—though it was indeed quite true that on the east shore Nat Hicks had caught a pike altogether admirable.

The talk went on. It did go on! Their voices were monotonous, thick, emphatic. They were harshly pompous, like men in the smoking-compartments of Pullman cars. They did not bore Carol. They frightened her. She panted, "They will be cordial to me, because my man belongs to their tribe. God help me if I were an outsider!"

Smiling as changelessly as an ivory figurine she sat quiescent, avoiding thought, glancing about the living-room and hall, noting their betrayal of unimaginative commercial prosperity. Kennicott said, "Dandy interior, eh? My idea of how a place ought to be furnished. Modern." She looked polite, and observed the oiled floors, hard-wood staircase, unused fireplace with tiles which resembled brown linoleum, cut-glass vases standing upon doilies, and the barred, shut, forbidding unit bookcases that were half filled with swashbuckler novels and unread-looking sets of Dickens, Kipling, O. Henry, and Elbert Hubbard.

She perceived that even personalities were failing to hold the party. The room filled with hesitancy as with a fog. People cleared their throats, tried to choke down yawns. The men shot their cuffs and the women stuck their combs more firmly into their back hair.

Then a rattle, a daring hope in every eye, the swinging of a door, the smell of strong coffee, Dave Dyer's mewing voice in a triumphant, "The eats!" They began to chatter. They had something to do. They could escape from themselves. They fell upon the food—chicken sandwiches, maple cake, drug-store ice cream. Even when the food was gone they remained cheerful. They could go home, any time now, and go to bed!

They went, with a flutter of coats, chiffon scarfs, and goodbys.

Carol and Kennicott walked home.

"Did you like them?" he asked.

"They were terribly sweet to me."

"Uh, Carrie——You ought to be more careful about shocking folks. Talking about gold stockings, and about showing your ankles to schoolteachers and all!" More mildly: "You gave 'em a good time, but I'd watch out for that, 'f I were you. Juanita Haydock is such a damn cat. I wouldn't give her a chance to criticize me."

"My poor effort to lift up the party! Was I wrong to try to amuse them?"

"No! No! Honey, I didn't mean——You were the only up-and-coming person in the bunch. I just mean——Don't get onto legs and all that immoral stuff. Pretty conservative crowd."

She was silent, raw with the shameful thought that the attentive circle might have been criticizing her, laughing at her.

"Don't, please don't worry!" he pleaded.

Silence.

"Gosh, I'm sorry I spoke about it. I just meant——But they were crazy about you. Sam said to me, 'That little lady of yours is the slickest thing that ever came to this town,' he said; and Ma Dawson—I didn't hardly know whether she'd like you or not, she's such a dried-up old bird, but she said, 'Your bride is so quick and bright, I declare, she just wakes me up.'"

Carol liked praise, the flavor and fatness of it, but she was so energetically being sorry for herself that she could not taste this commendation.

"Please! Come on! Cheer up!" His lips said it, his anxious shoulder said it, his arm about her said it, as they halted on the obscure porch of their house.

"Do you care if they think I'm flighty, Will?"

"Me? Why, I wouldn't care if the whole world thought you were this or that or anything else. You're my—well, you're my soul!"

He was an undefined mass, as solid-seeming as rock. She found his sleeve, pinched it, cried, "I'm glad! It's sweet to be wanted! You must tolerate my frivolousness. You're all I have!"

He lifted her, carried her into the house, and with her arms about his neck she forgot Main Street.

* * *

The Jolly Seventeen (the membership of which ranged from fourteen to twenty-six) was the social cornice of Gopher Prairie. It was the country club, the diplomatic set, the St. Cecilia, the Ritz oval room, the Club de Vingt. To belong to it was to be "in." Though its membership partly coincided with that of the Thanatopsis study club, the Jolly Seventeen as a separate entity guffawed at the Thanatopsis, and considered it middle-class and even "highbrow."

Most of the Jolly Seventeen were young married women, with their husbands as associate members. Once a week they had a women's afternoon-bridge; once a month the husbands joined them for supper and evening-bridge; twice a year they had dances at I. O. O. F. Hall. Then the town exploded. Only at the annual balls of the Firemen and of the Eastern Star was there such prodigality of chiffon scarfs and tangoing and heart-burnings, and these rival institutions were not select—hired girls attended the Firemen's Ball, with section-hands and laborers. Ella Stowbody had once gone to a Jolly Seventeen Soirée in the village hack, hitherto confined to chief mourners at funerals; and Harry Haydock and Dr. Terry Gould always appeared in the town's only specimens of evening clothes.

The afternoon-bridge of the Jolly Seventeen which followed Carol's lonely doubting was held at Juanita Haydock's new concrete bungalow, with its door of polished oak and beveled plate-glass, jar of ferns in the plastered hall, and in the living-room, a fumed oak Morris chair, sixteen color-prints, and a square varnished table with a mat made of cigar-ribbons on which was one Illustrated Gift Edition and one pack of cards in a burnt-leather case.

Carol stepped into a sirocco of furnace heat. They were already playing. Despite her flabby resolves she had not yet learned bridge. She was winningly apologetic about it to Juanita, and ashamed that she should have to go on being apologetic.

Mrs. Dave Dyer, a sallow woman with a thin prettiness, devoted to experiments in religious cults, illnesses, and scandal-bearing, shook her finger at Carol and trilled, "You're a naughty one! I don't believe you appreciate the honor, when you got into the Jolly Seventeen so easy!"

Mrs. Chet Dashaway nudged her neighbor at the second table. But Carol kept up the appealing bridal manner so far as possible. She twittered, "You're perfectly right. I'm a lazy thing. I'll make Will start teaching me this very evening." Her supplication had all the sound of birdies in the nest, and Easter church-bells, and frosted Christmas cards. Internally she snarled, "That ought to be saccharine enough." She sat in the smallest rocking-chair, a model of Victorian modesty. But she saw or she imagined that the women who had gurgled at her so welcomingly when she had first come to Gopher Prairie were nodding at her brusquely.

During the pause after the first game she petitioned Mrs. Jackson Elder, "Don't you think we ought to get up another bob-sled party soon?"

"It's so cold when you get dumped in the snow," said Mrs. Elder, indifferently.

"I hate snow down my neck," volunteered Mrs. Dave Dyer, with an unpleasant look at Carol and turning her back, she bubbled at Rita Simons, "Dearie, won't you run in this evening? I've got the loveliest new Butterick pattern I want to show you."

Carol crept back to her chair. In the fervor of discussing the game they ignored her. She was not used to being a wallflower. She struggled to keep from oversensitiveness, from becoming unpopular by the sure method of believing that she was unpopular; but she hadn't much reserve of patience, and at the end of the second game, when Ella Stowbody sniffily asked her, "Are you going to send to Minneapolis for your dress for the next soirée—heard you were," Carol said "Don't know yet" with unnecessary sharpness.

She was relieved by the admiration with which the *jeune fille* Rita Simons looked at the steel buckles on her pumps; but she resented Mrs. Howland's tart demand, "Don't you find that new couch of yours is too broad to be practical?" She nodded, then shook her head, and touchily left Mrs. Howland to get out of it any meaning she desired. Immediately she wanted to make peace. She was close to simpering in the sweetness with which she addressed Mrs. Howland: "I think that is the prettiest display of beef-tea your husband has in his store."

"Oh yes, Gopher Prairie isn't so much behind the times," gibed Mrs. Howland. Some one giggled.

Their rebuffs made her haughty; her haughtiness irritated them to franker rebuffs; they were working up to a state of painfully righteous war when they were saved by the coming of food.

Though Juanita Haydock was highly advanced in the matters of finger-bowls, doilies, and bath-mats, her "refreshments" were typical of all the afternoon-coffees. Juanita's best friends, Mrs. Dyer and Mrs. Dashaway, passed large dinner plates, each with a spoon, a fork, and a coffee cup without saucer. They apologized and discussed the afternoon's game as they passed through the thicket of women's feet. Then they distributed hot buttered rolls, coffee poured from an enamel-ware pot, stuffed olives, potato salad, and angel's-food cake. There was, even in the most strictly conforming Gopher Prairie circles, a certain option as to collations. The olives need not be stuffed. Doughnuts were in some houses well thought of as a substitute for the hot buttered rolls. But there was in all the town no heretic save Carol who omitted angel's-food.

They ate enormously. Carol had a suspicion that the thriftier housewives made the afternoon treat do for evening supper.

She tried to get back into the current. She edged over to Mrs. McGanum. Chunky, amiable, young Mrs. McGanum, with her breast and arms of a milkmaid, and her loud delayed laugh which burst startlingly from a sober face, was the daughter of old Dr. Westlake, and the wife of Westlake's partner, Dr. McGanum. Kennicott asserted that Westlake and McGanum and their contaminated families were tricky, but Carol had found them gracious. She asked for friendliness by crying to Mrs. McGanum, "How is the baby's throat now?" and she was attentive while Mrs. McGanum rocked and knitted and placidly described symptoms.

Vida Sherwin came in after school, with Miss Ethel Villets, the town librarian. Miss Sherwin's optimistic presence gave Carol more confidence. She talked. She informed the circle, "I drove almost down to Wahkeenyan with Will, a few days ago. Isn't the country lovely! And I do admire the Scandinavian farmers down there so: their big red barns and silos and milking-machines and everything. Do you all know that lonely Lutheran church, with the tin-covered spire, that stands out alone on a hill? It's so bleak; somehow it seems so brave. I do think the Scandinavians are the hardiest and best people——"

"Oh, do you *think* so?" protested Mrs. Jackson Elder. "My husband says the Svenskas that work in the planing-mill are perfectly terrible—so silent and cranky, and so selfish, the way they keep demanding raises. If they had their way they'd simply ruin the business."

"Yes, and they're simply *ghastly* hired girls!" wailed Mrs. Dave Dyer. "I swear, I work myself to skin and bone trying to please my hired girls—when I can get them! I do everything in the world for them. They can have their gentleman friends call on them in the kitchen any time, and they get just the same to eat as we do, if there's any left over, and I practically never jump on them."

Juanita Haydock rattled, "They're ungrateful, all that class of people. I do think the domestic problem is simply becoming awful. I don't know what the country's coming to, with these Scandahoofian clodhoppers demanding every cent you can save, and so ignorant and impertinent, and on my word, demanding bath-tubs and everything—as if they weren't mighty good and lucky at home if they got a bath in the wash-tub."

They were off, riding hard. Carol thought of Bea and waylaid them:

"But isn't it possibly the fault of the mistresses if the maids are ungrateful? For generations we've given them the leavings of food, and holes to live in. I don't want to boast, but I must say I don't have much trouble with Bea. She's so friendly. The Scandinavians are sturdy and honest——"

Mrs. Dave Dyer snapped, "Honest? Do you call it honest to hold us up for every cent of pay they can get? I can't say that I've had any of them steal anything (though you might call it stealing to eat so much that a roast of beef hardly lasts three days), but just the same I don't intend to let them think they can put anything over on *me!* I always make them pack and unpack their trunks down-stairs, right under my eyes, and then I know they aren't being tempted to dishonesty by any slackness on *my* part!"

"How much do the maids get here?" Carol ventured.

Mrs. B. J. Gougerling, wife of the banker, stated in a shocked manner, "Any place from three-fifty to five-fifty a week! I know positively that Mrs. Clark, after swearing that she wouldn't weaken and encourage them in their outrageous demands, went and paid five-fifty—think of it! practically a dollar a day for unskilled work and, of course, her food and room and a chance to do her own washing right in with the rest of the wash. *How much do you pay, Mrs. Kennicott?*"

"Yes! How much do you pay?" insisted half a dozen.

"W-why, I pay six a week," she feebly confessed.

They gasped. Juanita protested, "Don t you think it's hard on the rest of us when you pay so much?" Juanita's demand was re-inforced by the universal glower.

Carol was angry. "I don't care! A maid has one of the hardest jobs on earth. She works from ten to eighteen hours a day. She has to wash slimy dishes and dirty clothes. She tends the children and runs to the door with wet chapped hands and——"

Mrs. Dave Dyer broke into Carol's peroration with a furious, "That's all very well, but believe me, I do those things myself when I'm without a maid—and that's a good share of the time for a person that isn't willing to yield and pay exorbitant wages!"

Carol was retorting, "But a maid does it for strangers, and all she gets out of it is the pay——"

Their eyes were hostile. Four of them were talking at once. Vida

Sherwin's dictatorial voice cut through, took control of the revolution:

"Tut, tut, tut, tut! What angry passions—and what an idiotic discussion! All of you getting too serious. Stop it! Carol Kennicott, you're probably right, but you're too much ahead of the times. Juanita, quit looking so belligerent. What is this, a card party or a hen fight? Carol, you stop admiring yourself as the Joan of Arc of the hired girls, or I'll spank you. You come over here and talk libraries with Ethel Villets. Boooooo! If there's any more pecking, I'll take charge of the hen roost myself!"

They all laughed artificially, and Carol obediently "talked libraries."

A small-town bungalow, the wives of a village doctor and a village dry-goods merchant, a provincial teacher, a colloquial brawl over paying a servant a dollar more a week. Yet this insignificance echoed cellar-plots and cabinet meetings and labor conferences in Persia and Prussia, Rome and Boston, and the orators who deemed themselves international leaders were but the raised voices of a billion Juanitas denouncing a million Carols, with a hundred thousand Vida Sherwins trying to shoo away the storm.

Carol felt guilty. She devoted herself to admiring the spinsterish Miss Villets—and immediately committed another offense against the laws of decency.

"We haven't seen you at the library yet," Miss Villets reproved.

"I've wanted to run in so much but I've been getting settled and——I'll probably come in so often you'll get tired of me! I hear you have such a nice library."

"There are many who like it. We have two thousand more books than Wakamin."

"Isn't that fine. I'm sure you are largely responsible. I've had some experience, in St. Paul."

"So I have been informed. Not that I entirely approve of library methods in these large cities. So careless, letting tramps and all sorts of dirty persons practically sleep in the reading-rooms."

"I know, but the poor souls——Well, I'm sure you will agree with me in one thing: The chief task of a librarian is to get people to read."

"You feel so? My feeling, Mrs. Kennicott, and I am merely quoting the librarian of a very large college, is that the first duty of the *conscientious* librarian is to preserve the books."

"Oh!" Carol repented her "Oh." Miss Villets stiffened, and attacked:

"It may be all very well in cities, where they have unlimited funds, to let nasty children ruin books and just deliberately tear them up, and fresh young men take more books out than they are entitled to by the regulations, but I'm never going to permit it in this library!"

"What if some children are destructive? They learn to read. Books are cheaper than minds."

"Nothing is cheaper than the minds of some of these children that come in and bother me simply because their mothers don't keep them home where they belong. Some librarians may choose to be so wishy-washy and turn their libraries into nursing-homes and kindergartens, but as long as I'm in charge, the Gopher Prairie library is going to be quiet and decent, and the books well kept!"

Carol saw that the others were listening, waiting for her to be objectionable. She flinched before their dislike. She hastened to smile in agreement with Miss Villets, to glance publicly at her wrist-watch, to warble that it was "so late—have to hurry home—husband—such nice party—maybe you were right about maids, prejudiced because Bea so nice—such perfectly divine angel's-food, Mrs. Haydock must give me the recipe—good-by, such happy party——"

She walked home. She reflected, "It was my fault. I was touchy. And I opposed them so much. Only—— I can't! I can't be one of them if I must damn all the maids toiling in filthy kitchens, all the ragged hungry children. And these women are to be my arbiters, the rest of my life!"

She ignored Bea's call from the kitchen; she ran up-stairs to the unfrequented guest room; she wept in terror, her body a pale arc as she knelt beside a cumbrous black-walnut bed, beside a puffy mattress covered with a red quilt in a shuttered and airless room.

Eugene V. Debs, American socialist labor leader

JOHN DOS PASSOS

U.S.A.

(1930, 1932, 1936)

What, to paraphrase Crèvecoeur, is this twentieth-century American, this brand new man? John Dos Passos, in his novel-as-history U.S.A., sketches a new race of heroes, men born in one America and molding another, strange heroes who could have been of no other time.

Dos Passos' huge trilogy mixes conventional devices of the novel with reportage (The Camera Eye) – headlines, snatches of popular song, and capsule histories of representative Americans. Revived a generation later, this format, with variations, would be greeted with excitement as the "new journalism," the inevitable attempt to capture a modern experience so various and fragmented that no one part of it seems representative. Dos Passos' generation spent much time discussing a mythical beast called "the great American novel," the all-encompassing creation that would catch the flow of industrial America. But what fiction could capture Henry Ford and Rudolf Valentino or the world that knew both of them so well? Most writers since Dos Passos have protested how experience had already exceeded the limits of imagination. The American seemed to become a sensation-processing instrument in a world of nine-day wonders. Those, like Dos Passos' heroes, who held hard to some twisted shred of authenticity, found themselves uncomfortably far from home.

I
Meester Veelson

The year that Buchanan was elected President Thomas Woodrow Wilson
was born to a Presbyterian minister's daughter
in the manse at Staunton in the valley of Virginia; it was the old Scotch-Irish stock; the father was a Presbyterian minister, too, and a teacher of rhetoric in theological seminaries; the Wilsons lived in a universe of words linked into an incontrovertible firmament by two centuries of Calvinist divines,
God was the Word
and the Word was God.
Doctor Wilson was a man of standing who loved his home and his children and good books and his wife and correct syntax and talked to God every day at family prayers;
he brought his sons up
between the Bible and the dictionary.
The years of the Civil War
the years of fife and drum and platoonfire and proclamations
the Wilsons lived in Augusta, Georgia; Tommy was a backward child, didn't learn his letters till he was nine, but when he learned to read, his favorite reading was Parson Weems's
Life of Washington

In 1870 Doctor Wilson was called to the Theological Seminary at Columbia, South Carolina; Tommy attended Davidson College,
where he developed a good tenor voice;
then he went to Princeton and became a debater and editor of the *Princetonian*. His first published article in the *Nassau Literary Magazine* was an appreciation of Bismarck.

Afterwards he studied law at the University of Virginia; young Wilson wanted to be a Great Man, like Gladstone and the eighteenth-century English Parliamentarians; he wanted to hold the packed benches spellbound in the cause of Truth; but law practice irked him; he was more at home in the booky air of libraries, lecturerooms, college chapel, it was a relief to leave his law practice at Atlanta and take a Historical Fellowship at Johns Hopkins; there he wrote *Congressional Government.*
At twentynine he married a girl with a taste for painting (while he was courting her he coached her in how to use the broad "a") and got a job at Bryn Mawr teaching the girls History and Political Economy. When he got his Ph.D. from Johns Hopkins he moved to a professorship at Wesleyan, wrote articles, started a History of the United States,

spoke out for Truth Reform Responsible Government Democracy from the lecture platform, climbed all the steps of a brilliant university career; in 1901 the trustees of Princeton offered him the presidency;

he plunged into reforming the university, made violent friends and enemies, set the campus by the ears,

and the American people began to find on the front pages

the name of Woodrow Wilson.

In 1909 he made addresses on Lincoln and Robert E. Lee

and in 1910

the Democratic bosses of New Jersey, hardpressed by muckrakers and reformers, got the bright idea of offering the nomination for Governor to the stainless college president who attracted such large audiences

by publicly championing Right.

When Mr. Wilson addressed the Trenton convention that nominated him for Governor he confessed his belief in the common man (the smalltown bosses and the wardheelers looked at each other and scratched their heads); he went on, his voice growing firmer:

that is, the man by whose judgment I for one wish to be guided, so that as the tasks multiply, and as the days come when all will feel confusion and dismay, we may lift up our eyes to the hills out of these dark valleys where the crags of special privilege overshadow and darken our path, to where the sun gleams through the great passage in the broken cliffs, the sun of God,

the sun meant to regenerate men,

the sun meant to liberate them from their passion and despair and lift us to those uplands which are the promised land of every man who desires liberty and achievement.

The smalltown bosses and the wardheelers looked at each other and scratched their heads; then they cheered; Wilson fooled the wiseacres and doublecrossed the bosses, was elected by a huge plurality;

so he left Princeton only halfreformed to be Governor of New Jersey,

and became reconciled with Bryan

at the Jackson Day dinner: when Bryan remarked, "I of course knew that you were not with me in my position on the currency," Mr. Wilson replied, "All I can say, Mr. Bryan, is that you are a great big man."

He was introduced to Colonel House,

that amateur Merlin of politics who was spinning his webs at the Hotel Gotham,

and at the convention in Baltimore the next July the upshot of the puppetshow staged for sweating delegates by Hearst and House behind the scenes, and Bryan booming in the corridors with a handkerchief over his wilted collar, was that Woodrow Wilson was nominated for the presidency.

The bolt of the Progressives in Chicago from Taft to T. R. made his election sure;

so he left the State of New Jersey halfreformed

(pitiless publicity was the slogan of the Shadow Lawn Campaign)

and went to the White House

our twentyeighth President.

While Woodrow Wilson drove up Pennsylvania Avenue beside Taft, the great buttertub, who as President had been genially undoing T. R.'s reactionary efforts to put business under the control of the government,

J. Pierpont Morgan sat playing solitaire in his back office on Wall Street, smoking twenty black cigars a day, cursing the follies of democracy.

Wilson flayed the interests and branded privilege, refused to recognize Huerta and sent the militia to the Rio Grande,

to assume a policy of watchful waiting. He published *The New Freedom* and delivered his messages to Congress in person, like a college president addressing the faculty and students. At Mobile he said:

I wish to take this occasion to say that the United States will never again seek one additional foot of territory by conquest;

and he landed the marines at Vera Cruz.

We are witnessing a renaissance of public spirit, a reawakening of sober public opinion, a revival of the power of the people, the beginning of an age of thoughtful reconstruction . . .

but the World had started spinning round Sarajevo.

First it was *neutrality in thought and deed,* then *too proud to fight* when the *Lusitania* sinking and the danger to the Morgan loans and the stories of the British and French propagandists set all the financial centers in the East bawling for war, but the suction of the drumbeat and the guns was too strong; the best people took their fashions from Paris and their broad "a's" from London, and T. R. and the House of Morgan.

Five months after his re-election on the slogan *He kept us out of war,* Wilson pushed the Armed Ship Bill through Congress and declared that a state of war existed between the United States and the Central Powers:

Force without stint or limit, force to the utmost.

Wilson became the state (war is the health of the state), Washington his Versailles, manned the socialized government with dollar-a-year men out of the great corporations and ran the big parade

of men munitions groceries mules and trucks to France. Five million men stood at attention outside of their tarpaper barracks every sundown while they played *The Star-Spangled Banner.*

War brought the eighthour day, women's votes, prohibition, compulsory arbitration, high wages, high rates of interest, cost plus contracts, and the luxury of being a Gold Star Mother.

If you objected to making the world safe for cost plus democracy you went to jail with Debs.

Almost too soon the show was over, Prince Max of Baden was pleading for the Fourteen Points, Foch was occupying the bridgeheads on the Rhine, and the Kaiser, out of breath, ran for the train down the platform at Potsdam wearing a silk hat and some say false whiskers.

With the help of *Almighty God, Right, Truth, Justice, Freedom, Democracy, the Selfdetermination of Nations, No indemnities no annexations,*

and Cuban sugar and Caucasian manganese and Northwestern wheat and Dixie cotton, the British blockade, General Pershing, the taxicabs of Paris and the seventyfive gun,

we won the war.

On December 4, 1918, Woodrow Wilson, the first President to leave the territory of the United States during his presidency, sailed for France on board the *George Washington,*

the most powerful man in the world.

In Europe they knew what gas smelt like and the sweet sick stench of bodies buried too shallow and the gray look of the skin of starved children; they read in the papers that Meester Veelson was for peace and freedom and canned goods and butter and sugar;

he landed at Brest with his staff of experts and publicists after a rough trip on the *George Washington.*

La France héroique was there with the speeches, the singing schoolchildren, the mayors in their red sashes. (Did Meester Veelson see the gendarmes at Brest beating back the demonstration of dockyard workers who came to meet him with red flags?)

At the station in Paris he stepped from the train onto a wide red carpet that led him, between rows of potted palms, silk hats, legions of honor, decorated busts of uniforms, frockcoats, rosettes, boutonnières, to a Rolls-Royce. (Did Meester Veelson see the women in black, the cripples in their little carts, the pale anxious faces along the streets; did he hear the terrible anguish of the cheers as they hurried him and his new wife to the Hôtel de Murat, where in rooms full of brocade, gilt clocks, Buhl cabinets, and ormolu cupids the presidential suite had been prepared?)

While the experts were organizing the procedure of the peace conference, spreading green baize on the tables, arranging the protocols,

the Wilsons took a tour to see for themselves: the day after Christmas they were entertained at Buckingham Palace; at Newyear's they called on the Pope and on the microscopic Italian King at the Quirinal. (Did Meester Veelson know that in the peasants' wargrimed houses along the Brenta and the Piave they were burning candles in front of his picture cut out of the illustrated papers?) (Did Meester Veelson know that the people of Europe spelled a challenge to oppression out of the Fourteen Points, as centuries before they had spelled a challenge to oppression out of the ninetyfive articles Martin Luther nailed to the churchdoor in Wittenberg?)

January 18, 1919, in the midst of serried uniforms, cocked hats, and gold braid, decorations, epaulettes, orders of merit and knighthood, the High Contracting Parties, the Allied and Associated Powers, met in the Salon de l'Horloge at the Quai d'Orsay to dictate the peace,

but the grand assembly of the peace conference was too public a place to make peace in,

so the High Contracting Parties

formed the Council of Ten, went into the Gobelin Room, and, surrounded by Rubens's History of Marie de Medici,

began to dictate the peace.

But the Council of Ten was too public a place to make peace in,

so they formed the Council of Four.

Orlando went home in a huff,

and then there were three:

Clemenceau,

Lloyd George,

Woodrow Wilson.

Three old men shuffling the pack,

dealing out the cards:

the Rhineland, Danzig, the Polish Corridor, the Ruhr, selfdetermination of small nations, the Saar, League of Nations, mandates, the Mespot, Freedom of the Seas, Transjordania, Shantung, Fiume, and the Island of Yap:

machinegun fire and arson

starvation, lice, cholera, typhus;

oil was trumps.

Woodrow Wilson believed in his father's God,

so he told the parishioners in the little Lowther Street Congregational Church where his grandfather had preached in Carlisle in Scotland, a day so chilly that the newspapermen sitting in the old pews all had to keep their overcoats on.

On April 7 he ordered the *George Washington* to be held at Brest with steam up ready to take the American delegation home;

but he didn't go.

On April 19 sharper Clemenceau and sharper Lloyd George got him into their little cozy threecard game they called the Council of Four.

On June 28 the Treaty of Versailles was ready

and Wilson had to go back home to explain to the politicians, who'd been ganging up on him meanwhile in the Senate and House, and to sober public opinion and to his father's God how he'd let himself be trimmed and how far he'd made the world safe for democracy and the New Freedom.

From the day he landed in Hoboken, he had his back to the wall of the White House, talking to save his faith in words, talking to save his faith in the League of Nations, talking to save his faith in himself, in his father's God.

He strained every nerve of his body and brain, every agency of the government he had under his control (if anybody disagreed he was a crook or a red; no pardon for Debs).

In Seattle the wobblies whose leaders were in jail, in Seattle the wobblies whose leaders had been lynched, who'd been shot down like dogs, in Seattle the wobblies lined four blocks as Wilson passed, stood silent with their arms folded staring at the great liberal as he was hurried past in his car, huddled in his overcoat, haggard with fatigue, one side of his face twitching. Then men in overalls, the workingstiffs let him pass in silence after all the other blocks of handclapping and patriotic cheers.

In Pueblo, Colorado, he was a gray man hardly able to stand, one side of his face twitching:

Now that the mists of this great question have cleared away, I believe that men will see the Truth, eye for eye and face to face. There is one thing the American People always rise to and extend their hand to, that is, the truth of justice and of liberty and of peace. We have accepted that truth and we are going to be led by it, and it is going to lead us, and through us the world, out into pastures of quietness and peace such as the world never dreamed of before.

That was his last speech;

on the train to Wichita he had a stroke. He gave up the speaking tour that was to sweep the country for the League of Nations. After that he was a ruined paralyzed man barely able to speak;

the day he gave up the presidency to Harding the joint committee of the Senate and House appointed Henry Cabot Lodge, his lifelong enemy, to make the formal call at the executive office in the Capitol and ask the formal question whether the President had any message for the Congress assembled in joint session;

Wilson managed to get to his feet, lifting himself painfully by the two arms of the chair. "Senator Lodge, I have no further communication to make, thank you . . . Good morning," he said.

In 1924 on February 3, he died.

II
Lover of Mankind

Debs was a railroadman, born in a weatherboarded shack at Terre Haute.

He was one of ten children.

His father had come to America in a sailingship in '49,

an Alsatian from Colmar; not much of a moneymaker, fond of music and reading,

he gave his children a chance to finish public school and that was about all he could do.

At fifteen Gene Debs was already working as a machinist on the Indianapolis and Terre Haute Railway.

He worked as a locomotive fireman,

clerked in a store

joined the local of the Brotherhood of Locomotive Firemen, was elected secretary, traveled all over the country as organizer.

He was a tall shamblefooted man, had a sort of gusty rhetoric that set on fire the railroad workers in their pineboarded halls

made them want the world he wanted,

a world brothers might own

where everybody would split even:

I am not a labor leader. I don't want you to follow me or anyone else. If you are looking for a Moses to lead you out of the capitalist wilderness you will stay right where you are. I would not lead you into this promised land if I could, because if I could lead you in, someone else would lead you out.

That was how he talked to freighthandlers and gandywalkers, to firemen and switchmen and engineers, telling them it wasn't enough to organize the railroadmen, that all workers must be organized, that all workers must be organized in the workers' co-operative commonwealth.

Locomotive fireman on many a long night's run,

under the smoke a fire burned him up, burned in gusty words that beat in pineboarded halls; he wanted his brothers to be free men.

That was what he saw in the crowd that met him at the Old Wells Street Depot when he came out of jail after the Pullman strike,

those were the men that chalked up nine hundred thousand votes for him in nineteen-twelve and scared the frockcoats and the tophats and diamonded hostesses at Saratoga Springs, Bar Harbor, Lake Geneva with the bogy of a Socialist president.

But where were Gene Debs's brothers in nineteen eighteen when Woodrow Wilson had him locked up in Atlanta for speaking against war,

where were the big men fond of whiskey and fond of each other, gentle rambling tellers of stories over bars in small towns in the Middle West,

quiet men who wanted a house with a porch to putter around and a fat wife to cook for them, a few drinks and cigars, a garden to dig in, cronies to chew the rag with

and wanted to work for it

and others to work for it;

where were the locomotive firemen and engineers when they hustled him off to Atlanta Penitentiary?

And they brought him back to die in Terre Haute
to sit on his porch in a rocker with a cigar in his mouth,
beside him American Beauty roses his wife fixed in a bowl;
and the people of Terre Haute and the people in Indiana and the people of the Middle West were fond of him and afraid of him and thought of him as an old kindly uncle who loved them, and wanted to be with him and to have him give them candy,
but they were afraid of him as if he had contracted a social disease, syphilis or leprosy, and thought it was too bad,
but on account of the flag
and prosperity
and making the world safe for democracy,
they were afraid to be with him,
or to think much about him for fear they might believe him;
for he said:
While there is a lower class I am of it, while there is a criminal class I am of it, while there is a soul in prison I am not free.

* * *

III

Joe Hill

A young Swede named Hillstrom went to sea, got himself calloused hands on sailingships and tramps, learned English in the fo'c'stle of the steamers that make the run from Stockholm to Hull, dreamed the Swede's dream of the West;

when he got to America they gave him a job polishing cuspidors in a Bowery saloon.

He moved west to Chicago and worked in a machineshop.

He moved west and followed the harvest, hung around employment agencies, paid out many a dollar for a job in a construction camp, walked out many a mile when the grub was too bum, or the boss too tough, or too many bugs in the bunkhouse;

read Marx and the I.W.W. Preamble and dreamed about forming the structure of the new society within the shell of the old.

He was in California for the S.P. strike (*Casey Jones, two locomotives, Casey Jones*), used to play the concertina outside the bunkhouse door, after supper, evenings (*Longhaired preachers come out every night*), had a knack for setting rebel words to tunes (*And the union makes us strong*).

Along the coast in cookshacks flophouses jungles wobblies hoboes bindlestiffs began singing Joe Hill's songs. They sang 'em in the county jails of the State of Washington, Oregon, California, Nevada, Idaho, in the bullpens in Montana and Arizona, sang 'em in Walla Walla, San Quentin, and Leavenworth,

forming the structure of the new society within the jails of the old.

At Bingham, Utah, Joe Hill organized the workers of the Utah Construction Company in the One Big Union, won a new wagescale, shorter hours, better grub. (The angel Moroni didn't like labororganizers any better than the Southern Pacific did.)

The angel Moroni moved the hearts of the Mormons to decide it was Joe Hill shot a grocer named Morrison. The Swedish consul and President Wilson tried to get him a new trial, but the angel Moroni moved the hearts of the Supreme Court of the State of Utah to sustain the verdict of guilty. He was in jail a year, went on making up songs. In November 1915 he was stood up against the wall in the jail yard in Salt Lake City.

"Don't mourn for me, organize," was the last word he sent out to the workingstiffs of the I.W.W. Joe Hill stood up against the wall of the jail yard, looked into the muzzles of the guns, and gave the word to fire.

They put him in a black suit, put a stiff collar around his neck and a bow tie, shipped him to Chicago for a bangup funeral, and photographed his handsome stony mask staring into the future.

The first of May they scattered his ashes to the wind.

* * *

IV

Playboy

Jack Reed

was the son of a United States Marshal, a prominent citizen of Portland Oregon

He was a likely boy

so his folks sent him East to school

and to Harvard.

Harvard stood for the broad "a" and those contacts so useful in later life and good English prose . . . if the hedgehog can't be cultured at Harvard the hedgehog can't

at all and the Lowells only speak to the Cabots and the Cabots

and the Oxford Book of Verse.

Reed was a likely youngster, he wasn't a Jew or a Socialist and he didn't come from Roxbury; he was husky greedy had appetite for everything: a man's got to like many things in his life.

Reed was a man; he liked men he liked women he liked eating and writing and foggy nights and drinking and foggy nights and swimming and football and rhymed verse and being cheerleader ivy orator making clubs (not the very best clubs, his blood didn't run thin enough for the very best clubs)

and Copey's voice reading *The Man Who Would Be King,* the dying fall *Urnburial,* good English prose the lamps coming on across the Yard, under the elms in the twilight dim voices in lecturehalls,

the dying fall the elms the Discobulus the bricks of the old buildings and the commemorative gates and the goodies and the deans and the instructors all crying in thin voices refrain,

refrain; the rusty machinery creaked, the deans quivered under their mortarboards, the cogs turned to Class Day, and Reed was out in the world:

Washington Square!

Conventional turns out to be a cussword;

Villon seeking a lodging for the night in the Italian tenements on Sullivan Street, Bleecker, Carmine;

research proves R.L.S. to have been a great cocksman,

and as for the Elizabethans

to hell with them.

Ship on a cattleboat and see the world have adventures you can tell funny stories about every evening; a man's got to love . . . the quickening pulse the feel that today in foggy evenings footsteps taxicabs women's eyes . . . many things in his life.

Europe with a dash of horseradish, gulp Paris like an oyster;

but there's more to it than the Oxford Book of English Verse. Linc Steffens talked the co-operative commonwealth.

revolution in a voice as mellow as Copey's, Diogenes Steffens with Marx for a lantern going through the west looking for a good man, Socrates Steffens kept asking why not revolution?

Jack Reed wanted to live in a tub and write verses;

but he kept meeting bums workingmen husky guys he liked out of luck out of work why not revolution?

He couldn't keep his mind on his work with so many people out of luck;

in school hadn't he learned the Declaration of Independence by heart? Reed was a Westerner and words meant what they said; when he said something standing with a classmate at the Harvard Club bar, he meant what he said from the soles of his feet to the waves of his untidy hair (his blood didn't run thin enough for the Harvard Club and the Dutch Treat Club and respectable New York freelance Bohemia).

Life, liberty, and the pursuit of happiness;

not much of that round the silkmills when

in nineteen-thirteen,

he went over to Paterson to write up the strike, textile workers parading beaten up by the cops, the strikers in jail; before he knew it he was a striker parading beaten up by the cops in jail;

he wouldn't let the editor bail him out, he'd learn more with the strikers in jail.

He learned enough to put on the pageant of the Paterson Strike in Madison Square Garden.

He learned the hope of a new society where nobody would be out of luck.

why not revolution?

The *Metropolitan Magazine* sent him to Mexico

to write up Pancho Villa.

Pancho Villa taught him to write and the skeleton mountains and the tall organ cactus and the armored trains and the bands playing in little plazas full of dark girls in blue scarfs

and the bloody dust and the ping of rifleshots

in the enormous night of the desert, and the brown quietvoiced peons dying starving killing for liberty

for land for water for schools.

Mexico taught him to write.

Reed was a Westerner and words meant what they said.

The war was a blast that blew out all the Diogenes lanterns;

the good men began to gang up to call for machineguns. Jack Reed was the last of the great race of warcorrespondents who ducked under censorships and risked their skins for a story.

Jack Reed was the best American writer of his time, if anybody had wanted to know about the war they could have read about it in the articles he wrote

about the German front,

the Serbian retreat,

Saloniki;

behind the lines in the tottering empire of the Czar,

dodging the secret police,

jail in Cholm.

The brasshats wouldn't let him go to France because they said one night in the German trenches kidding with the Boche guncrew he'd pulled the string on a Hun gun pointed at the heart of France . . . playboy stuff but after all what did it matter who fired the guns or which way they were pointed? Reed was with the boys who were being blown to hell,

with the Germans the French the Russians the Bulgarians the seven little tailors in the Ghetto in Salonique,

and in nineteen-seventeen

he was with the soldiers and peasants

in Petrograd in October:

Smolny,

Ten Days That Shook the World;

no more Villa picturesque Mexico, no more Harvard Club playboy stuff, plans for Greek theaters, rhyming verse, good stories of an oldtime warcorrespondent,

this wasn't fun anymore

this was grim.

Delegate,
back in the States indictments, the Masses trial, the Wobbly trial, Wilson cramming the jails,
forged passports, speeches, secret documents, riding the rods across the cordon sanitaire, hiding in the bunkers on steamboats;
jail in Finland all his papers stolen,
no more chance to write verses now, no more warm chats with every guy you met up with, the college boy with the nice smile talking himself out of trouble with the judge;
at the Harvard Club they're all in the Intelligence Service making the world safe for the Morgan-Baker-Stillman combination of banks;
that old tramp sipping his coffee out of a tomatocan's a spy of the General Staff.
The world's no fun anymore,
only machinegunfire and arson
starvation lice bedbugs cholera typhus
no lint for bandages no chloroform or ether thousands dead of gangrened wounds cordon sanitaire and everywhere spies.
The windows of Smolny glow whitehot like a bessemer,
no sleep in Smolny,
Smolny the giant rollingmill running twentyfour hours a day rolling out men nations hopes millenniums impulses fears,
rawmaterial
for the foundations
of a new society.

A man has to do many things in his life.
Reed was a Westerner words meant what they said.
He threw everything he had and himself into Smolny,
dictatorship of the proletariat;
U.S.S.R.
The first workers republic
was established and stands.
Reed wrote, undertook missions (there were spies everywhere), worked till he dropped,
caught typhus and died in Moscow.

* * *

V

The Bitter Drink

Veblen,
a grayfaced shambling man lolling resentful at his desk with his cheek on his hand, in a low sarcastic mumble of intricate phrases subtly paying out the logical inescapable rope of matter-of-fact for a society to hang itself by,

dissecting out the century with a scalpel so keen, so comical, so exact that the professors and students ninetenths of the time didn't know it was there, and the magnates and the respected windbags and the applauded loudspeakers never knew it was there.

Veblen

asked too many questions, suffered from a constitutional inability to say yes.

Socrates asked questions, drank down the bitter drink one night when the first cock crowed,

but Veblen

drank it in little sips through a long life in the stuffiness of classrooms, the dust of libraries, the staleness of cheap flats such as a poor instructor can afford. He fought the bogy all right, pedantry, routine, timeservers at office desks, trustees, collegepresidents, the plump flunkies of the ruling businessmen, all the good jobs kept for yesmen, never enough money, every broadening hope thwarted. Veblen drank the bitter drink all right.

The Veblens were a family of freeholding farmers.

The freeholders of the narrow Norwegian valleys were a stubborn hardworking people, farmers, dairymen, fishermen, rooted in their fathers' stony fields, in their old timbered farmsteads with carved gables they took their names from, in the upland pastures where they grazed the stock in summer.

During the early nineteenth century the towns grew; Norway filled up with landless men, storekeepers, sheriffs, moneylenders, bailiffs, notaries in black with stiff collars and briefcases full of foreclosures under their arms. Industries were coming in. The townsmen were beginning to get profits out of the country and to finagle the farmers out of the freedom of their narrow farms.

The meanspirited submitted as tenants, daylaborers; but the strong men went out of the country

as their fathers had gone out of the country centuries before when Harald the Fairhaired and Saint Olaf hacked to pieces the liberties of the Northern men, who had been each man lord of his own creek, to make Christians and serfs of them,

only in the old days it was Iceland, Greenland, Vineland the Northmen had sailed west to; now it was America.

Both Thorstein Veblen's father's people and his mother's people had lost their farmsteads and with them the names that denoted them free men.

Thomas Anderson for a while tried to make his living as a traveling carpenter and cabinetmaker, but in 1847 he and his wife, Kari Thorsteinsdatter, crossed in a whalingship from Bremen and went out to join friends in the Scandihoovian colonies round Milwaukee.

Next year his brother Haldor joined him.

They were hard workers; in another year they had saved up money to pre-empt a claim on a hundred and sixty acres of uncleared land in

Sheboygan County, Wisconsin; when they'd gotten that land part cleared they sold it and moved to an all-Norway colony in Manitowoc County, near Cato, and a place named Valders after the valley they had all come from in the old country;

there in the house Thomas Anderson built with his own tools, the sixth of twelve children, Thorstein Veblen was born.

When Thorstein was eight years old, Thomas Anderson moved west again into the blacksoil prairies of Minnesota that the Sioux and the buffalo had only been driven off from a few years before. In the deed to the new farm Thomas Anderson took back the old farmstead name of Veblen.

He was a solid farmer, builder, a clever carpenter, the first man to import merino sheep and a mechanical reaper and binder; he was a man of standing in the group of Norway people farming the edge of the prairie, who kept their dialects, the manner of life of their narrow Norway valleys, their Lutheran pastors, their homemade clothes and cheese and bread, their suspicion and stubborn dislike of townsmen's ways.

The townspeople were Yankees mostly, smart to make two dollars grow where a dollar grew before, storekeepers, middlemen, speculators, moneylenders, with long heads for politics and mortgages; they despised the Scandihoovian dirtfarmers they lived off, whose daughters did their wives' kitchenwork.

The Norway people believed as their fathers had believed that there were only two callings for an honest man, farming or preaching.

Thorstein grew up a hulking lad with a reputation for laziness and wit. He hated the irk of everrepeated backbreaking chores round the farm. Reading he was happy. Carpentering he liked or running farm machinery. The Lutheran pastors who came to the house noticed that his supple mind slid easily round the corners of their theology. It was hard to get farmwork out of him; he had a stinging tongue and was famous for the funny names he called people; his father decided to make a preacher out of him.

When he was seventeen he was sent for out of the field where he was working. His bag was already packed. The horses were hitched up. He was being sent to Carleton Academy in Northfield, to prepare for Carleton College.

As there were several young Veblens to be educated, their father built them a house on a lot near the campus. Their food and clothes were sent to them from the farm. Cash money was something they never saw.

Thorstein spoke English with an accent. He had a constitutional inability to say yes. His mind was formed on the Norse sagas and on the matter-of-fact sense of his father's farming and the exact needs of carpenterwork and threshingmachines.

He could never take much interest in the theology, sociology, economics of Carleton College where they were busy trimming down the jagged dogmas of the old New England Bibletaught traders to make stencils to hang on the walls of commissionmerchants' offices.

Veblen's collegeyears were the years when Darwin's assertions of growth and becoming were breaking the set molds of the Noah's Ark world,

when Ibsen's women were tearing down the portières of the Victorian parlors,

and Marx's mighty machine was rigging the countinghouse's own logic to destroy the countinghouse.

When Veblen went home to the farm, he talked about these things with his father, following him up and down at his plowing, starting an argument while they were waiting for a new load for the wheat-thresher. Thomas Anderson had seen Norway and America; he had the squarebuilt mind of a carpenter and builder, and an understanding of tools and the treasured elaborated builtupseasonbyseason knowledge of a careful farmer.

a tough whetstone for the sharpening steel of young Thorstein's wits.

At Carleton College young Veblen was considered a brilliant unsound eccentric; nobody could understand why a boy of such attainments wouldn't settle down to the business of the day, which was to buttress property and profits with anything usable in the débris of Christian ethics and eighteenthcentury economics that cluttered the minds of college professors, and to reinforce the sacred, already shaky edifice with the new strong girderwork of science Herbert Spencer was throwing up for the benefit of the bosses.

People complained they never knew whether Veblen was joking or serious.

In 1880 Thorstein Veblen started to try to make his living by teaching. A year in an academy at Madison, Wisconsin, wasn't much of a success. Next year he and his brother Andrew started graduate work at Johns Hopkins. Johns Hopkins didn't suit, but boarding in an old Baltimore house with some ruined gentlewomen gave him a disdaining glimpse of an etiquette motheaten now but handed down through the lavish leisure of the slaveowning planters' mansions straight from the merrie England of the landlord cavaliers.

(The valleyfarmers had always been scornful of outlanders' ways.)

He was more at home at Yale, where in Noah Porter he found a New England roundhead granite against which his Norway granite rang in clear dissent. He took his Ph.D. there. But there was still some question as to what department of the academic world he could best make a living in.

He read Kant and wrote prize essays. But he couldn't get a job. Try as he would he couldn't get his mouth round the essential yes.

He went back to Minnesota with a certain intolerant knowledge of the amenities of the higher learning. To his slight Norwegian accent he'd added the broad "a."

At home he loafed about the farm and tinkered with inventions of new machinery and read and talked theology and philosophy with his father. In the Scandihoovian colonies the price of wheat and the belief in God and Saint Olaf were going down together. The farmers of the Northwest were starting their long losing fight against the parasite businessmen who were sucking them dry. There was a mortgage on the farm, interest on debts to pay, always fertilizer, new machines to buy to speed production to pump in a halfcentury the wealth out of the soil laid down in a million years of buffalograss. His brothers kept grumbling about this sardonic loafer who wouldn't earn his keep.

Back home he met again his college sweetheart, Ellen Rolfe, the niece of the president of Carleton College, a girl who had railroad-magnates and money in the family. People in Northfield were shocked when it came out that she was going to marry the drawling pernickety bookish badly dressed young Norwegian ne'erdowell.

Her family hatched a plan to get him a job as economist for the Santa Fe Railroad, but at the wrong moment Ellen Rolfe's uncle lost control of the line. The young couple went to live at Stacyville where they did everything but earn a living. They read Latin and Greek and botanized in the woods and along the fences and in the roadside scrub. They boated on the river and Veblen started his translation of the *Laxdaelasaga.* They read *Looking Backward* and articles by Henry George. They looked at their world from the outside.

In '91 Veblen got together some money to go to Cornell to do post-graduate work. He turned up there in the office of the head of the economics department wearing a coonskin cap and gray corduroy trousers and said in his low sarcastic drawl, "I am Thorstein Veblen,"

but it was not until several years later, after he was established at the new University of Chicago that had grown up next to the World's Fair, and had published *The Theory of the Leisure Class,* put on the map by Howells's famous review, that the world of the higher learning knew who Thorstein Veblen was.

Even in Chicago as the brilliant young economist he lived pioneer-fashion. (The valleyfarmers had always been scornful of outlanders' ways.) He kept his books in packingcases laid on their sides along the walls. His only extravagances were the Russian cigarettes he smoked and the red sash he sometimes sported. He was a man without smalltalk. When he lectured he put his cheek on his hand and mumbled out his long spiral sentences, reiterative like the eddas. His language was a mixture of mechanics' terms, scientific latinity, slang, and Roget's *Thesaurus*. The other profs couldn't imagine why the girls fell for him so.

The girls fell for him so that Ellen Rolfe kept leaving him. He'd take summer trips abroad without his wife. There was a scandal about a girl on an ocean liner.

Tongues wagged so (Veblen was a man who never explained, who never could get his tongue around the essential yes; the valleyfarmers had always been scornful of the outlanders' ways, and their opinions) that his wife left him and went off to live alone on a timberclaim in Idaho and the president asked for his resignation.

Veblen went out to Idaho to get Ellen Rolfe to go with him to California when he succeeded in getting a job at a better salary at Leland Stanford, but in Palo Alto it was the same story as in Chicago. He suffered from woman trouble and the constitutional inability to say yes and an unnatural tendency to feel with the workingclass instead of with the profittakers. There were the same complaints that his courses were not constructive or attractive to bigmoney bequests and didn't help his students to butter their bread, make Phi Beta Kappa, pick plums off the hierarchies of the academic grove. His wife left him for good. He wrote to a friend: "The president doesn't approve of my domestic arrangements; nor do I."

Talking about it he once said, "What is one to do if the woman moves in on you?"

He went back up to the shack in the Idaho woods.

Friends tried to get him an appointment to make studies in Crete, a chair at the University of Pekin, but always the bogy, routine, businessmen's flunkies in all the university offices . . . for the questioner the bitter drink.

His friend Davenport got him an appointment at the University of Missouri. At Columbia he lived like a hermit in the basement of the Davenports' house, helped with the work round the place, carpentered himself a table and chairs. He was already a bitter elderly man with a gray face covered with a net of fine wrinkles, a Vandyke beard and yellow teeth. Few students could follow his courses. The college authorities were often surprised and somewhat chagrined that when visitors came from Europe, it was always Veblen they wanted to meet.

These were the years he did most of his writing, trying out his ideas on his students, writing slowly at night in violet ink with a pen of his own designing. Whenever he published a book, he had to put up a guarantee with the publishers. In *The Theory of Business Enterprise, The Instinct of Workmanship, The Vested Interests and the Common Man,*

he established a new diagram of a society dominated by monopoly capital,

etched in irony

the sabotage of production by business,

the sabotage of life by blind need for money profits,

pointed out the alternatives: a warlike society strangled by the bureaucracies of the monopolies forced by the law of diminishing returns to grind down more and more the common man for profits,

or a new matter-of-fact commonsense society dominated by the needs of the men and women who did the work and the incredibly vast possibilities for peace and plenty offered by the progress of technology.

These were the years of Debs's speeches, growing laborunions, the I.W.W. talk about industrial democracy: these years Veblen still held to the hope that the workingclass would take over the machine of production before monopoly had pushed the western nations down into the dark again.

War cut across all that: under the cover of the bunting of Woodrow Wilson's phrases the monopolies cracked down. American democracy was crushed.

The war at least offered Veblen an opportunity to break out of the airless greenhouse of academic life. He was offered a job with the Food Administration, he sent the Navy Department a device for catching submarines by trailing lengths of stout bindingwire. (Meanwhile the government found his books somewhat confusing. The postoffice was forbidding the mails to *Imperial Germany and the Industrial Revolution* while propaganda agencies were sending it out to make people hate the Huns. Educators were denouncing *The Nature of Peace* while Washington experts were clipping phrases out of it to add to the Wilsonian smokescreen.)

For the Food Administration Thorstein Veblen wrote two reports: in one he advocated granting the demands of the I.W.W. as a wartime measure and conciliating the workingclass instead of beating up and jailing all the honest leaders; in the other he pointed out that the Food Administration was a businessman's racket and was not aiming for the most efficient organization of the country as a producing machine. He suggested that, in the interests of the efficient prosecution of the war, the government step into the place of the middleman and furnish necessities to the farmers direct in return for raw materials;

but cutting out business was not at all the Administration's idea of making the world safe for democracy,

so Veblen had to resign from the Food Administration.

He signed the protests against the trial of the hundred and one wobblies in Chicago.

After the armistice he went to New York. In spite of all the oppression of the war years, the air was freshening. In Russia the great storm of revolt had broken, seemed to be sweeping west; in the strong gusts from the new world in the east the warsodden multitudes began to see again. At Versailles allies and enemies, magnates, generals, flunkey politicians were slamming the shutters against the storm, against the new, against hope. It was suddenly clear for a second in the thundering glare what war was about, what peace was about.

In America, in Europe, the old men won. The bankers in their offices took a deep breath, the bediamonded old ladies of the leisure class went back to clipping their coupons in the refined quiet of their safe-deposit vaults,

the last puffs of the ozone of revolt went stale
in the whisper of speakeasy arguments.

Veblen wrote for the *Dial,*
lectured at the New School for Social Research.

He still had a hope that the engineers, the technicians, the nonprofiteers whose hands were on the switchboard might take up the fight where the workingclass had failed. He helped form the Technical Alliance. His last hope was the British general strike.

Was there no group of men bold enough to take charge of the magnificent machine before the pigeyed speculators and the yesmen at office desks irrevocably ruined it
and with it the hopes of four hundred years?

No one went to Veblen's lectures at the New School. With every article he wrote in the *Dial* the circulation dropped.

Harding's normalcy, the new era was beginning;
even Veblen made a small killing on the stockmarket.
He was an old man and lonely.
His second wife had gone to a sanitarium suffering from delusions of persecution.
There seemed no place for a masterless man

Veblen went back out to Palo Alto
to live in his shack in the tawny hills and observe from outside the last grabbing urges of the profit system taking on, as he put it, the systematized delusions of dementia praecox.
There he finished his translation of the *Laxdaelasaga.*

He was an old man. He was much alone. He let the woodrats take what they wanted from his larder. A skunk that hung round the shack was so tame he'd rub up against Veblen's leg like a cat.

He told a friend he'd sometimes hear in the stillness about him the voices of his boyhood talking Norwegian as clear as on the farm in Minnesota where he was raised. His friends found him harder than ever to talk to, harder than ever to interest in anything. He was running down. The last sips of the bitter drink.

He died on August 3, 1929.

Among his papers a penciled note was found:

It is also my wish, in case of death, to be cremated if it can conveniently be done, as expeditiously and inexpensively as may be, without ritual or ceremony of any kind; that my ashes be thrown loose into the sea or into some sizable stream running into the sea; that no tombstone, slab, epitaph, effigy, tablet, inscription or monument of any name or nature, be set up to my memory or name in any place or at any time; that no obituary, memorial, portrait or biography of me, nor any letters written to or by me be printed or published, or in any way reproduced, copied or circulated;

but his memorial remains
riveted into the language:
the sharp clear prism of his mind.

* * *

VI
The American Plan

Frederick Winslow Taylor (they called him Speedy Taylor in the shop) was born in Germantown, Pennsylvania, the year of Buchanan's election. His father was a lawyer, his mother came from a family of New Bedford whalers; she was a great reader of Emerson, belonged to the Unitarian Church and the Browning Society. She was a fervent abolitionist and believed in democratic manners; she was a housekeeper of the old school, kept everybody busy from dawn till dark. She laid down the rules of conduct:

selfrespect, selfreliance, selfcontrol
and a cold long head for figures.

But she wanted her children to appreciate the finer things, so she took them abroad for three years on the Continent, showed them cathedrals, grand opera, Roman pediments, the old masters under their brown varnish in their great frames of tarnished gilt.

Later Fred Taylor was impatient of these wasted years, stamped out of the room when people talked about the finer things; he was a testy youngster, fond of practical jokes, and a great hand at rigging up contraptions and devices.

At Exeter he was head of his class and captain of the ballteam, the first man to pitch overhand. (When umpires complained that overhand pitching wasn't in the rules of the game, he answered that it got results.)

As a boy he had nightmares; going to bed was horrible for him; he thought they came from sleeping on his back. He made himself a leather harness with wooden pegs that stuck into his flesh when he turned over. When he was grown he slept in a chair or in bed in a sitting position propped up with pillows. All his life he suffered from sleeplessness.

He was a crackerjack tennisplayer. In 1881, with his friend Clark, he won the National Doubles Championship. (He used a spoon-shaped racket of his own design.)

At school he broke down from overwork, his eyes went back on him. The doctor suggested manual labor. So instead of going to Harvard he went into the machineshop of a small pumpmanufacturing concern, owned by a friend of the family's, to learn the trade of patternmaker and machinist. He learned to handle a lathe and to dress and cuss like a workingman.

Fred Taylor never smoked tobacco or drank liquor or used tea or coffee; he couldn't understand why his fellowmechanics wanted to go on sprees and get drunk and raise cain Saturday nights. He lived at home; when he wasn't reading technical books he'd play parts in amateur theatricals or step up to the piano in the evening and sing a good tenor in *A Warrior Bold* or *A Spanish Cavalier.*

He served his first year's apprenticeship in the machineshop without pay; the next two years he made a dollar and a half a week, the last year two dollars.

Pennsylvania was getting rich off iron and coal. When he was twentytwo, Fred Taylor went to work at the Midvale Iron Works. At first he had to take a clerical job, but he hated that and went to work with a shovel. At last he got them to put him on a lathe. He was a good machinist, he worked ten hours a day and in the evenings followed an engineering course at Stevens. In six years he rose from machinist's helper to keeper of toolcribs to gangboss to foreman to mastermechanic in charge of repairs to chief draftsman and director of research to chief engineer of the Midvale Plant.

The early years he was a machinist with the other machinists in the shop, cussed and joked and worked with the rest of them, soldiered on the job when they did. Mustn't give the boss more than his money's worth. But when he got to be foreman, he was on the management's side of the fence, *gathering in on the part of those on the management's side all the great mass of traditional knowledge which in the past has been in the heads of the workmen and in the physical skill and knack of the workman.* He couldn't stand to see an idle lathe or an idle man.

Production went to his head and thrilled his sleepless nerves like liquor or women on a Saturday night. He never loafed and he'd be damned if anybody else would. Production was an itch under his skin.

He lost his friends in the shop; they called him niggerdriver. He was a stockily built man with a temper and a short tongue.

I was a young man in years, but I give you my word I was a great deal older than I am now, what with the worry, meanness, and contemptibleness of the whole damn thing. It's a horrid life for any man to live not being able to look any workman in the face without seeing hostility there, and a feeling that every man around you is your virtual enemy.

That was the beginning of the Taylor System of Scientific Management.

He was impatient of explanations, he didn't care whose hide he took off in enforcing the laws he believed inherent in the industrial process.

When starting an experiment in any field, question everything, question the very foundations upon which the art rests, question the simplest, the most selfevident, the most universally accepted facts; prove everything,

except the dominant Quaker Yankee (the New Bedford skippers were the greatest niggerdrivers on the whaling seas) rules of conduct. He boasted he'd never ask a workman to do anything he couldn't do.

He devised an improved steamhammer; he standardized tools and equipment, he filled the shop with college students with stopwatches and diagrams, tabulating, standardizing. *There's the right way of doing a thing and the wrong way of doing it; the right way means increased production, lower costs, higher wages, bigger profits:* the American plan.

He broke up the foreman's job into separate functions, speedbosses, gangbosses, timestudy men, order-of-work men

The skilled mechanics were too stubborn for him; what he wanted was a plain handyman who'd do what he was told. If he was a firstclass man and did firstclass work, Taylor was willing to let him have firstclass pay; that's where he began to get into trouble with the owners.

At thirtyfour he married and left Midvale and took a flyer for the big money in connection with a pulpmill started in Maine by some admirals and political friends of Grover Cleveland's;

the panic of '93 made hash of that enterprise,

so Taylor invented for himself the job of Consulting Engineer in Management and began to build up a fortune by careful investments.

The first paper he read before the American Society of Mechanical Engineers was anything but a success; they said he was crazy. *I have found,* he wrote in 1909, *that any improvement is not only opposed but aggressively and bitterly opposed by the majority of men.*

He was called in by Bethlehem Steel. It was in Bethlehem he made his famous experiments with handling pigiron; he taught a Dutchman named Schmidt to handle fortyseven tons instead of twelve and a half tons of pigiron a day and got Schmidt to admit he was as good as ever at the end of the day.

He was a crank about shovels, every job had to have a shovel of the right weight and size for that job alone; every job had to have a man of the right weight and size for that job alone; but when he began to pay his men in proportion to the increased efficiency of their work,

the owners, who were a lot of greedy smalleyed Dutchmen, began to raise Hail Columbia; when Schwab bought Bethlehem Steel in 1901

Fred Taylor
inventor of efficiency
who had doubled the production of the stampingmill by speeding up the main lines of shafting from ninetysix to twohundred and twentyfive revolutions a minute
was unceremoniously fired.

After that Fred Taylor always said he couldn't afford to work for money.
He took to playing golf (using golfclubs of his own design), doping out methods for transplanting huge boxtrees into the garden of his home.

At Boxly in Germantown he kept open house for engineers, factory-managers, industrialists;
he wrote papers,
lectured in colleges,
appeared before a congressional committee,
everywhere preached the virtues of scientific management and the Barth slide rule, the cutting-down of waste and idleness, the substitution for skilled mechanics of the plain handyman (like Schmidt the pigiron handler) who'd move as he was told
and work by the piece:
production;
more steel rails more bicycles more spools of thread more armorplate for battleships more bedpans more barbedwire more needles more lightningrods more ballbearings more dollarbills;
(the old Quaker families of Germantown were growing rich, the Pennsylvania millionaires were breeding billionaires out of iron and coal)
production would make every firstclass American rich who was willing to work at piecework and not drink or raise cain or think or stand mooning at his lathe.
Thrifty Schmidt the pigiron handler can invest his money and get to be an owner like Schwab and the rest of the greedy smalleyed Dutchmen and cultivate a taste for Bach and have hundredyearold boxtrees in his garden at Bethlehem or Germantown or Chestnut Hill,
and lay down the rules of conduct;
the American plan
But Fred Taylor never saw the working of the American plan;
in 1915 he went to the hospital in Philadelphia suffering from a breakdown.
Pneumonia developed; the nightnurse heard him winding his watch;
on the morning of his fiftyninth birthday, when the nurse went into his room to look at him at fourthirty,
he was dead with his watch in his hand.

General Motors sitdown strike at the Fisher Body plant in Flint, Michigan, 1937

RUTH McKENNEY

Industrial Valley

(1939)

The rise of labor to a position of organization and power was one of the most important single institutional changes of the twentieth century. The failure of socialism in the United States—indeed, the failure of all but a rather miniscule labor organization before the 1930s—has long been noted, especially by foreign observers, as a distinguishing feature of American society. Yet labor unions became the American substitute for a socialist movement. In 1931 a mere 3.1 million workers belonged to unions, and they lacked firm connection with any major party. By 1940 workers were unionized and the national Democratic party had become the party of labor. Few such changes take place without a revolution or at least a rebellion. In this case, the main form of alleged revolutionary activity was the sitdown strike.

In 1936 and 1937 commencing in Akron, Ohio—as Ruth McKenney's striking piece of reportage shows—wave after wave of strikes geared to this new sitdown tactic hit American industry. An agent of the Hotel & Restaurant Employees Union recalled how in those years "the phone would ring and the voice at the other end would say, 'My name is Mary Jones; I'm a soda clerk at Liggett's; we've thrown the manager out and we've got the keys. What do we do now?'" Sometimes, as in a famous incident on the overpass near Ford's River Rouge plant in 1937, serious violence erupted, and a few of the strikes shut down large industries for weeks at a time. Writers and radicals, cheering from the sidelines or serving as organizers, clamored for revolution; and for a time, it did look as if revolutionary anarchism might sweep across the land for the first time since the pre-World War I heyday of the I.W.W. But most of those who sat down and most of their leaders wanted neither revolution nor to take over the plants. What they wanted they got: union recognition, government support for their negotiations, and improvements in hours, pay, and working conditions. Samuel Gompers, surely the patron saint of American labor, had described his program for labor in one word: "More!" Since they united whole industries rather than separate crafts, the sitdowns moved far beyond Gompers in tactics and in their model of organization. But the strikers' goals were little different: they got more—much more—and enough, apparently, to satisfy them.

The First Sitdown — January 29-31, 1936

The mountaineer workers of Akron were fond of Alex Eigenmacht, the bullet-headed, blue-eyed Hungarian who ran the union print shop out near the Firestone plant. They liked him because he was the best story-teller in town. Even the gaudy movies hadn't spoiled the taste of the sons of the Southern hills for a good tale deftly spun. And Alex—rubberworkers had difficulty pronouncing his last name, so he went simply by his first—had a real talent for reciting the stories of his improbably adventurous life.

Union rubberworkers used to turn up an hour or so early at Alex's little office, and while they waited for the last of their leaflets to come off the little press out in the composing room, they listened solemnly, with just the ghost of pleased grins on their broad mouths, to tall tales of Alex fighting in the Austrian mountains; Alex in the Hungarian Red Army; Alex eluding—by the merest hairbreadth—German spies; Alex escaping the White Terror by the very skin of his teeth.

One day four truck-tire builders from Firestone ambled into the print-shop office to pick up some union notices. Alex was in an expansive mood and he began, in his poetic, slightly accented English, to tell them the story of the beginning of the World War.

Like some adventurous men, Alex had a talent for being in the right place at precisely the right moment. He had been a union printer in Serajevo the day the Austrian Crown Prince was blown to bits by the fatal bomb. A passionate Serbian nationalist, along with other members of his union, he had fought to prevent Serbia capitulating to the Austrian ultimatum.

"The men who threw that bomb," Alex told the listening rubberworkers, "were men fighting for freedom. My union decided to protest against the government's arresting them and trying them for murder." This was a new slant on old history and the Firestone union men leaned forward and said, "Yeah, go on."

The printers couldn't actually walk out on strike, Alex said, because they had heard that their boss had a whole crew of scabs lined up ready to take their places at a moment's notice. Besides, if they actually struck, they were quite likely to be arrested and thrown in jail. The times were tense and the Serbian government was trying to do everything to prevent the inevitable war.

"So we had an inside strike," Alex said casually. "We just sat around by our machines, and, by God, nobody could come in and take our jobs, and they couldn't arrest us either. We were on the job."

Alex went on, telling about engineers who struck and finally the mobilization. The pressman brought in the notices and the tirebuilders shook hands and said they liked the story.

Nearly three months later, on the cold winter day of January 28, 1936, Alex was startled to hear the door of his office banging in the wind. He went out to greet his old friends from the Firestone truck-tire department. Their faces were cracked with the wind, and they wore heavy scarfs and thick mittens and lumber-jackets.

"Sit down, sit down," Alex said pleasantly. "Pull up next to the radiator and warm yourselves up."

"Nope," one of them replied. "No time. Look, Alex, will you do us a favor?"

Alex had courtly continental manners. He said he would be delighted, it was an honor, what could he do?

"Tell us about that time in that town where the World War started when you guys struck but didn't walk out."

Alex hesitated, trying to recall the story. Then he nodded. "Sure," he said, "but what's up?"

"Just tell us," a big tirebuilder said.

So Alex, considerably bewildered by the air of mystery and excitement written all over the faces of these big tirebuilders, told them the story again, this time in great detail. They stopped him to ask questions.

"Well, didn't the boss try to throw you out?"

"He couldn't," Alex replied. "He was afraid of hurting his expensive machinery if there was any fighting inside."

"Uhmm," men in the little group said, and added, "Go on." When he was through, the tirebuilders pulled their scarfs tight around their ears, jerked their woolen caps down to their eyes. "Thank you," they said briskly and without another word, slammed out the door.

Left alone, Alex drummed on his desk with a pencil, put a thoughtful finger to his nose. Finally, he called up the Firestone local headquarters and asked, in the course of a casual conversation, if there was any trouble in the truck-tire department.

"Boy," said the man from union headquarters, "is there! Trouble and plenty of it!"

"What's it all about?" Alex asked pleasantly.

"Well, you know about how they tried to cut the base rate up there forty per cent to speed the boys up some more?" the union man said.

"Yeah," Alex replied, "so I heard. I was surprised at that. They usually don't trifle much with those babies in the truck-tire department. They're tough."

"You said it," the union man agreed. "Well, anyway, the boys raised holy hell about it, and finally we got Murphy—the factory super—to agree to only an eleven per cent cut."

"Yeah," Alex said. "So?"

"So the boys was still sore," the union man explained. "Sorer than hell. They've been speedin' them up for months now something terrible. My God, it's worth your life to work up there. Nobody but them big husky babies could take it. There isn't one of them in there under six feet two, and they all weigh better than two hundred and, believe me, they ain't fat, not the way they work."

"Yeah, yeah," Alex agreed.

"Well, so this eleven per cent cut didn't go so good. The boys figure if they don't stop this speedup now, they'll all be in the ashcan by the time they're thirty-five. The pace is something awful. Anyway, you know all the boys are scared now of this eight-hour-day thing, and they figure if they let the company get away with this cut, why, they'll start to think they can do anything and end up putting in the eight-hour day."

"Yeah. So?" Alex said.

"O.K., so the boys got together and decided to stall on the rate. You know, they got that group payment stuff up there, so when all the boys slow down, why, they can't cut their wages, see?"

"Yeah, sure."

"So last week Murphy sends a rat in to make the time," the union man went on. "You know the system. If a guy comes in and works like hell and even does sloppy work, the company don't care, and if he makes the base rate on the new schedule, why, then the whole outfit has to make it."

"Yeah, yeah," Alex said impatiently.

"O.K.," the union man went on. "So this skunk comes in and starts making time on the boys. Well, the second night he's in there, it's on the night shift, why, the boys begin to get pretty sore. Things begin to look as though this rat is going to get popped by some of the guys with bad tempers. So Clay Dicks comes over. He's the union committeeman in that department. Clay figures there's going to be trouble, and he wants to quiet the boys down, because he thinks it's not so good having union men slugging rats right in the shop. The company would probably use it as an excuse to fire them."

"Sure," Alex agreed.

"So Dicks tries to smooth the boys down. But obviously this skunk has been tipped off by the management, because he starts to pick on Dicks. Calls Clay a son-of-a-bitch and a lot more—plenty more."

"So?" Alex said, interested. Mountain men, he knew, did not take kindly to insults.

"Yeah. So Clay holds himself in pretty good. He gets the fellows back on their machines, and he says to this rat, 'I'll see you outside after the shift.' That don't suit the skunk so good, he wants to fight right then, which is just what Clay figures. This guy is out to get him canned, because he's the union committeeman."

"So?" Alex said again, getting excited.

"O.K. When the shift is over, Clay rings out at the timehouse. You know how that is. There's a little courtyard there just before the gates. Clay was figuring on meeting the rat right outside the fence and giving it to him. But all of a sudden, as he was walking toward the gate, this rat turns up and slugs Clay a dirty one, from the back."

"Uhmm."

"Yeah, so Clay takes a fall and then he gets up and gives it to this guy. Boy, the fellows said he just knocked the living daylights out of him, bounced him six feet across the ground."

"Good," Alex said, pleased.

"Not so good," his friend replied, "because, Jesus, Clay hardly had time to lay a hand on this dirty dog when suddenly from nowhere at all, mind you, just by coincidence, who should happen to be strolling around in the middle of the night but a big bunch of factory guards."

"My," said Alex.

"Yeah, so they pounce on Clay, and of course let the other guy go, and Murphy suspends Clay for a whole week, no pay, for fighting on company grounds, which is mighty convenient for Murphy, because here is the truck-tire department without their union committeeman just when they were trying to negotiate about this wage cut."

"Bad business."

"So the fellows is sore. Boy, they're boiling mad," the union man went on. "They're holding meetings here all the time, and Murphy says absolutely he won't take Dicks back, and the boys said he's got to, or else."

"Else what?" Alex inquired.

"I don't know," the union man replied, his voice suddenly blank.

"Yeah," Alex answered. "Well, thanks a lot." After he hung up he sat at his desk, drumming with his fingers, and staring out into the swirling snow. It was four o'clock. Alex bundled himself up in his heavy coat and went home.

The snow fell in patches all afternoon, and toward dusk, the winds grew fiercer. The six to twelve shift at Firestone came stamping into the factory, their ears wrapped in home-knit scarfs. The lights flashed on all over the great factory, and at six-fifteen the steady clatter and crash and whir of the early evening shift blotted out every human sound in the rubber shop.

Outside, in the gathering darkness, automobiles went carefully past the Firestone plant, poking their way along on the slippery windswept streets. People who lived in Akron were used to seeing the big rubber plants of southernmost Main Street, so only a few, as they rode by, even glanced at the great pile of yellow brick buildings. But passing strangers stared, and were filled with unrest. For the Firestone rubber shops, on the dusk of a winter's evening, were a commanding and beautiful sight. Arising black against a pale sky, they were illuminated by a thousand lights twinkling from their windows, making a soft glow on the snow-covered yards around them.

On this bitter night in January, the drafty hall of the union headquarters across the street from the Firestone plant was partly filled with restless tirebuilders. They were huddled, most of them still wearing their heavy lumber-jackets, around a fat stove at one end of the big room. A naked electric light bulb hung on a long cord from the ceiling, making a pool of yellow light near the stove. No pictures, no bulletins, no notices hung on the walls, except a badly lettered, homemade sign off in one corner, stating, "Buy union-made goods."

The men were talking quietly but with fierce excitement. They had just decided to give Murphy one more chance: Reinstate Dicks and give him back pay for his time lost, or else.

"He'll say 'or else what' and that would be bad," one of the men objected. He was, like his friends, tall above the average with tremendous shoulders, but very thin and gaunt, with deep hollows in his young weatherbeaten face and at his big neck bones.

"Yeah, that's right," someone answered from the outer circle around the stove. "We don't want to give him no hint. This has got to come off quick and easy. It's got to be a big surprise. That's what was the matter last year. We was all the time talkin' and didn't do nothin'."

"Yeah," a tirebuilder whose heavy boots were sizzling against the very belly of the stove replied, "yeah, and we let a lot of guys do the talkin' for us. This time we run it ourselves, and we don't tell nobody, and we don't ask nobody if it suits them either."

"Yep," the men in the circle murmured. They sat quietly in their wooden chairs, close to the smelly stove, thinking. They seemed tired. Mostly blond men, freckled on the high cheekbones, with blue eyes, big red ears covered with soft blond fuzz, big heavy noses and wide mouths, they had still, after years away from their mountains, the look of outdoor men. Awkward in repose, their big feet reached out in a dozen queer angles. But even as they lounged silently, their lanky bodies revealed swiftness of action, power in motion.

And indeed these men who sat now, brooding, were said by expert industrial engineers to be the most highly skilled workmen in American mass industry. They built truck tires, partly by machine, partly by hand. They worked at a speed unequaled even in the auto shops. Their tires shoed the busses and heavy motor vans of the world.

In the quiet, the faces of these men were profoundly unhappy. They had been pushed into making plans for desperate action, a final resistance against the way of their lives. Most of them were married, and had three or four young children. During the past years many of them had been off and on relief as they were taken on and laid off again at the factory. Since they were the aristocrats of the rubber shops, they made about $25 a week when they worked—if they worked. They could not feed their growing families on this average annual wage of a thousand dollars or less. With the eight-hour day in the offing, every fourth man would lose his job forever.

Just before midnight the men in the union hall buttoned their jackets and crossed the street to ring in. Murphy had said "No" again to a hasty telephone call. Their minds were made up. The signals were arranged. Everything was ready. Some of the men had trouble slipping their timecards into the punch. They were nervous and their throats felt dry. This was really a hell of a thing they were going to do. Nobody had ever done such a thing before—at least not in this country. It made a man sort of upset.

Promptly at midnight the truck-tire department started work. Under pools of light, the big men stood at their machines. A wheel slowly revolved, as they wound on strips of heavy rubber and fabric. Their hands flashed. Helpers came in quietly and laid piles of carefully folded material beside their machines. Just over their heads, a conveyor belt clattered slowly by. Suspended from the belt were huge thick hooks. Every few minutes, one of the darting hands ripped the finished tire from the machine, slammed it on a hook, and went back to the revolving wheel. Foremen walked slowly up and down the long lines of tirebuilders, checking material, glancing at the finished tires, sending machine repairmen to a faltering wheel.

No human sound came from this vast room. The clatter and shriek and roar of the conveyor belt and the revolving wheels, the drone of motors, the broken rush and squeaking halt of electric factory trucks, drowned out even a brief salute of one worker to another.

But as a flashing hand reached up to slam a tire on the hook, the worker had half a second when his body came near to the tirebuilder on the next machine.

"Two o'clock," a man muttered as he swung up his tire. The tirebuilder next to him did not look up from the revolving wheel. His hands never stopped their expert, rapid motions. He hardly nodded. But when his tire went up to the conveyor belt he said, his face a blank, with such a tight mouth that he might merely have been shifting his wad of chewing tobacco, "Two o'clock."

The man at the next machine never even looked his way. But, a moment later, and this was strange, for he was such an expert workman, he dropped his heavy tire tool. It clattered to the floor quite near the fourth machine. The foreman looked up, his ears trained to pick out of the constant uproar a different, unexpected noise. But he only saw a tirebuilder picking up his tool, brushing against a friend.

"Two o'clock," the clumsy tirebuilder murmured.

After the first hour, the foremen on the truck-tire floor were considerably annoyed when it appeared that two of their best workmen were apparently suffering from kidney trouble. At least they left the floor to go to the washroom; this was nearly unheard of the first hour. A tirebuilder could hardly afford to go to the washroom so early on the shift; because if he went more than once, his pay for the night would take a bad cut.

When they came back, one of them nodded, the barest kind of jerk of the head. Downstairs, in the auto tires, a man on the top machine was saying, as he reached over to grab material, "Two o'clock." And next to him, an auto tirebuilder was dropping his tool and picking it up, saying, through hardly moving lips, "Two o'clock."

A little after one-thirty, a foreman on the truck-tire floor went downstairs to talk to the super on the auto floor. "Everything O.K.?" he asked, shouting in his friend's ear, to be heard.

"I guess so," the foreman from auto tires replied. The two men stood together watching the rows of flashing hands, the rhythmically moving backs. The noise sounded in their ears as familiar music. They knew every variation and could separate the proper drone of the motors from a sudden brief whine of a machine gone sour. Tonight the noise sounded all right.

"I got the jitters, I guess," the super from upstairs said, shaking his big shocky head like a puzzled hunting dog.

"Me,too," the head from the auto tires answered. "I keep feeling there's something phony going on here. But I don't know. The fellows ain't talking any. They're making fast time tonight."

"It's goddamned funny they ain't talking," the upstairs foreman growled. "The last two nights they've been howling about this Dicks guy. Tonight they're as quiet as a bunch of ghosts."

"Yeah," the auto super replied. "I got a feeling somethin's wrong. Them guys is watching us right now."

The two foremen stared at the tirebuilders. Their hands wove the usual quick pattern. Their heads were bent over their piles. To a stranger's eye, they were lost in their work, each man a picture of useful concentration. But to the two foremen, there was something wrong. They felt the side-glances of these men. They felt the impact of a quick flash of eyes. They sensed hostility.

"Listen," the foreman from upstairs said, "if anything goes wrong, I'll close up the fire doors right away. You do the same."

"What's going to go wrong?" the auto super said.

"Nothing," the truck head growled, "but if it should, we don't want nothing to spread."

"Yeah." The auto foreman stood unhappily in the doorway as the upstairs super left. His eyes wandered from one hefty tirebuilder to another. Nothing wrong, he could see. But he felt queer. In his bones, he knew something was coming off. Jesus, it gave a man the creeps watching those guys at their machines and knowing they were watching you back, and hating you, and planning some goddamned trick to upset the shift and maybe lose you your job. He walked down the line, brushing past a dozen tirebuilders. They didn't even look up, but he could feel their backs stiffen as he passed. The sons-of-bitches, they were up to something. But what? What?

It was 1:45 A.M. on January 29, 1936.

Upstairs the foreman passed down the lines, his ears cocked for a murmur, for the barest whisper. He was determined to hustle the first guy he caught even muttering right off the floor and out the gate. Something was mighty wrong tonight; everybody on this whole line was sort of holding his breath. Zero hour. He smiled grimly. Zero hour for what? He was sure getting the jitters lately. But, my God, the company didn't realize how sore these boys were at the rate cut, and you couldn't tell them thick-headed guys in the front office. No, all they'd say was "We hold you accountable for unbroken production in your department." Jesus, was that the way to treat a good loyal company man, threaten to can him if anything went wrong?

The foreman paced slowly past his workmen, his eyes darting in and out of the machines, eager for any betraying gesture. He heard no word, and he saw no gesture. The hands flashed, the backs bent, the arms reached out in monotonous perfection. The foreman went back to his little desk and sat squirming on the smooth-seated swivel chair. He felt profoundly disturbed. Something, he knew, was coming off. But what? For God's sake, what?

It was 1:57 A.M. January 29, 1936.

The tirebuilders worked in smooth frenzy, sweat around their necks, under their arms. The belt clattered, the insufferable racket and din and monotonous clash and uproar went on in steady rhythm. The clock on the south wall, a big plain clock, hesitated, its minute hand jumped to two. A tirebuilder at the end of the line looked up, saw the hand jump. The foreman was sitting quietly staring at the lines of men working under the vast pools of light. Outside, in the winter night, the streets were empty, and the whir of the factory sounded faintly on the snow-swept yard.

The tirebuilder at the end of the line gulped. His hands stopped their quick weaving motions. Every man on the line stiffened. All over the vast room, hands hesitated. The foreman saw the falter, felt it instantly. He jumped up, but he stood beside his desk, his eyes darting quickly from one line to another.

This was it, then. But what was happening? Where was it starting? He stood perfectly still, his heart beating furiously, his throat feeling dry, watching the hesitating hands, watching the broken rhythm.

Then the tirebuilder at the end of the line walked three steps to the master safety switch and, drawing a deep breath, he pulled up the heavy wooden handle. With this signal, in perfect synchronization, with the rhythm they had learned in a great mass-production industry, the tirebuilders stepped back from their machines.

Instantly, the noise stopped. The whole room lay in perfect silence. The tirebuilders stood in long lines, touching each other, perfectly motionless, deafened by the silence. A moment ago there had been the weaving hands, the revolving wheels, the clanking belt, the moving hooks, the flashing tire tools. Now there was absolute stillness, no motion anywhere, no sound.

Out of the terrifying quiet came the wondering voice of a big tirebuilder near the windows: "Jesus Christ, it's like the end of the world."

He broke the spell, the magic moment of stillness. For now his awed words said the same thing to every man, "We done it! We stopped the belt! By God, we done it!" And men began to cheer hysterically, to shout and howl in the fresh silence. Men wrapped long sinewy arms around their neighbors' shoulders, screaming, "We done it! We done it!"

For the first time in history, American mass-production workers had stopped a conveyor belt and halted the inexorable movement of factory machinery.

"John Brown's body," somebody chanted above the cries. The others took it up. "But his soul," they sang, and some of them were nearly weeping, racked with sudden and deep emotion, "but his soul goes marchin' on."

Downstairs, the echo of the song burst on the first quiet. Men heard the faint music and picked up the familiar words. They leaned out the windows into the cold winter's night air. "He is trampling out the vintage where the grapes of wrath are stored," they sang.

Across the street, in the union hall, men ran to the door and heard the faint faraway song, and said, full of wonder and a deep pride, "Jesus Christ! They done it! Listen to 'em! They're singing! They're singing!"

Over the snow-swept yard, in the winds of January, the song floated out to the whole valley, a song that promised never to die away, a song that promised to live on, fresh and unafraid, in the hearts of workingmen, a song that promised to spread from Akron to Detroit, to New York, and across the whole land of America.

"Glory, Glory, Hallelujah!" the tirebuilders sang. "And his soul goes marchin' on."

The foremen heard the song and retreated. They locked the fire doors and, five minutes later, opened them on demand. They were amazed by the organization of these revolting workmen. After the first hysteria had died down, the confusion disappeared at once. The ringleader, the man who switched the current off, climbed on the foreman's desk and shouted, "O.K., fellows. Now any of you guys here who ain't with us can get the hell out right now. Go home and stay home and don't let's see your yellow-livered face around here again. Anybody want to leave?"

Nobody did. "O.K.," the speaker went on. "Now we got a lot of things to do. First, we got to have a committee to visit other departments, and let's have some volunteers who ain't chicken-livered." The whole truck-tire department wanted to go. The leader picked half a dozen. "You go downstairs and combine with the auto boys' committee and, listen, it's up to you guys to shut this whole goddamned plant down, see?"

"O.K.," the speaker continued quickly. "Now we got to have a committee to police the floor. We don't want no machinery broken we can get blamed for, and we got to keep the place clean. No gamblin' for money either, and absolutely no drinking. We frisk everybody who comes in, for bottles. We don't take nobody's word for it. A couple of drunks would make this sitdown strike look punk."

"Sitdown strike," the crowd repeated. It was a good phrase. The tirebuilders had never heard it before. They liked it.

"That's what I call it," the speaker said, "because we're sittin' down, ain't we, instead of working?"

"Yeah," the men answered and grinned.

"Now," the leader went on. "We're going to elect a committee to talk to Murphy. We figure we got to stay shut down until Murphy takes back Dicks and fixes the base rate."

There were murmurs of approval. The speaker added, "One more thing, and it's the biggest thing. Most of you fellows don't belong to the union. I ain't blamin' you. Some learns fast, some learns slow. But this strike was started by union fellows. The union ain't the same one that sold out the boys last year. We threw Green out on his ear, in case you haven't heard. The union belongs to us now. The only way we can get anywhere is to have an industrial union, and everybody in it. We got application cards, lots of 'em right here. Nobody has to join, but I should think it would be a pretty dumb cluck who couldn't see now, in the middle of this strike, that the union means business. O.K., that's all."

It was enough. By three o'clock, the tirebuilders on the late shift belonged to the U.R.W.A. in a body. Downstairs the union delegate was sitting at the foreman's desk issuing brand-new union cards to a long line of laughing excited men. The foreman himself was gone and with him his two assistants. They were sitting in the factory superintendent's office, floors away, twisting their fingers and saying, "Yeah, it's easy to say we should 'a' stopped them, but, my God, it's like a revolution. What can you do? There's hundreds of them and a half a dozen of us."

The factory superintendent's office was a glum place. Every few minutes a new foreman came in, his eyes blazing, his mouth twitching with rage. "I don't know how they found out," the new ones would say. "My God, I had the fire door locked, but all of a sudden, one of them was up there pulling the switch and right away they open the door and this goddamned roving committee comes in and starts to appoint a police committee and pass out union cards, and get them to elect somebody to this here negotiation committee."

Firestone Plant One gradually shut down completely. The departments that didn't actually sitdown and strike were paralyzed by lack of work or materials. The delicate mechanism of mass production was dealt a brutal fatal blow. Engineers had worked for years to synchronize every labor process in the great factory. The most remote departments were dependent on the flow of materials from some other faraway corner of the great plant. But once the line was broken, factory operations came to an uneven jerking halt.

As dawn came, the day-shift workers lined up at the timehouse, punching in their cards. Still dazed with sleep, they stumbled off streetcars, not knowing what had happened inside the walls of the great yellow brick factory. Yet they found out instantly. Murphy could never understand this grapevine telegraph. How did tirebuilders standing patiently in line instantly learn that everything had gone blooey up there in the factory? But they did. And they straightened up, joking and laughing and strutting as they walked. Murphy didn't know whether to let them in or not, and being confused, he did nothing. So the new shift came on, and joined the old sitdowners, the veterans, and listened jealously to their bragging tales of how *they* started it, *they* turned off the current. By noon the men who had come to work at dawn were also veterans, able to lord it over the newcomers.

Murphy was at his wit's end. Once he thought of turning off the steam. But when the tirebuilders heard the hissing sound stop, and felt the pipes grow cold, they began to beat such an inferno of noisy rapping on the pipes that Murphy was afraid. Suppose they got sore and busted up the machinery? He turned the steam back on.

The elevators kept running too. Murphy burned up, but what could he do? The tirebuilders rode downstairs in lordly fashion to the factory cafeteria, and ate good breakfasts, and rode back upstairs picking their teeth and talking in loud pleased voices. Maybe he should starve them out? Murphy thought. But, my God, there were 1,200 tirebuilders actually on strike and, as a matter of fact, most of the workers in the other departments were really striking too, only their departments had just closed down for lack of material. But Murphy knew 'em—they, too, were really strikers at heart. Well, that's a lot of men roaming around inside a factory. Suppose he closed the cafeteria. Could he close it? Maybe they'd fight to keep it open. They probably would. Even if he could close it, could he really starve them out? Wouldn't that make them even sorer and wouldn't the guys outside who sympathized—and there were plenty of them—wouldn't they rush the factory with food?

My God, Murphy thought, what does a factory superintendent do on a spot like this? He simply didn't know, this sad pioneer, this superintendent faced with America's first industrial sitdown strike.

The strikers themselves were surprised and jubilant when they found so little resistance. They owned the factory. Nobody dared say them nay. So they used power carefully. Clean-up squads kept the factory floors shining. The police committee looked darkly at a man who so much as swore. A tirebuilder, leaning on his machine to watch a tong game was warned by every other man on strike, "Watch out. Don't bust nothin'." Abashed sitdowners apologized to the union committee for suggesting poker at a penny limit.

By a little after noon, the tire floors were so crowded a man could hardly find a place to sit down. Three shifts were on sitdown duty and men from the fourth shift illicitly sneaked past the gates and came up to get in on the excitement. Runners carried news between the sitdowners and the union hall. So-and-so's wife had called up to say more power to you, stick it out.

About one o'clock the next morning, the end of the first day, the strike committee decided that some of the sitdowners should leave to get a little sleep. Apparently the management would continue to let strikers in and out of the big plant. The committee divided the men into shifts: about half the sitdowners marched out the factory to go into South Akron and Kenmore and get a clean shirt, some sleep, and a chance to tell the world what was happening at Firestone.

Next day they returned, looking fresh, to relieve their comrades standing guard over their machines. All during the second day the strikers sat around at machines singing, playing cards, listening to speeches, and signing union cards. They ate in the factory cafeteria, and some of them caught cat-naps on newspapers stretched out on cement floors.

While they ate and slept and played cards, the news of the sitdown strike spread through Akron. The newspapers carried awestruck and rather incomplete accounts of the amazing strike, but few feature writers penetrated to the sitdown area, no pictures were printed of wives kissing their husbands through fences. The newspapers stuck to baffled and sketchy reports of an incident that they did not understand very well but feared very much.

East Akron, South Akron, Kenmore Hill, and Barberton did not depend on the newspaper stories of the great sitdown strike. The sitdowners themselves came home for shaves and clean underwear, and they spread the story with feverish excitement. Goodyear tirebuilders sat patiently downstairs in little frame houses for hours waiting for a Firestone sitdowner to wake up and tell them all about it. The Firestone local hall was jammed day and night, and men worked twenty hours of twenty-four signing up new members and explaining how the sitdown worked.

The valleys seethed with the story. Women ran, bundled up in old coats, across their front yards, to call on their neighbors and tell them what was going on at Firestone. Little boys boasted in school recess that their Pops were sitting down in the truck-tire department, and other small boys all but burst with envy and rushed home screaming, "Pa, why can't you sitdown?"

The management of the rubber shops were stunned by the news. Here was something they had never heard of before, something frightening and queer. How did you deal with it? How did you break it up? One thing they were sure of: Firestone must be very firm. Not by any chance should the sitdowners be allowed to think they had won their peculiar strike. That would be fatal. That would give the new idea just the proper halo of success to make it spread, and then heaven only knew what would happen next.

The Firestone management agreed at first. For twenty-four hours Murphy refused even to discuss settlement with the negotiation committee. He said the plant would have to be cleared before he would talk about the Dicks case or the base rate either. The second twenty-four hours Murphy began to change his mind. It was all very well for Goodrich and Goodyear to beef about being firm and holding out and standing together. They were making tires, and he wasn't. Their factories were running smoothly and his was a bedlam.

Still Murphy hesitated. But at the beginning of the third full day of the sitdown, after fifty-three hours, his foremen brought terrible news. All of Plant Two was ready to sitdown in sympathy unless there was an immediate settlement. The Plant Two pitworkers had already voted to stand by their curing boxes and cut off the steam. Murphy shuddered, and in his mind's eye, he could see the beginning of a real strike, a strike for union recognition or something of the kind. His spies told him there was plenty of talk about spreading the strike and increasing the demands. Now this terrible news about the men in Plant Two!

Murphy sent for the negotiating committee and consigned to hell the opinions of his fellow factory superintendents at Goodrich and Goodyear. It was all very well to talk about a solid employer front, but in the face of something like this, a man had to act quickly or the whole situation would simply blow up in his face.

The settlement allowed Dicks' immediate reinstatement and three hours' pay for every day lost. It promised immediate negotiation on the base rate. It offered three hours' pay per day to all workers who had lost time during the sitdown.

When the committee, breathless and excited, brought the news to the men up in the truck-tire department for a vote, they could hardly talk, they were so jubilant. And the strikers were quite beside themselves. They were getting paid, paid, mind you, for sittingdown! And Dicks was back, with pay. And the rate would be negotiated. Glory Hallelujah!

The sitdowners marched out singing, and the sound of their voices went everywhere in the valley. The Firestone sitdowners had won! They won! They won! This sitdown business worked.

Migrant family of the Depression era

JOHN STEINBECK

The Grapes of Wrath

(1939)

In the fall of 1933, farms across the treeless plains that stretch from the Dakotas to Texas began to blow away. During World War I and in the twenties, modern machinery had transformed these grasslands, once the preserve of cowboys and their great herds of cattle, into a vast wheat bowl. Then in the thirties came four years of drought and heat followed by as many of drought and wind. Black wind-driven clouds of topsoil darkened the skies as far east as Albany, New York, turning the wheat bowl into a dust bowl. Hundreds of thousands of

people, many of them formerly independent farmers, suddenly found themselves without homes or livelihoods, with no choice but to pile their families and meager belongings into cars and pickup trucks and head west where the sky did not blacken and the ground stayed moist. They traveled, these poor farmers and their families, along Route 66 or up the Old Spanish Trail from El Paso through the mountain passes and into California, thinking they were on the brink of opportunity. Instead they discovered that they were "Okies": despised, feared, and unwanted except at the harvest season. "California," **sang Woody Guthrie,**

is a garden of Eden,
A paradise to live in or see.
But believe it or not
You won't find it so hot,
If you ain't got the do-re-mi.

The plight of these "Okies" offered a perfect model for the sufferings of the Depression. Here was the old America of small farms and hard work brought to grief by faults in the economic system, natural catastrophes, and the failure of men to extend their sympathies to the downtrodden. Out of all this, John Steinbeck fashioned the one epic novel of the Depression. A best seller in 1939, The Grapes of Wrath remains the lasting book of the era. While other writers struggled to create meaningful "proletarian" novels and produced only tracts for the time, Steinbeck somehow forced his sympathy for the whole fading world of agrarian America to dominate his outrage over the cruelty and destruction of the Great Depression. The Joads' odyssey had the character of folk epic: casualties of the Depression, the Joads were also figures from a deep past, looked upon as primitive Americans. Readers—in 1939 and since—could feel both close to and very distant from them in their battered truck on the sad American highway.

I

The spring is beautiful in California. Valleys in which the fruit blossoms are fragrant pink and white waters in a shallow sea. Then the first tendrils of the grapes, swelling from the old gnarled vines, cascade down to cover the trunks. The full green hills are round and soft as breasts. And on the level vegetable lands are the mile-long rows of pale green lettuce and the spindly little cauliflowers, the gray-green unearthly artichoke plants.

And then the leaves break out on the trees, and the petals drop from the fruit trees and carpet the earth with pink and white. The centers of the blossoms swell and grow and color: cherries and apples, peaches and pears, figs which close the flower in the fruit. All California quickens with produce, and the fruit grows heavy, and the limbs bend gradually under the fruit so that little crutches must be placed under them to support the weight.

Behind the fruitfulness are men of understanding and knowledge and skill, men who experiment with seed, endlessly developing the techniques for greater crops of plants whose roots will resist the million enemies of the earth: the molds, the insects, the rusts, the blights. These men work carefully and endlessly to perfect the seed, the roots. And there are the men of chemistry who spray the trees against pests, who sulphur the grapes, who cut out disease and rots, mildews and sicknesses. Doctors of preventive medicine, men at the borders who look for fruit flies, for Japanese beetle, men who quarantine the sick trees and root them out and burn them, men of knowledge. The men who graft the young trees, the little vines, are the cleverest of all, for theirs is a surgeon's job, as tender and delicate; and these men must have surgeons' hands and surgeons' hearts to slit the bark, to place the grafts, to bind the wounds and cover them from the air. These are great men.

Along the rows, the cultivators move, tearing the spring grass and turning it under to make a fertile earth, breaking the ground to hold the water up near the surface, ridging the ground in little pools for the irrigation, destroying the weed roots that may drink the water away from the trees.

And all the time the fruit swells and the flowers break out in long clusters on the vines. And in the growing year the warmth grows and the leaves turn dark green. The prunes lengthen like little green bird's eggs, and the limbs sag down against the crutches under the weight. And the hard little pears take shape, and the beginning of the fuzz comes out on the peaches. Grape blossoms shed their tiny petals and the hard little beads become green buttons, and the buttons grow heavy. The men who work in the fields, the owners of the little orchards, watch and calculate. The year is heavy with produce. And men are proud, for of their knowledge they can make the year heavy.

They have transformed the world with their knowledge. The short, lean wheat has been made big and productive. Little sour apples have grown large and sweet, and that old grape that grew among the trees and fed the birds its tiny fruit has mothered a thousand varieties, red and black, green and pale pink, purple and yellow; and each variety with its own flavor. The men who work in the experimental farms have made new fruits: nectarines and forty kinds of plums, walnuts with paper shells. And always they work, selecting, grafting, changing, driving themselves, driving the earth to produce.

And first the cherries ripen. Cent and a half a pound. Hell, we can't pick 'em for that. Black cherries and red cherries, full and sweet, and the birds eat half of each cherry and the yellowjackets buzz into the holes the birds made. And on the ground the seeds drop and dry with black shreds hanging from them.

The purple prunes soften and sweeten. My God, we can't pick them and dry and sulphur them. We can't pay wages, no matter what wages. And the purple prunes carpet the ground. And first the skins wrinkle a little and swarms of flies come to feast, and the valley is filled with the odor of sweet decay. The meat turns dark and the crop shrivels on the ground.

And the pears grow yellow and soft. Five dollars a ton. Five dollars for forty fifty-pound boxes; trees pruned and sprayed, orchards cultivated—pick the fruit, put it in boxes, load the trucks, deliver the fruit to the cannery—forty boxes for five dollars. We can't do it. And the yellow fruit falls heavily to the ground and splashes on the ground. The yellowjackets dig into the soft meat, and there is a smell of ferment and rot.

Then the grapes—we can't make good wine. People can't buy good wine. Rip the grapes from the vines, good grapes, rotten grapes, wasp-stung grapes. Press stems, press dirt and rot.

But there's mildew and formic acid in the vats.

Add sulphur and tannic acid.

The smell from the ferment is not the rich odor of wine, but the smell of decay and chemicals.

Oh, well. It has alcohol in it, anyway. They can get drunk.

The little farmers watched debt creep up on them like the tide. They sprayed the trees and sold no crop, they pruned and grafted and could not pick the crop. And the men of knowledge have worked, have considered, and the fruit is rotting on the ground, and the decaying mash in the wine vats is poisoning the air. And taste the wine—no grape flavor at all, just sulphur and tannic acid and alcohol.

This little orchard will be a part of a great holding next year, for the debt will have choked the owner.

This vineyard will belong to the bank. Only the great owners can survive, for they own the canneries too. And four pears peeled and cut in half, cooked and canned, still cost fifteen cents. And the canned pears do not spoil. They will last for years.

The decay spreads over the State, and the sweet smell is a great sorrow on the land. Men who can graft the trees and make the seed fertile and big can find no way to let the hungry people eat their produce. Men who have created new fruits in the world cannot create a system whereby their fruits may be eaten. And the failure hangs over the State like a great sorrow.

The works of the roots of the vines, of the trees, must be destroyed to keep up the price, and this is the saddest, bitterest thing of all. Carloads of oranges dumped on the ground. The people came for miles to take the fruit, but this could not be. How would they buy oranges at twenty cents a dozen if they could drive out and pick them up? And men with hoses squirt kerosene on the oranges, and they are angry at the crime, angry at the people who have come to take the fruit. A million people hungry, needing the fruit—and kerosene sprayed over the golden mountains.

And the smell of rot fills the country.

Burn coffee for fuel in the ships. Burn corn to keep warm, it makes a hot fire. Dump potatoes in the rivers and place guards along the banks to keep the hungry people from fishing them out. Slaughter the pigs and bury them, and let the putrescence drip down into the earth.

There is a crime here that goes beyond denunciation. There is a sorrow here that weeping cannot symbolize. There is a failure here that topples all our success. The fertile earth, the straight tree rows, the sturdy trunks, and the ripe fruit. And children dying of pellagra must die because a profit cannot be taken from an orange. And coroners must fill in the certificates—died of malnutrition—because the food must rot, must be forced to rot.

The people come with nets to fish for potatoes in the river, and the guards hold them back; they come in rattling cars to get the dumped oranges, but the kerosene is sprayed. And they stand still and watch the potatoes float by, listen to the screaming pigs being killed in a ditch and covered with quicklime, watch the mountains of oranges slop down to a putrefying ooze; and in the eyes of the people there is the failure; and in the eyes of the hungry there is a growing wrath. In the souls of the people the grapes of wrath are filling and growing heavy, growing heavy for the vintage.

II

In the Weedpatch camp, on an evening when the long, barred clouds hung over the set sun and inflamed their edges, the Joad family lingered after their supper. Ma hesitated before she started to do the dishes.

"We got to do somepin," she said. And she pointed at Winfield. "Look at 'im," she said. And when they stared at the little boy, "He's a-jerkin' an' a-twistin' in his sleep. Lookut his color." The members of the family looked at the earth again in shame. "Fried dough," Ma said. "One month we been here. An' Tom had five days' work. An' the rest of you scrabblin' out ever' day, an' no work. An' scairt to talk. An' the money gone. You're scairt to talk it out. Ever' night you jus' eat, an' then you get wanderin' away. Can't bear to talk it out. Well, you got to. Rosasharn ain't far from due, an' lookut her color. You got to talk it out. Now don't none of you get up till we figger somepin out. One day' more grease an' two days' flour, an' ten potatoes. You set here an' get busy!"

They looked at the ground. Pa cleaned his thick nails with his pocket knife. Uncle John picked at a splinter on the box he sat on. Tom pinched his lower lip and pulled it away from his teeth.

He released his lip and said softly, "We been a-lookin', Ma. Been walkin' out sence we can't use the gas no more. Been goin' in ever' gate, walkin' up to ever' house, even when we knowed they wasn't gonna be nothin'. Puts a weight on ya. Goin' out lookin' for somepin you know you ain't gonna find."

Ma said fiercely. "You ain't got the right to get discouraged. This here fambly's goin' under. You jus' ain't got the right."

Pa inspected his scraped nail. "We gota go," he said. "We didn' wanta go. It's nice here, an' folks is nice here. We're feared we'll have to go live in one a them Hoovervilles."

"Well, if we got to, we got to. First thing is, we got to eat."

Al broke in. "I got a tankful gas in the truck. I didn' let nobody get into that."

Tom smiled. "This here Al got a lot of sense along with he's randy-pandy."

"Now you figger," Ma said. "I ain't watchin' this here fambly starve no more. One day' more grease. That's what we got. Come time for Rosasharn to lay in, she got to be fed up. You figger!"

"This here hot water an' toilets—" Pa began.

"Well, we can't eat no toilets."

Tom said, "They was a fella come by today lookin' for men to go to Marysville. Pickin' fruit."

"Well, why don' we go to Marysville?" Ma demanded.

"I dunno," said Tom. "Didn' seem right, somehow. He was so anxious. Wouldn' say how much the pay was. Said he didn' know exactly."

Ma said, "We're a-goin' to Marysville. I don' care what the pay is. We're a-goin'."

"It's too far," said Tom. "We ain't got the money for gasoline. We couldn' get there. Ma, you say we got to figger. I ain't done nothin' but figger the whole time."

Uncle John said, "Feller says they's cotton a-comin' in up north, near a place called Tulare. That ain't very far, the feller says."

"Well, we got to git goin', an' goin' quick. I ain't a-settin' here no longer, no matter how nice." Ma took up her bucket and walked toward the sanitary unit for hot water.

"Ma gets tough," Tom said. "I seen her a-gettin' mad quite a piece now. She jus' boils up."

Pa said with relief, "Well, she brang it into the open, anyways. I been layin' at night a-burnin' my brains up. Now we can talk her out, anyways."

Ma came back with her bucket of steaming water. "Well," she demanded, "figger anything out?"

"Jus' workin' her over," said Tom. "Now s'pose we jus' move up north where that cotton's at. We been over this here country. We know they ain't nothin' here. S'pose we pack up an' shove north. Then when the cotton's ready, we'll be there. I kinda like to get my han's aroun' some cotton. You got a full tank, Al?"

"Almos'—'bout two inches down."

"Should get us up to that place."

Ma poised a dish over the bucket. "Well?" she demanded.

Tom said, "You win. We'll move on, I guess. Huh, Pa?"

"Guess we got to," Pa said.

Ma glanced at him. "When?"

"Well—no need waitin'. Might's well go in the mornin'."

"We got to go in the mornin'. I tol' you what's lef'."

"Now, Ma, don' think I don' wanta go. I ain't had a good gutful to eat in two weeks. 'Course I filled up, but I didn' take no good from it."

Ma plunged the dish into the bucket. "We'll go in the mornin'," she said.

Pa sniffed. "Seems like times is changed," he said sarcastically. "Time was when a man said what we'd do. Seems like women is tellin' now. Seems like it's purty near time to get out a stick."

Ma put the clean dripping tin-dish out on a box. She smiled down at her work. "You get your stick, Pa," she said. "Times when they's food an' a place to set, then maybe you can use your stick an' keep your skin whole. But you ain't a-doin' your job, either a-thinkin' or a-workin'. If you was, why, you could use your stick, an' women folks'd sniffle their nose an' creep-mouse aroun'. But you jus' get you a stick now an' you ain't lickin' no woman; you're a-fightin', 'cause I got a stick all laid out too."

Pa grinned with embarassment. "Now it ain't good to have the little fellas hear you talkin' like that," he said.

"You get some bacon inside the little fellas 'fore you come tellin' what else is good for 'em," said Ma.

Pa got up in disgust and moved away, and Uncle John followed him.

Ma's hands were busy in the water, but she watched them go, and she said proudly to Tom, "He's all right. He ain't beat. He's like as not to take a smack at me."

Tom laughed. "You jus' a-treadin' him on?"

"Sure," said Ma. "Take a man, he can get worried an' worried, an' it eats out his liver, an' purty soon he'll jus' lay down and die with his heart et out. But if you can take an' make 'im mad, why, he'll be awright. Pa, he didn' say nothin', but he's mad now. He'll show me now. He's awright."

Al got up. "I'm gonna walk down the row," he said.

"Better see the truck's ready to go," Tom warned him.

"She's ready."

"If she ain't, I'll turn Ma on ya."

"She's ready." Al strolled jauntily along the row of tents.

Tom sighed. "I'm a-gettin' tired, Ma. How 'bout makin' me mad?"

"You got more sense, Tom. I don' need to make you mad. I got to lean on you. Them others—they're kinda strangers, all but you. You won't give up, Tom."

The job fell on him. "I don' like it," he said. "I wanta go out like Al. An' I wanta get mad like Pa, an' I wanta get drunk like Uncle John."

Ma shook her head. "You can't, Tom. I know. I knowed from the time you was a little fella. You can't. They's some folks that's just theirself an' nothin' more. There's Al—he's jus' a young fella after a girl. You wasn't never like that, Tom."

"Sure I was," said Tom. "Still am."

"No you ain't. Ever'thing you do is more'n you. When they sent you to prison I knowed it. You're spoke for."

"Now, Ma—cut it out. It ain't true. It's all in your head."

She stacked the knives and forks on top of the plates. "Maybe. Maybe it's in my head. Rosasharn, you wipe up these here an' put 'em away."

The girl got breathlessly to her feet and her swollen middle hung out in front of her. She moved sluggishly to the box and picked up a washed dish.

Tom said, "Gettin' so tightful it's a-pullin' her eyes wide."

"Don't you go a-jollyin'," said Ma. "She's doin' good. You go 'long an' say goo'-by to anybody you wan'."

"O.K.," he said. "I'm gonna see how far it is up there."

Ma said to the girl, "He ain't sayin' stuff like that to make you feel bad. Where's Ruthie an' Winfiel'?"

"They snuck off after Pa. I seen 'em."

"Well, leave 'em go."

Rose of Sharon moved sluggishly about her work. Ma inspected her cautiously. "You feelin' pretty good? Your cheeks is kinda saggy."

"I ain't had milk like they said I ought."

"I know. We jus' didn' have no milk."

Rose of Sharon said dully, "Ef Connie hadn't went away, we'd a had a little house by now, with him studyin' an' all. Would a got milk like I need. Would a had a nice baby. This here baby ain't gonna be no good. I ought a had milk." She reached in her apron pocket and put something into her mouth.

Ma said, "I seen you nibblin' on somepin. What you eatin'?"

"Nothin'."

"Come on, what you nibblin' on?"

"Jus' a piece a slack lime. Foun' a big hunk."

"Why, tha's just like eatin' dirt."

"I kinda feel like I wan' it."

Ma was silent. She spread her knees and tightened her skirt. "I know," she said at last. "I et coal oncet when I was in a fambly way. Et a big piece of coal. Granma says I shouldn'. Don' you say that about the baby. You got no right even to think it."

"Got no husban'! Got no milk!"

Ma said, "If you was a well girl, I'd take a whang at you. Right in the face." She got up and went inside the tent. She came out and stood in front of Rose of Sharon, and she held out her hand. "Look!" The small gold earrings were in her hand. "These is for you."

The girl's eyes brightened for a moment, and then she looked aside. "I ain't pierced."

"Well, I'm a-gonna pierce ya." Ma hurried back into the tent. She came back with a cardboard box. Hurriedly she threaded a needle, doubled the thread and tied a series of knots in it. She threaded a second needle and knotted the thread. In the box she found a piece of cork.

"It'll hurt. It'll hurt."

Ma stepped to her, put the cork in back of the ear lobe and pushed the needle through the ear, into the cork.

The girl twitched. "It sticks. It'll hurt."

"No more'n that."

"Yes, it will."

"Well, then. Le's see the other ear first." She placed the cork and pierced the other ear.

"It'll hurt."

"Hush!" said Ma. "It's all done."

Rose of Sharon looked at her in wonder. Ma clipped the needles off and pulled one knot of each thread through the lobes.

"Now," she said. "Ever' day we'll pull one knot, and in a couple weeks it'll be all well an' you can wear 'em. Here—they're your'n now. You can keep 'em."

Rose of Sharon touched her ears tenderly and looked at the tiny spots of blood on her fingers. "It didn' hurt. Jus' stuck a little."

"You oughta been pierced long ago," said Ma. She looked at the girl's face, and she smiled in triumph. "Now get them dishes all done up. Your baby gonna be a good baby. Very near let you have a baby without yours ears was pierced. But you're safe now."

"Does it mean somepin?"

"Why, 'course it does," said Ma. "'Course it does."

Al strolled down the street toward the dancing platform. Outside a neat little tent he whistled softly, and then moved along the street. He walked to the edge of the grounds and sat down in the grass.

The clouds over the west had lost the red edging now, and the cores were black. Al scratched his legs and looked toward the evening sky.

In a few moments a blond girl walked near; she was pretty and sharp-featured. She sat down in the grass beside him and did not speak. Al put his hand on her waist and walked his fingers around.

"Don't," she said. "You tickle."

"We're goin' away tomorra," said Al.

She looked at him, startled. "Tomorra? Where?"

"Up north," he said lightly.

"Well, we're gonna git married, ain't we?"

"Sure, sometime."

"You said purty soon!" she cried angrily.

"Well, soon is when soon comes."

"You promised." He walked his fingers around farther. "Git away," she cried. "You said we was."

"Well, sure we are."

"An' now you're goin' away."

Al demanded, "What's the matter with you? You in a fambly way?"

"No, I ain't."

Al laughed. "I jus' been wastin' my time, huh?"

Her chin shot out. She jumped to her feet. "You git away from me, Al Joad. I don' wanta see you no more."

"Aw, come on. What's the matter?"

"You think you're jus'—hell on wheels."

"Now wait a minute."

"You think I got to go out with you. Well, I don't! I got lots a chances."

"Now wait a minute."

"No, sir—you git away."

Al lunged suddenly, caught her by the ankle, and tripped her. He grabbed her when she fell and held her and put his hand over her angry mouth. She tried to bite his palm, but he cupped it out over her mouth, and he held her down with his other arm. And in a moment she lay still, and in another moment they were giggling together in the dry grass.

"Why, we'll be a-comin' back purty soon," said Al. "An' I'll have a pocketful a jack. We'll go down to Hollywood an' see the pitchers."

She was lying on her back. Al bent over her. And he saw the bright evening star reflected in her eyes, and he saw the black cloud reflected in her eyes. "We'll go on the train," he said.

"How long ya think it'll be?" she asked.
"Oh, maybe a month," he said.

The evening dark came down and Pa and Uncle John squatted with the heads of families out by the office. They studied the night and the future. The little manager, in his white clothes, frayed and clean, rested his elbows on the porch rail. His face was drawn and tired.

Huston looked up at him. "You better get some sleep, mister."

"I guess I ought. Baby born last night in Unit Three. I'm getting to be a good midwife."

"Fella oughta know," said Huston. "Married fella got to know."

Pa said, "We're a-gittin' out in the mornin'."

"Yeah? Which way you goin'?"

"Thought we'd go up north a little. Try to get in the first cotton. We ain't had work. We're outa food."

"Know if they's any work?" Huston asked.

"No, but we're sure they ain't none here."

"They will be, a little later," Huston said. "We'll hold on."

"We hate to go," said Pa. "Folks been so nice here—an' the toilets an' all. But we got to eat. Got a tank of gas. That'll get us a little piece up the road. We had a bath ever' day here. Never was so clean in my life. Funny thing—use ta be I on'y got a bath ever' week an' I never seemed to stink. But now if I don't get one ever' day I stink. Wonder if takin' a bath so often makes that?"

"Maybe you couldn't smell yourself before," the manager said.

"Maybe. I wisht we could stay."

The little manager held his temples between his palms. "I think there's going to be another baby tonight," he said.

"We gonna have one in our fambly 'fore long," said Pa. "I wisht we could have it here. I sure wisht we could."

Tom and Willie and Jule the half-breed sat on the edge of the dance floor and swung their feet.

"I got a sack of Durham," Jule said. "Like a smoke?"

"I sure would," said Tom. "Ain't had a smoke for a hell of a time." He rolled the brown cigarette carefully, to keep down the loss of tobacco.

"Well, sir, we'll be sorry to see you go," said Willy. "You folks is good folks."

Tom lighted his cigarette. "I been thinkin' about it a lot. Jesus Christ, I wisht we could settle down."

Jule took back his Durham. "It ain't nice," he said. "I got a little girl. Thought when I come out here she'd get some schoolin'. But hell, we ain't in one place hardly long enough. Jes' gits goin' an' we got to drag on."

"I hope we don't get in no more Hoovervilles," said Tom. "I was really scairt, there."

"Deputies push you aroun'?"

"I was scairt I'd kill somebody," said Tom. "Was on'y there a little while, but I was a-stewin' aroun' the whole time. Depity come in an' picked up a frien', jus' because he talked outa turn. I was jus' stewin' all the time."

"Ever been in a strike?" Willie asked.

"No."

"Well, I been a-thinkin' a lot. Why don' them depities get in here an' raise hell like ever' place else? Think that little guy in the office is a-stoppin' 'em? No, sir."

"Well, what is?" Jule asked.

"I'll tell ya. It's 'cause we're all a-workin' together. Depity can't pick on one fella in this camp. He's pickin' on the whole darn camp. An' he don't dare. All we got to do is give a yell an' they's two hunderd men out. Fella organizin' for the union was a-talkin' out on the road. He says we could do that any place. Jus' stick together. They ain't raisin' hell with no two hunderd men. They're pickin' on one man."

"Yeah," said Jule, "an' suppose you got a union? You got to have leaders. They'll jus' pick up your leaders, an' where's your union?"

"Well," said Willie, "we got to figure her out some time. I been out here a year, an' wages is goin' right on down. Fella can't feed his fam'ly on his work now, an' it's gettin' worse all the time. It ain't gonna do no good to set aroun' an' starve. I don' know what to do. If a fella owns a team a horses, he don't raise no hell if he got to feed 'em when they ain't workin'. But if a fella got men workin' for him, he jus' don't give a damn. Horses is a hell of a lot more worth than men. I don' understan' it."

"Gets so I don' wanta think about it," said Jule. "An' I got to think about it. I got this here little girl. You know how purty she is. One week they give her a prize in this camp 'cause she's so purty. Well, what's gonna happen to her? She's gettin' spindly. I ain't gonna stan' it. She's so purty. I'm gonna bust out."

"How?" Willie asked. "What you gonna do—steal some stuff an' git in jail? Kill somebody an' git hung?"

"I don' know," said Jule. "Gits me nuts thinkin' about it. Gits me clear nuts."

"I'm a-gonna miss them dances," Tom said. "Them was some of the nicest dances I ever seen. Well, I'm gonna turn in. So long. I'll be seein' you someplace." He shook hands.

"Sure will," said Jule.

"Well, so long." Tom moved away into the darkness.

In the darkness of the Joad tent Ruthie and Winfield lay on their mattress, and Ma lay beside them. Ruthie whispered, "Ma!"

"Yeah? Ain't you asleep yet?"

"Ma—they gonna have croquet where we're goin'?"
"I don' know. Get some sleep. We want to get an early start."
"Well, I wisht we'd stay here where we're sure we got croquet."
"Sh!" said Ma.
"Ma, Winfiel' hit a kid tonight."
"He shouldn' of."
"I know. I tol' 'im, but he hit the kid right in the nose an', Jesus, how the blood run down!"
"Don' talk like that. It ain't a nice way to talk."
Winfield turned over. "That kid says we was Okies," he said in an outraged voice. "He says he wasn't no Okie 'cause he come from Oregon. Says we was goddamn Okies. I socked him."
"Sh! You shouldn'. He can't hurt you callin' names."
"Well, I won't let 'im," Winfield said fiercely.
"Sh! Get some sleep."
Ruthie said, "You oughta seen the blood run down—all over his clothes."
Ma reached a hand from under the blanket and snapped Ruthie on the cheek with her finger. The little girl went rigid for a moment, and then dissolved into sniffling, quiet crying.

In the sanitary unit Pa and Uncle John sat in adjoining compartments. "Might's well get in a good las' one," said Pa. "It's sure nice. 'Member how the little fellas was so scairt when they flushed 'em the first time?"
"I wasn't so easy myself," said Uncle John. He pulled his overalls neatly up around his knees. "I'm gettin' bad," he said. "I feel sin."
"You can't sin none," said Pa. "You ain't got no money. Jus' sit tight. Cos' you at leas' two bucks to sin, an' we ain't got two bucks amongst us."
"Yeah! But I'm a-thinkin' sin."
"Awright. You can think sin for nothin'."
"It's jus' as bad," said Uncle John.
"It's a whole hell of a lot cheaper," said Pa.
"Don't you go makin' light of sin."
"I ain't. You jus' go ahead. You always gets sinful jus' when hell's a-poppin'."
"I know it," said Uncle John. "Always was that way. I never tol' half the stuff I done."
"Well, keep it to yaself."
"These here nice toilets gets me sinful."
"Go out in the bushes then. Come on, pull up ya pants an' le's get some sleep." Pa pulled his overall straps in place and snapped the buckle. He flushed the toilet and watched thoughtfully while the water whirled in the bowl.

It was still dark when Ma roused her camp. The low night lights shone through the open doors of the sanitary units. From the tents along the road came the assorted snores of the campers.

Ma said, "Come on, roll out. We got to be on our way. Day's not far off." She raised the screechy shade of the lantern and lighted the wick. "Come on, all of you."

The floor of the tent squirmed into slow action. Blankets and comforts were thrown back and sleepy eyes squinted blindly at the light. Ma slipped on her dress over the underclothes she wore to bed. "We got no coffee," she said. "I got a few biscuits. We can eat 'em on the road. Jus' get up now, an' we'll load the truck. Come on now. Don't make no noise. Don' wanta wake the neighbors."

It was a few moments before they were fully aroused. "Now don' you get away," Ma warned the children. The family dressed. The men pulled down the tarpaulin and loaded up the truck. "Make it nice an' flat," Ma warned them. They piled the mattress on top of the load and bound the tarpaulin in place over its ridge pole.

"Awright, Ma," said Tom. "She's ready."

Ma held a plate of cold biscuits in her hand. "Awright. Here. Each take one. It's all we got."

Ruthie and Winfield grabbed their biscuits and climbed up on the load. They covered themselves with a blanket and went back to sleep, still holding the cold hard biscuits in their hands. Tom got into the driver's seat and stepped on the starter. It buzzed a little, and then stopped.

"Goddamn you, Al!" Tom cried. "You let the battery run down."

Al blustered, "How the hell was I gonna keep her up if I ain't got gas to run her?"

Tom chuckled suddenly. "Well, I don' know how, but it's your fault. You got to crank her."

"I tell you it ain't my fault."

Tom got out and found the crank under the seat. "It's my fault," he said.

"Gimme that crank." Al seized it. "Pull down the spark so she don't take my arm off."

"O.K. Twist her tail."

Al labored at the crank, around and around. The engine caught, spluttered, and roared as Tom choked the car delicately. He raised the spark and reduced the throttle.

Ma climbed in beside him. "We woke up ever'body in the camp," she said.

"They'll go to sleep again."

Al climbed in on the other side. "Pa 'n' Uncle John got up top," he said. "Goin' to sleep again."

Tom drove toward the main gate. The watchman came out of the office and played his flashlight on the truck. "Wait a minute."

"What ya want?"

"You checkin' out?"

"Sure."

"Well, I got to cross you off."

"O.K."

"Know which way you're goin'?"

"Well, we're gonna try up north."

"Well, good luck," said the watchman.

"Same to you. So long."

The truck edged slowly over the big hump and into the road. Tom retraced the road he had driven before, past Weedpatch and west until he came to 99, then north on the great paved road, toward Bakersfield. It was growing light when he came into the outskirts of the city.

Tom said, "Ever' place you look is restaurants. An' them places all got coffee. Lookit that all-nighter there. Bet they got ten gallons a coffee in there, all hot!"

"Aw, shut up," said Al.

Tom grinned over at him. "Well, I see you got yaself a girl right off."

"Well, what of it?"

"He's mean this mornin', Ma. He ain't good company."

Al said irritably. "I'm goin' out on my own purty soon. Fella can make his way lot easier if he ain't got a fambly."

Tom said, "You'd have yaself a fambly in nine months. I seen you playin' aroun'."

"Ya crazy," said Al. "I'd get myself a job in a garage an' I'd eat in restaurants——"

"An' you'd have a wife an' kid in nine months."

"I tell ya I wouldn'."

Tom said, "You're a wise guy, Al. You gonna take some beatin' over the head."

"Who's gonna do it?"

"They'll always be guys to do it," said Tom.

"You think jus' because you——"

"Now you jus' stop that," Ma broke in.

"I done it," said Tom. "I was a-badgerin' him. I didn't mean no harm, Al. I didn' know you like that girl so much."

"I don't like no girls much."

"Awright, then, you don't. You ain't gonna get no argument out of me."

The truck came to the edge of the city. "Look a them hot-dog stan's—hunderds of 'em," said Tom.

Ma said, "Tom! I got a dollar put away. You wan' coffee bad enough to spen' it?"

"No, Ma. I'm jus' foolin'."

"You can have it if you wan' it bad enough."

"I wouldn' take it."

Al said, "Then shut up about coffee."

Tom was silent for a time. "Seems like I got my foot in it all the time," he said. "There's the road we run up that night."

"I hope we don't never have nothin' like that again," said Ma. "That was a bad night."

"I didn' like it none either."

The sun rose on their right, and the great shadow of the truck ran beside them, flicking over the fence posts beside the road. They ran on past the rebuilt Hooverville.

"Look," said Tom. "They got new people there. Looks like the same place."

Al came slowly out of his sullenness. "Fella tol' me some a them people been burned out fifteen-twenty times. Says they jus' go hide down the willows an' then they come out an' build 'em another weed shack. Jus' like gophers. Got so use' to it they don't even get mad no more, this fella says. They jus' figger it's like bad weather."

"Sure was bad weather for me that night," said Tom. They moved up the wide highway. And the sun's warmth made them shiver. "Gettin' snappy in the mornin'," said Tom. "Winter's on the way. I jus' hope we can get some money 'fore it comes. Tent ain't gonna be nice in the winter."

Ma sighed, and then she straightened her head. "Tom," she said, "we gotta have a house in the winter. I tell ya we got to. Ruthie's awright, but Winfiel' ain't so strong. We got to have a house when the rains come. I heard it jus' rains cats aroun' here."

"We'll get a house, Ma. You res' easy. You gonna have a house."

"Jus' so's it's got a roof an' a floor. Jus' to keep the little fellas off'n the groun'."

"We'll try, Ma."

"I don' wanna worry ya now."

"We'll try, Ma."

"I jus' get panicky sometimes," she said. "I jus' lose my spunk."

"I never seen you when you lost it."

"Nights I do, sometimes."

There came a harsh hissing from the front of the truck. Tom grabbed the wheel tight and he thrust the brake down to the floor. The truck bumped to a stop. Tom sighed. "Well, there she is." He leaned back in the seat. Al leaped out and ran to the right front tire.

"Great big nail," he called.

"We got any tire patch?"

"No," said Al. "Used it all up. Got patch, but no glue stuff."

Tom turned and smiled sadly at Ma. "You shouldn' a tol' about that dollar," he said. "We'd a fixed her some way." He got out of the car and went to the flat tire.

Al pointed to a big nail protruding from the flat casing. "There she is!"

"If they's one nail in the county, we run over it."

"Is it bad?" Ma called.

"No, not bad, but we got to fix her."

The family piled down from the top of the truck. "Puncture?" Pa asked, and then he saw the tire and was silent.

Tom moved Ma from the seat and got the can of tire patch from underneath the cushion. He unrolled the rubber patch and took out the tube of cement, squeezed it gently. "She's almos' dry," he said. "Maybe they's enough. Awright, Al. Block the back wheels. Le's get her jacked up."

Tom and Al worked well together. They put stones behind the wheels, put the jack under the front axle, and lifted the weight off the limp casing. They ripped off the casing. They found the hole, dipped a rag in the gas tank and washed the tube around the hole. And then, while Al held the tube tight over his knee, Tom tore the cement tube in two and spread the little fluid thinly on the rubber with his pocket knife. He scraped the gum delicately. "Now let her dry while I cut a patch." He trimmed and beveled the edge of the blue patch. Al held the tube tight while Tom put the patch tenderly in place. "There! Now bring her to the running board while I tap her with a hammer." He pounded the patch carefully, then stretched the tube and watched the edges of the patch. "There she is! She's gonna hold. Stick her on the rim an' we'll pump her up. Looks like you keep your buck, Ma."

Al said, "I wisht we had a spare. We got to get us a spare, Tom, on a rim an' all pumped up. Then we can fix a puncture at night."

"When we get money for a spare we'll get us some coffee an' side-meat instead," Tom said.

The light morning traffic buzzed by on the highway, and the sun grew warm and bright. A wind, gentle and sighing, blew in puffs from the southwest, and the mountains on both sides of the great valley were indistinct in a pearly mist.

Tom was pumping at the tire when a roadster, coming from the north, stopped on the other side of the road. A brown-faced man dressed in a light gray business suit got out and walked across to the truck. He was bareheaded. He smiled, and his teeth were very white against his brown skin. He wore a massive gold wedding ring on the third finger of his left hand. A little gold football hung on a slender chain across his vest.

"Morning," he said pleasantly.

Tom stopped pumping and looked up. "Mornin'."

The man ran his fingers through his coarse, short, graying hair. "You people looking for work?"

"We sure are, mister. Lookin' even under boards."

"Can you pick peaches?"

"We never done it," Pa said.

"We can do anything," Tom said hurriedly. "We can pick anything there is."

The man fingered his gold football. "Well, there's plenty of work for you about forty miles north."

"We'd sure admire to get it," said Tom. "You tell us how to get there, an' we'll go a-lopin'."

"Well, you go north to Pixley, that's thirty-five or -six miles, and you turn east. Go about six miles. Ask anybody where the Hooper ranch is. You'll find plenty of work there."

"We sure will."

"Know where there's other people looking for work?"

"Sure," said Tom. "Down at the Weedpatch camp they's plenty lookin' for work."

"I'll take a run down there. We can use quite a few. Remember now, turn east at Pixley and keep straight east to the Hooper ranch."

"Sure," said Tom. "An' we thank ya, mister. We need work awful bad."

"All right. Get along as soon as you can." He walked back across the road, climbed into his open roadster, and drove away south.

Tom threw his weight on the pump. "Twenty apiece," he called. "One—two—three—four—" At twenty Al took the pump, and then Pa and then Uncle John. The tire filled out and grew plump and smooth. Three times around, the pump went. "Let 'er down an' le's see," said Tom.

Al released the jack and lowered the car. "Got plenty," he said. "Maybe a little too much."

They threw the tools into the car. "Come on, le's go," Tom called. "We're gonna get some work at last."

Ma got in the middle again. Al drove this time.

"Now take her easy. Don't burn her up, Al."

They drove on through the sunny morning fields. The mist lifted from the hilltops and they were clear and brown, with black-purple creases. The wild doves flew up from the fences as the truck passed. Al unconsciously increased his speed.

"Easy," Tom warned him. "She'll blow up if you crowd her. We got to get there. Might even get in some work today."

Ma said excitedly, "With four men a-workin' maybe I can get some credit right off. Fust thing I'll get is coffee, 'cause you been wanting that, an' then some flour an' bakin' powder an' some meat. Better not get no side-meat right off. Save that for later. Maybe Sat'dy. An' soap. Got to get soap. Wonder where we'll stay." She babbled on. "An' milk. I'll get some milk 'cause Rosasharn, she ought to have milk. The lady nurse says that."

A snake wiggled across the warm highway. Al zipped over and ran it down and came back to his own lane.

"Gopher snake," said Tom. "You oughtn't to done that."

"I hate 'em," said Al gaily. "Hate all kinds. Give me the stomach-quake."

The forenoon traffic on the highway increased, salesmen in shiny coupés with the insignia of their companies painted on the doors, red and white gasoline trucks dragging clinking chains behind them, great square-doored vans from wholesale grocery houses, delivering produce. The country was rich along the roadside. There were orchards, heavy leafed in their prime, and vineyards with the long green crawlers carpeting the ground between the rows. There were melon patches and grain fields. White houses stood in the greenery, roses growing over them. And the sun was gold and warm.

In the front seat of the truck Ma and Tom and Al were overcome with happiness. "I ain't really felt so good for a long time," Ma said. "'F we pick plenty peaches we might get a house, pay rent even, for a couple months. We got to have a house."

Al said, "I'm a-gonna save up. I'll save up an' then I'm a-goin' in a town an' get me a job in a garage. Live in a room an' eat in restaurants. Go to the movin' pitchers ever' damn night. Don' cost much. Cowboy pitchers." His hands tightened on the wheel.

The radiator bubbled and hissed steam. "Did you fill her up?" Tom asked.

"Yeah. Wind's kinda behind us. That's what makes her boil."

"It's a awful nice day," Tom said. "Use' ta work there in McAlester an' think all the things I'd do. I'd go in a straight line way to hell an' gone an' never stop nowheres. Seems like a long time ago. Seems like it's years ago I was in. They was a guard made it tough. I was gonna lay for 'im. Guess that's what makes me mad at cops. Seems like ever' cop got his face. He use' ta get red in the face. Looked like a pig. Had a brother out west, they said. Use' ta get fellas paroled to his brother, an' then they had to work for nothin'. If they raised a stink, they'd get sent back for breakin' parole. That's what the fellers said."

"Don' think about it," Ma begged him. "I'm a-gonna lay in a lot a stuff to eat. Lot a flour an' lard."

"Might's well think about it," said Tom. "Try to shut it out, an' it'll whang back at me. They was a screwball. Never tol' you 'bout him. Looked like Happy Hooligan. Harmless kinda fella. Always was gonna make a break. Fellas all called him Hooligan." Tom laughed to himself.

"Don' think about it," Ma begged.

"Go on," said Al. "Tell about the fella."

"It don't hurt nothin', Ma," Tom said. "This fella was always gonna break out. Make a plan, he would; but he couldn' keep it to hisself an' purty soon ever'body knowed it, even the warden. He'd make his break an' they'd take 'im by the han' an' lead 'im back. Well, one time he drawed a plan where he's goin' over. 'Course he showed it aroun', an' ever'body kep' still. An' he hid out, an' ever'body kep' still. So he's got himself a rope somewheres, an' he goes over the wall. They's six guards outside with a great big sack, an' Hooligan comes quiet down the rope an' they jus' hol' the sack out an' he goes right inside. They tie up the mouth an' take 'im back inside. Fellas laughed so hard they liked to died. But it busted Hooligan's spirit. He jus' cried an' cried, an' moped aroun' an' got sick. Hurt his feelin's so bad. Cut his wrists with a pin an' bled to death 'cause his feelin's was hurt. No harm in 'im at all. They's all kinds a screwballs in stir."

"Don't talk about it," Ma said. "I knowed Purty Boy Floyd's ma. He wan't a bad boy. Jus' got drove in a corner."

The sun moved up toward noon and the shadow of the truck grew lean and moved in under the wheels.

"Mus' be Pixley up the road," Al said. "Seen a sign a little back." They drove into the little town and turned eastward on a narrower road. And the orchards lined the way and made an aisle.

"Hope we can find her easy," Tom said.

Ma said, "That fella said the Hooper ranch. Said anybody'd tell us. Hope they's a store near by. Might get some credit, with four men workin'. I could get a real nice supper if they'd gimme some credit. Make up a big stew maybe."

"An' coffee," said Tom. "Might even get me a sack a Durham. I ain't had no tobacca of my own for a long time."

Far ahead the road was blocked with cars, and a line of white motorcycles was drawn up along the roadside. "Mus' be a wreck," Tom said.

As they drew near a State policeman, in boots and Sam Browne belt, stepped around the last parked car. He held up his hand and Al pulled to a stop. The policeman leaned confidentially on the side of the car. "Where you going?"

Al said, "Fella said they was work pickin' peaches up this way."

"Want to work, do you?"

"Damn right," said Tom.

"O.K. Wait here a minute." He moved to the side of the road and called ahead. "One more. That's six cars ready. Better take this batch through."

Tom called, "Hey! What's the matter?"

The patrol man lounged back. "Got a little trouble up ahead. Don't you worry. You'll get through. Just follow the line."

There came the splattering blast of motorcycles starting. The line of cars moved on, with the Joad truck last. Two motorcycles led the way, and two followed.

Tom said uneasily, "I wonder what's a matter."

"Maybe the road's out," Al suggested.

"Don' need four cops to lead us. I don' like it."

The motorcycles ahead speeded up. The line of old cars speeded up. Al hurried to keep in back of the last car.

"These here is our own people, all of 'em," Tom said. "I don' like this."

Suddenly the leading policemen turned off the road into a wide graveled entrance. The old cars whipped after them. The motorcycles roared their motors. Tom saw a line of men standing in the ditch beside the road, saw their mouths open as though they were yelling, saw their shaking fists and their furious faces. A stout woman ran toward the cars, but a roaring motorcycle stood in her way. A high wire gate swung open. The six old cars moved through and the gate closed behind them. The four motorcycles turned and sped back in the direction from which they had come. And now that the motors were gone, the distant yelling of the men in the ditch could be heard. Two men stood beside the graveled road. Each one carried a shotgun.

One called, "Go on, go on. What the hell are you waiting for?" The six cars moved ahead, turned a bend and came suddenly on the peach camp.

There were fifty little square, flat-roofed boxes, each with a door and a window, and the whole group in a square. A water tank stood high on one edge of the camp. And a little grocery store stood on the other side. At the end of each row of square houses stood two men armed with shotguns and wearing big silver stars pinned to their shirts.

The six cars stopped. Two bookkeepers moved from car to car. "Want to work?"

Tom answered, "Sure, but what is this?"

"That's not your affair. Want to work?"

"Sure we do."

"Name?"

"Joad."

"How many men?"

"Four."

"Women?"

"Two."

"Kids?"

"Two."

"Can all of you work?"

"Why—I guess so."

"O.K. Find house sixty-three. Wages five cents a box. No bruised fruit. All right, move along now. Go to work right away."

The cars moved on. On the door of each square red house a number was painted. "Sixty," Tom said. "There's sixty. Must be down that way. There, sixty-one, sixty-two— There she is."

Al parked the truck close to the door of the little house. The family came down from the top of the truck and looked about in bewilderment. Two deputies approached. They looked closely into each face.

"Name?"

"Joad," Tom said impatiently. "Say, what is this here?"

One of the deputies took out a long list. "Not here. Ever see these here? Look at the license. Nope. Ain't got it. Guess they're O.K."

"Now you look here. We don't want no trouble with you. Jes' do your work and mind your own business and you'll be all right." The two turned abruptly and walked away. At the end of the dusty street they sat down on two boxes and their position commanded the length of the street.

Tom stared after them. "They sure do wanta make us feel at home."

Ma opened the door of the house and stepped inside. The floor was splashed with grease. In the one room stood a rusty tin stove and nothing more. The tin stove rested on four bricks and its rusty stovepipe went up through the roof. The room smelled of sweat and grease. Rose of Sharon stood beside Ma. "We gonna live here?"

Ma was silent for a moment. "Why, sure," she said at last. "It ain't so bad once we wash it out. Get her mopped."

"I like the tent better," the girl said.

"This got a floor," Ma suggested. "This here wouldn' leak when it rains." She turned to the door. "Might as well unload," she said.

The men unloaded the truck silently. A fear had fallen on them. The great square of boxes was silent. A woman went by in the street, but she did not look at them. Her head was sunk and her dirty gingham dress was frayed at the bottom in little flags.

The pall had fallen on Ruthie and Winfield. They did not dash away to inspect the place. They stayed close to the truck, close to the family. They looked forlornly up and down the dusty street. Winfield found a piece of baling wire and he bent it back and forth until it broke. He made a little crank of the shortest piece and turned it around and around in his hands.

Tom and Pa were carrying the mattresses into the house when a clerk appeared. He wore khaki trousers and a blue shirt and a black necktie. He wore silver-bound eyeglasses, and his eyes, through the thick lenses, were weak and red, and the pupils were staring little bull's eyes. He leaned forward to look at Tom.

"I want to get you checked down," he said. "How many of you going to work?"

Tom said, "They's four men. Is this here hard work?"

"Picking peaches," the clerk said. "Piece work. Give five cents a box."

"Ain't no reason why the little fellas can't help?"

"Sure not, if they're careful."

Ma stood in the doorway. "Soon's I get settled down I'll come out an' help. We got nothin' to eat, mister. Do we get paid right off?"

"Well, no, not money right off. But you can get credit at the store for what you got coming."

"Come on, let's hurry," Tom said. "I want ta get some meat an' bread in me tonight. Where do we go, mister?"

"I'm going out there now. Come with me."

Tom and Pa and Al and Uncle John walked with him down the dusty street and into the orchard, in among the peach trees. The narrow leaves were beginning to turn a pale yellow. The peaches were little globes of gold and red on the branches. Among the trees were piles of empty boxes. The pickers scurried about, filling their buckets from the branches, putting the peaches in the boxes, carrying the boxes to the checking station; and at the stations, where the piles of filled boxes waited for the trucks, clerks waited to check against the names of the pickers.

"Here's four more," the guide said to a clerk.

"O.K. Ever picked before?"

"Never did," said Tom.

"Well, pick careful. No bruised fruit, no windfalls. Bruise your fruit an' we won't check 'em. There's some buckets."

Tom picked up a three-gallon bucket and looked at it. "Full a holes on the bottom."

"Sure," said the near-sighted clerk. "That keeps people from stealing them. All right—down in that section. Get going."

The four Joads took their buckets and went into the orchard. "They don't waste no time," Tom said.

"Christ Awmighty," Al said. "I ruther work in a garage."

Pa had followed docilely into the field. He turned suddenly on Al. "Now you jus' quit it," he said. "You been a-hankerin' an' a-complainin' an' a-bullblowin'. You get to work. You ain't so big I can't lick you yet."

Al's face turned red with anger. He started to bluster.

Tom moved near to him. "Come on, Al," he said quietly. "Bread an' meat. We got to get 'em."

They reached for the fruit and dropped them in the buckets. Tom ran at his work. One bucket full, two buckets. He dumped them in a box. Three buckets. The box was full. "I jus' made a nickel," he called. He picked up the box and walked hurriedly to the station. "Here's a nickel's worth," he said to the checker.

The man looked into the box, turned over a peach or two. "Put it over there. That's out," he said. "I told you not to bruise them. Dumped 'em outa the bucket, didn't you? Well, every damn peach is bruised. Can't check that one. Put 'em in easy or you're working for nothing."

"Why—goddamn it——"

"Now go easy. I warned you before you started."

Tom's eyes drooped sullenly. "O.K.," he said. "O.K." He went quickly back to the others. "Might's well dump what you got," he said. "Yours is the same as mine. Won't take 'em."

"Now, what the hell!" Al began.

"Got to pick easier. Can't drop 'em in the bucket. Got to lay 'em in."

They started again, and this time they handled the fruit gently. The boxes filled more slowly. "We could figger somepin out, I bet," Tom said. "If Ruthie an' Winfiel' or Rosasharn jus' put 'em in the boxes, we could work out a system." He carried his newest box to the station. "Is this here worth a nickel?"

The checker looked them over, dug down several layers. "That's better," he said. He checked the box in. "Just take it easy."

Tom hurried back. "I got a nickel," he called. "I got a nickel. On'y got to do that there twenty times for a dollar."

They worked on steadily through the afternoon. Ruthie and Winfield found them after a while. "You got to work," Pa told them. "You got to put the peaches careful in the box. Here, now, one at a time."

The children squatted down and picked the peaches out of the extra bucket, and a line of buckets stood ready for them. Tom carried the full boxes to the station. "That's seven," he said. "That's eight. Forty cents we got. Get a nice piece of meat for forty cents."

The afternoon passed. Ruthie tried to go away. "I'm tar'd," she whined. "I got to rest."

"You got to stay right where you're at," said Pa.

Uncle John picked slowly. He filled one bucket to two of Tom's. His pace didn't change.

In mid-afternoon Ma came trudging out. "I would a come before, but Rosasharn fainted," she said. "Jes' fainted away."

"You been eatin' peaches," she said to the children. "Well, they'll blast you out." Ma's stubby body moved quickly. She abandoned her bucket quickly and picked into her apron. When the sun went down they had picked twenty boxes.

Tom set the twentieth box down. "A buck," he said. "How long do we work?"

"Work til dark, long as you can see."

"Well, can we get credit now? Ma oughta go in an' buy some stuff to eat."

"Sure. I'll give you a slip for a dollar now." He wrote on a strip of paper and handed it to Tom.

He took it to Ma. "Here you are. You can get a dollar's worth of stuff at the store."

Ma put down her bucket and straightened her shoulders. "Gets you, the first time, don't it?"

"Sure. We'll all get used to it right off. Roll on in an' get some food."

Ma said, "What'll you like to eat?"

"Meat," said Tom. "Meat an' bread an' a big pot a coffee with sugar in. Great big piece a meat."

Ruthie wailed, "Ma, we're tar'd."

"Better come along in, then."

"They was tar'd when they started," Pa said. "Wild as rabbits they're a-gettin'. Ain't gonna be no good at all 'less we can pin 'em down."

"Soon's we get set down, they'll go to school," said Ma. She trudged away, and Ruthie and Winfield timidly followed her.

"We got to work ever' day?" Winfield asked.

Ma stopped and waited. She took his hand and walked along holding it. "It ain't hard work," she said. "Be good for you. An' you're helpin' us. If we all work, purty soon we'll live in a nice house. We all got to help."

"But I got so tar'd."

"I know. I got tar'd too. Ever'body gets wore out. Got to think about other stuff. Think about when you'll go to school."

"I don't wanta go to no school. Ruthie don't, neither. Them kids that goes to school, we seen 'em, Ma. Snots! Calls us Okies. We seen 'em. I ain't a-goin'."

Ma looked pityingly down on his straw hair. "Don' give us no trouble right now," she begged. "Soon's we get on our feet, you can be bad. But not now. We got too much, now."

"I et six of them peaches," Ruthie said.

"Well, you'll have the skitters. An' it ain't close to no toilet where we are."

The company's store was a large shed of corrugated iron. It had no display window. Ma opened the screen door and went in. A tiny man stood behind the counter. He was completely bald, and his head was blue-white. Large, brown eyebrows covered his eyes in such a high arch that his face seemed surprised and a little frightened. His nose was long and thin, and curved like a bird's beak, and his nostrils were blocked with light brown hair. Over the sleeves of his blue shirt he wore black sateen sleeve protectors. He was leaning on his elbows on the counter when Ma entered.

"Afternoon," she said.

He inspected her with interest. The arch over his eyes became higher. "Howdy."

"I got a slip here for a dollar."

"You can get a dollar's worth," he said, and he giggled shrilly. "Yes, sir. A dollar's worth. One dollar's worth." He moved his hand at the stock. "Any of it." He pulled his sleeve protectors up neatly.

"Thought I'd get a piece of meat."

"Got all kinds," he said. "Hamburg, like to have some hamburg? Twenty cents a pound, hamburg."

"Ain't that awful high? Seems to me hamburg was fifteen las' time I got some."

"Well," he giggled softly, "yes, it's high, an' same time it ain't high. Time you go on in town for a couple poun's of hamburg, it'll cos' you 'bout a gallon gas. So you see it ain't really high here, 'cause you got no gallon a gas."

Ma said sternly, "It didn' cos' you no gallon a gas to get it out here."

He laughed delightedly. "You're lookin' at it bass-ackwards," he said. "We ain't a-buyin' it, we're a-sellin' it. If we was buyin' it, why, that'd be different."

Ma put two fingers to her mouth and frowned with thought. "It looks all full a fat an' gristle."

"I ain't guaranteein' she won't cook down," the storekeeper said. "I ain't guaranteein' I'd eat her myself; but they's lots of stuff I wouldn' do."

Ma looked up at him fiercely for a moment. She controlled her voice. "Ain't you got some cheaper kind a meat?"

"Soup bones," he said. "Ten cents a pound."

"But them's jus' bones."

"Them's jes' bones," he said. "Make nice soup. Jes' bones."

"Got any boilin' beef?"

"Oh, yeah! Sure. That's two bits a poun'."

"Maybe I can't get no meat," Ma said. "But they want meat. They said they wanted meat."

"Ever'body wants meat—needs meat. That hamburg is purty nice stuff. Use the grease that comes out a her for gravy. Purty nice. No waste. Don't throw no bone away."

"How—how much is side-meat?"

"Well, now you're gettin' into fancy stuff. Christmas stuff. Thanksgivin' stuff. Thirty-five cents a poun'. I could sell you turkey cheaper, if I had some turkey."

Ma sighed. "Give me two pounds hamburg."

"Yes, ma'am." He scooped the pale meat on a piece of waxed paper. "An' what else?"

"Well, some bread."

"Right here. Fine big loaf, fifteen cents."

"That there's a twelve-cent loaf."

"Sure, it is. Go right in town an' get her for twelve cents. Gallon a gas. What else can I sell you, potatoes?"

"Yes, potatoes."

"Five pounds for a quarter."

Ma moved menacingly toward him. "I heard enough from you. I know what they cost in town."

The little man clamped his mouth tight. "Then go git 'em in town."

Ma looked at her knuckles. "What is this?" she asked softly. "You own this here store?"

"No. I jus' work here."

"Any reason you got to make fun? That help you any?" She regarded her shiny wrinkled hands. The little man was silent. "Who owns this here store?"

"Hooper Ranches, Incorporated, ma'am."

"An' they set the prices?"

"Yes, ma'am."

She looked up, smiling a little. "Ever'body comes in talks like me, is mad?"

He hesitated for a moment. "Yes, ma'am."

"An' that's why you make fun?"

"What cha mean?"

"Doin' a dirty thing like this. Shames ya, don't it? Got to act flip, huh?" Her voice was gentle. The clerk watched her, fascinated. He didn't answer. "That's how it is," Ma said finally. "Forty cents for meat, fifteen for bread, quarter for potatoes. That's eighty cents. Coffee?"

"Twenty cents the cheapest, ma'am."

"An' that's the dollar. Seven of us workin', an' that's supper." She studied her hand. "Wrap 'em up," she said quickly.

"Yes, ma'am," he said. "Thanks." He put the potatoes in a bag and folded the top carefully down. His eyes slipped to Ma, and then hid in his work again. She watched him, and she smiled a little.

"How'd you get a job like this?" she asked.

"A fella got to eat," he began; and then, belligerently, "A fella got a right to eat."

"What fella?" Ma asked.

He placed the four packages on the counter. "Meat," he said. "Potatoes, bread, coffee. One dollar, even." She handed him her slip of paper and watched while he entered the name and the amount in a ledger. "There," he said. "Now we're all even."

Ma picked up her bags. "Say," she said. "We got no sugar for the coffee. My boy Tom, he wants sugar. Look!" she said. "They're a-workin' out there. You let me have some sugar an' I'll bring the slip in later."

The little man looked away—took his eyes as far from Ma as he could. "I can't do it," he said softly. "That's the rule. I can't. I'd get in trouble. I'd get canned."

"But they're a-workin' out in the field now. They got more'n a dime comin'. Gimme ten cents' of sugar. Tom, he wanted sugar in his coffee. Spoke about it."

"I can't do it, ma'am. That's the rule. No slip, no groceries. The manager, he talks about that all the time. No, I can't do it. No, I can't. They'd catch me. They always catch fellas. Always. I can't."

"For a dime?"

"For anything, ma'am." He looked pleadingly at her. And then his face lost its fear. He took ten cents from his pocket and rang it up in the cash register. "There," he said with relief. He pulled a little bag from under the counter, whipped it open and scooped some sugar into it, weighed the bag, and added a little more sugar. "There you are," he said. "Now it's all right. You bring in your slip an' I'll get my dime back."

Ma studied him. Her hand went blindly out and put the little bag of sugar on the pile in her arm. "Thanks to you," she said quietly. She started for the door, and when she reached it, she turned about. "I'm learnin' one thing good," she said. "Learnin' it all a time, ever' day. If you're in trouble or hurt or need—go to poor people. They're the only ones that'll help—the only ones." The screen door slammed behind her.

The little man leaned his elbows on the counter and looked after her with his surprised eyes. A plump tortoise-shell cat leaped up on the counter and stalked lazily near to him. It rubbed sideways against his arms, and he reached out with his hand and pulled it against his cheek. The cat purred loudly, and the tip of its tail jerked back and forth.

Tom and Al and Pa and Uncle John walked in from the orchard when the dusk was deep. Their feet were a little heavy against the road.

"You wouldn' think jus' reachin' up an' pickin'd get you in the back," Pa said.

"Be awright in a couple days," said Tom. "Say, Pa, after we eat I'm a-gonna walk out an' see what all that fuss is outside the gate. It's been a-workin' on me. Wanta come?"

"No," said Pa. "I like to have a little while to jus' work an' not think about nothin'. Seems like I jus' been beatin' my brains to death for a hell of a long time. No, I'm gonna set awhile, an' then go to bed."

"How 'bout you, Al?"

Al looked away. "Guess I'll look aroun' in here, first," he said.

"Well, I know Uncle John won't come. Guess I'll go her alone. Got me all curious."

Pa said, "I'll get a hell of a lot curiouser 'fore I'll do anything about it—with all them cops out there."

"Maybe they ain't there at night," Tom suggested.

"Well, I ain't gonna find out. An' you better not tell Ma where you're a-goin'. She'll jus' squirt her head off worryin'."

Tom turned to Al. "Ain't you curious?"

"Guess I'll jes' look aroun' this here camp," Al said.

"Lookin' for girls, huh?"

"Mindin' my own business," Al said acidly.

"I'm still a-goin'," said Tom.

They emerged from the orchard into the dusty street between the red shacks. The low yellow light of kerosene lanterns shone from some of the doorways, and inside, in the half-gloom, the black shapes of people moved about. At the end of the street a guard still sat, his shotgun resting against his knee.

Tom paused as he passed the guard. "Got a place where a fella can get a bath, mister?"

The guard studied him in the half-light. At last he said, "See that water tank?"

"Yeah."

"Well, there's a hose over there."

"Any warm water?"

"Say, who in hell you think you are, J. P. Morgan?"

"No," said Tom. "No, I sure don't. Good night, mister."

The guard grunted contemptuously. "Hot water, for Christ's sake. Be wantin' tubs next." He stared glumly after the four Joads.

A second guard came around the end house. "'S'matter, Mack?"

"Why, them goddamn Okies. 'Is they warm water?' he says."

The second guard rested his gun butt on the ground. "It's them gov'ment camps," he said. "I bet that fella been in a gov'ment camp. We ain't gonna have no peace till we wipe them camps out. They'll be wantin' clean sheets, first thing we know."

Mack asked, "How is it out at the main gate—hear anything?"

"Well, they was out there yellin' all day. State police got it in hand. They're runnin' the hell outa them smart guys. I heard they's a long lean son-of-a-bitch spark-pluggin' the thing. Fella says they'll get him tonight, an' then she'll go to pieces."

"We won't have no job if it comes too easy," Mack said.

"We'll have a job, all right. These goddamn Okies! You got to watch 'em all the time. Things get a little quiet, we can always stir 'em up a little."

"Have trouble when they cut the rate here, I guess."

"We sure will. No, you needn' worry about us havin' work—not while Hooper's snubbin' close."

The fire roared in the Joad house. Hamburger patties splashed and hissed in the grease, and the potatoes bubbled. The house was full of smoke, and the yellow lantern light threw heavy black shadows on the walls. Ma worked quickly about the fire while Rose of Sharon sat on a box resting her heavy abdomen on her knees.

"Feelin' better now?" Ma asked.

"Smell a cookin' gets me. I'm hungry, too."

"Go set in the door," Ma said. "I got to have that box to break up anyways."

The men trooped in. "Meat, by God!" said Tom. "And coffee. I smell her. Jesus, I'm hungry! I et a lot of peaches, but they didn' do no good. Where can we wash, Ma?"

"Go down to the water tank. Wash down there. I jus' sent Ruthie an' Winfiel' to wash." The men went out again.

"Go on now, Rosasharn," Ma ordered. "Either you set in the door or else on the bed. I got to break that box up."

The girl helped herself up with her hands. She moved heavily to one of the mattresses and sat down on it. Ruthie and Winfield came in quietly, trying by silence and by keeping close to the wall to remain obscure.

Ma looked over at them. "I got a feelin' you little fellas is lucky they ain't much light," she said. She pounced at Winfield and felt his hair. "Well, you got wet, anyway, but I bet you ain't clean."

"They wasn't no soap," Winfield complained.

"No, that's right. I couldn' buy no soap. Not today. Maybe we can get soap tomorra." She went back to the stove, laid out the plates, and began to serve the supper. Two patties apiece and a big potato. She placed three slices of bread on each plate. When the meat was all out of the frying pan she poured a little of the grease on each plate.

The men came in again, their faces dripping and their hair shining with water.

"Leave me at her," Tom cried.

They took the plates. They ate silently; wolfishly, and wiped up the grease with the bread. The children retired into the corner of the room, put their plates on the floor, and knelt in front of the food like little animals.

Tom swallowed the last of his bread. "Got any more, Ma?"

"No," she said. "That's all. You made a dollar, an' that's a dollar's worth."

"That?"

"They charge extry out here. We got to go in town when we can."

"I ain't full," said Tom.

"Well, tomorra you'll get in a full day. Tomorra night—we'll have plenty."

Al wiped his mouth on his sleeve. "Guess I'll take a look around," he said.

"Wait, I'll go with you." Tom followed him outside. In the darkness Tom went close to his brother. "Sure you don' wanta come with me?"

"No. I'm gonna look aroun' like I said."

"O.K.," said Tom. He turned away and strolled down the street. The smoke from the houses hung low to the ground, and the lanterns threw their pictures of doorways and windows into the street. On the doorsteps people sat and looked out into the darkness. Tom could see their heads turn as their eyes followed him down the street. At the street end the dirt road continued across a stubble field, and the black lumps of haycocks were visible in the starlight. A thin blade of moon was low in the sky toward the west, and the long cloud of the milky way trailed clearly overhead. Tom's feet sounded softly on the dusty road, a dark patch against the yellow stubble. He put his hands in his pockets and trudged along toward the main gate. An embankment came close to the road. Tom could hear the whisper of water against the grasses in the irrigation ditch. He climbed up the bank and looked down on the dark water, and saw the stretched reflections of the stars. The State road was ahead. Car lights swooping past showed where it was. Tom set out again toward it. He could see the high wire gate in the starlight.

A figure stirred beside the road. A voice said, "Hello—who is it?"

Tom stopped and stood still. "Who are you?"

A man stood up and walked near. Tom could see the gun in his hand. Then a flashlight played on his face. "Where you think you're going?"

"Well, I thought I'd take a walk. Any law against it?"

"You better walk some other way."

Tom asked, "Can't I even get out of here?"

"Not tonight you can't. Want to walk back, or shall I whistle some help an' take you?"

"Hell," said Tom, "it ain't nothin' to me. If it's gonna cause a mess, I don't give a darn. Sure, I'll go back."

The dark figure relaxed. The flash went off. "Ya see, it's for your own good. Them crazy pickets might get you."

"What pickets?"

"Them goddamn reds."

"Oh," said Tom. "I didn' know 'bout them."

"You seen 'em when you come, didn' you?"

"Well, I seen a bunch a guys, but they was so many cops I didn' know. Thought it was a accident."

"Well, you better git along back."

"That's O.K. with me, mister." He swung about and started back. He walked quietly along the road a hundred yards, and then he stopped and listened. The twittering call of a raccoon sounded near the irrigation ditch and, very far away, the angry howl of a tied dog. Tom sat down beside the road and listened. He heard the high soft laughter of a night hawk and the stealthy movement of a creeping animal in the stubble. He inspected the skyline in both directions, dark frames both ways, nothing to show against. Now he stood up and walked slowly to the right of the road, off into the stubble field, and he walked bent down, nearly as low as the haycocks. He moved slowly and stopped occasionally to listen. At last he came to the wire fence, five strands of taut barbed wire. Beside the fence he lay on his back, moved his head under the lowest strand, held the wire up with his hands and slid himself under, pushing against the ground with his feet.

He was about to get up when a group of men walked by on the edge of the highway. Tom waited until they were far ahead before he stood up and followed them. He watched the side of the road for tents. A few automobiles went by. A stream cut across the fields, and the highway crossed it on a small concrete bridge. Tom looked over the side of the bridge. In the bottom of the deep ravine he saw a tent and a lantern was burning inside. He watched it for a moment, saw the shadows of people against the canvas walls. Tom climbed a fence and moved down into the ravine through brush and dwarf willows; and in the bottom, beside a tiny stream, he found a trail. A man sat on a box in front of the tent.

"Evenin'," Tom said.

"Who are you?"

"Well—I guess, well—I'm jus' goin' past."

"Know anybody here?"

"No. I tell you I was jus' goin' past."

A head stuck out of the tent. A voice said, "What's the matter?"

"Casy!" Tom cried. "Casy! For Chris' sake, what you doin' here?"

"Why, my God, it's Tom Joad! Come on in, Tommy. Come on in."

"Know him, do ya?" the man in front asked.

"Know him? Christ, yes. Knowed him for years. I come west with him. Come on in, Tom." He clutched Tom's elbow and pulled him into the tent.

Three other men sat on the ground, and in the center of the tent a lantern burned. The men looked up suspiciously. A dark-faced, scowling man held out his hand. "Glad to meet ya," he said. "I heard what Casy said. This the fella you was tellin' about?"

"Sure. This is him. Well, for God's sake! Where's your folks? What you doin' here?"

"Well," said Tom, "we heard they was work this-a-way. An' we come, an' a bunch a State cops run us into this here ranch an' we been a-pickin' peaches all afternoon. I seen a bunch a fellas yellin'. They wouldn' tell me nothin', so I come out here to see what's goin' on. How'n hell'd you get here, Casy?"

The preacher leaned forward and the yellow lantern light fell on his high pale forehead. "Jail house is a kinda funny place," he said. "Here's me, been a-goin' into the wilderness like Jesus to try find out somepin. Almost got her sometimes, too. But it's in the jail house I really got her." His eyes were sharp and merry. "Great big ol' cell, an' she's full all a time. New guys come in, and guys go out. An' 'course I talked to all of 'em."

"'Course you did," said Tom. "Always talk. If you was up on the gallows you'd be passin' the time a day with the hangman. Never seen sech a talker."

The men in the tent chuckled. A wizened little man with a wrinkled face slapped his knee. "Talks all the time," he said. "Folks kinda likes to hear 'im, though."

"Use' ta be a preacher," said Tom. "Did he tell that?"

"Sure, he told."

Casy grinned. "Well, sir," he went on, "I begin gettin' at things. Some a them fellas in the tank was drunks, but mostly they was there 'cause they stole stuff; an' mostly it was stuff they needed an' couldn' get no other way. Ya see?" he asked.

"No," said Tom.

"Well, they was nice fellas, ya see. What made 'em bad was they needed stuff. An' I begin to see, then. It's need that makes all the trouble. I ain't got it worked out. Well, one day they give us some beans that was sour. One fella started yellin', an' nothin' happened. He yelled his head off. Trusty come along an' looked in an' went on. Then another fella yelled. Well, sir, then we all got yellin'. And we all got on the same tone, an' I tell ya, it jus' seemed like that tank bulged an' give and swelled up. By God! Then somepin happened! They come a-runnin', and they give us some other stuff to eat—give it to us. Ya see?"

"No," said Tom.

Casy put his chin down on his hands. "Maybe I can't tell you," he said. "Maybe you got to find out. Where's your cap?"

"I come out without it."

"How's your sister?"

"Hell, she's big as a cow. I bet she got twins. Gonna need wheels under her stomach. Got to holdin' it with her han's, now. You ain' tol' me what's goin' on."

The wizened man said, "We struck. This here's a strike."

"Well, fi' cents a box ain't much, but a fella can eat."

"Fi' cents?" the wizened man cried. "Fi' cents! They payin you fi' cents?"

"Sure. We made a buck an' a half."

A heavy silence fell in the tent. Casy stared out the entrance, into the dark night. "Lookie, Tom," he said at last. "We come to work there. They says it's gonna be fi' cents. They was a hell of a lot of us. We got there an' they says they're payin' two an' a half cents. A fella can't even eat on that, an' if he got kids—So we says we won't take it. So they druv us off. An' all the cops in the worl' come down on us. Now they're payin' you five. When they bust this here strike—ya think they'll pay five?"

"I dunno," Tom said. "Payin' five now."

"Lookie," said Casy. "We tried to camp together, an' they druv us like pigs. Scattered us. Beat the hell outa fellas. Druv us like pigs. They run you in like pigs, too. We can't las' much longer. Some people ain't et for two days. You goin' back tonight?"

"Aim to," said Tom.

"Well—tell the folks in there how it is, Tom. Tell 'em they're starvin' us an' stabbin' theirself in the back. 'Cause sure as cowflops she'll drop to two an' a half jus' as soon as they clear us out."

"I'll tell 'em," said Tom. "I don' know how. Never seen so many guys with guns. Don' know if they'll even let a fella talk. An' folks don' pass no time of day. They jus' hang down their heads an' won't even give a fella a howdy."

"Try an' tell 'em, Tom. They'll get two an' a half, jus' the minute we're gone. You know what two an' a half is—that's one ton of peaches picked an' carried for a dollar." He dropped his head. "No—you can't do it. You can't get your food for that. Can't eat for that."

"I'll try to get to tell the folks."

"How's your ma?"

"Purty good. She liked that gov'ment camp. Baths an' hot water."

"Yeah—I heard."

"It was pretty nice there. Couldn' find no work, though. Had a leave."

"I'd like to go to one," said Casy. "Like to see it. Fella says they ain't no cops."

"Folks is their own cops."

Casy looked up excitedly. "An' was they any trouble? Fightin', stealin', drinkin'?"

"No," said Tom.

"Well, if a fella went bad—what then? What'd they do?"

"Put 'im outa the camp."

"But they wasn' many?"

"Hell, no," said Tom. "We was there a month, an' on'y one."

Casy's eyes shone with excitement. He turned to the other men. "Ya see?" he cried. "I tol' you. Cops cause more trouble than they stop. Look, Tom. Try an' get the folks in there to come on out. They can do it in a couple days. Them peaches is ripe. Tell 'em."

"They won't," said Tom. "They're a-gettin' five, an' they don' give a damn about nothin' else."

"But jus' the minute they ain't strikebreakin' they won't get no five."

"I don' think they'll swalla that. Five they're a-gettin'. Tha's all they care about."

"Well, tell 'em anyways."

"Pa wouldn' do it," Tom said. "I know 'im. He'd say it wasn't none of his business."

"Yes," Casy said disconsolately. "I guess that's right. Have to take a beatin' 'fore he'll know."

"We was outa food," Tom said. "Tonight we had meat. Not much, but we had it. Think Pa's gonna give up his meat on account a other fellas? An' Rosasharn oughta get milk. Think Ma's gonna wanta starve that baby jus' 'cause a bunch a fellas is yellin' outside a gate?"

Casy said sadly, "I wisht they could see it. I wisht they could see the on'y way they can depen' on their meat—Oh, the hell! Get tar'd sometimes. God-awful tar'd. I knowed a fella. Brang 'im in while I was in the jail house. Been tryin' to start a union. Got one started. An' then them vigilantes bust it up. An' know what? Them very folks he been tryin' to help tossed him out. Wouldn' have nothin' to do with 'im. Scared they'd get saw in his comp'ny. Says, 'Git out. You're a danger on us.' Well, sir, it hurt his feelin's purty bad. But then he says, 'It ain't so bad if you know.' He says, 'French Revolution—all them fellas that figgered her out got their heads chopped off. Always that way,' he says. 'Jus' as natural as rain. You didn' do it for fun no way. Doin' it 'cause you have to. 'Cause it's you. Look a Washington,' he says. 'Fit the Revolution, an' after, them sons-a-bitches turned on him. An' Lincoln the same. Same folks yellin' to kill 'em. Natural as rain.'"

"Don't soun' like no fun," said Tom.

"No, it don't. This fella in jail, he says, 'Anyways, you do what you can. An',' he says, 'the on'y thing you got to look at is that ever' time they's a little step fo'ward, she may slip back a little, but she never slips clear back. You can prove that,' he says, 'an' that makes the whole thing right. An' that means they wasn't no waste even if it seemed like they was.'"

"Talkin'," said Tom. "Always talkin'. Take my brother Al. He's out lookin' for a girl. He don't care 'bout nothin' else. Couple days he'll get him a girl. Think about it all day an' do it all night. He don't give a damn 'bout steps up or down or sideways."

"Sure," said Casy. "Sure. He's jus' doin' what he's got to do. All of us like that."

The man seated outside pulled the tent flap wide. "Goddamn it, I don' like it," he said.

Casy looked out at him. "What's the matter?"

"I don' know. I jus' itch all over. Nervous as a cat."

"Well, what's the matter?"

"I don' know. Seems like I hear somepin, an' then I listen an' they ain't nothin' to hear."

"You're jus jumpy," the wizened man said. He got up and went outside. And in a second he looked into the tent. "They's a great big ol' black cloud a-sailin' over. Bet she's got thunder. That's what's itchin' him—'lectricity." He ducked out again. The other two men stood up from the ground and went outside.

Casy said softly, "All of 'em's itchy. Them cops been sayin' how they're gonna beat the hell outa us an' run us outa the county. They figger I'm a leader 'cause I talk so much."

The wizened face looked in again. "Casy, turn out that lantern an' come outside. They's somepin."

Casy turned the screw. The flame drew down into the slots and popped and went out. Casy groped outside and Tom followed him. "What is it?" Casy asked softly.

"I dunno. Listen!"

There was a wall of frog sounds that merged with silence. A high, shrill whistle of crickets. But through this background came other sounds—faint footsteps from the road, a crunch of clods up on the bank, a little swish of brush down the stream.

"Can't really tell if you hear it. Fools you. Get nervous," Casy reassured them. "We're all nervous. Can't really tell. You hear it, Tom?"

"I hear it," said Tom. "Yeah, I hear it. I think they's guys comin' from ever' which way. We better get outa here."

The wizened man whispered, "Under the bridge span—out that way. Hate to leave my tent."

"Le's go," said Casy.

They moved quietly along the edge of the stream. The black span was a cave before them. Casy bent over and moved through. Tom behind. Their feet slipped into the water. Thirty feet they moved, and their breathing echoed from the curved ceiling. Then they came out on the other side and straightened up.

A sharp call, "There they are!" Two flashlight beams fell on the men, caught them, blinded them. "Stand where you are." The voices came out of the darkness. "That's him. That shiny bastard. That's him."

Casy stared blindly at the light. He breathed heavily. "Listen," he said. "You fellas don' know what you're doin'. You're helpin' to starve kids."

"Shut up, you red son-of-a-bitch."

A short heavy man stepped into the light. He carried a new white pick handle.

Casy went on, "You don' know what you're a-doin'."

The heavy man swung with the pick handle. Casy dodged down into the swing. The heavy club crashed into the side of his head with a dull crunch of bone, and Casy fell sideways out of the light.

"Jesus, George. I think you killed him."

"Put the light on him," said George. "Serve the son-of-a-bitch right." The flashlight beam dropped, searched and found Casy's crushed head.

Tom looked down at the preacher. The light crossed the heavy man's legs and the white new pick handle. Tom leaped silently. He wrenched the club free. The first time he knew he had missed and struck a shoulder, but the second time his crushing blow found the head, and as the heavy man sank down, three more blows found his head. The lights danced about. There were shouts, the sound of running feet, crashing through brush. Tom stood over the prostrate man. And then a club reached his head, a glancing blow. He felt the stroke like an electric shock. And then he was running along the stream, bending low. He heard the splash of footsteps following him. Suddenly he turned and squirmed up into the brush, deep into a poison-oak thicket. And he lay still. The footsteps came near, the light beams glanced along the stream bottom. Tom wriggled up through the thicket to the top. He emerged in an orchard. And still he could hear the calls, the pursuit in the stream bottom. He bent low and ran over the cultivated earth; the clods slipped and rolled under his feet. Ahead he saw the bushes that bounded the field, bushes along the edges of an irrigation ditch. He slipped through the fence, edged in among vines and blackberry bushes. And then he lay still, panting hoarsely. He felt his numb face and nose. The nose was crushed, and a trickle of blood dripped from his chin. He lay still on his stomach until his mind came back. And then he crawled slowly over the edge of the ditch. He bathed his face in the cool water, tore off the tail of his blue shirt and dipped it and held it against his torn cheek and nose. The water stung and burned.

The black cloud had crossed the sky, a blob of dark against the stars. The night was quiet again.

Tom stepped into the water and felt the bottom drop from under his feet. He threshed the two strokes across the ditch and pulled himself heavily up the other bank. His clothes clung to him. He moved and made a slopping noise; his shoes squished. Then he sat down, took off his shoes and emptied them. He wrung the bottoms of his trousers, took off his coat and squeezed the water from it.

Along the highway he saw the dancing beams of the flashlights, searching the ditches. Tom put on his shoes and moved cautiously across the stubble field. The squishing noise no longer came from his shoes. He went by instinct toward the other side of the stubble field, and at last he came to the road. Very cautiously he approached the square of houses.

Once a guard, thinking he heard a noise, called, "Who's there?"

Tom dropped and froze to the ground, and the flashlight beam passed over him. He crept silently to the door of the Joad house. The door squalled on its hinges. And Ma's voice, calm and steady and wide awake:

"What's that?"

"Me. Tom."

"Well, you better get some sleep. Al ain't in yet."

"He must a foun' a girl."

"Go on to sleep," she said softly. "Over under the window."

He found his place and took off his clothes to the skin. He lay shivering under his blanket. And his torn face awakened from its numbness, and his whole head throbbed.

It was an hour more before Al came in. He moved cautiously near and stepped on Tom's wet clothes.

"Sh!" said Tom.

Al whispered, "You awake? How'd you get wet?"

"Sh," said Tom. "Tell you in the mornin'."

Pa turned on his back, and his snoring filled the room with gasps and snorts.

"You're col'," Al said.

"Sh. Go to sleep." The little square of the window showed gray against the black of the room.

Tom did not sleep. The nerves of his wounded face came back to life and throbbed, and his cheek bone ached, and his broken nose bulged and pulsed with pain that seemed to toss him about, to shake him. He watched the little square window, saw the stars slide down over it and drop from sight. At intervals he heard the footsteps of the watchmen.

At last the roosters crowed, far away, and gradually the window lightened. Tom touched his swollen face with his fingertips, and at his movement Al groaned and murmured in his sleep.

The dawn came finally. In the houses, packed together, there was a sound of movement, a crash of breaking sticks, a little clatter of pans. In the graying gloom Ma sat up suddenly. Tom could see her face, swollen with sleep. She looked at the window, for a long moment. And then she threw the blanket off and found her dress. Still sitting down, she put it over her head and held her arms up and let the dress slide down to her waist. She stood up and pulled the dress down around her ankles. Then, in bare feet, she stepped carefully to the window and looked out, and while she stared at the growing light, her quick fingers unbraided her hair and smoothed the strands and braided them up again. Then she clasped her hands in front of her and stood motionless for a moment. Her face was lighted sharply by the window. She turned, stepped carefully among the mattresses, and found the lantern. The shade screeched up, and she lighted the wick.

Pa rolled over and blinked at her. She said, "Pa, you got more money?"

"Huh? Yeah. Paper wrote for sixty cents."

"Well, git up an' go buy some flour an' lard. Quick, now."

Pa yawned. "Maybe the store ain't open."

"Make 'em open it. Got to get somepin in you fellas. You got to get out to work."

Pa struggled into his overalls and put on his rusty coat. He went sluggishly out the door, yawning and stretching.

The children awakened and watched from under their blanket, like mice. Pale light filled the room now, but colorless light, before the sun. Ma glanced at the mattresses. Uncle John was awake, Al slept heavily. Her eyes moved to Tom. For a moment she peered at him, and then she moved quickly to him. His face was puffed and blue, and the blood was dried black on his lips and chin. The edges of the torn cheek were gathered and tight.

"Tom," she whispered, "what's the matter?"

"Sh!" he said. "Don't talk loud. I got in a fight."

"Tom!"

"I couldn' help it, Ma."

She knelt down beside him. "You in trouble?"

He was a long time answering. "Yeah," he said. "In trouble. I can't go out to work. I got to hide."

The children crawled near on their hands and knees, staring greedily. "What's the matter'th him, Ma?"

"Hush!" Ma said. "Go wash up."

"We got no soap."

"Well, use water."

"What's the matter'th Tom?"

"Now you hush. An' don't you tell nobody."

They backed away and squatted down against the far wall, knowing they would not be inspected.

Ma asked, "Is it bad?"

"Nose busted."

"I mean the trouble?"

"Yeah. Bad!"

Al opened his eyes and looked at Tom. "Well, for Chris' sake! What was you in?"

"What's a matter?" Uncle John asked.

Pa clumped in. "They was open all right." He put a tiny bag of flour and his package of lard on the floor beside the stove. "'S'a matter?" he asked.

Tom braced himself on one elbow for a moment, and then he lay back. "Jesus, I'm weak. I'm gonna tell ya once. So I'll tell all of ya. How 'bout the kids?"

Ma looked at them, huddled against the wall. "Go wash ya face."

"No," Tom said. "They got to hear. They got to know. They might blab if they don' know."

"What the hell is this?" Pa demanded.

"I'm a-gonna tell. Las' night I went out to see what all the yellin' was about. An' I come on Casy."

"The preacher?"

"Yeah, Pa. The preacher, on'y he was a-leadin' the strike. They come for him."

Pa demanded, "Who come for him?"

"I dunno. Same kinda guys that turned us back on the road that night. Had pick handles." He paused. "They killed 'im. Busted his head. I was standin' there. I went nuts. Grabbed the pick handle." He looked bleakly back at the night, the darkness, the flashlights, as he spoke. "I—I clubbed a guy."

Ma's breath caught in her throat. Pa stiffened. "Kill 'im?" he asked softly.

"I—don't know. I was nuts. Tried to."

Ma asked, "Was you saw?"

"I dunno. I dunno. I guess so. They had the lights on us."

For a moment Ma stared into his eyes. "Pa," she said, "break up some boxes. We got to get breakfas'. You got to go to work. Ruthie, Winfiel'. If anybody asts you—Tom is sick—you hear? If you tell—he'll—get sent to jail. You hear?"

"Yes, ma'am."

"Keep your eye on 'em, John. Don' let 'em talk to nobody." She built the fire as Pa broke the boxes that had held the goods. She made her dough, put a pot of coffee to boil. The light wood caught and roared its flame in the chimney.

Pa finished breaking the boxes. He came near to Tom. "Casy—he was a good man. What'd he wanta mess with that stuff for?"

Tom said dully, "They come to work for fi' cents a box."

"That's what we're a-gettin'."

"Yeah. What we was a-doin' was breakin' strike. They give them fellas two an' a half cents."

"You can't eat on that."

"I know," Tom said wearily. "That's why they struck. Well, I think they bust that strike las' night. We'll maybe be gettin' two an' a half cents today."

"Why, the sons-a-bitches——"

"Yeah! Pa. You see? Casy was still a—good man. Goddamn it, I can't get that pitcher outa my head. Him layin' there—head jus' crushed flat an' oozin'. Jesus!" He covered his eyes with his hand.

"Well, what we gonna do?" Uncle John asked.

Al was standing up now. "Well, by God, I know what I'm gonna do. I'm gonna get out of it."

"No, you ain't, Al," Tom said. "We need you now. I'm the one. I'm a danger now. Soon's I get on my feet I got to go."

Ma worked at the stove. Her head was half turned to hear. She put grease in the frying pan, and when it whispered with heat, she spooned the dough into it.

Tom went on, "You got to stay, Al. You got to take care a the truck."

"Well, I don' like it."

"Can't help it, Al. It's your folks. You can help 'em. I'm a danger to 'em."

Al grumbled angrily. "I don' know why I ain't let to get me a job in a garage."

"Later, maybe." Tom looked past him, and he saw Rose of Sharon lying on the mattress. Her eyes were huge—opened wide. "Don't worry," he called to her. "Don't you worry. Gonna get you some milk today." She blinked slowly, and didn't answer him.

Pa said, "We got to know, Tom. Think ya killed this fella?"

"I don' know. It was dark. An' somebody smacked me. I don't know. I hope so. I hope I killed the bastard."

"Tom!" Ma called. "Don' talk like that."

From the street came the sound of many cars moving slowly. Pa stepped to the window and looked out. "They's a whole slew a new people comin' in," he said.

"I guess they bust the strike, awright," said Tom. "I guess you'll start at two an' a half cents."

"But a fella could work at a run, an' still he couldn' eat."

"I know," said Tom. "Eat win'fall peaches. That'll keep ya up."

Ma turned the dough and stirred the coffee. "Listen to me," she said. "I'm gettin' cornmeal today. We're a-gonna eat cornmeal mush. An' soon's we get enough for gas, we're movin' away. This ain't a good place. An' I ain't gonna have Tom out alone. No, sir."

"Ya can't do that, Ma. I tell you I'm jus' a danger to ya."

Her chin was set. "That's what we'll do. Here, come eat this here, an' then get out to work. I'll come out soon's I get washed up. We got to make some money."

They ate the fried dough so hot that it sizzled in their mouths. And they tossed the coffee down and filled their cups and drank more coffee.

Uncle John shook his head over his plate. "Don't look like we're a-gonna get shet of this here. I bet it's my sin."

"Oh, shut up!" Pa cried. "We ain't got the time for your sin now. Come on now. Le's get out to her. Kids, you come he'p. Ma's right. We got to go outa here."

When they were gone, Ma took a plate and a cup to Tom. "Better eat a little somepin."

"I can't, Ma. I'm so darn sore I couldn' chew."

"You better try."

"No, I can't, Ma."

She sat down on the edge of his mattress. "You got to tell me," she said. "I got to figger how it was. I got to keep straight. What was Casy a-doin'? Why'd they kill 'im?"

"He was jus' standin' there with the lights on 'im."

"What'd he say? Can ya 'member what he says?"

Tom said, "Sure. Casy said, 'You got no right to starve people.' An' then this heavy fella called him a red son-of-a-bitch. An' Casy says, 'You don' know what you're a-doin'.' An' then this guy smashed 'im."

"Yeah!"

Ma looked down. She twisted her hands together. "That's what he said—'You don' know what you're doin'?'"

"Yeah!"

Ma said, "I wisht Granma could a heard."

"Ma—I didn' know what I was a-doin', no more'n when you take a breath. I didn' even know I was gonna do it."

"It's awright. I wisht you didn' do it. I wisht you wasn' there. But you done what you had to do. I can't read no fault on you." She went to the stove and dipped a cloth in the heating dishwater. "Here," she said. "Put that there on your face."

He laid the warm cloth over his nose and cheek, and winced at the heat. "Ma, I'm a-gonna go away tonight. I can't go puttin' this on you folks."

Ma said angrily, "Tom! They's a whole lot I don' un'erstan'. But goin' away ain't gonna ease us. It's gonna bear us down." And she went on, "They was the time when we was on the lan'. They was a boundary to us then. Ol' folks died off, an' little fellas come, an' we was always one thing—we was the fambly—kinda whole and clear. An' now we ain't clear no more. I can't get straight. They ain't nothin' keeps us clear. Al—he's a-hankerin' an' a jibbitin' to go off on his own. An' Uncle John is jus' a-draggin' along. Pa's lost his place. He ain't the head no more. We're crackin' up, Tom. There ain't no fambly now. An' Rosasharn—" She looked around and found the girl's wide eyes. "She gonna have her baby an' they won't be no fambly. I don' know. I been a-tryin' to keep her goin'. Winfiel'—what's he gonna be, this-a-way? Gettin' wild, an' Ruthie too—like animals. Got nothin' to trus'. Don' go, Tom. Stay an' help."

"O.K.," he said tiredly. "O.K. I shouldn', though. I know it."

Ma went to her dishpan and washed the tin plates and dried them. "You didn' sleep."

"No."

"Well, you sleep. I seen your clothes was wet. I'll hang 'em by the stove to dry." She finished her work. "I'm goin' now. I'll pick. Rosasharn, if anybody comes, Tom's sick, you hear? Don' let nobody in. You hear?" Rose of Sharon nodded. "We'll come back at noon. Get some sleep, Tom. Maybe we can get outa here tonight." She moved swiftly to him. "Tom, you ain't gonna slip out?"

"No, Ma."

"You sure? You won't go?"

"No, Ma. I'll be here."

"Awright. 'Member, Rosasharn." She went out and closed the door firmly behind her.

Tom lay still—and then a wave of sleep lifted him to the edge of unconsciousness and dropped him slowly back and lifted him again.

"You—Tom!"

"Huh? Yeah!" He started awake. He looked over at Rose of Sharon. Her eyes were blazing with resentment. "What you want?"

"You killed a fella!"

"Yeah. Not so loud! You wanta rouse somebody?"

"What da I care?" she cried. "That lady tol' me. She says what sin's gonna do. She tol' me. What chance I got to have a nice baby? Connie's gone, an' I ain't gettin' good food. I ain't gettin' milk." Her voice rose hysterically. "An' now you kill a fella. What chance that baby got to get bore right? I know—gonna be a freak—a freak! I never done no dancin'."

Tom got up. "Sh!" he said. "You're gonna get folks in here."

"I don' care. I'll have a freak! I didn' dance no hug-dance."

He went near to her. "Be quiet."

"You get away from me. It ain't the first fella you killed, neither." Her face was growing red with hysteria. Her words blurred. "I don' wanta look at you." She covered her head with her blanket.

Tom heard the choked, smothered cries. He bit his lower lip and studied the floor. And then he went to Pa's bed. Under the edge of the mattress the rifle lay, a lever-action Winchester .38, long and heavy. Tom picked it up and dropped the lever to see that a cartridge was in the chamber. He tested the hammer on half-cock. And then he went back to his mattress. He laid the rifle on the floor beside him, stock up and barrel pointing down. Rose of Sharon's voice thinned to a whimper. Tom lay down again and covered himself, covered his bruised cheek with the blanket and made a little tunnel to breathe through. He sighed, "Jesus, oh, Jesus!"

Outside, a group of cars went by, and voices sounded.

"How many men?"

"Jes' us—three. Whatcha payin'?"

"You go to house twenty-five. Number's right on the door."
"O.K., mister. Whatcha payin'?"
"Two and a half cents."
"Why, goddamn it, a man can't make his dinner!"
"That's what we're payin'. There's two hundred men coming from the South that'll be glad to get it."
"But, Jesus, mister!"
"Go on now. Either take it or go on along. I got no time to argue."
"But——"
"Look, I didn' set the price. I'm just checking you in. If you want it, take it. If you don't, turn right around and go along."
"Twenty-five, you say?"

HENRY ROTH

Call It Sleep

(1934)

In 1907, the year that David Schearl, the young hero of Call It Sleep, arrived with his mother from Russia, he was one of 1,285,000 immigrants—more than in any other single year. No story—real or fictional—can pretend to represent the experience of so vast and heterogeneous a group. Roth, in his careful artistry, establishes early that "there was something quite untypical" about his subjects' behavior. Nonetheless, this remarkable novel, published in 1934 and then republished to wide acclaim in 1960, offers an aperture through which to view some of the human meanings of this great historical movement.

The immigrants were not "uncultured" as Americans of the

era assumed; rather their native culture was, like poor David's straw hat with the polka dot ribbons, instantly converted into a badge of shame the moment they arrived in the new world. Roth reinforces the point with his astute rendering of speech. The Schearl's native Yiddish is presented in a pure and cultured English prose. But "In the street David spoke English," and that English is an extraordinary Brooklynese: "So wot makes id?" "Kentcha see? Id's coz id's a machine."

The immigrant ghettoes—the Lower East Side, the Little Italies, and Little Bohemias of the early twentieth century—have long since entered the illusory world of nostalgia. This is the "world of our fathers" to new generations of Americans seeking their roots. The suffering is forgotten—along with the losers like Albert Schearl—and the assimilation of tens of millions of immigrants is an American success story. Roth's vision of acculturation by degradation is a part of that history that few now alive remember or acknowledge.

Prologue

(I pray thee ask no questions this is that Golden Land)

The small white steamer, *Peter Stuyvesant*, that delivered the immigrants from the stench and throb of the steerage to the stench and the throb of New York tenements, rolled slightly on the water beside the stone quay in the lee of the weathered barracks and new brick buildings of Ellis Island. Her skipper was waiting for the last of the officials, laborers and guards to embark upon her before he cast off and started for Manhattan. Since this was Saturday afternoon and this the last trip she would make for the week-end, those left behind might have to stay over till Monday. Her whistle bellowed its hoarse warning. A few figures in overalls sauntered from the high doors of the immigration quarters and down the grey pavement that led to the dock.

It was May of the year 1907, the year that was destined to bring the greatest number of immigrants to the shores of the United States. All that day, as on all the days since spring began, her docks had been thronged by hundreds upon hundreds of foreigners, natives from almost every land in the world, the joweled close-cropped Teuton, the full-bearded Russian, the scraggly-whiskered Jew, and among them Slovack peasants with docile faces, smooth-cheeked and swarthy Armenians, pimply Greeks, Danes with wrinkled eyelids. All day her decks had been colorful, a matrix of the vivid costumes of other lands, the speckled green-and-yellow aprons, the flowered kerchief, embroidered homespun, the silver-braided sheepskin vest, the gaudy scarfs, yellow boots, fur caps, caftans, dull gabardines. All day the guttural, the high-pitched voices, the astonished cries, the gasps of wonder, reiterations of gladness had risen from her decks in a motley billow of sound. But now her decks were empty, quiet, spreading out under the sunlight almost as if the warm boards were relaxing from the strain and the pressure of the myriads of feet. All those steerage passengers of the ships that had docked that day who were permitted to enter had already entered—except two, a woman and a young child she carried in her arms. They had just come aboard escorted by a man.

About the appearance of these late comers there was very little that was unusual. The man had evidently spent some time in America and was now bringing his wife and child over from the other side. It might have been thought that he had spent most of his time in lower New York, for he paid only the scantest attention to the Statue of Liberty or to the city rising from the water or to the bridges spanning the East River—or perhaps he was merely too agitated to waste much time on these wonders. His clothes were the ordinary clothes the ordinary New Yorker wore in that period—sober and dull. A black derby accentuated the sharpness and sedentary pallor of his face; a jacket, loose on his tall spare frame, buttoned up in a V close to the throat; and above the V a tightly knotted black tie was mounted in the groove of a high starched collar. As for his wife, one guessed that she was a European more by the timid wondering look in her eyes as she gazed from her husband to the harbor, than by her clothes. For her clothes were American—a black skirt, a white shirt-waist and a black jacket. Obviously her husband had either taken the precaution of sending them to her while she was still in Europe or had brought them with him to Ellis Island where she had slipped them on before she left.

Only the small child in her arms wore a distinctly foreign costume, an impression one got chiefly from the odd, outlandish, blue straw hat on his head with its polka dot ribbons of the same color dangling over each shoulder.

Except for this hat, had the three newcomers been in a crowd, no one probably, could have singled out the woman and child as newly arrived immigrants. They carried no sheets tied up in huge bundles, no bulky wicker baskets, no prized feather beds, no boxes of delicacies, sausages, virgin-olive oils, rare cheeses; the large black satchel beside them was their only luggage. But despite this, despite their even less than commonplace appearance, the two overalled men, sprawled out and smoking cigarettes in the stern, eyed them curiously. And the old peddler woman, sitting with basket of oranges on knee, continually squinted her weak eyes in their direction.

The truth was there was something quite untypical about their behavior. The old peddler woman on the bench and the overalled men in the stern had seen enough husbands meeting their wives and children after a long absence to know how such people ought to behave. The most volatile races, such as the Italians, often danced for joy, whirled each other around, pirouetted in an ecstasy: Swedes sometimes just looked at each other, breathing through open mouths like a panting dog; Jews wept, jabbered, almost put each other's eyes out with the recklessness of their darting gestures; Poles roared and gripped each other at arm's length as though they meant to tear a handful of flesh; and after one pecking kiss, the English might be seen gravitating toward, but never achieving an embrace. But these two stood silent, apart; the man staring with aloof, offended eyes grimly down at the water—or if he turned his face toward his wife at all, it was only to glare in harsh contempt at the blue straw hat worn by the child in her arms, and then his hostile eyes would sweep about the deck to see if anyone else were observing them. And his wife beside him regarding him uneasily, appealingly. And the child against her breast looking from one to the other with watchful, frightened eyes. Altogether it was a very curious meeting.

They had been standing in this strange and silent manner for several minutes, when the woman, as if driven by the strain into action, tried to smile, and touching her husband's arm said timidly, "And this is the Golden Land." She spoke in Yiddish.

The man grunted, but made no answer.

She took a breath as if taking courage, and tremulously, "I'm sorry, Albert, I was so stupid." She paused waiting for some flicker of unbending, some word, which never came. "But you look so lean, Albert, so haggard. And your mustache—you've shaved."

His brusque glance stabbed and withdrew. "Even so."

"You must have suffered in this land." She continued gentle despite his rebuke. "You never wrote me. You're thin. Ach! Then here in the new land is the same old poverty. You've gone without food. I can see it. You've changed."

"Well that don't matter," he snapped, ignoring her sympathy. "It's no excuse for your not recognizing me. Who else would call for you? Do you know anyone else in this land?"

"No," placatingly. "But I was so frightened, Albert. Listen to me. I was so bewildered, and that long waiting there in that vast room since morning. Oh, that horrible waiting! I saw them all go, one after the other. The shoemaker and his wife. The coppersmith and his children from Strij. All those on the *Kaiserin Viktoria*. But I—I remained. To-morrow will be Sunday. They told me no one could come to fetch me. What if they sent me back? I was frantic!"

"Are you blaming me?" His voice was dangerous.

"No! No! Of course not Albert! I was just explaining."

"Well then let me explain," he said curtly. "I did what I could. I took the day off from the shop. I called that cursed Hamburg-American Line four times. And each time they told me you weren't on board."

"They didn't have any more third-class passage, so I had to take the steerage—"

"Yes, now I know. That's all very well. That couldn't be helped. I came here anyway. The last boat. And what do you do? You refused to recognize me. You don't know me." He dropped his elbows down on the rail, averted his angry face. "That's the greeting I get."

"I'm sorry, Albert," she stroked his arm humbly. "I'm sorry."

"And as if those blue-coated mongrels in there weren't mocking me enough, you give them that brat's right age. Didn't I write you to say seventeen months because it would save the half fare! Didn't you hear me inside when I told them?"

"How could I, Albert?" she protested. "How could I? You were on the other side of that—that cage."

"Well why didn't you say seventeen months anyway? Look!" he pointed to several blue-coated officials who came hurrying out of a doorway out of the immigration quarters. "There they are." An ominous pride dragged at his voice. "If he's among them, that one who questioned me so much, I could speak to him if he came up here."

"Don't bother with him, Albert," she exclaimed uneasily. "Please, Albert! What have you against him? He couldn't help it. It's his work."

"Is it?" His eyes followed with unswerving deliberation the blue-coats as they neared the boat. "Well he didn't have to do it so well."

"And after all, I did lie to him, Albert," she said hurriedly trying to distract him.

"The truth is you didn't," he snapped, turning his anger against her. "You made your first lie plain by telling the truth afterward. And made a laughing-stock of me!"

"I didn't know what to do." She picked despairingly at the wire grill beneath the rail. "In Hamburg the doctor laughed at me when I said seventeen months. He's so big. He was big when he was born." She smiled, the worried look on her face vanishing momentarily as she stroked her son's cheek. "Won't you speak to your father, David, beloved?"

The child merely ducked his head behind his mother.

His father stared at him, shifted his gaze and glared down at the officials, and then, as though perplexity had crossed his mind he frowned absently. "How old did he say he was?"

"The doctor? Over two years—and as I say he laughed."

"Well what did he enter?"

"Seventeen months—I told you."

"Then why didn't you tell them seventeen—" He broke off, shrugged violently. "Baah! You need more strength in this land." He paused, eyed her intently and then frowned suddenly. "Did you bring his birth certificate?"

"Why—" She seemed confused. "It may be in the trunk—there on the ship. I don't know. Perhaps I left it behind." Her hand wandered uncertainly to her lips. "I don't know. Is it important? I never thought of it. But surely father could send it. We need only write."

"Hmm! Well, put him down." His head jerked brusquely toward the child. "You don't need to carry him all the way. He's big enough to stand on his own feet."

She hesitated, and then reluctantly set the child down on the deck. Scared, unsteady, the little one edged over to the side opposite his father, and hidden by his mother, clung to her skirt.

"Well, it's all over now." She attempted to be cheerful. "It's all behind us now, isn't it, Albert? Whatever mistakes I made don't really matter any more. Do they?"

"A fine taste of what lies before me!" He turned his back on her and leaned morosely against the rail. "A fine taste!"

They were silent. On the dock below, the brown hawsers had been slipped over the mooring posts, and the men on the lower deck now dragged them dripping from the water. Bells clanged. The ship throbbed. Startled by the hoarse bellow of her whistle, the gulls wheeling before her prow rose with slight creaking cry from the green water, and as she churned away from the stone quay skimmed across her path on indolent, scimitar wing. Behind the ship the white wake that stretched to Ellis Island grew longer, raveling wanly into melon-green. On one side curved the low drab Jersey coast-line, the spars and masts on the waterfront fringing the sky; on the other side was Brooklyn, flat, water-towered; the horns of the harbor. And before them, rising on her high pedestal from the scaling swarmy brilliance of sunlit water to the west, Liberty. The spinning disk of the late afternoon sun slanted behind her, and to those on board who gazed, her features were charred with shadow, her depths exhausted, her masses ironed to one single plane. Against the luminous sky the rays of her halo were spikes of darkness roweling the air; shadow flattened the torch she bore to a black cross against flawless light—the blackened hilt of a broken sword. Liberty. The child and his mother stared again at the massive figure in wonder.

The ship curved around in a long arc toward Manhattan, her bow sweeping past Brooklyn and the bridges whose cables and pillars superimposed by distance, spanned the East River in diaphanous and rigid waves. The western wind that raked the harbor into brilliant clods blew fresh and clear—a salt tang in the lull of its veerings. It whipped the polka-dot ribbons on the child's hat straight out behind him. They caught his father's eye.

"Where did you find that crown?"

Startled by his sudden question his wife looked down. "That? That was Maria's parting gift. The old nurse. She bought it herself and then sewed the ribbons on. You don't think it's pretty?"

"Pretty? Do you still ask?" His lean jaws hardly moved as he spoke. "Can't you see that those idiots lying back there are watching us already? They're mocking us! What will the others do on the train? He looks like a clown in it. He's the cause of all this trouble anyway!"

The harsh voice, the wrathful glare, the hand flung toward the child frightened him. Without knowing the cause, he knew that the stranger's anger was directed at himself. He burst into tears and pressed closer to his mother.

"Quiet!" the voice above him snapped.

Cowering, the child wept all the louder.

"Hush, darling!" His mother's protecting hands settled on his shoulders.

"Just when we're about to land!" her husband said furiously. "He begins this! This howling! And now we'll have it all the way home, I suppose! Quiet! You hear?"

"It's you who are frightening him, Albert!" she protested.

"Am I? Well, let him be quiet. And take that straw gear off his head."

"But Albert, it's cool here."

"Will you take that off when I—" A snarl choked whatever else he would have uttered. While his wife looked on aghast, his long fingers scooped the hat from the child's head. The next instant it was sailing over the ship's side to the green waters below. The overalled men in the stern grinned at each other. The old orange-peddler shook her head and clucked.

"Albert!" his wife caught her breath. "How could you?"

"I could!" he rapped out. "You should have left it behind!" His teeth clicked, and he glared about the deck.

She lifted the sobbing child to her breast, pressed him against her. With a vacant stunned expression, her gaze wandered from the grim smouldering face of her husband to the stern of the ship. In the silvery-green wake that curved trumpet-wise through the water, the blue hat still bobbed and rolled, ribbon stretched out on the waves. Tears sprang to her eyes. She brushed them away quickly, shook her head as if shaking off the memory, and looked toward the bow. Before her the grimy cupolas and towering square walls of the city loomed up. Above the jagged roof tops, the white smoke, whitened and suffused by the slanting sun, faded into the slots and wedges of the sky. She pressed her brow against her child's, hushed him with whispers. This was that vast incredible land, the land of freedom, of immense opportunity, that Golden Land. Again she tried to smile.

"Albert," she said timidly, "Albert."

"Hm?"

"Gehen vir voinen du? In Nev York?"

"Nein. Bronzeville. Ich hud dir schoin geschriben."

She nodded uncertainly, sighed . . .

Screws threshing, backing water, the *Peter Stuyvesant* neared her dock—drifting slowly and with canceled momentum as if reluctant.

I

Standing before the kitchen sink and regarding the bright brass faucets that gleamed so far away, each with a bead of water at its nose, slowly swelling, falling, David again became aware that this world had been created without thought of him. He was thirsty, but the iron hip of the sink rested on legs tall almost as his own body, and by no stretch of arm, no leap, could he ever reach the distant tap. Where did the water come from that lurked so secretly in the curve of the brass? Where did it go, gurgling in the drain? What a strange world must be hidden behind the walls of a house! But he was thirsty.

"Mama!" he called, his voice rising above the hiss of sweeping in the frontroom. "Mama, I want a drink."

The unseen broom stopped to listen. "I'll be there in a moment," his mother answered. A chair squealed on its castors; a window chuckled down; his mother's approaching tread.

Standing in the doorway on the top step (two steps led up into the frontroom) his mother smilingly surveyed him. She looked as tall as a tower. The old grey dress she wore rose straight from strong bare ankle to waist, curved round the deep bosom and over the wide shoulders, and set her full throat in a frame of frayed lace. Her smooth, sloping face was flushed now with her work, but faintly so, diffused, the color of a hand beneath wax. She had mild, full lips, brown hair. A vague, fugitive darkness blurred the hollow above her cheekbone, giving to her face and to her large brown eyes, set in their white ovals, a reserved and almost mournful air.

"I want a drink, mama," he repeated.

"I know," she answered, coming down the stairs. "I heard you." And casting a quick, sidelong glance at him, she went over to the sink and turned the tap. The water spouted noisily down. She stood there a moment, smiling obscurely, one finger parting the turbulent jet, waiting for the water to cool. Then filling a glass, she handed it down to him.

"When am I going to be big enough?" he asked resentfully as he took the glass in both hands.

"There will come a time," she answered, smiling. She rarely smiled broadly; instead the thin furrow along her upper lip would deepen. "Have little fear."

With eyes still fixed on his mother, he drank the water in breathless, uneven gulps, then returned the glass to her, surprised to see its contents scarcely diminished.

"Why can't I talk with my mouth in the water?"

"No one would hear you. Have you had your fill?"

He nodded, murmuring contentedly.

"And is that all?" she asked. Her voice held a faint challenge.

"Yes," he said hesitantly, meanwhile scanning her face for some clue.

"I thought so," she drew her head back in droll disappointment.

"What?"

"It is summer," she pointed to the window, "the weather grows warm. Whom will you refresh with the icy lips the water lent you?"

"Oh!" he lifted his smiling face.

"You remember nothing," she reproached him, and with a throaty chuckle, lifted him in her arms.

Sinking his fingers in her hair, David kissed her brow. The faint familiar warmth and odor of her skin and hair.

"There!" she laughed, nuzzling his cheek, "but you've waited too long; the sweet chill has dulled. Lips for me," she reminded him, "must always be cool as the water that wet them." She put him down.

"Sometime I'm going to eat some ice," he said warningly, "then you'll like it."

She laughed. And then soberly, "Aren't you ever going down into the street? The morning grows old."

"Aaa!"

"You'd better go. Just for a little while. I'm going to sweep here, you know."

"I want my calendar first," he pouted, invoking his privilege against the evil hour.

"Get it then. But you've got to go down afterwards."

He dragged a chair over beneath the calendar on the wall, clambered up, plucked off the outworn leaf, and fingered the remaining ones to see how far off the next red day was. Red days were Sundays, days his father was home. It always gave David a little qualm of dread to watch them draw near.

"Now you have your leaf," his mother reminded him. "Come." She stretched out her arms.

He held back. "Show me where my birthday is."

"Woe is me!" She exclaimed with an impatient chuckle. "I've shown it to you every day for weeks now."

"Show me again."

She rumpled the pad, lifted a thin plaque of leaves. "July—" she murmured, "July 12th . . . There!" She found it. "July 12th, 1911. You'll be six then."

David regarded the strange figures gravely. "Lots of pages still," he informed her.

"Yes."

"And a black day too."

"On the calendar," she laughed, "only on the calendar. Now do come down!"

Grasping her arm, he jumped down from the chair. "I must hide it now." He explained.

"So you must. I see I'll never finish my work today."

Too absorbed in his own affairs to pay much heed to hers, he went over to the pantry beneath the cupboard, opened the door and drew out a shoe-box, his treasure chest.

"See how many I've got already?" he pointed proudly to the fat sheaf of rumpled leaves inside the box.

"Wonderful!" She glanced at the box in perfunctory admiration. "You peel off the year as one might a cabbage. Are you ready for your journey?"

"Yes." He put away the box without a trace of alacrity.

"Where is your sailor blouse?" she murmured looking about. "With the white strings in it? What have I—?" She found it. "There is still a little wind."

David held up his arms for her to slip the blouse over his head.

"Now, my own," she said, kissing his reemerging face. "Go down and play." She led him toward the door and opened it. "Not too far. And remember if I don't call you, wait until the whistle blows."

He went out into the hallway. Behind him, like an eyelid shutting, the soft closing of the door winked out the light. He assayed the stairs, lapsing below him into darkness, and grasping one by one each slender upright to the banister, went down. David never found himself alone on these stairs, but he wished there were no carpet covering them. How could you heard the sound of your own feet in the dark if a carpet muffled every step you took? And if you couldn't hear the sound of your own feet and couldn't see anything either, how could you be sure you were actually there and not dreaming? A few steps from the bottom landing, he paused and stared rigidly at the cellar door. It bulged with darkness. Would it hold? . . . It held! He jumped from the last steps and raced through the narrow hallway to the light of the street. Flying through the doorway was like butting a wave. A dazzling breaker of sunlight burst over his head, swamped him in reeling blur of brilliance, and then receded . . . A row of frame houses half in thin shade, a pitted gutter, a yawning ashcan, flotsam on the shore, his street.

Blinking and almost shaken, he waited on the low stoop a moment, until his whirling vision steadied. Then for the first time, he noticed that seated on the curbstone near the house was a boy, whom an instant later, he recognized. It was Yussie who had just moved into David's house and who lived on the floor above. Yussie had a very red, fat face. His big sister walked with a limp and wore strange iron slats on one of her legs. What was he doing, David wondered, what did he have in his hands? Stepping down from the stoop, he drew near, and totally disregarded, stood beside him.

Yussie had stripped off the outer shell of an alarm clock. Exposed, the brassy, geometric vitals ticked when prodded, whirred and jingled falteringly.

"It still c'n go," Yussie gravely enlightened him. David sat down. Fascinated, he stared at the shining cogs that moved without moving their hearts of light. "So wot makes id?" he asked. In the street David spoke English.

"Kentcha see? Id's coz id's a machine."

"Oh!"

"It wakes op mine fodder in de mawning."

"It wakes op mine fodder too."

"It tells yuh w'en yuh sh'd eat an' w'en yuh have tuh go tuh sleep. It shows yuh w'ea, but I tooked it off."

"I god a calenduh opstai's." David informed him.

"Puh! Who ain' god a calenduh?"

"I save mine. I godda big book outa dem, wit numbuhs on id."

"Who can't do dat?"

"But mine fodder made it," David drove home the one unique point about it all.

"Wot's your fodder?"

"Mine fodder is a printer."

"Mine fodder woiks inna joolery shop. In Brooklyn. Didja ever live in Brooklyn?"

"No." David shook his head.

"We usetuh—right near my fodder's joolery shop on Rainey Avenyuh. W'ea does your fodder woik?"

David tried to think. "I don't know." He finally confessed, hoping that Yussie would not pursue the subject further.

He didn't. Instead "I don' like Brownsville," he said. "I like Brooklyn bedder."

David felt relieved.

"We usetuh find cigahs innuh gudduh," Yussie continued. "An we usetuh t'row 'em on de ladies, an we usetuh run. Who you like bedder, ladies or gents?"

"Ladies."

"I like mine fodder bedder," said Yussie. "My mudder always holluhs on me." He pried a nail between two wheels. A bright yellow gear suddenly snapped off and fell to the gutter at his feet. He picked it up, blew the dust off, and rose. "Yuh want?"

"Yea," David reached for it.

Yussie was about to drop it into his outstretched palm, but on second thought, drew back. "No. Id's liddle like a penny. Maybe I c'n pud id inna slot machine 'n' gid gum. Hea, yuh c'n take dis one." He fished a larger gear out of his pocket, gave it to David. "Id's a quarter. Yuh wanna come?"

David hesitated. "I godduh waid hea till duh wissle blows."

"W'a wissle?"

"By de fectory. All togedder."

"So?"

"So den I c'n go opstai's."

"So w'y?"

"Cuz dey blow on twelve a'clock an' den dey blow on five a'clock. Den I c'n go op."

Yussie eyed him curiously. "I'm gonna gid gum," he said, shrugging off his perplexity. "In duh slod machine." And he ambled off in the direction of the candy store on the corner.

Holding the little wheel in his hand, David wondered again why it was that every boy on the street knew where his father worked except himself. His father had so many jobs. No sooner did you learn where he was working then he was working somewhere else. And why was he always saying, "They look at me crookedly, with mockery in their eyes! How much can a man endure? May the fire of God consume them!" A terrifying picture rose in David's mind—the memory of how once at the supper table his mother had dared to say that perhaps the men weren't really looking at him crookedly, perhaps he was only imagining it. His father had snarled then. And with one sudden sweep of his arm had sent food and dishes crashing to the floor. And other pictures came in its train, pictures of the door being kicked open and his father coming in looking pale and savage and sitting down like old men sit down, one trembling hand behind him groping for the chair. He wouldn't speak. His jaws, and even his joints, seemed to have become fused together by a withering rage.

David often dreamed of his father's footsteps booming on the stairs, of the glistening doorknob turning, and of himself clutching at knives he couldn't lift from the table.

Brooding, engrossed in his thoughts, engrossed in the rhythmic, accurate teeth of the yellow cog in his hand, the thin bright circles whirling restlessly without motion, David was unaware that a little group of girls had gathered in the gutter some distance away. But when they began to sing, he started and looked up. Their faces were sober, their hands locked in one another; circling slowly in a ring they chanted in a plaintive nasal chorus:

"Waltuh, Waltuh, Wiuhlflowuh,
Growin' up so high;
So we are all young ladies,
An' we are ready to die."

Again and again, they repeated their burden. Their words obscure at first, emerged at last, gathered meaning. The song troubled David strangely. Walter Wildflower was a little boy. David knew him. He lived in Europe, far away, where David's mother said he was born. He had seen him standing on a hill, far away. Filled with a warm, nostalgic mournfulness, he shut his eyes. Fragments of forgotten rivers floated under the lids, dusty roads, fathomless curve of trees, a branch in a window under flawless light. A world somewhere, somewhere else.

"Waltuh, Waltuh, Wiuhlflowuh,
Growin' up so high,"

His body relaxed, yielding to the rhythm of the song and to the golden June sunlight. He seemed to rise and fall on waves somewhere without him. Within him a voice spoke with no words but with the shift of slow flame: . . .

"So we are all young ladies,
An' we are ready to die."

From the limp, uncurling fingers, the cog rolled to the ground, rang like a coin, fell over on its side. The sudden sound moored him again, fixed him to the quiet, suburban street, the curbstone. The inarticulate flame that had pulsed within him, wavered and went out. He sighed, bent over and picked up the wheel.

When would the whistle blow he wondered. It took long today. . . .

II

As far back as he could remember, this was the first time that he had ever gone anywhere alone with his father, and already he felt desolated, stirred with dismal forebodings, longing desperately for his mother. His father was so silent and so remote that he felt as though he were alone even at his side. What if his father should abandon him, leave him in some lonely street. The thought sent shudders of horror through his body. No! No! He couldn't do that!

At last they reached the trolley lines. The sight of people cheered him again, dispelling his fear for a while. They boarded a car, rode what seemed to him a long time and then got off in a crowded street under an elevated. Nervously gripping David's arm, his father guided him across the street. They stopped before the stretched iron wicker of a closed theatre. Colored billboards on either side of them, the odor of stale perfume behind. People hurrying, trains roaring. David gazed about him frightened. To the right of the theatre, in the window of an ice cream parlor, gaudy, colored popcorn danced and drifted, blown by a fan. He looked up apprehensively at his father. He was pale, grim. The fine veins in his nose stood out like a pink cobweb.

"Do you see that door?" He shook him into attention. "In the grey house. See? That man just came out of there."

"Yes, Papa."

"Now you go in there and go up the stairs and you'll see another door. Go right in. And to the first man you see inside, say this: I'm Albert Schearl's son. He wants you to give me the clothes in his locker and the money that's coming to him. Do you understand? When they've given it to you bring it down here. I'll be waiting for you. Now what will you say?" he demanded abruptly.

David began to repeat his instructions in Yiddish.

"Say it in English, you fool!"

He rendered them in English. And when he had satisfied his father that he knew them, he was sent in.

"And don't tell them I'm out here," he was warned as he left. "Remember you came alone!"

Full of misgivings, unnerved at the ordeal of facing strangers alone, strangers of whom his own father seemed apprehensive, he entered the hallway, climbed the stairs. One flight up, he pushed open the door and entered a small room, an office. From somewhere back of this office, machinery clanked and rattled. A bald-headed man smoking a cigar looked up as he came in.

"Well, my boy," he asked smiling, "what do you want?"

For a moment all of his instructions flew out of his head. "My—my fodder sent me hea." He faltered.

"Your father? Who's he?"

"I—I'm Albert Schearl's son," he blurted out. "He sent me I shuh ged his clo's f'om de locker an' his money you owing him."

"Oh, you're Albert Schearl's son," said the man, his expression changing. "And he wants his money, eh?" He nodded with the short vibrating motion of a bell. "You've got some father, my boy. You can tell him that for me. I didn't get a chance. He's crazy. Anybody who— What does he do at home?"

David shook his head guiltily, "Nuttin."

"No?" he chuckled. "Nothin', hey? Well—" he broke off and went over to a small arched window in the rear. "Joe!" he called. "Oh Joe! Come here a minute, will you?"

In a few seconds a gray-haired man in overalls came in.

"Call me, Mr. Lobe?"

"Yea, will you get Schearl's things out of his locker and wrap 'em up for me. His kid's here."

The other man's face broke into a wide, brown-toothed grin. "Is zat his kid?" As if to keep from laughing his tongue worried the quid of tobacco in his cheek.

"Yea."

"He don' look crazy." He burst into a laugh.

"No." Mr. Lobe subdued him with a wave of his hand. "He's a nice kid."

"Your ol' man near brained me wid a hammer," said the man addressing David. "Don' know wot happened, nobody said nuttin." He grinned. "Never saw such a guy, Mr. Lobe. Holy Jesus, he looked like he wuz boinin' up. Didja see de rail he twisted wid his hands? Maybe I oughta to give it to 'im fer a souvenir?"

Mr. Lobe grinned. "Let the kid alone," he said quietly. "Get his stuff."

"O.K." Still chuckling, the gray-haired man went out.

"Sit down, my boy," said Mr. Lobe, pointing to a seat. "We'll have your father's things here in a few minutes."

David sat down. In a few minutes, a girl, bearing a paper in her hand, came into the office.

"Say, Marge," said Mr. Lobe, "find out what Schearl gets, will you."

"Yes, Mr. Lobe." She regarded David, "What's that, his boy?"

"Mmm."

"Looks like him, don't he?"

"Maybe."

"I'd have him arrested," said the girl opening up a large ledger.

"What good would that do?"

"I don't know, it might put some sense into his head."

Mr. Lobe shrugged. "I'm only too glad he didn't kill anybody."

"He ought to be in a padded cell," said the girl scribbling something on a paper.

Mr. Lobe made no response.

"He gets six sixty-two." She put down her pencil. "Shall I get it?"

"Mmm."

The girl went over to a large black safe in a corner, drew out a box, and when she had counted out some money, put it into a small envelope and gave it to Mr. Lobe.

"Come here," he said to David. "What's your name?"

"David."

"David and Goliath," he smiled. "Well, David, have you got a good deep pocket? Let's see." He picked up the tails of David's jacket. "There, that's the one I want." And fingering the small watch-pocket at the waist. "We'll put it in there." He folded the envelope and wedged it in. "Now don't take it out. Don't tell anybody you've got it till you get home, understand? The idea, sending a kid his age on an errand like this."

David, staring ahead of him, under Mr. Lobe's arm, was aware of two faces, peering in at the little window in the back. The eyes of both were fastened on him, regarding him with a curious and amused scrutiny of men beholding for the first time some astonishing freak. They both grinned when the girl, happening to turn in their direction, saw them; one of the men winked and cranked his temple with his hand. As Mr. Lobe turned, both disappeared. A moment later, the gray-haired man returned with a paper-wrapped bundle.

"Here's all I c'n find, Mr. Lobe. His towel, and his shoit an' a jacket."

"All right, Joe," Mr. Lobe took the package from him and turned to David. "Here you are, my boy. Put it under your arm and don't lose it." He tucked it under David's arm. "Not heavy, is it? No? That's good." He opened the door to let David pass. "Good bye." A dry smile whisked over his features. "Pretty tough for you."

Grasping the bundle firmly under his arm, David went slowly down the stairs. So that was how his father quit a place! He held a hammer in hand, he would have killed somebody. David could almost see him, the hammer raised over his head, his face contorted in terrific wrath, the rest cringing away. He shuddered at the image in his mind, stopped motionless on the stair, terrified at having to confront the reality. But he must go down; he must meet him; it would be worse for him if he remained on the stair any longer. He didn't want to go, but he had to. If only the stairs were twice as high.

He hurried down, came out into the street. His father, his back pressed close to the iron wicker, was waiting for him, and when he saw him come out, motioned to him to hurry and began walking away. David ran after him, caught up to him finally, and his father, without slackening his pace, relieved him of the bundle.

"They took long enough," he said, casting a malevolent glance over his shoulder. It was evident from his face that he had worked himself into a rage during the interval that David had left him. "They gave you the money?"

"Yes, Papa."

"How much?"

"Six—six dollars, the girl—"

"Did they say anything to you?" His teeth clenched grimly, "About me?"

"No, Papa," he answered hurriedly. "Nothing, Papa. They just gave me the—the money and I went down."

"Where is it?"

"Over here," he pointed to the pocket.

"Well, give it to me!"

With difficulty, David uprooted the envelope from his pocket. His father snatched it from him, counted the money.

"And so they said nothing, eh?" He seemed to demand a final confirmation. "None of the men spoke to you, did they? Only that bald-headed pig with the glasses?" He was watching him narrowly.

"No, Papa. Only that man. He just gave me the money." He knew that while his father's eyes rested on him he must look frank, he must look wide-eyed, simple.

"Very well!" His lips stretched for a brief instant in fleeting satisfaction. "Good!"

They stopped at the corner and waited for the trolley. . . .

David never said anything to anyone of what he had discovered, not even to his mother—it was all too terrifying, too unreal to share with someone else. He brooded about it till it entered his sleep, till he no longer could tell where his father was flesh and where dream. Who would believe him if he said, I saw my father lift a hammer; he was standing on a high roof of darkness, and below him were faces uplifted, so many, they stretched like white cobbles to the end of the world; who would believe him? He dared not.

III

The table had been set with the best dishes. There was a chicken roasting in the oven. His mother was pouring the last of the Passover's lustrous red wine from the wicker-covered bottle into the fat flagon. She had been quiet till now, but as she set the bottle down in the center of the table, she turned to David who was watching her. "I feel something I don't know what," she said. "Troubled." She looked at the floor a moment, gazing mournfully at nothing; then turned up her palm as if asking herself, "why," and sighing let her hands fall again, as if unanswered. "Perhaps it is because I think my work is fated to be lost."

David wondered a moment why she had said that, and then he remembered. That man was coming, that man whose name had been on his father's lips for the last week—ever since he had gotten his new job. That man was a foreman. His father said that they came from the same region in far-off Austria. How strange it was that they should come from far away and find each other in the same shop, and find each other living in the same neighborhood in Brownsville. His father had said that he had found a true friend now, but his mother had sighed. And now she sighed again and said that her work was fated to be lost. David hoped that she would be wrong. He wanted to be like the other boys in the street. He wanted to be able to say where his father worked.

Soon he heard his father's voice on the stairs. His mother rose, looked about her hastily to see whether all was prepared and then went to the door and opened it. The two men came in, his father first and the other man after him.

"Well, here we are," said his father with nervous heartiness. "This is my wife. This is Joe Luter, my countryman. And that over there," he pointed to David, "is what will pray for me after my death. Make yourself at home."

"A fine home you have here," said the other smiling at David's mother. "Very, very fine," he beamed.

"It's livable," answered David's mother.

"A fine boy too." He eyed David approvingly.

"Well!" said his father abruptly, "Let's have some dinner soon, eh?"

While his father was urging Luter to drink some wine, David examined the newcomer. In height he was not as tall as his father, but was much broader, fleshier, and unlike his father had a fair paunch. His face was somehow difficult to get accustomed to. It was not because it was particularly ugly or because it was scarred, but because one felt one's own features trying to imitate it while one looked at it. His mouth so very short and the bow of his lips so very thick and arched that David actually felt himself waiting for it to relax. And the way his nostrils swelled up and out almost fatigued one and one hoped the deep dimples in his cheek would soon fill out. His speech was very slow and level, his whole attitude, tolerant and attentive, and because of this and because of the permanent wreathing of his features, he gave one the impression of great affability and good nature. In fact, as it soon turned out, he was not only affable, but very appreciative and very polite and commended in very warm tones the wine and the cake that was served with it, the neatness of the house as compared to his landlady's and finally congratulated David's father on having so excellent a wife.

When supper was served, he refused to begin eating until David's mother had sat down—which embarrassed her since she always served the others first—and then during the meal was very considerate of everyone, passing meat and bread and salt before it was asked for. When he spoke, he included everyone in the conversation, sometimes by asking questions, sometimes by fixing his eyes upon one. All of which disconcerted David not a little. Accustomed as he was to almost silent meals, to being either ignored or taken for granted, he resented this forcing of self-awareness upon him, this intruding of questions like a false weave into the fabric and pattern of his thought. But chiefly he found himself resenting Mr. Luter's eyes. They seemed to be independent of his speech, far outstripping it in fact; for instead of glancing at one, they fixed one and then held on until the voice caught up. It became a kind of uneasy game with David, a kind of secret tag, to beat Luter's gaze before it caught him, to look down at the tablecloth or at his mother the very moment he felt these eyes veering toward him.

Conversation touched on many subjects, drifting from the problems of the printing trade and the possibilities of a union among the printers to the problems and possibilities (and blessings, said Luter with a smile) of marriage. And then from this land to the old land and back again to this. And whether David's mother kept a kosher house—at which she smiled—and whether David's father still had time to don phylacteries in the morning and what synagogue he attended—at which his father snorted, amused. Most of what they said interested David only vaguely. What did fascinate him, however, was the curious effect that Luter had on his father. For once that brusque, cold manner of his had thawed a little. A faint though guarded deference mitigated somewhat the irrevocable quality with which his voice always bound his words. He would ask at the end of a statement he had just made, "Don't you think so?" Sometimes he would begin by saying, "It seems to me." It was strange. It disturbed David. He didn't know whether to be grateful to Luter for softening the harsh, inflexible edge of his father's temperament, or to be uneasy. Somehow it was a little unreal to see his father expand this way, uncoil warily like a tense spring slowly released. And urged on by only a sympathetic look from Luter, to hear him speak of his youth, he, who was so taciturn and thin-lipped, whom David never could think of as having a youth, speaking of his youth, of the black and white bulls he had tended for his father (and try to hide a frown at the word, father, he, who never hid displeasure), how they had fed them mash from his father's yeast mill, how he had won a prize with them from the hand of Franz Joseph, the King. Why did Luter need to look that way to make his father speak? Why did Luter only need to say, "I don't like the earth. It's for peasants," to make his father laugh, to make his father answer. "*I think* I do. *I think* when you come out of a house and step on the bare earth among the fields you're the same man you were when you were inside the house. But when you step out on pavements, you're someone else. You can feel your face change. *Hasn't that happened to you?*" And all that Luter needed to say was, "Yes. You're right, Albert," and his father would take a deep breath of satisfaction. It was strange. Why had no one else ever succeeded in doing that? Why not his mother? Why not himself? No one except Luter.

His questions went unanswered. He only knew that when supper was over he wanted very much to like Luter. He wanted to like any man who praised his mother and guided his father into untrodden paths of amiability. He wanted to like him, but he couldn't. But that would pass, he assured himself. As soon as Luter came again he would like him. Yes, the very next time. He was sure of it. He wanted to. As soon as he got used to his eyes. Yes.

A little while after dinner, Luter got up to go. His father protested that he had just come, that he ought to stay at least another hour.

"I also have to work in the morning," Luter reminded him. "Otherwise I would stay. It's heaven compared to my landlady's." And then he turned to David's mother, and in his slow way, smiling, extended his hand. "I want to thank you a thousand times, Mrs. Schearl, I haven't had so good a dinner or so much to eat since my last uncle was married."

She reddened as she shook hands with him and laughed. "You've praised everything but the water you drank."

"Yes." He laughed also. "And the salt. But I was afraid you wouldn't believe me if I said their flavor surpassed all others."

And after exchanging "Good-nights" and patting David's head (which David wasn't quite reconciled to) he left.

"Ha!" his father exclaimed exultantly after he had gone. "I told you this cursed wandering from job to job would end. I'm working for Dolman's Press to stay. Now time may bring something—who knows. There are two other foremen there. I'm as good a pressman as any of them. I know more about that iron juggler than they do. Who knows? Who knows? A little money. In time I might even suggest to him that we try— Well! In time! In time!"

"He looks like a very decent man," said his mother.

"Wait till you really know him!"

And from Luter's departure to his bedtime, David never remembered spending so serene an hour in his father's presence. . . .

IV

"Not a single one?" Luter was asking with some surprise. "Not in the old land either?"

The old land. David's thoughts turned outward. Anything about the old land was always worth listening to.

"Not one," his mother answered. "Nothing ever came to my hamlet except the snow and the rain. Not that I minded. Except once—yes. A man with a gramophone—the kind you listened to with ear pieces. It cost a penny to listen to it, and it wasn't even worth that. I never heard anything labor so and squawk. But the peasants were awed. They swore there was a devil in the box."

Luter laughed. "And that's all you had seen before you came here to this turmoil?"

"I've seen little enough of *it!* I know that I myself live on one hundred and twenty-six Boddeh Stritt—"

"Bahday Street!" Her husband corrected her. "I've told you scores of times."

"Boddeh Stritt," she resumed apologetically. He shrugged. "It's such a strange name—bath street in German. But here I am. I know there is a church on a certain street to my left, the vegetable market is to my right, behind me are the railroad tracks and the broken rocks, and before me, a few blocks away is a certain store window that has a kind of white-wash on it—and faces in the white-wash, the kind children draw. Within this pale is my America, and if I ventured further I should be lost. In fact," she laughed, "were they even to wash that window, I might never find my way home again."

His father made an impatient gesture. "Speaking of Yiddish plays," he said, "I did see one. It was when I stayed with my father in Lemberg, the days of the great fair. They called it the Revenge of Samson. I can see him yet, blind, but shaggy again, waiting his time against the pagans. It moved me greatly."

"For my part," said Luter, "I go to the theatre to laugh. Shall I go there and be tormented when life itself is a plague? No, give me rather a mad jester or the antics of a spry wench."

"I don't care for that." His father was brief.

"Well, I'm not mad about it either, you understand, but I was just saying sometimes when one is gloomy it does the heart good. Don't you think great laughter heals the soul, Mrs. Schearl?"

"I suppose so."

"There, you see! But listen, I have an idea. You know that the People's Theatre always gives Dolman the job of printing its placards. Well, it has a stage that is never empty of tears—at least one good death rattle is heard every night. And if you like that sort of play, why I can talk to the agent or whatever he's called and squeeze a whole month's pass out of him. You know they change every week."

"I don't know whether I want to." His father frowned dubiously.

"Why, certainly! It won't be any trouble at all. And it won't cost you a cent. I'll get a pass for two, you watch me. I wish I had known this before."

"Don't trouble about me," said his mother. "Many thanks, but I couldn't possibly go away and leave David here alone."

"Oh, that can be solved!" he assured her. "That's the least of your worries. But first let me get the pass." Luter left early that evening, before David was put to bed. And when he was gone, his father turned to his mother and said, "Well, did I make a mistake when I said this man was my friend? Did I? Here is one who knows how to express friendship, here as well as in the shop. Tell me, do I know a decent man when I see him?"

"You do," was the mild answer.

"And you with your fear of taking strangers into the house!" he continued scornfully. "Could you ever have a better boarder than he?"

"It isn't that. I'm glad to serve him dinners regularly. But I do know that most often it's better for friends to be a little apart than always together."

"Nonsense!" He retorted. "It's your silly pride."

V

Trinkets held in the mortar of desire, the fancy a trowel, the whim the builder. A wall, a tower, stout, secure, incredible, immuring the spirit from a flight of arrows, the mind, experience, shearing the flow of time as a rock shears water. The minutes skirted by, unknown.

His mother and father had left for the theatre, and he was alone with Luter. He would not see his mother again until morning, and morning, with his mother gone, had become remote and tentative. The tears had started to his eyes when she left, and Luter had said "Come child, do you begrudge your mother the little pleasure she may get to-night?" David had stared sullenly at the floor, aware that a great resentment against Luter was gathering within him. Had not Luter been the agent of his mother's going? And now how dared he reprove him for weeping when she was gone! How did he know what it felt like to be left alone? It wasn't *his* mother.

"Now you look just like your father." Luter had laughed. "He has just such lips when he frowns."

There had been something in his voice that had had a peculiar sting to it. Hurt, David had turned away and gotten out his box in the pantry in which he saved both the calendar leaves he collected and whatever striking odds and ends he found in the street. His mother called them his gems and often asked him why he liked things that were worn and old. It would have been hard to tell her. But there was something about the way in which the link of a chain was worn or the thread on a bolt or a castor-wheel that gave him a vague feeling of pain when he ran his fingers over them. They were like worn shoe-soles or very thin dimes. You never saw them wear, you only knew they were worn, obscurely aching.

He fingered one of his newly-found acquisitions. It was one of those perforated metal corks that the barber used to squirt perfumed water on one's head. One could blow through it, peep through it, it could be strung on a thread. He dropped it back into the box and picked up instead the stretched helix of a small window-shade spring. If one had these on one's feet instead of shoes, one might bound instead of walk. High as the roof; far away at once. Like Puss in Boots. But if the mouse changed back into an ogre inside the puss—just before he died—I'm a mouse—an ogre!— Then poor Puss would have swelled and swelled and—

Luter sighed. Startled, David looked up. I'm a mouse—I'm an ogre! The thought lingered. He eyed Luter furtively. Unaware that he was being watched, Luter had put down his paper and was staring ahead of him. Something curious had happened to his expression. The usually upturned, affable lines of his face either curved the other way now, downward, or where not curved were sharp, wedge-shaped at the eyes and mouth. And the eyes themselves, which were always so round and soft, had narrowed now, so narrow, the eyeballs looked charred, remote. His upper teeth gnawed the skin of his lips, drawing his face into a brooding frown. It worried David. A faint thrill of disquiet ran through him. He suddenly felt an intense desire to have someone else present in his house. It didn't have to be his mother. Anybody would do—Yussie from upstairs. Even his father.

Luter rose. David hastily dropped his gaze. Deliberate, brown-clad legs approached (what?) passed by him (he relaxed) stopped before the wall (peered over his shoulder) the calendar. Luter thumbed the leaves (black, black, black, red, black, black) held up a thin sheaf, and with puckered lips, stared at the date as though something far more intricate and absorbing than the mere figures were depicted there. Then he lowered the upturned leaves slowly, cautiously (Why? Why so carefully? They had only one place they could fall to) and rubbed his hands.

On his way back to the chair, he glanced down at the empty shoe-box between David's knees, emptied of everything except its calendar-leaves.

"Well!" His voice seemed amused, yet not entirely so, as if crossed by a slight start of surprise. "What are those? Do you get them from there?"

"Yes." David looked up uneasily. "I save them."

"Yesterday's days? What do you want with them? To scribble on?"

"No. Just save."

"Chm!" His laughing snort sounded unpleasant to David. "If I had so few days as you have I wouldn't bother about them. And when you're as old as I am—" he stopped, indulged in a short chuckle that pecked like a tiny hammer—"you'll know that the only thing that matters are the days ahead."

David tried not to look resentful for fear Luter would accuse him again of looking like his father. He wished he would go away. But instead Luter nodded, and smiling to himself, glanced at the clock.

"It's time for you to go to bed now. It's long after eight."

He poured the various trinkets back into the box, went over to the pantry and stowed them away in the corner.

"Do you know how to undress yourself?"

"Yes."

"You'd better go in and 'pee' first," he advised, smiling. "How does your mother say it?"

"She says numbuh one."

Luter chuckled. "Then she's learned a little English."

After he had gone to the bathroom, David went into his bedroom, and undressed and got into his night-gown.

Luter looked in. "All right?" he asked.

"Yes," he answered climbing into bed.

Luter shut the door.

Darkness was different without his mother near. People were different too.

BOOKER T WASHINGTO
1856 1915
HE LIFTED THE VEIL OF IGNOR
FROM HIS PEOPLE AND POINT
THE WAY TO PROGRESS THROU
EDUCATION AND INDUSTRY

"The Founder"

RALPH ELLISON

A Black's Education

(1947)

Ralph Ellison's Invisible Man, first published in 1947, is—according to many critics—the most important novel written in post-World War II America. Few would question its primacy among novels by and about black America. In it, Ellison offers an allegorical portrait of the black man through his years of "invisibility" before the civil rights revolution of the late 1950s and 1960s. We see the old rural South, the educational world of Booker T. Washington (as in the selection printed below), the migration to the city, and the essentially futile search for place and identity. It is the black man's cry of

"Goodbye to All That," a rejection of every illusion which white America cruelly visited upon black America.

Booker T. Washington – the "Founder" – eulogized below by the bland Mr. Barbee, sought in the late nineteenth and early twentieth centuries to carve a place in American life for Negroes through accommodation, subservience, and vocational education. Washington was a powerful speaker and a shrewd politician who manipulated both white philanthropists and his black followers. He achieved much that was concrete and significant: a black educational establishment and a tradition of self-help and economic advancement. These gains came, however, at a high price: they cost the black man his dignity and the assertion of his political rights.

Ellison's fictional account of Tuskegee, the institution Washington founded, presents – through the eyes of a student who has just been notified of his expulsion (because of an inadvertent error that hurt the school in the eyes of its benefactors) – the sense of Washington's program that must have been common to southern blacks: that there was nothing else; that what in retrospect seems like a capitulation to racism was, to many, the only image of opportunity they had. For all the falseness of Barbee and Bledsoe, the unfortunate protagonist has no doubt that they alone hold the keys to the kingdom of advancement in white America.

At the sound of vespers I moved across the campus with groups of students, walking slowly, their voices soft in the mellow dusk. I remember the yellowed globes of frosted glass making lacy silhouettes on the gravel and the walk of the leaves and branches above us as we moved slow through the dusk so restless with scents of lilac, honeysuckle and verbena, and the feel of spring greenness; and I recall the sudden arpeggios of laughter lilting across the tender, springtime grass—gay-welling, far-floating, fluent, spontaneous, a bell-like feminine fluting, then suppressed; as though snuffed swiftly and irrevocably beneath the quiet solemnity of the vespered air now vibrant with somber chapel bells. Dong! Dong! Dong! Above the decorous walking around me, sounds of footsteps leaving the verandas of far-flung buildings and moving toward the walks and over the walks to the asphalt drives lined with whitewashed stones, those cryptic messages for men and women, boys and girls heading quietly toward where the visitors waited, and we moving not in the mood of worship but of judgment; as though even here in the filtering dusk, here beneath the deep indigo sky, here, alive with looping swifts and darting moths, here in the hereness of the night not yet lighted by the moon that looms blood-red behind the chapel like a fallen sun, its radiance shedding not upon the here-dusk of twittering bats, nor on the there-night of cricket and whippoorwill, but focused short-rayed upon our place of convergence; and we drifting forward with rigid motions, limbs stiff and voices now silent, as though on exhibit even in the dark, and the moon a white man's bloodshot eye.

And I move more rigid than all the others with a sense of judgment; the vibrations of the chapel bells stirring the depths of my turmoil, moving toward its nexus with a sense of doom. And I remember the chapel with its sweeping eaves, long and low as though risen bloody from the earth like the rising moon; vine-covered and earth-colored as though more earth-sprung than man-sprung. And my mind rushing for relief away from the spring dusk and flower scents, away from the time-scene of the crucifixion to the time-mood of the birth; from spring-dusk and vespers to the high, clear, lucid moon of winter and snow glinting upon the dwarfed pines where instead of the bells, the organ and the trombone choir speak carols to the distances drifted with snow, making of the night air a sea of crystal water lapping the slumbering land to the farthest reaches of sound, for endless miles, bringing the new dispensation even to the Golden Day, even unto the house of madness. But in the hereness of dusk I am moving toward the doomlike bells through the flowered air, beneath the rising moon.

Into the doors and into the soft lights I go, silently, past the rows of puritanical benches straight and torturous, finding that to which I am assigned and bending my body to its agony. There at the head of the platform with its pulpit and rail of polished brass are the banked and pyramided heads of the student choir, faces composed and stolid above uniforms of black and white; and above them, stretching to the ceiling, the organ pipes looming, a gothic hierarchy of dull gilded gold.

Around me the students move with faces frozen in solemn masks, and I seem to hear already the voices mechanically raised in the songs the visitors loved. (Loved? Demanded. Sung? An ultimatum accepted and ritualized, an allegiance recited for the peace it imparted, and for that perhaps loved. Loved as the defeated come to love the symbols of their conquerors. A gesture of acceptance, of terms laid down and reluctantly approved.) And here, sitting rigid, I remember the evenings spent before the sweeping platform in awe and in pleasure, and in the pleasure of awe; remember the short formal sermons intoned from the pulpit there, rendered in smooth articulate tones, with calm assurance purged of that wild emotion of the crude preachers most of us knew in our home towns and of whom we were deeply ashamed, these logical appeals which reached us more like the thrust of a firm and formal design requiring nothing more than the lucidity of uncluttered periods, the lulling movement of multisyllabic words to thrill and console us. And I remember, too, the talks of visiting speakers, all eager to inform us of how fortunate we were to be a part of the "vast" and formal ritual. How fortunate to belong to this family sheltered from those lost in ignorance and darkness.

Here upon this stage the black rite of Horatio Alger was performed to God's own acting script, with millionaires come down to portray themselves; not merely acting out the myth of their goodness, and wealth and success and power and benevolence and authority in cardboard masks, but themselves, these virtues concretely! Not the wafer and the wine, but the flesh and the blood, vibrant and alive, and vibrant even when stooped, ancient and withered. (And who, in face of this, would not believe? Could even doubt?)

And I remember too, how we confronted those others, those who had set me here in this Eden, whom we knew though we didn't know, who were unfamiliar in their familiarity, who trailed their words to us through blood and violence and ridicule and condescension with drawling smiles, and who exhorted and threatened, intimidated with innocent words as they described to us the limitations of our lives and the vast boldness of our aspirations, the staggering folly of our impatience to rise even higher; who, as they talked, aroused furtive visions within me of blood-froth sparkling their chins like their familiar tobacco juice, and upon their lips the curdled milk of a million black slave mammies' withered dugs, a treacherous and fluid knowledge of our being, imbibed at our source and now regurgitated foul upon us. This was our world, they said as they described it to us, this our horizon and its earth, its seasons and its climate, its spring and its summer, and its fall and harvest some unknown millennium ahead; and these its floods and cyclones and they themselves our thunder and lightning; and this we must accept and love and accept even if we did not love. We must accept—even when those were absent, and the men who made the railroads and ships and towers of stone, were before our eyes, in the flesh, their voices different, unweighted with recognizable danger and their delight in our songs more sincere seeming, their regard for our welfare marked by an almost benign and impersonal indifference. But the words of the others were stronger than the strength of philanthropic dollars, deeper than shafts sunk in the earth for oil and gold, more awe-inspiring than the miracles fabricated in scientific laboratories. For their most innocent words were acts of violence to which we of the campus were hypersensitive though we endured them not.

And there on the platform I too had stridden and debated, a student leader directing my voice at the highest beams and farthest rafters, ringing them, the accents staccato upon the ridgepole and echoing back with a tinkling, like words hurled to the trees of a wilderness, or into a well of slate-gray water; more sound than sense, a play upon the resonances of buildings, an assault upon the temples of the ear:

Ha! to the gray-haired matron in the final row. Ha! Miss Susie, Miss Susie Gresham, back there looking at that co-ed smiling at that he-ed—listen to me, the bungling bugler of words, imitating the trumpet and the trombone's timbre, playing thematic variations like a baritone horn. Hey! old connoisseur of voice sounds, of voices without messages, of newsless winds, listen to the vowel sounds and the crackling dentals, to the low harsh gutturals of empty anguish, now riding the curve of a preacher's rhythm I heard long ago in a Baptist church, stripped now of its imagery: No suns having hemorrhages, no moons weeping tears, no earthworms refusing the sacred flesh and dancing in the earth on Easter morn. Ha! singing achievement, Ha! booming success, intoning, Ha! acceptance, Ha! a river of word-sounds filled with drowned passions, floating, Ha! with wrecks of unachievable ambitions and stillborn revolts, sweeping their ears, Ha! ranged stiff before me, necks stretched forward with listening ears, Ha! a-spraying the ceiling and a-drumming the dark-stained after rafter, that seasoned crossarm of torturous timber mellowed in the kiln of a thousand voices; playing Ha! as upon a xylophone; words marching like the student band, up the campus and down again, blaring triumphant sounds empty of triumphs. Hey, Miss Susie! the sound of words that were no words, counterfeit notes singing achievements yet unachieved, riding upon the wings of my voice out to you, old matron, who knew the voice sounds of the Founder and knew the accents and echo of his promise; your gray old head cocked with the young around you, your eyes closed, face ecstatic, as I toss the word sounds in my breath, my bellows, my fountain, like bright-colored balls in a water spout—hear me, old matron, justify now this sound with your dear old nod of affirmation, your closed-eye smile and bow of recognition, who'll never be fooled with the mere content of words, not my words, not these pinfeathered flighters that stroke your lids till they flutter with the ecstasy with but the mere echoed noise of the promise. And after the singing and outward marching, you seize my hand and sing out quavering, "Boy, some day you'll make the Founder proud!" Ha! Susie Gresham, Mother Gresham, guardian of the hot young woman on the puritan benches who couldn't see your Jordan's water for their private steam; you, relic of slavery whom the campus loved but did not understand, aged, of slavery, yet bearer of something warm and vital and all-enduring, of which in that island of shame we were not ashamed—it was to you on the final row I directed my rush of sound, and it was you of whom I thought with shame and regret as I waited for the ceremony to begin.

The honored guests moved silently upon the platform, herded toward their high, carved chairs by Dr. Bledsoe with the decorum of a portly head waiter. Like some of the guests, he wore striped trousers and a swallow-tail coat with black-braided lapels topped by a rich ascot tie. It was his regular dress for such occasions, yet for all its elegance, he managed to make himself look humble. Somehow, his trousers inevitably bagged at the knees and the coat slouched in the shoulders. I watched him smiling at first one and then another of the guests, of whom all but one were white; and as I saw him placing his hand upon their arms, touching their backs, whispering to a tall angular-faced trustee who in turn touched his arm familiarly, I felt a shudder. I too had touched a white man today and I felt that it had been disastrous, and I realized then that he was the only one of us whom I knew—except perhaps a barber or a nursemaid—who could touch a white man with impunity. And I remembered too that whenever white guests came upon the platform he placed his hand upon them as though exercising a powerful magic. I watched his teeth flash as he took a white hand; then, with all seated, he went to his place at the end of the row of chairs.

Several terraces of students' faces above them, the organist, his eyes glinting at the console, was waiting with his head turned over his shoulder, and I saw Dr. Bledsoe, his eyes roaming over the audience, suddenly nod without turning his head. It was as though he had given a downbeat with an invisible baton. The organist turned and hunched his shoulders. A high cascade of sound bubbled from the organ, spreading, thick and clinging, over the chapel, slowly surging. The organist twisted and turned on his bench, with his feet flying beneath him as though dancing to rhythms totally unrelated to the decorous thunder of his organ.

And Dr. Bledsoe sat with a benign smile of inward concentration. Yet his eyes were darting swiftly, first over the rows of students, then over the section reserved for teachers, his swift glance carrying a threat for all. For he demanded that everyone attend these sessions. It was here that policy was announced in broadest rhetoric. I seemed to feel his eyes resting upon my face as he swept the section in which I sat. I looked at the guests on the platform; they sat with that alert relaxation with which they always met our upturned eyes. I wondered to which of them I might go to intercede for me with Dr. Bledsoe, but within myself I knew that there was no one.

In spite of the array of important men beside him, and despite the posture of humility and meekness which made him seem smaller than the others (although he was physically larger), Dr. Bledsoe made his presence felt by us with a far greater impact. I remembered the legend of how he had come to the college, a barefoot boy who in his fervor for education had trudged with his bundle of ragged clothing across two states. And how he was given a job feeding slop to the hogs but had made himself the best slop dispenser in the history of the school; and how the Founder had been impressed and made him his office boy. Each of us knew of his rise over years of hard work to the presidency, and each of us at some time wished that he had walked to the school or pushed a wheelbarrow or performed some other act of determination and sacrifice to attest his eagerness for knowledge. I remembered the admiration and fear he inspired in everyone on the campus; the pictures in the Negro press captioned "EDUCATOR," in type that exploded like a rifle shot, his face looking out at you with utmost confidence. To us he was more than just a president of a college. He was a leader, a "statesman" who carried our problems to those above us, even unto the White House; and in days past he had conducted the President himself about the campus. He was our leader and our magic, who kept the endowment high, the funds for scholarships plentiful and publicity moving through the channels of the press. He was our coal-black daddy of whom we were afraid.

As the organ voices died, I saw a thin brown girl arise noiselessly with the rigid control of a modern dancer, high in the upper rows of the choir, and begin to sing a cappella. She began softly, as though singing to herself of emotions of utmost privacy, a sound not addressed to the gathering, but which they overheard almost against her will. Gradually she increased its volume, until at times the voice seemed to become a disembodied force that sought to enter her, to violate her, shaking her, rocking her rhythmically, as though it had become the source of her being, rather than the fluid web of her own creation.

I saw the guests on the platform turn to look behind them, to see the thin brown girl in white choir robe standing high against the organ pipes, herself become before our eyes a pipe of contained, controlled and sublimated anguish, a thin plain face transformed by music. I could not understand the words, but only the mood, sorrowful, vague and ethereal, of the singing. It throbbed with nostalgia, regret and repentance, and I sat with a lump in my throat as she sank slowly down; not a sitting but a controlled collapsing, as though she were balancing, sustaining the simmering bubble of her final tone by some delicate rhythm of her heart's blood, or by some mystic concentration of her being, focused upon the sound through the contained liquid of her large uplifted eyes.

There was no applause, only the appreciation of a profound silence. The white guests exchanged smiles of approval. I sat thinking of the dread possibility of having to leave all this, of being expelled; imagining the return home and the rebukes of my parents. I looked out at the scene now from far back in my despair, seeing the platform and its actors as through a reversed telescope; small doll-like figures moving through some meaningless ritual. Someone up there, above the alternating moss-dry and grease-slick heads of the students rowed before me, was making announcements from a lectern on which a dim light shone. Another figure rose and led a prayer. Someone spoke. Then around me everyone was singing *Lead me, lead me to a rock that is higher than I.* And as though the sound contained some force more impervious than the image of the scene of which it was the living connective tissue, I was pulled back to its immediacy.

One of the guests had risen to speak. A man of striking ugliness; fat, with a bullet-head set on a short neck, with a nose much too wide for its face, upon which he wore black-lensed glasses. He had been seated next to Dr. Bledsoe, but so concerned had I been with the president that I hadn't really seen him. My eyes had focused only upon the white men and Dr. Bledsoe. So that now as he arose and crossed slowly to the center of the platform, I had the notion that part of Dr. Bledsoe had arisen and moved forward, leaving his other part smiling in the chair.

He stood before us relaxed, his white collar gleaming like a band between his black face and his dark garments, dividing his head from his body; his short arms crossed before his barrel, like a black little Buddha's. For a moment he stood with his large head lifted, as though thinking; then he began speaking, his voice round and vibrant as he told of his pleasure in being allowed to visit the school once more after many years. Having been preaching in a northern city, he had seen it last in the final days of the Founder, when Dr. Bledsoe was the "second in command." "Those were wonderful days," he droned. "Significant days. Days filled with great portent."

As he talked he made a cage of his hands by touching his fingertips, then with his small feet pressing together, he began a slow, rhythmic rocking; tilting forward on his toes until it seemed he would fall, then back on his heels, the lights catching his black-lensed glasses until it seemed that his head floated free of his body and was held close to it only by the white band of his collar. And as he tilted he talked until a rhythm was established.

Then he was renewing the dream in our hearts:

". . . this barren land after Emancipation," he intoned, "this land of darkness and sorrow, of ignorance and degradation, where the hand of brother had been turned against brother, father against son, and son against father; where master had turned against slave and slave against master; where all was strife and darkness, an aching land. And into this land came a humble prophet, lowly like the humble carpenter of Nazareth, a slave and a son of slaves, knowing only his mother. A slave born, but marked from the beginning by a high intelligence and princely personality; born in the lowest part of this barren, war-scarred land, yet somehow shedding light upon it where'er he passed through. I'm sure you have heard of his precarious infancy, his precious life almost destroyed by an insane cousin who splashed the babe with lye and shriveled his seed and how, a mere babe, he lay nine days in a deathlike coma and then suddenly and miraculously recovered. You might say that it was as though he had risen from the dead or been reborn.

"Oh, my young friends," he cried, beaming, "my young friends, it is indeed a beautiful story. I'm sure you've heard it many times: Recall how he came upon his initial learning through shrewd questioning of his little masters, the elder masters never suspecting; and how he learned his alphabet and taught himself to read and solve the secret of words, going instinctively to the Holy Bible with its great wisdom for his first knowledge. And you know how he escaped and made his way across mountain and valley to that place of learning and how he persisted and worked noontimes, nights and mornings for the privilege of studying, or, as the old folk would say, of 'rubbing his head against the college wall.' You know of his brilliant career, how already he was a moving orator; then his penniless graduation and his return after years to this country.

"And then his great struggle beginning. Picture it, my young friends: The clouds of darkness all over the land, black folk and white folk full of fear and hate, wanting to go forward, but each fearful of the other. A whole region is caught in a terrible tension. Everyone is perplexed with the question of what must be done to dissolve this fear and hatred that crouched over the land like a demon waiting to spring, and you know how he came and showed them the way. Oh, yes, my friends. I'm sure you've heard it time and time again; of this godly man's labors, his great humility and his undimming vision, the fruits of which you enjoy today; concrete, made flesh; his dream, conceived in the starkness and darkness of slavery, fulfilled now even in the air you breathe, in the sweet harmonies of your blended voices, in the knowledge which each of you—daughters and granddaughters, sons and grandsons, of slaves—all of you partaking of it in bright and well-equipped classrooms. You must see this slave, this black Aristotle, moving slowly, with sweet patience, with a patience not of mere man, but of God-inspired faith—see him moving slowly as he surmounts each and every opposition. Rendering unto Caesar that which was Caesar's, yes; but steadfastly seeking for you that bright horizon which you now enjoy . . .

"All this," he said, spreading his fingers palm down before him, "has been told and retold throughout the land, inspiring a humble but fast-rising people. You have heard it and it—this true story of rich implication, this living parable of proven glory and humble nobility—and it, as I say, has made you free. Even you who have come to this shrine only this semester know it. You have heard his name from your parents, for it was he who led them to the path, guiding them like a great captain; like that great pilot of ancient times who led his people safe and unharmed across the bottom of the blood-red sea. And your parents followed this remarkable man across the black sea of prejudice, safely out of the land of ignorance, through the storms of fear and anger, shouting, LET MY PEOPLE GO! when it was necessary, whispering it during those times when whispering was wisest. And he was heard."

I listened, my back pressing against the hard bench, with a numbness, my emotions woven into his words as upon a loom.

"And remember how," he said, "when he entered a certain state at cotton-picking time, his enemies had plotted to take his life. And recall how during his journey he was stopped by the strange figure of a man whose pitted features revealed no inkling of whether he was black or white . . . Some say he was a Greek. Some a Mongolian. Others a mulatto—and others still, a simple white man of God. Whoever, and whatsoever, and we must not rule out the possibility of an emissary direct from above—oh, yes!—and remember how he appeared suddenly, startling both Founder and horse as he gave warning, telling the Founder to leave the horse and buggy there in the road and proceed immediately to a certain cabin, then slipped silently away, so silently, my young friends, that the Founder doubted his very existence. And you know how the great man continued through the dusk, determined though puzzled as he approached the town. He was lost, lost in reverie until the crack of the first rifle sounded, then the almost fatal volley that creased his skull—oh my!—and left him stunned and apparently lifeless.

"I have heard him tell with his own lips how consciousness returned while they were still upon him examining their foul deed, and how he lay biting his heart lest they hear it and wipe out their failure with a *coup-de-grace,* as the French would say. Ha! And I'm sure you've each of you lived with him through his escape," he said, seeming to look directly into my watered eyes. "You awakened when he awakened, rejoiced when he rejoiced at their leaving without further harm; arising when he arose; seeing with his eyes the prints of their milling footsteps and the cartridges dropped in the dust about the imprint of his fallen body; yes, and the cold, dust-encrusted, but not quite fatal blood. And you hurried with him full of doubt to the cabin designated by the stranger, where he met that seemingly demented black man . . . You remember that old one, laughed at by the children in the town's square, old, comic-faced, crafty, *cotton*-headed. And yet it was he who bound up your wounds with the wounds of the Founder. He, the old slave, showing a surprising knowledge of such matters—*germology* and *scabology*—ha! ha!—he called it, and what a youthful skill of the hands! For he shaved our skull, and cleansed our wound and bound it neat with bandages stolen from the home of an unsuspecting leader of the mob, ha! And you recall how you plunged with the Founder, the Leader, deep into the black art of escape, guided at first, indeed, initiated, by the seemingly demented one who had learned his craft in slavery. You left with the Founder in the black of night, and I know it. You hurried silently along the river bottom, stung by mosquitoes, hooted by owls, zoomed by bats, buzzed by snakes that rattled among the rocks, mud and fever, darkness and sighing. You hid all the following day in the cabin where thirteen slept in three small rooms, standing until darkness in the fireplace chimney, back in all the soot and ashes—ha! ha!—guarded by the granny who dozed at the hearth seemingly without a fire. You stood in the blackness and when they came with their baying hounds they thought her demented. But she knew, she knew! She knew the fire! She knew the fire! She knew the fire that burned without consuming! My God, yes!"

"My God, yes!" a woman's voice responded, adding to the structure of his vision within me.

"And you left him on the morning, hidden in a wagonload of cotton, in the very center of the fleece, where you breathed the hot air through the barrel of the emergency shotgun; the cartridges, which thank God it was unnecessary to use, held fanwise and ready between the spread fingers of your hand. And you went into this town with him and were hidden by the friendly aristocrat one night, and on the next by the white blacksmith who held no hatred—surprising contradictions of the underground. Escaping, yes! helped by those who knew you and those who didn't know. Because for some it was enough to see him; others helped without even that, black and white. But mostly it was our own who aided, because you were their own and we have always helped our own. And so, my young friends, my sisters and brothers, you went with him, in and out of cabins, by night and early morning, through swamps and hills. On and on, passed from black hand to black hand and some white hands, and all the hands molding the Founder's freedom and our own freedom like voices shaping a deep-felt song. And you, each of you, were with him. Ah, how well you know it, for it was you who escaped to freedom. Ah, yes, and you know the story."

I saw him resting now, and beaming out across the chapel, his huge head turning to all its corners like a beacon, his voice still echoing as I fought back my emotion. For the first time the evocation of the Founder saddened me, and the campus seemed to rush past me, fast retreating, like the fading of a dream at the sundering of slumber. Beside me, the student's eyes swam with a distorting cataract of tears, his features rigid as though he struggled within himself. The fat man was playing upon the whole audience without the least show of exertion. He seemed completely composed, hidden behind his black-lensed glasses, only his mobile features gesturing his vocal drama. I nudged the boy beside me.

"Who is he?" I whispered.

He gave me a look of annoyance, almost of outrage. "Reverend Homer A. Barbee, Chicago," he said.

Now the speaker rested his arm upon the lectern and turned toward Dr. Bledsoe:

"You've heard the bright beginning of the beautiful story, my friends. But there is the mournful ending, and perhaps in many ways the richer side. The setting of this glorious son of the morning."

He turned to Dr. Bledsoe, "It was a fateful day, Dr. Bledsoe, sir, if I may recall it to you, for we were there. Oh yes, my young friends," he said, turning to face us again with a sad proud smile. "I knew him well and loved him, and I was there.

"We had toured through several states to which he was carrying the message. The people had come to hear the prophet, the multitude had responded. The old-fashioned people; women in aprons and Mother Hubbards of calico and gingham, men in their overalls and patched alpacas; a sea of upturned and puzzled faces looking out from beneath old battered straw hats and limp sunbonnets. They who had come by oxen and mule team and by walking long distances. It was the month of September and unseasonably cold. He had spoken peace and confidence into their troubled souls, had set a star before them and we were passing on to other scenes, still carrying the message.

"Ah, those days of ceaseless travel, those youthful days, those springtime days; fertile, blossomy, sun-filled days of promise. Ah, yes, those indescribably glorious days, in which the Founder was building the dream not only here in this then barren valley, but hither and yonder throughout the land instilling the dream in the hearts of the people. Erecting the scaffolding of a nation. Broadcasting his message that fell like seed on fallow ground, sacrificing himself, fighting and forgiving his enemies of both complexions—oh yes, he had them, of both complexions. But going forward filled with the importance of his message, filled with his dedicated mission; and in his zeal, perhaps in his mortal pride, ignoring the advice of his physician. I see in my mind's eye the fatal atmosphere of that jam-packed auditorium: The Founder holds the audience within the gentle palm of his eloquence, rocking it, soothing it, instructing it; and there below, the rapt faces blushed by the glow of the big pot-bellied stove now turned cherry-red with its glowing; yes, the spellbound rows caught in the imperious truth of his message. And I hear now, again, the great humming hush as his voice reached the end of a mighty period, and one of the listeners, a snowy-headed man, leaps to his feet crying out, 'Tell us what is to be done, sir! For God's sake, tell us! Tell us in the name of the son they snatched from me last week!' And all through the room the voices arising, imploring, 'Tell us, tell us!' And the Founder is suddenly mute with tears."

Old Barbee's voice rang out, as suddenly he made charged and incomplete movements about the platform, acting out his words. And I watched with a sick fascination, knowing part of the story, yet a part of me fighting against its sad inevitable conclusion.

"And the Founder pauses, then steps forward with his eyes spilling his great emotion. With his arm upraised, he begins to answer and totters. Then all is commotion. We rush forward and lead him away.

"The audience leaps to its feet in consternation. All is terror and turmoil, a moan and a sighing. Until, like a clap of thunder, I hear Dr. Bledsoe's voice ring out whip-like with authority, a song of hope. And as we stretch the Founder upon a bench to rest, I hear Dr. Bledsoe stomping out the time with mighty strokes upon the hollow platform, commanding not in words but in the great gut-tones of his magnificent basso—oh, but wasn't he a singer? Isn't he a singer still today?—and they stand, they calm, and with him they sing out against the tottering of their giant. Sing out their long black songs of blood and bones:

"Meaning HOPE!

"Of hardship and pain:

"Meaning FAITH!

"Of humbleness and absurdity:

"Meaning ENDURANCE!

"Of ceaseless struggle in darkness, meaning:

"TRIUMPH . . .

"Ha!" Barbee cried, slapping his hands, "Ha! Singing verse after verse, until the leader revived!" (Slap, slap of his hands.)

"Addressed them"—

(Slap!) "My God, my God!"

"Assured them"—(Slap!)

"That"—(Slap!)

"He was only tired of his ceaseless efforts." (Slap!) "Yes, and dismisses them, sending each on his way rejoicing, giving each a parting handshake of fellowship . . ."

I watched Barbee pace in a semi-circle, his lips compressed, his face working with emotion, his palms meeting but making no sound.

"Ah, those days in which he tilled his mighty fields, those days in which he watched the crops take hold and grow, those youthful, summery, sun-bright days . . ."

Barbee's voice sighed off in nostalgia. The chapel hardly breathed as he sighed deeply. Then I watched him produce a snowy handkerchief, remove his dark glasses and wipes his eyes, and through the increasing distance of my isolation, I watched the men in the seats of honor slowly shake their spellbound heads. Then Barbee's voice began again, disembodied now, and it was as though he had never paused, as though his words, reverberating within us, had continued their rhythmic flow though their source was for a moment stilled:

"Oh, yes, my young friends, oh, yes," he continued with a great sadness. "Man's hope can paint a purple picture, can transform a soaring vulture into a noble eagle or a moaning dove. Oh, yes! But I *knew,*" he shouted, startling me. "In spite of that *great, anguished hope within me, I knew—knew* that the great spirit was declining, was approaching its lonely winter; the great sun going down. For sometimes it is given one to know these things . . . And I staggered under the awful burden of that knowledge and I cursed myself because I bore it. But such was the Founder's enthusiasm—oh, yes!—that as we sped from country town to country town through the glorious Indian summer, I soon forgot. And then . . . And then . . . and . . . then . . ."

I listened to his voice fall to a whisper; his hands were outspread as though he were leading an orchestra into a profound and final diminuendo. Then his voice rose again, crisply, almost matter-of-factly, accelerated:

"I remember the start of the train, how it seemed to groan as it started up the steep grade into the mountain. It was cold. Frost formed its icy patterns upon the window's edges. And the whistle of the train was long-drawn and lonely, a sigh issuing from the depths of the mountain.

"In the car up ahead, in the Pullman assigned him by the very president of the line, the Leader lay tossing. He had been struck with a sudden and mysterious sickness. And I knew in spite of the anguish within me that the sun goeth down, for the heavens themselves conveyed that knowledge. The rush of the train, the clicking of wheels upon the steel. I remember how I looked out of the frosted pane and saw the looming great North Star and lost it, as though the sky had shut its eye. The train was curving the mountain, the engine loping like a great black hound, parallel with the last careening cars, panting forth its pale white vapor as it hurled us ever higher. And shortly the sky was black, without a moon . . ."

As his "mooo-o-on" echoed over the chapel, he drew his chin against his chest until his white collar disappeared, leaving him a figure of balanced unbroken blackness, and I could hear the rasp of air as he inhaled.

"It was as though the very constellations knew our impending sorrow," he bugled, his head raised to the ceiling, his voice full-throated. "For against that great—wide—sweep of sable there came the burst of a single jewel-like star, and I saw it shimmer, and break, and streak down the cheek of that coal-black sky like a reluctant and solitary tear . . ."

He shook his head with great emotion, his lips pursed as he moaned, "Mmmmmmmmmm," turning toward Dr. Bledsoe as though he did not quite see him. "At that fateful moment . . . Mmmmmm, I sat with your great president . . . Mmmmmmmmmm! He was deep in meditation as we awaited word from the men of science, and he said to me of that dying star,

"'Barbee, friend, did you see?'

"And I answered, 'Yes, Doctor, I saw.'

"And at our throats already we felt the cold hands of sorrow. And I said to Dr. Bledsoe, 'Let us pray.' And as we knelt there on the swaying floor our words were less prayers than sounds of mute and terrible sorrow. And it was then, as we pulled to our feet, staggering with the motion of that speeding train, that we saw the physician moving toward us. And we looked with bated breath into the blank and expressionless features of the man of science, asking with our total beings: Do you bring us hope or disaster? And it was then and there he informed us that the Leader was nearing his destination . . .

"It was said, the cruel blow had fallen and we were left numb, but the Founder was still for the moment with us and still in command. And, of all in the traveling party, he sent for him who sits there before you, and for me as a man of God. But he wanted mainly his friend of midnight consultations, his comrade of many battles, who over the weary years had remained steadfast in defeat as in victory.

"Even now I can see it, the dark passage lit with dim lights and Dr. Bledsoe swaying as he went before me. At the door stood the porter and the conductor, a black man and a white man of the South, both crying. Both weeping. And he looked up as we entered, his great eyes resigned but still aflame with nobility and courage against the white of his pillow; and he looked at his friend and smiled. Smiled warmly at his old campaigner, his loyal champion, his adjunct, that marvelous singer of the old songs who had rallied his spirit during times of distress and discouragement, who with his singing of the old familiar melodies soothed the doubts and fears of the multitude; he who had rallied the ignorant, the fearful and suspicious, those still wrapped in the rags of slavery; him, there, your leader, who calmed the children of the storm. And as the Founder looked up at his companion, he smiled. And reaching out his hand to his friend and companion as I now stretch out my hand to you, he said, 'Come closer. Come closer.' And he moved closer, until he stood beside the berth, and the light slanting across his shoulder as he knelt beside him. And the hand reached out and gently touched him and he said, 'Now, you must take on the burden. Lead them the rest of the way.' And oh, the cry of that train and the pain too big for tears!

"When the train reached the summit of the mountain, he was no longer with us. And as the train dropped down the grade he had departed.

"It had become a veritable train of sorrow. Dr. Bledsoe there, sat weary in mind and heavy of heart. What should he do? The leader was dead and he thrown suddenly at the head of the troops like a cavalryman catapulted into the saddle of his general felled in a charge of battle—vaulted onto the back of his fiery and half-broken charger. Ah! And that great, black, noble beast, walleyed with the din of battle and twitching already with its sense of loss. What command should he give? Should he return with his burden, home, to where already the hot wires were flashing, speaking, rattling the mournful message? Should he turn and bear the fallen soldier down the cold and alien mountain to this valley home? Return with the dear eyes dulled, the firm hand still, the magnificent voice silent, the Leader cold? Return to the warm valley, to the green grounds he could no longer light with his mortal vision? Should he follow his Leader's vision though he had now himself departed?

"Ah, of course you know the story: How he bore the body into the strange city, and the speech he made as his Leader lay in state, and how when the sad news spread, a day of mourning was declared for the whole municipality. Oh, and how rich and poor, black and white, weak and powerful, young and old, all came to pay their homage—many realizing the Leader's worth and their loss only now with his passing. And how, with his mission done, Dr. Bledsoe returned, keeping his sorrowful vigil with his friend in an humble baggage car; and how the people came to pay their respects at the stations . . . A slow train. A sorrowful train. And all along the line, in mountain and valley, wherever the rails found their fateful course, the people were one in their common mourning, and like the cold steel rails, were spiked down to their sorrow. Oh, what a sad departure!

"And what an even sadder arrival. See with me, my young friends, hear with me: The weeping and wailing of those who shared his labors. Their sweet Leader returned to them, rock-cold in the iron immobility of death. He who had left them quick, in the prime of his manhood, author of their own fire and illumination, returned to them cold, already a bronzed statue. Oh, the *despair,* my young friends. The black despair of black people! I see them now; wandering about these grounds, where each brick, each bird, each blade of grass was a reminder of some precious memory; and each memory a hammer stroke driving home the blunt spikes of their sorrow. Oh, yes, some now are here gray-haired among you, still dedicated to his vision, still laboring in the vineyard. But then with the black-draped coffin lying in state among them—inescapably reminding them—they felt the dark night of slavery settling once more upon them. They smelt that old obscene stink of darkness, that old slavery smell, worse than the rank halitosis of hoary death. Their sweet light enclosed in a black-draped coffin, their majestic sun snatched behind a cloud.

"Oh, and the sad sound of weeping bugles! I can hear them now, stationed at the four corners of the campus, sounding taps for the fallen general; announcing and reannouncing the sad tidings, telling and retelling the sad revelation one to the other across the still numbness of the air, as though they could not believe it, could neither comprehend nor accept it; bugles weeping like a family of tender women lamenting their loved one. And the people came to sing the old songs and to express their unspeakable sorrow. Black, black, black! Black people in blacker mourning, the funeral crape hung upon their naked hearts; singing unashamedly their black folk's songs of sorrow, moving painfully, overflowing the curving walks, weeping and wailing beneath the drooping trees and their low murmuring voices like the moans of winds in a wilderness. And finally they gathered on the hill slope and as far as the tear-wet eyes could see, they stood with their heads bowed, singing.

"Then silence. The lonesome hole banked with poignant flowers. The dozen white-gloved hands waiting taut upon the silken ropes. That awful silence. The final words are spoken. A single wild rose tossed farewell, bursts slowly, its petals drifting snowlike upon the reluctantly lowered coffin. Then down into the earth; back to the ancient dust; back to the cold black clay . . . mother . . . of us all."

As Barbee paused the silence was so complete that I could hear the power engines far across the campus throbbing the night like an excited pulse. Somewhere in the audience an old woman's voice began a plaintive wail; the birth of a sad, unformulated song that died stillborn in a sob.

Barbee stood with his head thrown back, his arms rigid at his sides, his fists clenched as though fighting desperately for control. Dr. Bledsoe sat with his face in his hands. Near me someone blew his nose. Barbee took a tottering step forward.

"Oh, yes. Oh, yes," he said. "Oh, yes. That too is part of the glorious story. But think of it not as a death, but as a birth. A great seed had been planted. A seed which has continued to put forth its fruit in its season as surely as if the great creator had been resurrected. For in a sense he was, if not in the flesh, in the spirit. And in a sense in the flesh too. For has not your present leader become his living agent, his physical presence? Look about you if you doubt it. My young friends, my dear young friends! How can I tell you what manner of man this is who leads you? How can I convey to you how well he has kept his pledge to the Founder, how conscientious has been his stewardship?

"First, you must see the school as it was. Already a great institution, to be sure; but then the buildings were eight, now they are twenty; then the faculty was fifty, now it is two hundred; then the student body was a few hundred, where now I'm told you are three thousand. And now where you have roads of asphalt for the passage of rubber tires, then the roads were of crushed stone for the passage of oxen, and mule teams, and horse-drawn wagons. I have not the words to tell you how my heart swelled to return to this great institution after so great a while to move among its wealth of green things, its fruitful farmland and fragrant campus. Ah! and the marvelous plant supplying power to an area larger than many towns—all operated by *black hands.* Thus, my young friends, does the light of the Founder still burn. Your leader has kept his promise a thousandfold. I commend him in his own right, for he is the co-architect of a great and noble experiment. He is a worthy successor to his great friend and it is no accident that his great and intelligent leadership has made him our leading statesman. His is a form of greatness worthy of your imitation. I say to you, pattern yourselves upon him. Aspire, each of you, to some day follow in his footsteps. Great deeds are yet to be performed. For we are a young, though a fast-rising, people. Legends are still to be created. Be not afraid to undertake the burdens of your leader, and the work of the Founder will be one of ever unfolding glory, the history of the race a saga of mounting triumphs."

Barbee stood with his arms outstretched now, beaming over the audience, his Buddha-like body still as an onyx boulder. There was sniffling throughout the chapel. Voices murmured with admiration and I felt more lost than ever. For a few minutes old Barbee had made me see the vision and now I knew that leaving the campus would be like the parting of flesh. I watched him lower his arms now and start back to his chair, moving slowly with his head cocked as though listening to distant music. I had lowered my head to wipe my eyes when I heard the shocked gasp arise.

Looking up, I saw two of the white trustees moving swiftly across the platform to where Barbee floundered upon Dr. Bledsoe's legs. The old man slid forward upon his hands and knees as the two white men took his arms; and now as he stood I saw one of them reach for something on the floor and place it in his hands. It was when he raised his head that I saw it. For a swift instant, between the gesture and the opaque glitter of his glasses, I saw the blinking of sightless eyes. Homer A. Barbee was blind.

Uttering apologies, Dr. Bledsoe helped him to his chair. Then as the old man rested back with a smile, Dr. Bledsoe walked to the edge of the platform and lifted his arms. I closed my eyes as I heard the deep moaning sound that issued from him, and the rising crescendo of the student body joining in. This time it was music sincerely felt, not rendered for the guests, but for themselves; a song of hope and exaltation. I wanted to rush from the building, but didn't dare. I sat stiff and erect, supported by the hard bench, relying upon it as upon a form of hope.

I could not look at Dr. Bledsoe now, because old Barbee had made me both feel my guilt and accept it. For although I had not intended it, any act that endangered the continuity of the dream was an act of treason.

I did not listen to the next speaker, a tall white man who kept dabbing at his eyes with a handkerchief and repeating his phrases in an emotional and inarticulate manner. Then the orchestra played excerpts from Dvořák's *New World Symphony* and I kept hearing "Swing Low, Sweet Chariot" resounding through its dominant theme—my mother's and grandfather's favorite spiritual. It was more than I could stand, and before the next speaker could begin I hurried past the disapproving eyes of teachers and matrons, out into the night.

A mockingbird trilled a note from where it perched upon the hand of the moonlit Founder, flipping its moon-mad tail above the head of the eternally kneeling slave. I went up the shadowy drive, heard it trill behind me. The street lamps glowed brilliant in the moonlit dream of the campus, each light serene in its cage of shadows.

I might well have waited until the end of the services, for I hadn't gone far when I heard the dim, bright notes of the orchestra striking up a march, followed by a burst of voices as the students filed out into the night. With a feeling of dread I headed for the administration building, and upon reaching it, stood in the darkened doorway. My mind fluttered like the moths that veiled the street lamp which cast shadows upon the bank of grass below me. I would now have my real interview with Dr. Bledsoe, and I recalled Barbee's address with resentment. With such words fresh in his mind, I was sure Dr. Bledsoe would be far less sympathetic to my plea. I stood in the darkened doorway trying to probe my future if I were expelled. Where would I go, what would I do? How could I ever return home?

STUDENTS FOR A DEMOCRATIC SOCIETY

The Port Huron Statement

(1962)

The radical tradition in America is a series of episodes, not a continuous story. Where conservatives and liberals never cease reaching back for real or imaginary forbears, radicals have generally insisted on forgetting the history of radicalism as the first act in any new beginning. In the early 1960s, when the Students for a Democratic Society spread from campus to campus, drawing together activists in the civil rights and peace movements, the group received compliments for pre-

cisely this tendency to forget the radical past. It was "pragmatic," "non-ideological," and "non-programmatic." The movement worried little about its intellectual underpinnings; its main concern was action. The Port Huron Statement, drawn up at the first SDS convention in 1962, achieved wide circulation on the campuses as an "agenda for a generation."

The document, written principally by Tom Hayden, is impressive in surprising ways. Its tentative assertions, social science language, and generally nationalistic and cooperative stance contrast sharply with the image of campus militancy of the later 1960s. In its quiet way, however, it states the main themes of the youth political movement: rejection of bureaucracy, anticommunism, alienation, and the lack of community. It is clearly the beginning of a quest, not a set of final answers. Where that quest led was one of the fascinating subjects of the decade. It raises the inevitable question – to what extent did the young radicals relive the experience of earlier radicals because they began by rejecting its lessons?

Introduction: Agenda For a Generation

We are people of this generation, bred in at least modest comfort, housed now in universities, looking uncomfortably to the world we inherit.

When we were kids the United States was the wealthiest and strongest country in the world; the only one with the atom bomb, the least scarred by modern war, an initiator of the United Nations that we thought would distribute Western influence throughout the world. Freedom and equality for each individual, government of, by, and for the people—these American values we found good, principles by which we could live as men. Many of us began maturing in complacency.

As we grew, however, our comfort was penetrated by events too troubling to dismiss. First, the permeating and victimizing fact of human degradation, symbolized by the Southern struggle against racial bigotry, compelled most of us from silence to activism. Second, the enclosing fact of the Cold War, symbolized by the presence of the Bomb, brought awareness that we ourselves, and our friends, and millions of abstract "others" we knew more directly because of our common peril, might die at any time. We might deliberately ignore, or avoid, or fail to feel all other human problems, but not these two, for these were too immediate and crushing in their impact, too challenging in the demand that we as individuals take the responsibility for encounter and resolution.

While these and other problems either directly oppressed us or rankled our consciences and became our own subjective concerns, we began to see complicated and disturbing paradoxes in our surrounding America. The declaration "all men are created equal . . ." rang hollow before the facts of Negro life in the South and the big cities of the North. The proclaimed peaceful intentions of the United States contradicted its economic and military investments in the Cold War status quo.

We witnessed, and continue to witness, other paradoxes. With nuclear energy whole cities can easily be powered, yet the dominant nation-states seem more likely to unleash destruction greater than that incurred in all wars of human history. Although our own technology is destroying old and creating new forms of social organization, men still tolerate meaningless work and idleness. While two-thirds of mankind suffers undernourishment, our own upper classes revel amidst superfluous abundance. Although world population is expected to double in forty years, the nations still tolerate anarchy as a major principle of international conduct and uncontrolled exploitation governs the sapping of the earth's physical resources. Although mankind desperately needs revolutionary leadership, America rests in national stalemate, its goals ambiguous and tradition-bound instead of informed and clear, its democratic system apathetic and manipulated rather than "of, by, and for the people."

Not only did tarnish appear on our image of American virtue, not only did disillusion occur when the hypocrisy of American ideals was discovered, but we began to sense that what we had originally seen as the American Golden Age was actually the decline of an era. The worldwide outbreak of revolution against colonialism and imperialism, the entrenchment of totalitarian states, the menace of war, overpopulation, international disorder, supertechnology—these trends were testing the tenacity of our own commitment to democracy and freedom and our abilities to visualize their application to a world in upheaval.

Our work is guided by the sense that we may be the last generation in the experiment with living. But we are a minority—the vast majority of our people regard the temporary equilibriums of our society and world as eternally-functional parts. In this is perhaps the outstanding paradox: we ourselves are imbued with urgency, yet the message of our society is that there is no viable alternative to the present. Beneath the reassuring tones of the politicians, beneath the common opinion that America will "muddle through," beneath the stagnation of those who have closed their minds to the future, is the pervading feeling that there simply are no alternatives, that our times have witnessed the exhaustion not only of Utopias, but of any new departures as well. Feeling the press of complexity upon the emptiness of life, people are fearful of the thought that at any moment things might be thrust out of control. They fear change itself, since change might smash whatever invisible framework seems to hold back chaos for them now. For most Americans, all crusades are suspect, threatening. The fact that each individual sees apathy in his fellows perpetuates the common reluctance to organize for change. The dominant institutions are complex enough to blunt the minds of their potential critics, and entrenched enough to swiftly dissipate or entirely repel the energies of protest and reform, thus limiting human expectancies. Then, too, we are a materially improved society, and by our own improvements we seem to have weakened the case for further change.

Some would have us believe that Americans feel contentment amidst prosperity—but might it not be better be called a glaze above deeply felt anxieties about their role in the new world? And if these anxieties produce a developed indifference to human affairs, do they not as well produce a yearning to believe there *is* an alternative to the present, that something *can* be done to change circumstances in the school, the workplaces, the bureaucracies, the government? It is to this latter yearning, at once the spark and engine of change, that we direct our present appeal. The search for truly democratic alternatives to the present, and a commitment to social experimentation with them, is a worthy and fulfilling human enterprise, one which moves us and, we hope, others today. On such a basis do we offer this document of our convictions and analysis: as an effort in understanding and changing the conditions of humanity in the late twentieth century, an effort rooted in the ancient, still unfulfilled conception of man attaining determining influence over his circumstances of life. . . .

The Students

In the last few years, thousands of American students demonstrated that they at least felt the urgency of the times. They moved actively and directly against racial injustices, the threat of war, violations of individual rights of conscience and, less frequently, against economic manipulation. They succeeded in restoring a small measure of controversy to the campuses after the stillness of the McCarthy period. They succeeded, too, in gaining some concessions from the people and institutions they opposed, especially in the fight against racial bigotry.

The significance of these scattered movements lies not in their success or failure in gaining objectives—at least not yet. Nor does the significance lie in the intellectual "competence" or "maturity" of the students involved—as some pedantic elders allege. The significance is in the fact the students are breaking the crust of apathy and overcoming the inner alienation that remain the defining characteristics of American college life.

If student movements for change are still rareties on the campus scene, what is commonplace there? The real campus, the familiar campus, is a place of private people, engaged in their notorious "inner emigration." It is a place of commitment to business-as-usual, getting ahead, playing it cool. It is a place of mass affirmation of the Twist, but mass reluctance toward the controversial public stance. Rules are accepted as "inevitable," bureaucracy as "just circumstances," irrelevance as "scholarship," selflessness as "martyrdom," politics as "just another way to make people, and an unprofitable one, too."

Almost no students value activity as citizens. Passive in public, they are hardly more idealistic in arranging their private lives: Gallup concludes they will settle for "low success, and won't risk high failure." There is not much willingness to take risks (not even in business), no settling of dangerous goals, no real conception of personal identity except one manufactured in the image of others, no real urge for personal fulfillment except to be almost as successful as the very successful people. Attention is being paid to social status (the quality of shirt collars, meeting people, getting wives or husbands, making solid contacts for later on); much, too, is paid to academic status (grades, honors, the med school rat race). But neglected generally is real intellectual status, the personal cultivation of the mind.

"Students don't even give a damn about the apathy," one has said. Apathy toward apathy begets a privately-constructed universe, a place of systematic study schedules, two nights each week for beer, a girl or two, and early marriage; a framework infused with personality, warmth, and under control, no matter how unsatisfying otherwise.

Under these conditions university life loses all relevance to some. Four hundred thousand of our classmates leave college every year.

But apathy is not simply an attitude; it is a product of social institutions, and of the structure and organization of higher education itself. The extracurricular life is ordered according to *in loco parentis* theory, which ratifies the Administration as the moral guardian of the young.

The accompanying "let's pretend" theory of student extracurricular affairs validates student government as a training center for those who want to spend their lives in political pretense, and discourages initiative from the more articulate, honest, and sensitive students. The bounds and style of controversy are delimited before controversy begins. The university "prepares" the student for "citizenship" through perpetual rehearsals and, usually, through emasculation of what creative spirit there is in the individual.

The academic life contains reinforcing counterparts to the way in which extracurricular life is organized. The academic world is founded on a teacher-student relation analogous to the parent-child relation which characterizes *in loco parentis.* Further, academia includes a radical separation of the student from the material of study. That which is studied, the social reality, is "objectified" to sterility, dividing the student from life—just as he is restrained in active involvement by the deans controlling student government. The specialization of function and knowledge, admittedly necessary to our complex technological and social structure, has produced an exaggerated compartmentalization of study and understanding. This has contributed to an overly parochial view, by faculty, of the role of its research and scholarship, to a discontinuous and truncated understanding, by students, of the surrounding social order; and to a loss of personal attachment, by nearly all, to the worth of study as a humanistic enterprise.

There is, finally, the cumbersome academic bureaucracy extending throughout the academic as well as the extracurricular structures, contributing to the sense of outer complexity and inner-powerlessness that transforms the honest searching of many students to a ratification of convention and, worse, to a numbness to present and future catastrophes. The size and financing systems of the university enhance the permanent trusteeship of the administrative bureaucracy, their power leading to a shift within the university toward the value standards of business and the administrative mentality. Huge foundations and other private financial interests shape the under-financed colleges and universities, not only making them more commercial, but less disposed to diagnose society critically, less open to dissent. Many social and physical scientists, neglecting the liberating heritage of higher learning, develop "human relations" or "morale-producing" techniques for the corporate economy, while others exercise their intellectual skills to accelerate the arms race.

Tragically, the university could serve as a significant source of social criticism and an initiator of new modes and molders of attitudes. But the actual intellectual effect of the college experience is hardly distinguishable from that of any other communications channel—say, a television set—passing on the stock truths of the day. Students leave college somewhat more "tolerant" than when they arrived, but basically unchallenged in their values and political orientations. With administrators ordering the institution, and faculty the curriculum, the student learns by his isolation to accept elite rule within the university, which prepares him to accept later forms of minority control. The real function of the educational system—as opposed to its more rhetorical function of "searching for truth"—is to impart the key information and styles that will help the student get by, modestly but comfortably, in the big society beyond.

The Society Beyond

Look beyond the campus, to America itself. That student life is more intellectual, and perhaps more comfortable, does not obscure the fact that the fundamental qualities of life on the campus reflect the habits of society at large. The fraternity president is seen at the junior manager levels; the sorority queen has gone to Grosse Pointe; the serious poet burns for a place, any place, to work; the once-serious and never-serious poets work at the advertising agencies. The desperation of people threatened by forces about which they know little and of which they can say less; the cheerful emptiness of people "giving up" all hope of changing things; the faceless ones polled by Gallup who listed "international affairs" fourteenth on their list of "problems" but who also expected thermonuclear war in the next few years; in these and other forms, Americans are in withdrawal from public life, from any collective effort at directing their own affairs.

Some regard these national doldrums as a sign of healthy approval of the established order—but is it approval by consent or manipulated acquiescence? Others declare that the people are withdrawn because compelling issues are fast disappearing—perhaps there are fewer breadlines in America, but is Jim Crow gone, is there enough work and work more fulfilling, is world war a diminishing threat, and what of the revolutionary new peoples? Still others think the national quietude is a necessary consequence of the need for elites to resolve complex and specialized problems of modern industrial society—but, then, why should *business* elites help decide foreign policy, and who controls the elites anyway, and are they solving mankind's problems? Others, finally, shrug knowingly and announce that full democracy never worked anywhere in the past—but why lump qualitatively different civilizations together, and how can a social order work well if its best thinkers are skeptics, and is man really doomed forever to the domination of today?

There are no convincing apologies for the contemporary malaise. While the world tumbles toward final war, while men in other nations are trying desperately to alter events, while the very future qua future is uncertain—America is without community, impulse, without the inner momentum necessary for an age when societies cannot successfully perpetuate themselves by their military weapons, when democracy must be viable because of the quality of life, not its quantity of rockets.

The apathy here is, first *subjective*—the felt powerlessness of ordinary people, the resignation before the enormity of events. But subjective apathy is encouraged by the *objective* American situation—the actual structural separation of people from power, from relevant knowledge, from pinnacles of decision-making. Just as the university influences the student way of life, so do major social institutions create the circumstances in which the isolated citizen will try hopelessly to understand his world and himself.

The very isolation of the individual—from power and community and ability to aspire—means the rise of a democracy without publics. With the great mass of people structurally remote and psychologically hesitant with respect to democratic institutions, those institutions themselves attenuate and become, in the fashion of the vicious circle, progressively less accessible to those few who aspire to serious participation in social affairs. The vital democratic connection between community and leadership, between the mass and the several elites, has been so wrenched and perverted that disastrous policies go unchallenged time and again.

Politics Without Publics

The American political system is not the democratic model of which its glorifiers speak. In actuality it frustrates democracy by confusing the individual citizen, paralyzing policy discussion, and consolidating the irresponsible power of military and business interests.

A crucial feature of the political apparatus in America is that greater differences are harbored within each major party than the differences existing between them. Instead of two parties presenting distinctive and significant differences of approach, what dominates the system is a natural interlocking of Democrats from Southern states with the more conservative elements of the Republican party. This arrangement of forces is blessed by the seniority system of Congress which guarantees congressional committee domination by conservatives—ten of 17 committees in the Senate and 13 of 21 in the House of Representatives are chaired currently by Dixiecrats.

The party overlap, however, is not the only structural antagonist of democracy in politics. First, the localized nature of the party system does not encourage discussion of national and international issues: thus problems are not raised by and for people, and political representatives usually are unfettered from any responsibilities to the general public except those regarding parochial matters. Second, whole constituencies are divested of the full political power they might have: Many Negroes in the South are prevented from voting, migrant workers are disenfranchised by various residence requirements, some urban and suburban dwellers are victimized by gerrymandering, and poor people are too often without the power to obtain political representation. Third, the focus of political attention is significantly distorted by the enormous lobby force, composed predominantly of business interests, spending hundreds of millions each year in an attempt to conform facts about productivity, agriculture, defense, and social services, to the wants of private economic groupings.

What emerges from the party contradiction and insulation of privately-held power is the organized political stalemate: calcification dominates flexibility as the principle of parliamentary organization, frustration is the expectancy of legislators intending liberal reform, and Congress becomes less and less central to national decision-making especially in the area of foreign policy. In this context, confusion and blurring is built into the formulation of issues, long-range priorities are not discussed in the rational manner needed for policy-making, the politics of personality and "image" becomes a more important mechanism than the construction of issues in a way that affords each voter a challenging and real option. The American voter is buffeted from all directions by pseudo-problems, by the structurally-initiated sense that nothing political is subject to human mastery. Worried by his mundane problems which never get solved, but constrained by the common belief that politics is an agonizingly slow accommodation of views, he quits all pretense of bothering.

A most alarming fact is that few, if any, politicians are calling for changes in these conditions. Only a handful even are calling on the President to "live up to" platform pledges; no one is demanding structural changes, such as the shuttling of Southern Democrats out of the Democratic Party. Rather than protesting the state of politics, most politicians are reinforcing and aggravating that state. While in practice they rig public opinion to suit their own interests, in word and ritual they enshrine "the sovereign public" and call for more and more letters. Their speeches and campaign actions are banal, based on a degrading conception of what people want to hear. They respond not to dialogue, but to pressure: and knowing this, the ordinary citizen sees even greater inclination to shun the political sphere. The politician is usually a trumpeter to "citizenship" and "service to the nation," but since he is unwilling to seriously rearrange power relationships, his trumpetings only increase apathy by creating no outlets. Much of the time the call to "service" is justified not in idealistic terms, but in the crasser terms of "defending the free world from communism"—thus making future idealistic impulses harder to justify in anything but Cold War terms.

In such a setting of status quo politics, where most if not all government activity is rationalized in Cold War anticommunist terms, it is somewhat natural that discontented, super-patriotic groups would emerge through political channels and explain their ultra-conservatism as the best means of Victory over Communism. They have become a politically influential force within the Republican Party, at a national level through Senator Goldwater, and at a local level through their important social and economic roles. Their political views are defined generally as the opposite of the supposed views of communists: complete individual freedom in the economic sphere, non-participation by the government in the machinery of production. But actually "anticommunism" becomes an umbrella by which to protest liberalism, internationalism, welfareism, the active civil rights and labor movements. It is to the disgrace of the United States that such a movement should become a prominent kind of public participation in the modern world—but, ironically, it is somewhat to the interests of the United States that such a movement should be a public constituency pointed toward realignment of the political parties, demanding a conservative Republican Party in the South and an exclusion of the "leftist" elements of the national GOP.

The Economy

American capitalism today advertises itself as the Welfare State. Many of us comfortably expect pensions, medical care, unemployment compensation, and other social services in our lifetimes. Even with one-fourth of our productive capacity unused, the majority of Americans are living in relative comfort—although their nagging incentive to "keep up" makes them continually dissatisfied with their possessions. In many places, unrestrained bosses, uncontrolled machines, and sweatshop conditions have been reformed or abolished and suffering tremendously relieved. But in spite of the benign yet obscuring effects of the New Deal reforms and the reassuring phrases of government economists and politicians, the paradoxes and myths of the economy are sufficient to irritate our complacency and reveal to us some essential causes of the American malaise.

We live amidst a national celebration of economic prosperity while poverty and deprivation remain an unbreakable way of life for millions in the "affluent society," including many of our own generation. We hear glib references to the "welfare state," "free enterprise," and "shareholder's democracy" while military defense is the main item of "public" spending and obvious oligopoly and other forms of minority rule defy real individual initiative or popular control. Work, too, is often unfulfilling and victimizing, accepted as a channel to status or plenty, if not a way to pay the bills, rarely as a means of understanding and controlling self and events. In work and leisure the individual is regulated as part of the system, a consuming unit, bombarded by hard-sell, soft-sell, lies and semi-true appeals to his basest drives. He is always told that he is a "free" man bacause of "free enterprise." . . .

The Military-Industrial Complex

The most spectacular and important creation of the authoritarian and oligopolistic structure of economic decision-making in America is the institution called "the military-industrial complex" by former President Eisenhower—the powerful congruence of interest and structure among military and business elites which affects so much of our development and destiny. Not only is ours the first generation to live with the possibility of world-wide cataclysm—it is the first to experience the actual social preparation for cataclysm, the general militarization of American society. In 1948 Congress established Universal Military Training, the first peacetime conscription. The military became a permanent institution. Four years earlier, General Motors' Charles E. Wilson had heralded the creation of what he called the "permanent war economy," the continuous use of military spending as a solution to economic problems unsolved before the post-war boom, most notably the problem of the seventeen million jobless after eight years of the New Deal. This has left a "hidden crisis" in the allocation of resources by the American economy.

Since our childhood these two trends—the rise of the military and the installation of a defense-based economy—have grown fantastically. The Department of Defense, ironically the world's largest single organization, is worth $160 billion, owns 32 million acres of America and employs half the 7.5 million persons directly dependent on the military for subsistence, has an $11 billion payroll which is larger than the net annual income of all American corporations. Defense spending in the Eisenhower era totaled $350 billions and President Kennedy entered office pledged to go even beyond the present defense allocation of 60 cents from every public dollar spent. Except for a war-induced boom immediately after "our side" bombed Hiroshima, American economic prosperity has coincided with a growing dependence on military outlay—from 1941 to 1959 America's Gross National Product of $5.25 trillion included $700 billion in goods and services purchased for the defense effort, about one-seventh of the accumulated GNP. This pattern has included the steady concentration of military spending among a few corporations. In 1961, 86 percent of Defense Department contracts were awarded without competition. The ordnance industry of 100,000 people is completely engaged in military work; in the aircraft industry, 94 percent of 750,000 workers are linked to the war economy; shipbuilding, radio and communications equipment industries commit 40 percent of their work to defense; iron and steel, petroleum, metal-stamping and machine shop products, motors and generators, tools and hardware, copper, aluminum and machine tools industries all devote at least 10 percent of their work to the same cause.

The intermingling of Big Military and Big Industry is evidenced in the 1,400 former officers working for the 100 corporations who received nearly all the $21 billion spent in procurement by the Defense Department in 1961. The overlap is most poignantly clear in the case of General Dynamics, the company which received the best 1961 contracts, employed the most retired officers (187), and is directed by a former Secretary of the Army. A *Fortune* magazine profile of General Dynamics said: "The unique group of men who run Dynamics are only incidentally in rivalry with other U.S. manufacturers, with many of whom they actually act in concert. Their chief competitor is the USSR. The core of General Dynamics' corporate philosophy is the conviction that national defense is a more or less permanent business." Little has changed since Wilson's proud declaration of the Permanent War Economy back in the 1944 days when the top 200 corporations possessed 80 percent of all active prime war-supply contracts.

Military-Industrial Politics

The military and its supporting business foundation have found numerous forms of political expression, and we have heard their din endlessly. There has not been a major Congressional split on the issue of continued defense spending spirals in our lifetime. The triangular relations of the business, military, and political arenas cannot be better expressed than in Dixiecrat Carl Vinson's remarks as his House Armed Services Committee reported out a military construction bill of $808 million throughout the 50 states, for 1960–61: "There is something in this bill for everyone," he announced. President Kennedy had earlier acknowledged the valuable anti-recession features of the bill.

Imagine, on the other hand, $808 million suggested as an antirecession measure, but being poured into programs of social welfare: the impossibility of receiving support for such a measure identifies a crucial feature of defense spending—it is beneficial to private enterprise, while welfare spending is not. Defense spending does not "compete" with the private sector; it contains a natural obsolescence; its "confidential" nature permits easier boondoggling; the tax burdens to which it leads can be shunted from corporation to consumer as a "cost of production." Welfare spending, however, involves the government in competition with private corporations and contractors; it conflicts with immediate interests of private pressure groups; it leads to taxes on business. Think of the opposition of private power companies to current proposals for river and valley development, or the hostility of the real estate lobby to urban renewal; or the attitude of the American Medical Association to a paltry medical care bill; or of all business lobbyists to foreign aid; these are the pressures leading to the schizophrenic public-military, private-civilian economy of our epoch. The politicians, of course, take the line of least resistance and thickest support: warfare, instead of welfare, is easiest to stand up for: after all, the Free World is at stake (and our constituency's investments, too). . . .

The Stance of Labor

Amidst all this, what of organized labor, the historic institutional representative of the exploited, the presumed "countervailing power" against the excesses of Big Business? The contemporary social assault on the labor movement is of crisis proportions. To the average American, "big labor" is a growing cancer equal in impact to Big Business—nothing could be more distorted, even granting a sizeable union bureaucracy. But in addition to public exaggerations, the labor crisis can be measured in several ways. First, the high expectations of the newborn AFL-CIO of 30 million members by 1965 are suffering a reverse unimaginable five years ago. The demise of the dream of "organizing the unorganized" is dramatically reflected in the AFL-CIO decision, just two years after its creation, to slash its organizing staff in half. From 15 million members when the AFL and CIO merged, the total has slipped to 13.5 million. During the post-war generation, union membership nationally has increased by four million—but the total number of workers has jumped by 13 million. Today only 40 percent of all non-agricultural workers are protected by any form of organization. Second, organizing conditions are going to worsen. Where labor now is strongest—in industries—automation is leading to an attrition of available work. As the number of jobs dwindles, so does labor's power of bargaining, since management can handle a strike in an automated plant more easily than the older mass-operated ones.

More important, perhaps, the American economy has changed

radically in the last decade, as suddenly the number of workers producing goods became fewer than the number in "nonproductive" areas—government, trade, finance, services, utilities, transportation. Since World War II "white collar" and "service" jobs have grown twice as fast as have "blue collar" production jobs. Labor has almost no organization in the expanding occupational areas of the new economy, but almost all of its entrenched strength in contracting areas. As big government hires more, as business seeks more office workers and skilled technicians, and as growing commercial America demands new hotels, service stations and the like, the conditions will become graver still. Further, there is continuing hostility to labor by the Southern states and their industrial interests—meaning "runaway" plants, cheap labor threatening the organized trade union movement, and opposition from Dixiecrats to favorable labor legislation in Congress. Finally, there is indication that Big Business, for the sake of public relations if nothing more, has acknowledged labor's "right" to exist, but has deliberately tried to contain labor at its present strength, preventing strong unions from helping weaker ones or from spreading to unorganized sectors of the economy. Business is aided in its efforts by proliferation of "right-to-work" laws at state levels (especially in areas where labor is without organizing strength to begin with), and anti-labor legislation in Congress.

In the midst of these besetting crises, labor itself faces its own problems of vision and program. Historically, there can be no doubt as to its worth in American politics—what progress there has been in meeting human needs in this century rests greatly with the labor movement. And to a considerable extent the social democracy for which labor has fought externally is reflected in its own essentially democratic character: representing millions of people, not millions of dollars; demanding their welfare, not eternal profit.

Today labor remains the most liberal "mainstream" institution—but often its liberalism represents vestigial commitments, self-interestedness, unradicalism. In some measure labor has succumbed to institutionalization, its social idealism waning under the tendencies of bureaucracy, materialism, business ethics. The successes of the last generation perhaps have braked, rather than accelerated labor's zeal for change. Even the House of Labor has bay windows: not only is this true of the labor elites, but as well of some of the rank-and-file. Many of the latter are indifferent unionists, uninterested in meetings, alienated from the complexities of the labor-management negotiating apparatus, lulled to comfort by the accessibility of luxury and the opportunity of long-term contracts. "Union democracy" is not simply inhibited by labor-leader elitism, but by the related problem of rank-and-file apathy to the tradition of unionism. The crisis of labor is reflected in the co-existence within the unions of militant Negro discontents and discriminatory locals, sweeping critics of the obscuring "public interest" marginal tinkering of government and willing handmaidens of conservative political leadership, austere sacrificers and business-like operators, visionaries and anachronisms—tensions between extremes that keep alive the possibilities for a more militant unionism. Too there are seeds of rebirth in the "organizational crisis" itself: the technologically unemployed, the unorganized white collar men and women, the migrants and farm workers, the unprotected Negroes, the poor, all of whom are isolated now from the power structure of the economy, but who are the potential base for a broader and more forceful unionism.

Horizon

In summary: a more reformed, more human capitalism, functioning at three-fourths capacity while one-third of America and two-thirds of the world goes needy, domination of politics and the economy by fantastically rich elites, accommodation and limited effectiveness by the labor movement, hard-core poverty and unemployment, automation confirming the dark ascension of machine over man instead of shared abundance, technological change being introduced into the economy by the criteria of profitability—this has been our inheritance. However inadequate, it has instilled quiescence in liberal hearts—partly reflecting the extent to which misery has been overcome, but also the eclipse of social ideals. Though many of us are "affluent," poverty, waste, elitism, manipulation are too manifest to go unnoticed, too clearly unnecessary to go accepted. To change the Cold War status quo and other social evils, concern with the challenges to the American economic machine must expand. Now, as a truly better social state becomes visible, a new poverty impends: a poverty of vision, and a poverty of political action to make that vision reality. Without new vision, the failure to achieve our potentialities will spell the inability of our society to endure in a world of obvious, crying needs and rapid change. . . .

Towards American Democracy

Every effort to end the Cold War and expand the process of world industrialization is an effort hostile to people and institutions whose interests lie in perpetuation of the East-West military threat and the postponement of change in the "have not" nations of the world. Every such effort, too, is bound to establish greater democracy in America. The major goals of a domestic effort would be:

1. *America must abolish its political party stalemate.*

Two genuine parties, centered around issues and essential values, demanding allegiance to party principles shall supplant the current system of organized stalemate which is seriously inadequate to a world in flux. . . . What is desirable is sufficient party disagreement to dramatize major issues, yet sufficient party overlap to guarantee stable transitions from administration to administration.

Every time the President criticizes a recalcitrant Congress, we must ask that he no longer tolerate the Southern conservatives in the Democratic Party. Every time a liberal representative complains that "we can't expect everything at once" we must ask if we received much of anything from Congress in the last generation. Every time he refers to "circumstances beyond control" we must ask why he fraternizes with racist scoundrels. Every time he speaks of the "unpleasantness of personal and party fighting" we should insist that pleasantry with Dixiecrats is inexcusable when the dark peoples of the world call for American support.

2. *Mechanisms of voluntary association must be created through which political information can be imparted and political participation encouraged.*

Political parties, even if realigned, would not provide adequate outlets for popular involvement. Institutions should be created that engage people with issues and express political preference, not as now with huge business lobbies which exercise undemocratic *power* but which carry political *influence* (appropriate to private, rather than public, groupings) in national decision-making enterprise. Private in nature, these should be organized around single issues (medical care, transportation systems reform, etc.), concrete interest (labor and minority group organizations); multiple issues or general issues. These do not exist in America in quantity today. If they did exist, they would be a significant politicizing and educative force bringing people into touch with public life and affording them means of expression and action. Today, giant lobby representatives of business interests are dominant, but not educative. The Federal government itself should counter the latter forces whose intent is often public deceit for private gain, by subsidizing the preparation and decentralized distribution of objective materials on all public issues facing government.

3. *Institutions and practices which stifle dissent should be abolished, and the promotion of peaceful dissent should be actively promoted.*

The First Amendment freedoms of speech, assembly, thought, religion and press should be seen as guarantees, not threats, to national security. While society has the right to prevent active subversion of its laws and institutions, it has the duty as well to promote open discussion of all issues—otherwise it will be in fact promoting real subversion as the only means of implementing ideas. To eliminate the fears and apathy from national life it is necessary that the institutions bred by fear and apathy be rooted out: the House Un-American Activities Committee, the Senate Internal Security Committee, the loyalty oaths on Federal loans, the Attorney General's list of subversive organizations, the Smith and McCarran Acts. The process of eliminating the blighting institutions is the process of restoring democratic participation. Their existence is a sign of the decomposition and atrophy of participation.

4. *Corporations must be made publicly responsible.*

It is not possible to believe that true democracy can exist where a minority utterly controls enormous wealth and power. The influence of corporate elites on foreign policy is neither reliable nor democratic; a way must be found to subordinate private American foreign investment to a democratically-constructed foreign policy. . . .

Labor and government as presently constituted are not sufficient to "regulate" corporations. A new re-ordering, a new calling of responsibility is necessary: more than changing "work rules" we must consider changes in the rules of society by challenging the unchallenged politics of American corporations. Before the government can really begin to control business in a "public interest," the public must gain more substantial control of government: this demands a movement for political as well as economic realignments. We are aware that simple government "regulation," if achieved, would be inadequate without increased worker participation in management decision-making, strengthened and independent regulatory power, balances of partial and/or complete public ownership, various means of humanizing the conditions and types of work itself, sweeping welfare programs and regional *public* development authorities. These are examples of measures to re-balance the economy toward public—and individual—control.

5. *The allocation of resources must be based on social needs. A truly "public sector" must be established, and its nature debated and planned.*

At present the majority of America's "public sector," the largest part of our public spending, is for the military. When great social needs are so pressing, our concept of "government spending" is wrapped up in the "permanent war economy." . . .

The main *private* forces of economic expansion cannot guarantee a steady rate of growth, nor acceptable recovery from recession—especially in a demilitarizing world. Government participation will inevitably expand enormously, because the stable growth of the economy demands increasing "public" investments yearly. Our present outpour of more than $500 billion might double in a generation, irreversibly involving government solutions. And in future recessions, the compensatory fiscal action by the government will be the only means of avoiding the twin disasters of greater unemployment and a slackening rate of growth. Furthermore, a close relationship with the European Common Market will involve competition with numerous planned economies and may aggravate American unemployment unless the economy here is expanding swiftly enough to create new jobs.

All these tendencies suggest that not only solutions to our present social needs but our future expansion rests upon our willingness to enlarge the "public sector" greatly. Unless we choose war as an economic solvent, future public spending will be of non-military nature—a major intervention into civilian production by the government. . . .

6. *America should concentrate on its genuine social priorities: abolish squalor, terminate neglect, and establish an environment for people to live in with dignity and creativeness.*

A. A program against *poverty* must be just as sweeping as the nature of poverty itself. It must not be just palliative, but directed to the abolition of the structural circumstances of poverty. At a bare minimum it should include a *housing* act far larger than the one supported by the Kennedy Administration, but one that is geared more to low- and middle-income needs than to the windfall aspirations of small and large private entrepreneurs, one that is more sympathetic to the quality of communal life than to the efficiency of city-split highways. Second, *medical care* must become recognized as a lifetime human right just as vital as food, shelter and clothing—the Federal government should guarantee health insurance as a basic social service turning medical treatment into a social habit, not just an occasion of crisis, fighting sickness among the aged, not just by making medical care financially feasible but by reducing sickness among children and younger people. Third, existing institutions should be expanded so the Welfare State cares for *everyone's* welfare according to need. *Social Security* payments should be extended to everyone and should be proportionately greater for the poorest. A *minimum wage* of at least $1.50 should be extended to all workers (including the 16 million currently not covered at all). Programs for equal *educational opportunity* are as important a part of the battle against poverty.

B. A full-scale public initiative for civil rights should be undertaken despite the clamor among conservatives (and liberals) about gradualism, property rights, and law and order. The executive and legislative branches of the Federal government should work by enforcement *and* enactment against any form of exploitation of minority groups. No Federal cooperation with racism is tolerable—from financing of schools, to the development of Federally-supported industry, to the social gatherings of the President. Laws hastening school desegregation, voting rights, and economic protection for Negroes are needed right now. The moral force of the Executive Office should be exerted against the Dixiecrats specifically, and the national complacency about the race question generally. Especially in the North, where one-half of the country's Negro people now live, civil rights is not a problem to be solved in isolation from other problems. The fight against poverty, against slums, against the stalemated Congress, against McCarthyism, are all fights against the discrimination that is nearly endemic to all areas of American life.

C. The promise and problems of long-range *Federal economic development* should be studied more constructively. It is an embarrassing parodox that the Tennessee Valley Authority is a wonder to most foreign visitors but a "radical" and barely influential project to most Americans. The Kennedy decision to permit private facilities to transmit power from the $1 billion Colorado River Storage Project is a disastrous one, interposing privately-owned transmitters between publicly-owned generators and their publicly (and cooperatively) owned distributors. The contrary trend, to public ownership of power, should be generated in an experimental way.

The Area Redevelopment Act of 1961 is a first step in recognizing the underdeveloped areas of the United States. It is only a drop in the bucket financially and is not keyed to public planning and public works on a broad scale. It consists only of a few loan programs to lure industries and some grants to improve public facilities to lure these industries. The current public works bill in Congress is needeed—and a more sweeping, higher-priced program of regional development with a proliferation of "TVAs" in such areas as the Appalachian region are needed desperately. However, it has been rejected already by Mississippi because the improvement it bodes for the unskilled Negro worker. This program should be enlarged, given teeth, and pursued rigorously by Federal authorities.

D. We must meet the growing complex of "city" problems; over 90 percent of Americans will live in urban areas within two decades. Juvenile delinquency, untended mental illness, crime increase, slums, urban tenantry and non-rent controlled housing, the isolation of the individual in the city—all are problems of the city and are major symptoms of the present system of economic priorities and lack of public planning. Private property control (the real estate lobby and a few selfish landowners and businesses) is as devastating in the cities as corporations are on the national level. But there is no comprehensive way to deal with these problems now amidst competing units of government, dwindling tax resources, suburban escapism (saprophitic to the sick central cities), high infrastructure costs and no one to pay them.

The only solutions are national and regional. "Federalism" has thus far failed here because states are rural-dominated; the Federal government has had to operate by bootlegging and trickle-down measures dominated by private interests, with their appendages through annexation or federation. A new external challenge is needed, not just a Department of Urban Affairs but a thorough national *program* to help the cities. The *model* city must be projected—more community decision-making and participation, true integration of classes, races, vocations—provision for beauty, access to nature and the benefits of the central city as well, privacy without privatism, decentralized "units" spread horizontally with central, regional democratic control—provision for the basic facility-needs, for everyone, with units of planned *regions* and thus public, democratic control over the growth of the civic community and the allocation of resources.

E. *Mental health institutions* are in dire need; there were fewer mental hospital beds in relation to the numbers of mentally-ill in 1959 than there were in 1948. Public hospitals, too, are seriously wanting; existing structures alone need an estimated $1 billion for rehabilitation. Tremendous staff and faculty needs exist as well, and there are not enough medical students enrolled today to meet the anticipated needs of the future.

F. Our *prisons* are too often the enforcers of misery. They must be either re-oriented to rehabilitative work through public supervision or be abolished for their dehumanizing social effects. Funds are needed, too, to make possible a decent prison environment.

G. *Education* is too vital a public problem to be completely entrusted to the province of the various states and local units. In fact, there is no good reason why America should not progress now toward internationalizing rather than localizing, its education system—children and young adults studying everywhere in the world, through a United Nations program, would go far to create mutual understanding. In the meantime, the need for teachers and classrooms in America is fantastic. This is an area where "minimal" requirements should hardly be considered as a goal—there always are improvements to be made in the education system, e.g., smaller classes and many more teachers for them, programs to subsidize the education for the poor but bright, etc.

H. America should eliminate *agricultural policies* based on scarcity and pent-up surplus. In America and foreign countries there exist tremendous needs for more food and balanced diets. The Federal government should finance small farmers' cooperatives, strengthen programs of rural electrification, and expand policies for the distribution of agricultural surpluses throughout the world (by Food-for-Peace and related UN programming). Marginal farmers must be helped to either become productive enough to survive "industrialized agriculture" or given help in making the transition out of agriculture—the current Rural Area Development program must be better coordinated with a massive national "area redevelopment" program.

I. *Science* should be employed to constructively transform the conditions of life throughout the United States and the world. Yet at the present time the Department of Health, Education, and Welfare and the National Science Foundation together spend only $300 million annually for scientific purposes in contrast to the $6 billion spent by the Defense Department and the Atomic Energy Commission. One-half of all research and development in America is directly devoted to military purposes. Two imbalances must be corrected—that of military over nonmilitary investigation, and that of biological-natural-physical science over the sciences of human behavior. Our political system must then include planning for the human use of science: by anticipating the political consequences of scientific innovation, by directing the discovery and exploration of space, by adapting science to improved production of food, to international communications systems, to technical problems of disarmament, and so on. For the newly-developing nations, American science should focus on the study of cheap sources of power, housing and building materials, mass educational techniques, etc. Further, science and scholarship should be seen less as an apparatus of conflicting power blocs, but as a bridge toward supra-national community: the International Geophysical Year is a model for continuous further cooperation between the science communities of all nations.

Violence in the streets of Chicago during the Democratic National Convention, August 1968

DANIEL WALKER

The Walker Report

(1968)

Rights In Conflict: The Violent Confrontation of Demonstrators and Police in the Parks and Streets of Chicago During the Week of the Democratic National Convention of 1968. A Report Submitted by Daniel Walker, Director of the Chicago Study Team, to the National Commission on the Causes and Prevention of Violence, **is an example of the lengthily-titled long public reports with even longer accompanying documents which became the least expected best-sellers of the 1960s and perhaps that era's characteristic genre. The "Walker Report" appeared but four months after the events it described and only nine months after the publication of the Report of the National Advisory Commission on Civil Disorders, (the "Kerner Commission Report") which studied the ghetto riots of 1967 – the fourth con-**

secutive summer of major disorders. Nor was the "Kerner Report" the first such best-seller. The Warren Commission study of President Kennedy's assassination had already created a major literature of defense and criticism of its findings that Lee Harvey Oswald had acted alone, and twenty-six volumes of accompanying documents had been published to substantiate the commission's conclusions.

Observers of American culture realized that the constant national crises of the decade had generated a new form of literature. Never had public documents seemed so relevant to a large educated public: a report on national goals at the end of the fifties, an important study of juvenile delinquency that influenced the development of the War on Poverty, and later a controversial report on pornography as well as somewhat differently motivated but in many ways similar documents like the Pentagon Papers and the Watergate Tapes. Parallel to these documents was the "New Journalism," an extension of traditional journalism into fiction and visionary projections from the real-life material that the writer viewed through the filter of national media and widely shared myths. Tom Wolfe seemed to live the drug culture as participant-observer in The Electric Kool-Aid Acid Test (1969); Norman Mailer actually marched with "The Armies of the Night" in the book of that name about the massive demonstration against the Pentagon in October, 1967. This mentality of "I was there; I didn't just see it on TV and I can prove it by my own personal witness" strangely informs the public documents much as it does this more personal genre. Both kinds of writing found a wide audience probably because they were a check on the readers' direct observation of the same events on television. The sense that one had seen it all yet did not have any way to tell what was real lingered throughout the sixties and seventies, generating myths and conspiratorial fantasies. The climax came with Watergate, an epistemological political drama in which millions climbed mountains of fact to peer through clouds of constitutional abstractions in search of a "smoking gun." National reports were a public way—as the new journalism was a private way—to clear the air.

The "Walker Report" is perhaps the best written, most gripping document of all this literature. 212 people created the report in 53 days. Rather than seeming hasty or sloppy, the narrative has a pace that reflects the mood and the speed of its composition. It is probably the best introduction to the crisis of the 1960s, catching all the anger and frustration of the era of racial rioting, stalemate in Vietnam, and the souring of the mid-decade dreams of achieving prosperity and social justice together. It portrays the so-called "counterculture" at its height, when political revolutionaries and exponents of a private revolution in life-styles made common cause against a shaky "establishment" aptly symbolized by Mayor Richard J. Daley of Chicago. This confrontation, so neatly symbolic of the country's tensions then, was also formative of its future politics. Out of these events came both the election of Richard Nixon in 1968 and the Watergate scandal that drove him from office in 1974. For it was Nixon's fear of the radicals that led to the illegal activities which he was then forced to cover up, which in turn forced him to cover-up that cover-up when the Watergate break-in occurred. Abbie Hoffman, interviewed in Chicago in 1968, explained the philosophy which would find an even better foil in Richard Nixon than in Richard Daley: "Urban guerrilla warfare is a psychological attempt to trick the enemy into developing a policy of over-kill . . . on the part of the aggressor, on the part of those people in power and what they do is you see then, is start to gobble themselves up." What Hoffman did not predict was that by the time Richard Nixon had gobbled himself up through overkill, the counterculture would already have been digested into American culture.

About the Report

The facts included in this report are taken primarily from 3,437 statements of eyewitnesses and participants in the events chronicled. Our staff took 1,410 of the statements; another 2,017 were taken by the Federal Bureau of Investigation and made available to us. A few others were provided by such agencies as the U.S. Attorney's office in Chicago. In total, about 20,000 pages of witness statements were reviewed.

Persons interviewed, both in Chicago and throughout the nation, included police officers, National Guardsmen, U.S. Army personnel, demonstrators and their leaders, government officials, convention delegates, news media representatives and bystanders.

The staff also viewed about 180 hours of motion picture film provided by television networks and local stations, the Chicago Police Department and private sources. More than 12,000 still photographs were examined. Official records of the National Guard and Police Department were reviewed.

Thousands of news accounts were examined but none was used as a fact source. They appear in the report only when the fact of publication is itself material—for example, the accounts of demonstrators' plans which had an effect on the city's security planning.

We have, with considerable reluctance, included the actual obscenities used by participants—demonstrators and police alike. Extremely obscene language was a contributing factor to the violence described in this report, and its frequency and intensity were such that to omit it would inevitably understate the effect it had.

The Chicago staff started on September 27, 1968, and only by disregarding clock and families was it able to complete the report 53 days later.

Daniel Walker, Director
Chicago, Illinois
November 18, 1968

Foreword

The right to dissent is fundamental to democracy. But the expression of that right has become one of the most serious problems in contemporary democratic government. That dilemma was dramatized in Chicago during the Democratic National Convention of 1968—the dilemma of a city coping with the expression of dissent.

Unlike other recent big city riots, including those in Chicago itself, the events of convention week did not consist of looting and burning, followed by mass arrests. To a shocking extent they consisted of crowd-police battles in the parks as well as the streets. And the shock was intensified by the presence in the crowds (which included some anarchists and revolutionaries) of large numbers of innocent dissenting citizens.

The initial response, precipitated by dramatic television coverage, was a horrified condemnation of city and police. When demonstrators compared the Chicago police to the Soviet troops then occupying Prague, news commentators sympathetically relayed that comparison to the world. Not since Birmingham and Selma had there been so heated a mood of public outrage.

An immediate counterresponse, however, expressed the feeling that the demonstrators got what they deserved, and the thinking that the city had no alternative. Many observers thought that, in view of the provocation and the circumstances, police had performed admirably and with restraint.

The commentary far outlasted the convention. Major writers in some of the world's most respected periodicals denounced the city, the police, and the Democratic leaders. For its part, the City of Chicago issued "The Strategy of Confrontation," a paper detailing the threat to the city, itemizing provocations, describing a battery of bizarre weapons allegedly intended for use against law enforcement officers, and charging the American news media with biased coverage. The city also prepared a one-hour film shown nationally on television.

These conflicting responses, and the nature of the dilemma imposed upon Chicago, make this study necessary. Our purpose is to present the facts so that thoughtful readers can decide what lessons come out of them; for it is urgent that any such lessons be speedily incorporated into American public life. The *Chicago Tribune* began its special report on convention week with the line, "Not everyone wins." They might have added that there are circumstances in which *no one* wins, in which everyone loses. Such circumstances make up this report.

We have addressed ourselves to questions like the following. What were the objectives of the planned demonstrations, and who planned them? How did the city prepare itself? What types of people made up the crowds in the parks? Were physical and verbal attacks typical of demonstrator behavior? And did they precipitate police violence or follow it? Was the clubbing done by a few tired policemen goaded into "overreacting," or was there large-scale police brutality? Is there evidence that newsmen were singled out for assault? Was Chicago itself conducive to violence, or was it merely where the convention, and the cameras, happened to be?

We believe we have laid a factual foundation for meaningful answers to those questions.

Our charge was not to decide what ought to have been done, or to balance the rights and wrongs, or to recommend a course of action for the future. Having sought out the facts, we intend to let them speak for themselves. But we urge the reader, in assessing these facts, to bear in mind that the physical confrontations in Chicago will be repeated elsewhere until we learn to deal with the dilemma they represent.

In principle at least, most Americans acknowledge the right to dissent. And, in principle at least, most dissenters acknowledge the right of a city to protect its citizens and its property. But what happens when these undeniable rights are brought—deliberately by some—into conflict?

Convention week in Chicago is what happens, and the challenge it brings is plain: to keep *peaceful assembly* from becoming a contradiction in terms.

A Summary

During the week of the Democratic National Convention, the Chicago police were the targets of mounting provocation by both word and act. It took the form of obscene epithets, and of rocks, sticks, bathroom tiles and even human feces hurled at police by demonstrators. Some of these acts had been planned; others were spontaneous or were themselves provoked by police action. Furthermore, the police had been put on edge by widely published threats of attempts to disrupt both the city and the Convention.

That was the nature of the provocation. The nature of the response was unrestrained and indiscriminate police violence on many occasions, particularly at night.

That violence was made all the more shocking by the fact that it was often inflicted upon persons who had broken no law, disobeyed no order, made no threat. These included peaceful demonstrators, onlookers, and large numbers of residents who were simply passing through, or happened to live in, the areas where confrontations were occurring.

Newsmen and photographers were singled out for assault, and their equipment deliberately damaged. Fundamental police training was ignored; and officers, when on the scene, were often unable to control their men. As one police officer put it: "What happened didn't have anything to do with police work."

The violence reached its culmination on Wednesday night.

A report prepared by an inspector from the Los Angeles Police Department, present as an official observer, while generally praising the police restraint he had observed in the parks during the week, said this about the events that night:

"There is no question but that many officers acted without restraint and exerted force beyond that necessary under the circumstances. The leadership at the point of conflict did little to prevent such conduct and the direct control of officers by first line supervisors was virtually non-existent."

He is referring to the police-crowd confrontation in front of the Conrad Hilton Hotel. Most Americans know about it, having seen the 17-minute sequence played and replayed on their television screens.

But most Americans do not know that the confrontation was followed by even more brutal incidents in the Loop side streets. Or that it had been preceded by comparable instances of indiscriminate police attacks on the North Side a few nights earlier when demonstrators were cleared from Lincoln Park and pushed into the streets and alleys of Old Town.

How did it start? With the emergence long before convention week of three factors which figured significantly in the outbreak of violence. These were: threats to the city; the city's response; and the conditioning of Chicago police to expect that violence against demonstrators, as against rioters, would be condoned by city officials.

The threats to the City were varied. Provocative and inflammatory statements, made in connection with activities planned for convention week, were published and widely disseminated. There were also intelligence reports from informants.

Some of this information was absurd, like the reported plan to contaminate the city's water supply with LSD. But some were serious; and both were strengthened by the authorities' lack of any mechanism for distinguishing one from the other.

The second factor—the city's response—matched, in numbers and logistics at least, the demonstrators' threats.

The city, fearful that the "leaders" would not be able to control their followers, attempted to discourage an inundation of demonstrators by not granting permits for marches and rallies and by making it quite clear that the "law" would be enforced.

Government—federal, state and local—moved to defend itself from the threats, both imaginary and real. The preparations were detailed and far ranging: from stationing firemen at each alarm box within a six block radius of the Amphitheatre to staging U.S. Army armored personnel carriers in Soldier Field under Secret Service control. Six thousand Regular Army troops in full field gear, equipped with rifles, flame throwers, and bazookas were airlifted to Chicago on Monday, August 26. About 6,000 Illinois National Guard troops had already been activated to assist the 12,000 member Chicago Police Force.

Of course, the Secret Service could never afford to ignore threats of assassination of Presidential candidates. Neither could the city, against the background of riots in 1967 and 1968, ignore the ever-present threat of ghetto riots, possibly sparked by large numbers of demonstrators, during convention week.

The third factor emerged in the city's position regarding the riots following the death of Dr. Martin Luther King and the April 27th peace march to the Civic Center in Chicago.

The police were generally credited with restraint in handling the first riots—but Mayor Daley rebuked the Superintendent of Police. While it was later modified, his widely disseminated "shoot to kill arsonists and shoot to maim looters" order undoubtedly had an effect.

The effect on police became apparent several weeks later, when they attacked demonstrators, bystanders and media representatives at a Civic Center peace march. There were published criticisms—but the city's response was to ignore the police violence.

That was the background. On August 18, 1968, the advance contingent of demonstrators arrived in Chicago and established their base, as planned, in Lincoln Park on the city's Near North Side. Throughout the week, they were joined by others—some from the Chicago area, some from states as far away as New York and California. On the weekend before the convention began, there were about 2,000 demonstrators in Lincoln Park; the crowd grew to about 10,000 by Wednesday.

There were, of course, the hippies—the long hair and love beads, the calculated unwashedness, the flagrant banners, the open lovemaking and disdain for the constraints of conventional society. In dramatic effect, both visual and vocal, these dominated a crowd whose members actually differed widely in physical appearance, in motivation, in political affiliation, in philosophy. The crowd included Yippies come to "do their thing," youngsters working for a political candidate, professional people with dissenting political views, anarchists and determined revolutionaries, motorcycle gangs, black activists, young thugs, police and secret service undercover agents. There were demonstrators waving the Viet Cong flag and the red flag of revolution and there were the simply curious who came to watch and, in many cases, became willing or unwilling participants.

To characterize the crowd, then, as entirely hippy-Yippie, entirely "New Left," entirely anarchist, or entirely youthful political dissenters is both wrong and dangerous. The stereotyping that did occur helps to explain the emotional reaction of both police and public during and after the violence that occurred.

Despite the presence of some revolutionaries, the vast majority of the demonstrators were intent on expressing by peaceful means their dissent either from society generally or from the administration's policies in Vietnam.

Most of those intending to join the major protest demonstrations scheduled during convention week did not plan to enter the Amphitheatre and disrupt the proceedings of the Democratic convention, did not plan aggressive acts of physical provocation against the authorities, and did not plan to use rallies of demonstrators to stage an assault against any person, institution, or place of business. But while it is clear that most of the protesters in Chicago had no intention of initiating violence, this is not to say that they did not expect it to develop.

It was the clearing of the demonstrators from Lincoln Park that led directly to the violence: symbolically, it expressed the city's opposition to the protesters; literally, it forced the protesters into confrontation with police in Old Town and the adjacent residential neighborhoods.

The Old Town area near Lincoln Park was a scene of police ferocity exceeding that shown on television on Wednesday night. From Sunday night through Tuesday night, incidents of intense and indiscriminate violence occurred in the streets after police had swept the park clear of demonstrators.

Demonstrators attacked too. And they posed difficult problems for police as they persisted in marching through the streets, blocking traffic and intersections. But it was the police who forced them out of the park and into the neighborhood. And on the part of the police there was enough wild club swinging, enough cries of hatred, enough gratuitous beating to make the conclusion inescapable that individual policemen, and lots of them, committed violent acts far in excess of the requisite force for crowd dispersal or arrest. To read dispassionately the hundreds of statements describing at firsthand the events of Sunday and Monday nights is to become convinced of the presence of what can only be called a police riot.

Here is an eyewitness talking about Monday night:

"The demonstrators were forced out onto Clark Street and once again a traffic jam developed. Cars were stopped, the horns began to honk, people couldn't move, people got gassed inside their cars, people got stoned inside their cars, police were the objects of stones, and taunts, mostly taunts. As you must understand, most of the taunting of the police was verbal. There were stones thrown of course, but for the most part it was verbal. But there were stones being thrown and of course the police were responding with tear gas and clubs and everytime they could get near enough to a demonstrator they hit him.

"But again you had this police problem within–this really turned into a police problem. They pushed everybody out of the park, but this night there were a lot more people in the park than there had been during the previous night and Clark Street was just full of people and in addition now was full of gas because the police were using gas on a much larger scale this night. So the police were faced with the task, which took them about an hour or so, of hitting people over the head and gassing them enough to get them out of Clark Street, which they did."

But police action was not confined to the necessary force, even in clearing the park:

A young man and his girl friend were both grabbed by officers. He screamed, "We're going, we're going," but they threw him into the pond. The officers grabbed the girl, knocked her to the ground, dragged her along the embankment and hit her with their batons on her head, arms, back and legs. The boy tried to scramble up the embankment to her, but police shoved him back in the water at least twice. He finally got to her and tried to pull her in the water, away from the police. He was clubbed on the head five or six times. An officer shouted, "Let's get the fucking bastards!" but the boy pulled her in the water and the police left.

Like the incident described above, much of the violence witnessed in Old Town that night seems malicious or mindless:

There were pedestrians. People who were not part of the demonstration were coming out of a tavern to see what the demonstration was . . . and the officers indiscriminately started beating everybody on the street who was not a policeman.

Another scene:

There was a group of about six police officers that moved in and started beating two youths. When one of the officers pulled back his nightstick to swing, one of the youths grabbed it from behind and started beating on the officer. At this point about ten officers left everybody else and ran after this youth, who turned down Wells and ran to the left.

But the officers went to the right, picked up another youth, assuming he was the one they were chasing, and took him into an empty lot and beat him. And when they got him to the ground, they just kicked him ten times—the wrong youth, the innocent youth who had been standing there.

A federal legal official relates an experience of Tuesday evening.

I then walked one block north where I met a group of 12–15 policemen. I showed them my identification and they permitted me to walk with them. The police walked one block west. Numerous people were watching us from their windows and balconies. The police yelled profanities at them, taunting them to come down where the police would beat them up. The police stopped a number of people on the street demanding identification. They verbally abused each pedestrian and pushed one or two without hurting them. We walked back to Clark Street and began to walk north where the police stopped a number of people who appeared to be protesters, and ordered them out of the area in a very abusive way. One protester who was walking in the opposite direction was kneed in the groin by a policeman who was walking towards him. The boy fell to the ground and swore at the policeman who picked him up and threw him to the ground. We continued to walk toward the command post. A derelict who appeared to be very intoxicated, walked up to the policeman and mumbled something that was incoherent. The policeman pulled from his belt a tin container and sprayed its contents into the eyes of the derelict, who stumbled around and fell on his face.

It was on these nights that the police violence against media representatives reached its peak. Much of it was plainly deliberate. A newsman was pulled aside on Monday by a detective acquaintance of his who said: "The word is being passed to get newsmen." Individual newsmen were warned, "You take my picture tonight and I'm going to get you." Cries of "get the camera" preceded individual attacks on photographers.

A newspaper photographer describes Old Town on Monday at about 9:00 P.M.:

When the people arrived at the intersection of Wells and Division, they were not standing in the streets. Suddenly a column of policemen ran out from the alley. They were reinforcements. They were under control but there seemed to be no direction. One man was yelling, 'Get them up on the sidewalks, turn them around.' Very suddenly the police charged the people on the sidewalks and began beating their heads. A line of cameramen was 'trapped' along with the crowd along the sidewalks, and the police went down the line chopping away at the cameras.

A network cameraman reports that on the same night:

I just saw this guy coming at me with his nightstick and I had the camera up. The tip of his stick hit me right in the mouth, then I put my tongue up there and I noticed that my tooth was gone. I turned around then to try to leave and then this cop came up behind me with his stick and he jabbed me in the back.

All of a sudden these cops jumped out of the police cars and started just beating the hell out of people. And before anything else happened to me, I saw a man holding a Bell & Howell camera with big wide letters on it, saying 'CBS.' He apparently had been hit by a cop. And cops were standing around and there was blood streaming down his face. Another policeman was running after me and saying, 'Get the fuck out of here.' And I heard another guy scream, 'Get their fucking cameras.' And the next thing I know I was being hit on the head, and I think on the back, and I was just forced down on the ground at the corner of Division and Wells.

If the intent was to discourage coverage, it was successful in at least one case. A photographer from a news magazine says that finally, "I just stopped shooting, because every time you push the flash, they look at you and they are screaming about, 'Get the fucking photographers and get the film.'"

There is some explanation for the media-directed violence. Camera crews on at least two occasions did stage violence and fake injuries. Demonstrators did sometimes step up their activities for the benefit of TV cameras. Newsmen and photographers' blinding lights did get in the way of police clearing streets, sweeping the park and dispersing demonstrators. Newsmen did, on occasion, disobey legitimate police orders to "move" or "clear the streets." News reporting of events did seem to the police to be anti-Chicago and anti-police.

But was the response appropriate to the provocation?

Out of 300 newsmen assigned to cover the parks and streets of Chicago during convention week, more than 60 (about 20%) were involved in incidents resulting in injury to themselves, damage to their equipment, or their arrest. Sixty-three newsmen were physically attacked by police; in 13 of these instances, photographic or recording equipment was intentionally damaged.

The violence did not end with either demonstrators or newsmen on the North Side on Sunday, Monday and Tuesday. It continued in Grant Park on Wednesday. It occurred on Michigan Avenue in front of the Conrad Hilton Hotel, as already described. A high-ranking Chicago police commander admits that on that occasion the police "got out of control." This same commander appears in one of the most vivid scenes of the entire week, trying desperately to keep individual policemen from beating demonstrators as he screams, "For Christ's sake, stop it!"

Thereafter, the violence continued on Michigan Avenue and on the side streets running into Chicago's Loop. A federal official describes how it began:

> *"I heard a 10-1 call [policeman in trouble] on either my radio or one of the other hand sets carried by men with me and then heard 'Car 100—sweep.' With a roar of motors, squads, vans and three-wheelers came from east, west and north into the block north of Jackson. The crowd scattered. A big group ran west on Jackson, with a group of blue shirted policemen in pursuit, beating at them with clubs. Some of the crowd would jump into doorways and the police would rout them out. The action was very tough. In my judgment, unnecessarily so. The police were hitting with a vengeance and quite obviously with relish. . . ."*

What followed was a club-swinging melee. Police ranged the streets striking anyone they could catch. To be sure, demonstrators threw things at policemen and at police cars; but the weight of violence was overwhelmingly on the side of the police. A few examples will give the flavor of that night in Chicago:

> *"At the corner of Congress Plaza and Michigan,"* states a doctor, *"was gathered a group of people, numbering between thirty and forty. They were trapped against a railing [along a ramp leading down from Michigan Avenue to an underground parking garage] by several policemen on motorcycles. The police charged the people on motorcycles and struck about a dozen of them, knocking several of them down. About twenty standing there jumped over the railing. On the other side of the railing was a three-to-four-foot drop. None of the people who were struck by the motor-*

cycles appeared to be seriously injured. However, several of them were limping as if they had been run over on their feet."

A UPI reporter witnessed these attacks, too. He relates in his statement that one officer, "with a smile on his face and a fanatical look in his eyes, was standing on a three-wheel cycle, shouting, 'Wahoo, wahoo,' and trying to run down people on the sidewalk." The reporter says he was chased thirty feet by the cycle.

A priest who was in the crowd says he saw a "boy, about fourteen or fifteen, white, standing on top of an automobile yelling something which was unidentifiable. Suddenly a policeman pulled him down from the car and beat him to the ground by striking him three or four times with a nightstick. Other police joined in . . . and they eventually shoved him to a police van.

"A well-dressed woman saw this incident and spoke angrily to a nearby police captain. As she spoke, another policeman came up from behind her and sprayed something in her face with an aerosol can. He then clubbed her to the ground. He and two other policemen then dragged her along the ground to the same paddy wagon and threw her in."

"I ran west on Jackson," a witness states. "West of Wabash, a line of police stretching across both sidewalks and the street charged after a small group I was in. Many people were clubbed and maced as they ran. Some weren't demonstrators at all, but were just pedestrians who didn't know how to react to the charging officers yelling 'Police!'"

"A wave of police charged down Jackson," another witness relates. "Fleeing demonstrators were beaten indiscriminately and a temporary, makeshift first aid station was set up on the corner of State and Jackson. Two men lay in pools of blood, their heads severely cut by clubs. A minister moved amongst the crowd, quieting them, brushing aside curious onlookers, and finally asked a policeman to call an ambulance, which he agreed to do. . . ."

An Assistant U.S. Attorney later reported that "the demonstrators were running as fast as they could but were unable to get out of the way because of the crowds in front of them. I observed the police striking numerous individuals, perhaps 20 to 30. I saw three fall down and then overrun by the police. I observed two demonstrators who had multiple cuts on their heads. We assisted one who was in shock into a passer-by's car."

Police violence was a fact of convention week. Were the policemen who committed it a minority? It appears certain that they were—but one which has imposed some of the consequences of its actions on the majority, and certainly on their commanders. There has been no public condemnation of these violators of sound police procedures and common decency by either their commanding officers or city officials. Nor (at the time this Report is being completed—almost three months after the convention) has any disciplinary action been taken against most of them. That some policemen lost control of themselves under exceedingly provocative circumstances can perhaps be understood:

but not condoned. If no action is taken against them, the effect can only be to discourage the majority of policemen who acted responsibly, and further weaken the bond between police and community.

Although the crowds were finally dispelled on the nights of violence in Chicago, the problems they represent have not been. Surely this is not the last time that a violent dissenting group will clash head-on with those whose duty it is to enforce the law. And the next time the whole world will still be watching.

The Gathering Forces: A Prelude to Convention Week

The events examined in this report cannot be understood apart from the social context and the city in which they occurred.

Near the center of the city, the Chicago River flows west out of Lake Michigan and, in about a mile, forks into a north branch and a south branch. Beyond the fork is the West Side, now largely populated by Negroes and Spanish Americans. Just south of the river is the Loop, a downtown area of banks and businesses, theaters and restaurants, and the seats of government of both Chicago and Cook County. Also in the Loop are most of the hotels which house the 1,300,000 visitors who come each year. The largest of these hotels, the Conrad Hilton, faces Grant Park, which lies between Michigan Avenue and the lake.

Downtown Chicago has relatively few permanent residents. Half of the city's population lives on the sprawling South Side, where a "Black Belt" of Negroes extends for almost ten miles, bound on the east by Lake Michigan and on the west by white ethnic neighborhoods. As in other American urban centers, the Negroes are concentrated into a few overcrowded sections. On the North Side thousands of Negroes live in uneasy proximity to bohemians and affluent whites.

Racial tensions have been high in Chicago in recent years. Riots broke out in 1966 and again in April, 1968, after Dr. Martin Luther King's assassination. Arson and looting were widespread during the April, 1968, riots. The police had, however, benefited from the findings of the President's National Commission on Civil Disorders and from the experience of police departments in coping with previous riots in Chicago and other major cities. The Mayor's Chicago Riot Study Committee, appointed after the April disturbances, cited the restraint exercised by the Chicago Police Department as a major factor in preventing the riots from becoming even more violent and widespread. Shortly after the April riots, however, Mayor Richard J. Daley held a press conference in which he seemed to criticize the Police Department for precisely that restraint, asserting that the police should shoot to kill arsonists and shoot to maim looters.

While the Mayor later modified his statement in conformance with restrictions imposed by Illinois law on police use of deadly force, his initial remark was widely reported both in Chicago and throughout the nation. Undoubtedly it had some effect on the attitude of Chicago policemen towards their role in riots and other disorders.

On April 27, 1968, several Chicago peace organizations held a demonstration march in the Loop to protest the war in Vietnam. There was controversy concerning the permit for this march, which was made up of some 6,500 persons and ended in a confrontation with the police at the Civic Center. Eyewitnesses maintain that the police used excessive force in dispersing these demonstrators at the Civic Center and that police officers clubbed several bystanders. Whatever the truth with respect to specific incidents, it is quite clear that the police used direct physical force to dispel the demonstrators. Their tactics on that occasion were severely criticized in the report of a citizens' committee headed by Dr. Edward J. Sparling, president emeritus of Roosevelt University.

These recent and local circumstances reflected the gathering national forces propelling public dissent. While it is not the purpose of this report to analyze those forces, we must recognize that they impinged significantly upon convention week in Chicago.

Among those national forces were the civil rights movement, the peace movement, the changing role of universities, the changing emphasis of organized religion, the growth of an affluent middle class, the ubiquity of television, the stresses of urbanization, and the failure of federal, state and city governments to find solutions to social problems fast enough to satisfy aspirations raised by the solutions they *have* found. But the issue most immediately relevant to convention week in Chicago was the war in Vietnam.

Following the Montgomery, Alabama, bus boycott of 1955, the Reverend Martin Luther King, Jr. emerged as a leader in the cause of both civil rights and nonviolence. There was nothing new about boycotts or sit-ins or the fusion of civil rights and pacifism. But for the first time a nonviolent confrontation was widely publicized enough to become a rallying point for mass dissent and for what could loosely be called a "movement."

The civil rights protests of the fifties were in some respects like the Chicago confrontation of 1968. They were heterogenous; they resulted in violence; they involved students and clergy; they depended on novel strategies for outmaneuvering the authorities; they were given wide television coverage; and they were blamed by the authorities on "outside agitators."

In the sixties, Negroes demanded, and took, control of their own movement. White students found other points of rebellion right on campus, in the machine-like impersonality of the large university, with its emphasis on research rather than instruction—research that, moreover, was often tied to the war in Vietnam. In a general way the issue was one of student participation in their own affairs. But while some students wanted a place in the system, others wanted to replace the system.

Still others—students, nonstudents, ex-students—equally alienated from the system, turned their backs on it and became "hippies."

Many students came to distrust a society that, in their eyes, took refuge in liquor but forbade marijuana, that preached individualism but sought security in large corporations, that talked peace but dropped napalm, and that nurtured, they believed, a climate favorable for the recent assassinations of the most prominent civil rights leader and a presidential candidate. Enjoying an unprecedented sexual freedom (partly because of the steady liberalization of mores and partly because of the easy availability of effective contraceptive devices), they challenged the way society talked about sex. Thus, at Berkeley the demand for free speech included the right of obscene speech. Others seized obscenity as an offensive weapon, one that they brought to Chicago.

To ignore society was to simultaneously challenge it—with communal living, with drugs, with rhetoric, with music, exemplified by Bob Dylan's lyrical warning that "The Times They Are a-Changin'."

Conventional behavior and traditional values were under attack at every level. They always have been. But never before had a generation been in so strong a position to launch an attack on the society they were inheriting.

One reason was affluence, which meant free time and unprecedented mobility.

Another reason was education and experience in protest techniques, not all of them nonviolent.

But perhaps the most influential contributing factor to the strength of dissent was the existence of communications media of all kinds. There is no question that the protesters in Chicago, as elsewhere, "played to the cameras" or that they often did it very effectively and, this, too, had been learned in earlier protests. What "the whole world was watching," after all, was not a confrontation but the picture of a confrontation, to some extent directed by a generation that had grown up with television and learned to use it.

It was also a generation facing the draft. And the issue of war in Vietnam brought large groups of young people to Chicago to express dissent. They were joined by citizens of all ages.

On October 8, 1967, it was announced that the Democratic National Convention would be held in Chicago. At the time, it seemed most likely that President Lyndon Johnson and Vice President Hubert Humphrey would be nominated to run again.

From the start there were misgivings about the location. McCormick Place, Chicago's giant lakefront convention hall, had been destroyed by fire. The Chicago Amphitheatre, the only appropriate substitute, was over five miles from the major hotels which would house the convention delegates. Moreover, the Amphitheatre was close to one of the city's ghettos and there had been ghetto violence across the country the previous summer.

As the convention week neared, new complications appeared and further misgivings were expressed. The April riots had shaken Chicago. A bitter telephone workers strike remained unsettled. Most of the city's taxi cabs were idled by strike and a public transit workers walkout added to the confusion anticipated. Plans for massive protest demonstrations had been disclosed and thousands of young dissidents, including hippies, black militants and motorcycle gangs from the West Coast were expected to converge on the city. In the meantime, assassination plots, sabotage and disruptive activities were rumored and extensive precautions unveiled in recourse.

But suggestions for relocating the convention were swept aside—the convention, scheduled for August 26 through August 29, would unfold in Chicago, where the nation's problems were waiting to greet the delegates, almost literally face to face.

By the eve of convention week, the political scenes had shifted dramatically. President Johnson announced on March 31, 1968, that he would not accept renomination. In the meantime, Senator Eugene McCarthy had won a significant primary vote in New Hampshire. McCarthy continued to rally significant support, especially among younger citizens, campaigning principally in opposition to the current administration's policy in Vietnam. Senator Robert Kennedy joined the race for the Democratic nomination and he, too, followed by Senator McGovern, vigorously challenged the Johnson-Humphrey administration's Vietnam policy. The antiwar movement had, in a sense, become politically legitimatized.

When Vice President Humphrey entered the race there was little question that the Democratic National Convention was to be the arena for a sharply contested debate on United States involvement in Vietnam. Chicago was to become the focal point for an abrupt confrontation of national policies, both within and without the framework of the Democratic Party.

While the various factions within the party were preparing for convention week, anti-war activists and dissident groups of various sorts were considering plans to stage demonstrations. Many of those expected to join these demonstrations were supporters of Senators McCarthy, Kennedy and McGovern. Others viewed the Democratic Party as unresponsive to the public will and inexorably connected with what they considered to be an inhuman war.

Among the dissidents planning to come in protest were violent revolutionaries, pro-Peking sympathizers, communists, anarchists, militant extremists, as well as pacifists, poor people's campaigners, civil rights workers and moderate left-wingers.

For those who had forsaken electoral politics, the convention offered a convenient occasion to rally supporters and to broadcast their disillusionment.

There were also hippies, and among them were hippies turned

inside out: becoming concerned with their relationship with the "other society," they cast themselves in the role of self-styled revolutionaries. A few of the more deliberate and creative of these invented an acronym, YIPPIE! and a "non-organization" to go with it.

The tactics planned by radical dissenters reflect various attitudes, ranging from complete pacifism to hard-core militance. And their motives vary from individual to individual and association to association. In the main, though, the disruptive tactics, whether violent or not, were intended to expose the inhumanity, injustice, prejudice, hypocrisy or militaristic repression with which dissenters take issue. Disruptive tactics obviously impose a high cost upon society and its leaders and eventually, the dissidents argue, the price will become too great.

It is clear that the great majority of protesters in Chicago had no preconceived intention to initiate violence. This is not to say, however, that they did not expect it to develop.

Most of those who intended to join the major protest demonstrations scheduled during convention week did not plan to enter the Amphitheatre and disrupt the proceedings of the Democratic convention, did not plan aggressive acts of physical provocation against the authorities and did not plan to use rallies of demonstrators to stage an assault against any person, institution or place of business.

During the months preceding the convention, provocative and inflammatory statements, made in connection with activities planned for the forthcoming convention week, were published and widely disseminated through underground channels and by exposure in the general media. Numerous articles, speeches and disclosed conversations promised threatening acts of public disorder and terrorism which could not be responsibly dismissed. Those committed to such actions, however, appear to have been unable to combine a broadly based following nor a well-organized plan.

* * *

A Festival of Life

While plans were being made by antiwar and other dissident groups for activities in Chicago during convention week, preparations were under way within the hippie communities in New York, Chicago, on the West Coast and elsewhere for a massive convocation. The vision was one of a carnival-like party in one of Chicago's lakefront parks, a festive counter-convention offering entertainment, discussion forums, information exchanges, workshops in problems facing dissenting youth and other attractions of interest to the nation's subculture dropouts. The festival was seen as continuing day and night throughout convention week, and the prospect excited hippies across the country. For those who were already coming, the festival was an added attraction; for others, it was to be a demonstration in itself—

the demonstration of an alternative "life style," the surfacing of an underground culture, "a renaissance of youth," as they called it.

Long-haired, political activists who had participated in the Pentagon march on October 21, 1967, viewed that demonstration as a turning point, "a new kind of experience in which creativity was unleashed." "People were devising their own schemes," Abbie Hoffman, one of the flamboyant spokesmen for the "underground" movement, recalls.

"Hippie-types" had joined the more formalized protest groups and had added a new dimension which they considered to be satirical. Their statements, while objectionable to many, made good newspaper print. "We saw a chance of developing a real populous involvement among the people within the revolution," Abbie Hoffman said. "Revolution for the hell of it!" "Theatre in the streets!"

This theatrical concept was a primary ingredient of their approach. The audience would be the American public, the means of communication would be the mass media, manipulated to create distorted images of themselves. The stage would be the streets and the message would be a demonstration of disrespect, irreverence and ridicule. It is an approach most graphically described in Abbie Hoffman's words:

> *You got a TV set? That's a jungle. You think that gives a shit about words, lineal concepts? We get on that tube . . . we get information out, and our information is heavy, and it sticks, and it's exciting, it's alive. . . .* (New York Free Press, October 3–9, 1968)

These active hippies, many of them with backgrounds in the creative arts, journalism and the theater, meant to put creativity into protest demonstrations, with an emphasis on individual participation. Hoffman describes how:

> *People will be attempting to use guerrilla theater techniques, people will be attempting to use satire, people will be attempting to talk to other people and people will be passing out newspapers, and some will be stoned and some will be fucking on the grass, and people will do whatever they want to do. There is no reason why people come to demonstrations . . . no single cause. It's multifaceted and it's generally a feeling of disgust with what's going on in this country, in every area conceivable that's controlled by the power. . . .*
>
> *I use guerrilla theatre as a medium for creating what I call blank space. Blank space is where you use media so that the observer, the audience becomes a participant, becomes involved.*

These activists styled themselves as revolutionaries, promoting a movement within their own dropout community aimed at demonstrating to the "other society" that they were serious about the way of life they had chosen; and that they wanted the freedom to follow their own ways—free love, free traffic in drugs, free music and art, free stores and all.

Again, Abbie Hoffman:

> *You see in the whole hippie movement the possibility that people in this country, young white kids, can make their own revolution around their own dreams, their own visions, their own needs. We're already living in the future, we're living 30 years ahead, and, you see, we like it; you see, we like it so much that we're willing to die to defend it and that's where it's at and that's why we're gonna win. . . .*
>
> *There's no doubts about it. We're going to wreck this fuckin' society. If we don't, this society is going to wreck itself anyway so, we might as well have some fun doin' it.*

Hippies were talking about fighting, "by any means necessary," against repression of their concept of life.

Shortly after Chicago was announced as the convention city, hippie activists began thinking about how to channel the new outward-looking energy within their community into a demonstration directed against President Johnson's administration and what was expected to be this convention in Chicago.

One of these activists, Jerry Rubin, invited others to come to Chicago as early as November.

In the apartment of Abbie Hoffman, on New York's lower East Side, a small group got together to discuss specific plans for organizing massive participation of the hippie community. The date was New Year's Eve, or *Christmas* Eve. There is disagreement among those present, including Hoffman, Rubin and writer Paul Krassner.

Hoffman describes the scene:

> *There we were, all stoned, rolling around the floor . . . yippie! . . . Somebody says oink and that's it, pig, it's a natural, man, we gotta win. . . . Let's try success, I mean, when we went to the Pentagon we were going to get it to rise 300 feet in the air . . . so we said how about doing one that will win.*
>
> *And so, YIPPIE was born, the Youth International Party. What about if we create a myth, program it into the media, you know . . . when that myth goes in, its always connected to Chicago August 25 . . . come and do your thing, excitement, bullshit, everything, anything . . . commitment, engagement, Democrats, pigs, the whole thing. All you do is change the H in Hippie to a Y for Yippie, and you got it . . . you can study the media and you say well, the H is switching, now they're talking about Yippies. New phenomena, a new thing on the American scene. . . . Why? That's our question. Our slogan is why? You know as long as we can make up a story about it that's exciting, full of shit, mystical, magical, you have to accuse us of going to Chicago to perform magic.*

The idea was to get people involved and the expectations were high. President Johnson had become the personified object of hippie discontent. The Festival of Life was conceived as a contrast to what they called the "Convention of Death" to be held at the Amphitheatre. The Festival of Life, featuring 30 or 40 popular rock groups, would be the drawing card for perhaps hundreds of thousands of young people around the country. They viewed it as a massive demonstration of an alternative life style, and recognized that it would undoubtedly require major security precautions on the part of the city. But, they say, this was part of their plan—the Democratic National Convention re-nominating President Johnson under military guard—an achievement for the "Politics of Absurdity."

The "Politics of Absurdity" is represented by *"Be Realistic, Demand the Impossible,"* a Yippie flyer prepared for convention week and distributed in Lincoln Park. Its demands include the ludicrous, the outrageous, and the routine.

> *An immediate end to the War in Vietnam . . . the abolition of the military draft. . . . An end to the cultural and economic domination of minority groups. . . . The legalization of marijuana and all other psychedelic drugs. . . . A prison system based on the concept of rehabilitation rather than punishment. . . . The total disarmament of all the people beginning with the police. . . . The abolition of Money. . . . A conservation program geared towards preserving our natural resources and committed to the elimination of pollution of our crowded cities . . . free birth control information and devices but also abortions when desired . . . student power to determine his course of study. . . . The open and free use of the media. . . . An end to all censorship. . . . We believe that people should fuck all the time, anytime, whomever they wish . . . a national referendum system conducted via television or a telephone voting system. . . . A program that encourages and promotes the arts. . . .*

Was all of this simply a put-on, or was there a serious political motive? Said Jerry Rubin, "I think we succeeded in making the Pentagon look ridiculous—forcing troops carrying bayonets to "protect" it from unarmed, hairy, young people. Our strategy for Chicago was more or less the same."

Rubin, 30, is a former Cincinnati newspaper reporter, now active in the pro-Maoist Progressive Labor Party in California. He had participated in organizing the Pentagon march in October, which ended in violence, and was involved in various violent demonstrations in Berkeley, California. He is also reported to have been one of the sponsors of the April, 1967 peace demonstration in New York.

The objectives of Yippie were explained by Hoffman:

> *1. The blending of pot and politics grass leaves movement—a cross-fertilization of the hippie and New Left philosophy. 2. A connecting link that would tie as much as the underground as was willing into some gigantic national get-together. 3. The development of a model for an alternative society. 4. The need to make some statement, especially in revolutionary*

action-theater terms, about LBJ, the Democratic Party, electoral politics, and the state of the nation.

—Realist, *September, 1968.*

Hoffman, 31, had been active in the Movement for some time. Once a psychologist, he left his job to participate in civil rights demonstrations in the South. Along with Rubin, he had more recently taken part in demonstrations in Berkeley, New York and at the Pentagon.

Paul Krassner describes Yippie as "a national disorganization whose sole purpose would be the Theatre of Disruption," explaining:

. . . [It was] a gesture to show that they felt they had to protect the convention. We didn't know they were going to do the thing with the barbed wire, but they played their roles perfectly . . . our mere appearance there, thousands of freaky looking people is in itself a disruption . . . For example, when they knew we were running a pig, they put an armed guard on the pig in the zoo. It just made them look ridiculous. We wanted to make them look ridiculous because we felt they were.

Krassner, 36, for ten years has published *The Realist,* a satirical underground magazine with a circulation of over 100,000. A close friend of Hoffman and Rubin, he has covered major demonstrations across the country for some time. This literature was always fanciful, confusing and belligerent, a blend of playfulness and militancy, whimsy and contempt. Half serious and half in jest, it is always calculated to excite reaction. It was consciously threatening and deliberately unpredictable.

By early January, plans for the Festival of Life had progressed rapidly, and underground newspapers carried articles promoting the event.

The following example is from the *New York Free Press:*

We've got to get crazy. Craziest motherfuckers they ever seen in this country. Cause that's the only way we're gonna beat them. So fucking crazy that they can't understand it at ALL. They know something's up, something's going on down there, something's happening, some change coming on in this country, just like Dylan says, "There's something happening but you don't know what it is, do you, Mr. Jones?"

We won't tell 'em what it is. What do you want to tell them for? Don't tell 'em shit. NEVER.

. . . That's the problem you have when you focus in on an issue, when you make a demand. They can deal with a demand.

We put a finger up their ass and tell them, "I ain't telling you what I want," then they got a problem.

The Festival of Life plan travelled rapidly throughout the hippie communities by word of mouth. Letters came into New York from various parts of the country, asking how to become a Yippie. The answer: "How do you become a Yippie? Say you're a Yippie, and you're a Yippie! Just say you're a Yippie leader and do your own thing!"

There was great enthusiasm and organizational activity during the early months of 1968, particularly in New York. Posters and flyers and buttons were distributed. A benefit was held and afterwards a Yippie office opened. Weekly meetings began and committees for entertainment, theater, press, food, housing and other preparations were set up.

When those who had taken an active role in organizing the Festival travelled and spoke to other groups, Chicago was mentioned. Folk and rock musical groups also promoted the Festival.

Sometime in February, Jerry Rubin made contact with a Chicago hippie group centered around *The Seed,* a local underground newspaper, and solicited their help to promote the Festival and to make local arrangements.

Further plans were worked out during this period. There would be a giant music fair, a nude-in on the beach, workshops of various sorts, including draft resistance, use of LSD, underground newspapers and other matter uniquely of interest to the dropout community. There would be poetry sessions, information exchanges, political forums and a convention of underground intellectuals to discuss the direction of a new society. The protest march to the Amphitheatre, being planned by National Mobilization, was considered, but not scheduled as part of the proposed program for the Festival of Life. Each individual was left to "do his own thing."

In February, the New York Yippies staged their first event: a raid on the Stony Brook campus of the State University of New York, intended to satirize a previous dope raid by the police. It was disruptive and gave Yippies the publicity they sought.

By March, the Yippies had made contact with an impressive number of prominent radio personalities, poets, folk singers, theater people and somewhere between 20 to 40 rock groups, all tentatively committed to come to Chicago.

On March 21, the Yippies staged another event in New York, a nighttime party at Grand Central Station. Although there was little promotion, around 5,000 people showed up. The result was sustained disruption, a police confrontation, violence and more publicity for Yippies. There were more than 50 arrests and many injured.

On the following day Abbie Hoffman, Jerry Rubin, and Paul Krassner went to Chicago to attend the Lake Villa meeting of various New Left and black groups to discuss convention week plans. They had been invited by National Mobilization. The three Yippies announced that they were coming to Chicago and that they expected tens, maybe hundreds of thousands to join their Festival of Life.

Most of the participants in that conference had trouble communicating with the Yippie contingent. One of the Yippie spokesmen is reported to have said:

America is dead, you all know it, and yet you're getting involved in a dance with a dead lady. The Democratic Party is going to foul you up. The only way you're going to change America is to involve people with their emotions, not their minds. Chicago Sun-Times, *March 25.*

Abbie Hoffman commented on what he had to say at the meeting:

We demanded such relevant things . . . (as) the abolition of pay toilets—that was one of our key items . . . they didn't understand what I was talking about I'm sure. They're the Left, they're into heavy words, words mean something—I'm into emotion. I'm into symbols and gestures and I don't have a program and I don't have an ideology and I'm not a part of the Left.

So while the "Left" continued to debate whether or not they were coming to Chicago and what they were going to do when they got there, the Yippie organizers took a positive attitude—they were coming, to be sure, with music and myth and with their threats to disrupt the city.

Before leaving Chicago, the three Yippies renewed personal contact with the *Seed* group. They worked up a permit application for the use of a Chicago park during the convention.

After President Johnson's announced withdrawal from the presidential campaign on March 31, 1968, there was a marked decline of interest in the Festival of Life. The New York Yippie spokesmen, after a period of several months of little organizational activity, actually decided to drop the idea of coming to Chicago. During this period, underground publications carried articles criticizing the Yippie plans, stressing local action as the proper focus. In the meantime, the softer side of the Yippie-hippie community pointed to the violent Grand Central Station incident, to the severe encounter of the April 27 peace marchers with the Chicago police and to the tough statements on police action being made by Mayor Daley. A violent confrontation with the Chicago police seemed likely if the Festival of Life were to take place, and many simply didn't want to travel hundreds of miles to join a tumultuous battle of police and demonstrators in a Chicago park. The more militant side of Yippie professed, however, that if some were "into violence, that was their thing," and it shouldn't concern anyone.

Planning for the Festival of Life, consequently, proceeded at a slower pace; persons that were still interested were referred to the Chicago *Seed* group or asked to work on it locally.

On the weekend of May 10, Abbie Hoffman flew to Chicago. He conferred with the *Seed* people. They talked about local preparations, and Hoffman encouraged the Chicagoans to plan weekly music festivals in the park to accustom local residents to the "long hair" community, thus preparing them for the August influx. It was also hoped that such "little" festivals would lessen the danger of disturbance by "greasers," lower middle-class white gangs about whom the Yippies were particularly apprehensive.

Following this meeting, the Chicago *Seed* group decided to abandon a public association with "Yippie." On April 25, a meeting of the group under the aegis of Yippie! had been raided by the Chicago police. Twenty-one were arrested. A subsequent benefit at the Electric Theatre was also raided, and again there were more arrests, this time about 30. Because of the reputation the New York Yippies were building for violence and disruption, and because productive negotiations for the August Festival under the auspices of Yippie were considered dubious, the Chicago group formed the Free City Survival Committee. It was this committee which would officially continue negotiations with the city through June, July and the first week of August and which would carry on with local preparations for the Festival of Life.

The Free City Survival Committee worked closely with the Chicago Commission on Youth Welfare, the Park District and the police. It also conducted weekly music festivals in Lincoln Park beginning in mid-May. Some of these occasions attracted more than 1,000 people.

For Yippie activists in New York and California, this late spring period offered activities, particularly at Columbia and Berkeley, that took priority over the Festival of Life. The rash of convention related underground literature, designed to develop the Yippie myth, to create mystery and excitement and thus expand enthusiasm for Chicago, had come and gone.

Then, after Senator Robert Kennedy's assassination and with schools closed for the summer recess, interest in the Festival of Life was suddenly revived. "People wanted to know when the hell we were going," Abbie Hoffman remembered, "and I would say, 'A week after Kennedy's assassination I became convinced that I was going to Chicago.'"

* * *

In what was described as a "Daring Expose—Top Secret Yippie Plans for Lincoln Park," a schedule of events for the Festival of Life was outlined, and is reproduced below:

> August 20–August 24 (AM): Training in snake dancing, karate, non-violent self-defense. Information booth in Park.
> August 24 (PM): Yippie Mayor R. Daley presents fireworks on Lake Michigan.
> August 25 (AM): Welcoming of the Democratic delegates—downtown hotels (to be announced).
> August 25 (PM): MUSIC FESTIVAL—Lincoln Park.
> August 26 (AM): Workshop in drug problems, underground communications, how to live free, guerrilla theatre, self-defense, draft

resistance, communes, etc. (Potential workshop leaders should call the Seed, 837 N. LaSalle Street, 943-5282.)

Scenario sessions to plan small group activities.

August 26 (PM): Beach Party ON THE LAKE ACROSS from Lincoln Park (North Avenue Beach).—folksinging, barbecues, swimming, lovemaking.

August 27 (dawn): Poetry, mantras, religious ceremony.

August 27 (AM): Workshops and Scenario sessions. Film showing and mixed media—Coliseum, 1513 S. Wabash.

August 27 (PM): Benefit concert—Coliseum. Rally and Nomination of Pigasus and LBJ birthday—Lincoln Park.

August 28 (dawn): Poetry and folk singing.

August 28 (AM): Yippie Olympics, Miss Yippie Contest, catch the candidate, pin the tail on the donkey, pin the rubber on the Pope, and other normal, healthy games.

August 28 (PM): Plans to be announced at a later date. 4 P.M.—Mobilization Rally scheduled for Grant Park. March to the convention.

August 29–30: Events scheduled depend on Wednesday night. Return to park for sleeping.

* * *

How the City Prepared

Even under normal circumstances, a national political convention demands extensive security preparations. In order to protect officials, delegates and their families, extraordinary precautions must be taken at the convention site, at the hotels and along the routes that provide access to them.

But the circumstances in 1968 were not normal.

As we have documented in the previous chapter, the announcement that the convention would be held in Chicago was almost immediately followed by the prospect of mass demonstrations involving hundreds of thousands of people and threatened disruption of the city, ghetto riots and assassinations. The problem was enlarged by the possibility that the President himself would appear at the convention, a possibility that was never entirely ruled out.

The following pages describe the security measures taken by the Chicago Police Department and other law enforcement agencies, by the National Guard and by other governmental bodies.

Overall Security Planning

In January, 1968, a Convention Planning Committee was set up by the Police Department to organize police planning and to coordinate the preparations of city, state and federal agencies. Included on the committee were representatives of the Police Department, Secret Service, Military Intelligence, the Mayor's Office, the Fire Department and other governmental agencies. The committee met every two weeks through May and weekly thereafter until mid-August.

The committee concentrated upon the Amphitheatre and Loop areas, and transportation between them, with lesser attention being given to other parts of the city except as they specifically related to those areas.

Throughout its deliberations the Planning Committee concerned itself with a large variety of security measures—such as identification for security personnel, access to the Amphitheatre, traffic and transportation problems, dispelling of anxieties among Amphitheatre area residents which might be created by "rumors or overzealous press reports," arrangements for media representatives, utilization of plainclothes policemen on the floor of the Amphitheatre and procedure in case of mass arrests or mass injuries.

Throughout the planning and the convention week the Police Department worked closely with the National Guard, Secret Service, Democratic National Committee and other agencies. It is clear that many decisions were not made solely by the city officials. Some were made on a group basis. Thus, while the mission of the Secret Service was specifically protection of the President, the candidates, and their families, it gave an opinion, when asked, on security matters not directly related to protection of its principals. For example, when asked about its opinion on enforcement of existing laws and ordinances, such as those relating to park usage and street marches, the Secret Service strongly encouraged strict enforcement.

In addition to the Planning Committee meetings, periodic command staff meetings were held during the summer. These were concerned primarily with police planning; the only non-police agency in attendance was the Secret Service. Information concerning the possible types and locations of demonstrations was divulged and plans were discussed.

Early in August, the results of the Planning Committee action were turned over to the men who were assigned operational commands for the convention week. Implementation and continuing development of the plans they received was accomplished by the operational commanders with the assistance of members of the Planning Committee.

Intelligence Information

The city regularly received information concerning activities planned or threatened for the convention week which, if implemented, could have a direct impact on not only the convention but on the city itself. This information—which came from a variety of federal and local governmental agencies—was disseminated after evaluation to persons concerned with security measures at the decision-making level.

Some of the information was available to the mass media, and they gave extensive coverage to it. We have already described some of the published plans and threats.

Similar information came from confidential sources. Examples are:

1. Reports that black power groups were allegedly meeting to discuss the convention and the assassination of leading political figures.
2. Unnamed black militant groups in the East were reported to have discussed renting apartments near the Amphitheatre for use as sniping posts.
3. An organization was reportedly organized to secure weapons and explosives and to plan a revolution to coincide with the convention.
4. A report that the National Mobilization Committee intended to prevent Vice President Humphrey from utilizing surface transportation to reach the convention.
5. An allegation from militant white racists to the effect that black militants intended to invade white Chicago neighborhoods and "lay siege" to the city.
6. Reports that black gangs were allegedly accumulating weapons to attack police precinct stations in order to draw police forces away from the convention.
7. Reports that black nationalists in California were alleged to have devised a plot to assassinate certain prominent Negroes in Chicago in order to create disruption throughout the city.
8. Reports that weapons had been sent to Chicago to be used to assassinate one of the presidential candidates.
9. Reports that various organizations planned to put LSD into the Chicago water supply.

An unidentified document in police intelligence files describes in detail the Chicago Avenue Armory and the surrounding neighborhood, and suggests where materials could be obtained to obstruct movement of personnel out of the armory. It also suggests escape routes:

> *. . . 750 of us could easily block all doors symbolically, also possible provocation: detour Lake Shore Drive traffic into immediate neighborhood with wooden horses, etc., then stop cars with other wooden horses, then saturate with people, then let air out of tires of more and more cars until tanks, etc., in armory can't get out. A few cars sacrificed for most direct blocking of garage doors. Aluminum door could be bent out of operation. Could NWU [Northwestern University] form a sanctuary? Source of cadre?*
>
> *Lots of fire hydrants for further confusion, first aid for gas attacks. Construction site(s) would provide barricade materials. Apartment houses*

and hotels provide many blind alleys, which connect, for possible escape through confusion . . .

The Intelligence Division sought information from police departments in other cities around the country to ascertain and estimate the number and propensities of militant activists in those cities who might come to Chicago during the convention week. This effort began during the early summer and continued through the convention.

Some of the intelligence reports contained information of a type not unlike that described in the August 6, 1968 issue of *Saga* magazine, detailing the alleged plans of more than 85 known groups and organizations. Tactics described in the articles included: putting ground glass into food served in downtown restaurants, disrupting communications and electrical service and fire bombing buildings. Guerrilla warfare of the type prevalent in Vietnam was referred to as a possibility.

Intelligence authorities recognized that material of the type described above, as well as the published threats related earlier, could not all be taken seriously. They realized that the published and nonpublished plans and threats were comprised of both fact and fiction. But since their responsibility takes in the protection of the entire public, they could not take the risk of underestimating any intelligence, however absurd it might seem to a private citizen. There were attempts made to verify information received, and the authorities concluded that there was enough fact to require intensive security precautions. The Secret Service, of course, never can afford to ignore threats of assassination of presidential candidates.

The Intelligence Division of the Chicago Police Department believed prior to the convention that most of the demonstrating groups would be politically motivated white groups, rather than black civil rights groups. They found no evidence of high-level coordination, cooperation or liaison between the two categories and formed the impression that they would not join in creating disorder at the convention. However, against the background of violence in 1967 and 1968, the city felt that it could not ignore the ever-present threat of ghetto riots being sparked by demonstrator activity during the convention week.

In determining the security precautions needed to cope with large numbers of demonstrators, the intelligence agencies apparently made little effort to distinguish between the philosophies and intents of various groups. They were concerned not with whether a group advocated violence or adhered to nonviolent tenets, but with the dangers inherent in large crowds of demonstrators, regardless of whether all members espouse violence. They believed that even an orderly crowd of peaceful demonstrators could easily develop into a mob and could be led by a few determined agitators of violent action.

* * *

Confrontation

One incident which contributed to the week's uncertainty and the demonstrators' edginess was the August 22 killing of a 17-year-old American Indian, Jerome Johnson. Johnson, from Sioux Falls, South Dakota, was shot to death by police at North Avenue and Wells Street, just a few blocks southwest of the park. Police detectives said they fired their guns when the fleeing youth, identified as a Yippie, fired a .32 caliber revolver at them. The shooting caused one of the marshal trainers to say:

> *We don't want to go overboard in ascribing malevolent intentions to the police, but obviously things are going to be getting very rough here. We've got to be prepared.*

On Friday, August 23, several hundred persons were reported in the park. National Mobilization leaders and representatives of SDS (Students For A Democratic Society) were discussing first aid precautions, the availability of legal aid in the event of mass arrests and precautions against tear gas. Legal aid was to be provided through the Legal Defense Committee, made up of volunteer lawyers and law students.

The same day, Jerry Rubin caused a stir when he and several followers released a pig named "Pigasus" in the Chicago Civic Center Plaza. They said Pigasus was their candidate for president and that his platform was garbage: "Who knows more about that than a pig?" "If our president gets out of line," they vowed, "we'll eat him." Pigasus was confiscated by the police and locked up at the Chicago Humane Society. Six persons were arrested.

* * *

Wednesday—The Culmination of Violence

Dawn broke over Grant Park Wednesday through a thin mist and ground fog, thickened by smoke from the sputtering fires. Many of the "campers" dozed in sleeping bags or huddled in blankets, some of which had been supplied by sympathetic guests at the Hilton. Here and there small knots of people sat on the grass talking, playing guitars or reading. Some were in trees. As the demonstrators awoke, they washed in the park's fountains, some showering under the water cascading from one level of a fountain to another.

Along Michigan Avenue, the assistant Guard squad leader remembers three boys in "hippie clothes" and a "pretty girl, well-kempt and clean looking" were giving the V-sign to passengers in buses stopped for traffic lights and asking them to return the sign. "When it wasn't returned," the witness says, "the boys would swear at the people and call them 'fucking ass-holes' and 'mother fuckers.'"

A girl who had been among demonstrators in Lincoln Park Tuesday night claims that early Wednesday outside the Hilton a policeman assaulted her "with no provocation." In an account substantiated by a friend who was with her, the girl said the officer walked up to them, called her a "bitch" and struck her in the mouth with his fist.

Morning Clean-Up and Afternoon Speeches

At about 9:30 a.m., so that city work crews could clean the area, about 20 policemen carrying nightsticks entered the park and told everyone there to clear out. "Aside from jeers of 'pigs . . . fascist pigs,' there was no trouble," the Guardsman recalls. "Most people obeyed and the nightsticks were never used." One college student who was present says some of the demonstrators joined in the clean-up, and that street department employees furnished sticks with nails in the end so that the volunteers could pick up papers. These sticks were later identified by some witnesses as part of the weaponry in the hands of the protesters.

At 9:45 a.m., with the sun shining pleasantly, police replaced the Guard on duty in front of the Hilton. Later, at about 1 p.m., a National Guard command post was set up on the roof of the Field Museum, south of Grant Park on the lakefront and overlooking the bandshell area. The 2nd Battalion of the 129th Infantry took up positions in back of the museum on the west side and the 2nd Battalion of the 127th Artillery assembled on the east side of the museum. It has been charged that the Guard units in the Grant Park area "whitened" from Tuesday to Wednesday, meaning that Negro Guardsmen were no longer present. This in fact happened, but there is no evidence that it was done by conscious design. The 33rd MP (on duty Tuesday night) has a number of Negro Guardsmen, while the 2/129th and 2/122nd are essentially white.

In the early afternoon the crowd numbered about 700 persons, the speeches continued. Bobby Seale of the Black Panthers demanded, among other things, the freeing of Huey Newton and the painting of the White House black. He exhorted his listeners to "burn the city" . . . "tear it down." He counseled: "We can lead them on a merry-go-round like you have."

At about 1:30 p.m., a young man using his omnipresent, battery-powered speaker (another carried the sound equipment on his head) began urging the demonstrators to move over to the bandshell in the far southeast corner of the park area, about two blocks due east of the south edge of the Hilton, but separated from the hotel by Michigan Avenue, the railroad cut and Columbus Drive. Some who followed his pleas were equipped with helmets and gas masks. Some sticks, on which signs could be mounted, were also in evidence. Many "revolution" posters were visible in the crowd moving off toward the bandshell.

* * *

The Crowd on Michigan Avenue

At 7:14 p.m., as the first groups of demonstrators crossed the bridge toward Michigan Avenue, they noticed that the mule train of the Poor People's Campaign was just entering the intersection of Michigan and Jackson, headed south. The train consisted of three wagons, each drawn by two mules, and was accompanied by a number of SCLC blacks in fieldwork attire. The wagons were painted, "Jobs & Food for All." The train had a permit to parade within the Loop and south on Michigan Avenue.

The train was accompanied by 24 policemen on foot, five on three-wheelers, and four in two squadrols. A police official was in front with the caravan's leaders. The sight of the train seemed to galvanize the disorganized Grant Park crowd and those streaming over the bridge broke into cheers and shouts. "Peace now!" bellowed the demonstrators. "Dump the Hump!" This unexpected enthusiastic horde in turn stimulated the mule train marchers. Drivers of the wagons stood and waved to the crowd, shouting: "Join us! Join us!" To a young man watching from the 23rd floor of the Hilton Hotel, "the caravan seemed like a magnet to demonstrators leaving the park."

A medic accompanying the march reports that "at this time it appeared that the marshals had lost control and the group was moving more or less under mob psychology."

At this the exodus from Grant Park swelled to a torrent and Michigan rapidly filled out with now revitalized, shouting demonstrators. The two squadrols, driving at the rear of the train, were unable to move to the front because of the crush of the crowd.

Led by Viet Cong red and black flags, and the loud-speaker, and constantly joined by more people escaping from Grant Park, all came slowly south on Michigan with the mule train in the middle of this sea of people. The crowd, estimated at "several thousand" by a police official, filled out an entire city block and chanted "We want peace." As the demonstrators marched, says an Assistant U.S. Attorney, "four or five policemen ran into the crowd swinging nightsticks. I saw a couple of policemen strike some of the individuals." Few policemen were, however, present on the street.

The Balbo-Michigan Crowd Builds Up

When the crowd's first rank reached the intersection of Balbo and Michigan, the northeast corner of the Hilton, it was close to the approximately 2,000 to 3,000 demonstrators and spectators massed east of a police line along the two blocks of Grant Park opposite the Hilton and 500 others contained between another police line and the hotel's east face.

An additional single line of police was formed diagonally across Michigan at the south line of Balbo to divert the new oncoming crowd off the street and into Grant Park. A portion of the crowd had spilled west on Balbo toward Wabash, a block west of Michigan, where there was another police line across Balbo.

The police were armed with riot helmets, batons, mace, an aerosol tear gas can and their service revolvers (which they always carry).

Behind the police lines, parked in front of the Hilton, was a fire department high pressure pumper truck hooked up to a hydrant. Pairs of uniformed firemen were also in the vicinity.

The growing crowds, according to the U.S. Attorney's report, were a blend of "young and old, hippies, Yippies, straights, newsmen and cameramen," even two mobile TV units. TV cameras also were situated on an entrance canopy jutting out from the north side of the Hilton. The smell of tear gas from the Congress bridge encounter still hung heavy in the air.

When the line of march reached the police line across Michigan, it stopped and the crowd began to bunch up in the intersection. It quickly overflowed into all available adjacent areas. All traffic was immobilized, both on Michigan and the cross streets. The forces that would clash at 7:57 p.m. in the unreal glow of TV lights were in final deployment.

Some in the crowd were equipped with helmets and gas masks and armed with rocks, sticks, bottles and other weapons. Volunteer "medic" teams were on hand among the demonstrators.

While the crowd was not organized in any traditional sense, it had leaders—some self-appointed, some the marshals. Dellinger and other demonstration leaders had disappeared after the dispersal of the line of march at Balbo and Columbus. Among other things, these "leaders" had exhorted the marchers by loudspeaker, while the crowd was pushing south on Michigan with the mule train, to sit down on the pavement if the police tried to prevent their eventual passage to the Amphitheatre.

Facing this vast, virtually encircling congregation of 4,000 to 4,500 people were about 300 police. One demonstrator says that when three policemen on three-wheel motorcycles tried to get through the crowd, the throng surrounded them and covered the cycles with Yippie posters, such as "Vote the Pig Vote." The officers finally were let through when they said they were off duty and on their way home.

A police officer recalls that shortly after 7 p.m. he attempted to clear the intersection by saying, "Get up on the curb, please" and "Clear the streets, please." Initially, he said, "there was compliance with this request" until a tall, slender youth, about 20 years old, "appeared on the scene and told the people to disregard the police request and come back into the street." They obeyed.

The police officer approached the youth and asked him to cooperate with the police. According to the officer, the young man pushed him with both hands. Quickly the two were "surrounded by a large group." Two of them knocked the officer to the ground. In his opinion, he was in danger of being "stomped." Other officers quickly rescued him, but his ankle was badly injured in the scuffle.

From within the crowd were rising the usual shouts from some of the demonstrators: "Hell no, we won't go!" . . . "Fuck these Nazis!" . . . "Fuck you, L.B.J.!" . . . "No more war!" . . . "Pigs, pigs, pigs." . . . "The streets belong to the people!" . . . "Let's go to the Amphitheatre!" . . . "Move on, Move on!" . . . "You can't stop us." . . . "From the hotel," recalls a student, "people who sympathized were throwing confetti and pieces of paper out of the windows and they were blinking their room lights."

The history professor quoted earlier, standing on the northwest corner of the Balbo-Michigan intersection, said: "The police would move periodically north on Michigan, forcing the crowd back, or move east on Balbo, or would split the group north and south." But then they would return to their positions and "the crowd would flow back."

Isolated Incidents

Occasionally during the early evening, groups of demonstrators would flank the police lines or find a soft spot and punch through, heading off on their own for the Amphitheatre. On the periphery of the Hilton and on thoroughfares and side streets further southwest, a series of brief but sometimes violent encounters occurred.

For example, says the manager of a private club on Michigan Avenue, "a large band of long-haired demonstrators . . . tore down the American flag" overhanging the entrance to the club "and took it into Michigan Avenue attempting to tear it." A veteran who happened by, grabbed the flag and returned it to the club. He reports that they tried to strike him.

At about 7 p.m. from the window of a motel room in the 1100 block of South Michigan, a senator's driver noticed a group of demonstrators walking south, chanting: "Hell no, we won't go!" and "Fuck the draft." They were hurling insults at passing pedestrians and when one answered back, the witness says, "five demonstrators charged out of Michigan Avenue onto the sidewalk, knocked the pedestrian down, formed a circle around his fallen body, locked their arms together and commenced kicking him in a vicious manner. When they had finished kicking their victim, they unlocked their arms and immediately melted back into the crowd. . . ."

Within six minutes this action was repeated against four other pedestrians, the witness says. One of them was smashed with a city trash basket "as he lay prostrate on the sidewalk after being knocked down and kicked."

At another Michigan Avenue motel, demonstrators objecting to a "Young Citizens for Humphrey" display in the lobby hurled unidentified objects at the front of the building, breaking a large plate glass window, according to the manager.

A few blocks away, at Wabash and Roosevelt, a university student observed what he describes as "an orderly march" down Wabash. He said that a police squad car drove into the crowd in an effort to break up the march. He states that "a police bus followed the car through the crowd and, when it reached the outer periphery of the crowd, the bus stopped and unloaded the police. The police then began chasing the marchers."

Several policemen chased one young man, he recalls. "When they caught him, they all beat him with their nightsticks."

A running fray broke out on Wabash near 14th Street. There, says a law student, plainclothes men piled from police cars. "They came out with clubs and immediately began attacking the people. There wasn't any provocation. . . . A lot of the policemen were attacking girls, since they were running the slowest."

Police cars and CTA buses loaded with policemen converged on the area. A demonstrator picked up a brick or rock, the law student says and "threw it through the windshield of one of the police cars."

Demonstrators scattered through alleys and sidestreets. Some arrests were made, but much of the crowd escaped and many returned to the Hilton Hotel area.

During a similar encounter between demonstrators and lawmen, a magazine editor says, police grabbed a boy with a knapsack over his shoulder. An officer opened the knapsack and dumped its contents onto the sidewalk. When he found a brassiere among the contents, he told the demonstrator, "I knew you were a fag." The police then proceeded to arrest several of the boy's companions.

Back at the Conrad Hilton

Vice President Humphrey was now inside the Conrad Hilton Hotel and the police commanders were afraid that the crowd might either attempt to storm the hotel or march south on Michigan Avenue, ultimately to the Amphitheatre. The Secret Service had received an anonymous phone call that the Amphitheatre was to be blown up. A line of police was established at 8th and Michigan at the south end of the hotel and the squads of police stationed at the hotel doors began restricting access to those who could display room keys. Some hotel guests, including delegates and Senator McCarthy's wife, were turned away.

By 7:30 p.m., the SCLC people, too, were growing apprehensive. They were becoming concerned for the mule train because of the press of demonstrators and the crowd's escalating emotionalism. Also a rumor was passing around that the Blackstone Rangers and the East Side Disciples, two of Chicago's most troublesome street gangs, were on their way to the scene. (This was later proven to be untrue; neither of these South Side gangs was present in any numbers in either Lincoln Park or Grant Park.)

At this point, a Negro male was led through the police line by a police officer. He spoke to the police officer, a city official and a deputy superintendent of police. He told them that he was in charge of the mule train and that his people wanted no part of this mob. He said he had 80 people with him, that they included old people and children, and he wanted to get them out of the mob. The police officer later stated the group wanted to go past the Hilton, circle it, and return to the front of the hotel where Reverend Ralph Abernathy could address the crowd.

At this time, says the police sergeant who had thrown the smoke bomb into the bandshell crowd, and who now was on duty at the Hilton, people were screaming foul language of every type at the police and shouting, "Who's your wife with now?" . . . "Where's your wife tonight?" Some were spitting on the officers and daring them to come and hit them. "The obscenities," says an attorney who was present, "were frequently returned in kind by the police."

In response to the mule train leader's plea, the deputy superintendent of police ordered a police escort to lead the wagons through the crowd. Flying wedges of officers pushed back the resisting crowd and the train was let through the police skirmish line at Balbo. It then moved up in front of the hotel.

In a few minutes, Reverend Ralph Abernathy appeared and, according to the police officer's statement, "said he wanted to be taken out of the area as he feared for the safety of his group." The police officer directed that the train be moved south on Michigan to 11th Street and then, through a series of turns through the Loop, to the West Side.

Before the train moved out, a leader of the mule train addressed the crowd with a bullhorn provided by police. He said: "We have nothing against you joining our demonstration, and we have nothing against joining your demonstration . . . I think it was very violent for the police to tear gas you."

The demonstrators did not pay much attention to him but, instead, seemed bent on making their march to the Amphitheatre. Obscenities and vulgar epithets were shouted at the police. There were also chants of "One, two, three, four; stop this damn war"; "Dump the Hump"; "Daley must go"; "Ho, Ho, Ho Chi Minh"; "The streets belong to the people"; and "Prague, Prague, Prague!"

A policeman on Michigan later said that at about this time a "female hippie" came up to him, pulled up her skirt and said, "You haven't had a piece in a long time."

A policeman standing in front of the Hilton remembers seeing a blond female who was dressed in a short red minidress make lewd, sexual motions in front of a police line. Whenever this happened, he says, the policemen moved back to prevent any incident. The crowd, however, egged her on, the patrolman says. He thought that "she and the crowd wanted an arrest to create a riot." Earlier in the same general area a male youth had stripped bare and walked around carrying his clothes on a stick.

An attorney who was present at the intersection, a member of the ACLU, later said that "perhaps ten people were on lampposts and shoulders of other people, waving at the cameras. . . . The noise was very loud. . . . I felt this was a violent crowd that came to fight and was looking for trouble."

The intersection at Balbo and Michigan was in total chaos at this point. The street was filled with people. Darkness had fallen but the scene was lit by both police and television lights. As the mule train left, part of the group tried to follow the wagons through the police line and were stopped. According to the deputy superintendent of police, there was much pushing back and forth between the policemen and the demonstrators. He said that this is where real physical contact began. An old car bearing a sign announcing a draft card burning rally edged up to the police lines.

Continual announcements were made at this time over a police amplifier for the crowd to "clear the street and go up on the sidewalk or into the park area for their demonstrations." The broadcast said "Please gather in the park on the east side of the street. You may have your peaceful demonstration and speechmaking there." The demonstrators were also advised that if they did not heed these orders they would face arrest. The response from many in the crowd, according to a police observer, was to scream and shout obscenities. A Chicago attorney who was watching the scene recalls that when the announcements were broadcast, "No one moved."

"There was roughly a ten-yard distance between the police line and the demonstrators," recalls an Assistant U.S. attorney. "Two policemen periodically walked across the gap, took hold of a demonstrator and walked him to a paddy wagon behind the police line. They arrested approximately ten protesters this way. We saw them hit a few with their nightsticks as they were pushing them into the paddy wagon but it appeared that none of the protesters was injured."

A police observer recalls that the deputy superintendent then made another announcement: "Will any nondemonstrators, anyone who is not a part of this group, any newsmen, please leave the group." Despite the crowd noise, the loud-speaker announcements were "loud and plainly heard," according to this officer. Police state that the messages to clear the street were repeated—officers "walked to the front of the crowd and repeated these messages to individuals all along the line, all the while pointing over to the east side of the street where we wanted them to go."

Presently, a police officer states, he glanced back and noticed that part of the crowd had moved forward and had "completely surrounded" the police car from which the announcements were being broadcast. Police rushed to the car and helped clear a path so that it could be driven slowly north through the crowd. Before it reached the north side of Balbo, according to the officer, its windshield, side windows and headlights had been pasted with McCarthy stickers. "When we finally got into the car and it began to move," said the officer, "it became apparent that the right rear tire was almost flat." The valve had been loosened. The car limped away in search of a filling station.

The deputy superintendent of police states that at this point demonstrators staged "massive sit-downs" in Michigan Avenue. While some sit-downs occurred, the films and still photographs do not show any that were "massive." But this was a tactic that had been discussed earlier among the crowd, should the march to the Amphitheatre ultimately be thwarted. The sitters, according to the deputy, were hampering the orderly movements of his police. "People in the streets were having face-to-face confrontations with the police officers, telling them that they did not have to move and that they were not going to move," he says. As police announcements were made to leave the street, demonstrators with loud-speakers of their own shouted to the crowd, "You don't have to go. Hell no, don't go!"

The crowd was becoming increasingly ugly. The deputy superintendent states that demonstrators were pushing police lines back, spitting in officers' faces and pelting them with rocks, bottles, shoes, glass and other objects.

While this was happening on Michigan Avenue, a separate police line had begun to move east toward the crowd from the block of Balbo that lies between Michigan and Wabash along the north side of the Hilton.

About 7:45 p.m., the police radio had crackled with "10-1," the emergency code for "police officer needs help." A police captain was reporting imminent danger in front of the Hilton and, in response to his call, a reserve platoon had been ordered to the northwest corner of the hotel on Balbo. Shortly after that, all available vans in the vicinity were ordered to converge on the Hilton.

The reserve platoon, numbering some 40 policemen, had arrived by special CTA bus at Wabash and Balbo, one block west of Michigan, at 7:55 p.m., under the command of a deputy chief of police. The men came from a skirmish with demonstrators at 14th and Wabash, several blocks southwest of the Hilton, where they had arrived after another unit had broken up an attempted march on the Amphitheatre and had rounded up a group of demonstrators. Some had also been on duty at Columbus and Balbo in Grant Park that afternoon.

As the bus unloaded, the unit formed up building-to-building across Balbo in four ranks of ten led by a deputy chief and a lieutenant.

At the same time, Sidney Peck with his bullhorn was urging people to follow him west on Balbo in an effort to flee the Michigan intersection. "We saw the police approaching," Peck states. He says he called people back and urged the police "not to move against them." Over the loud-speaking equipment, Peck shouted, "Sit down and no violence will happen. Don't use any violence."

The deputy chief states, on the other hand, that he saw marchers coming toward his men. He felt that "a disorderly mob surging west on Balbo from Michigan, taking up the whole street and sidewalks, shouting and screaming slogans and insults [was] taking over the Blackstone and Hilton Hotel entrances with the intention of taking over these hotels."

The police unit moved east on Balbo toward Michigan Avenue at a fast walk. As they did so, the throng on Balbo backed east toward the intersection or crowded onto the sidewalk. By the time the officers reached the west edge of Michigan, they slowed to a determined walk.

A 19-year-old boy, working as a chauffeur for Senator McGovern's staff, relates: "An officer was counting off 'Hut, two, three, four,' and several of the men were chanting along with him. . . . The policemen were walking slowly with their nightsticks extended, held in both hands. I did not see anything thrown from the demonstrators at the police at this time or any charge by the demonstrators at the police."

As a response to seeing the police phalanx, however, says a law student, who was standing near the front of the mob, the chant, "Pigs . . . pigs . . . pigs" went up.

Policemen in the line of march claim that they suffered more than verbal abuse. One officer states that in the vicinity of the Haymarket, a cocktail lounge in the Hilton's northeast corner with an entrance on Balbo, a bottle shattered about 18 inches behind him. He thought it was dropped from a hotel window. When the line reached Michigan, he said, he heard someone say, "Mother fucker, I'm going to kill you." He saw a man, about 33 years old, bearded and wearing a helmet, standing with a wine bottle in his hand, . . . "ready to swing at me. I knocked the bottle out of his hand at that point, someone behind me hit me with some heavy object in the back, and I fell to one knee." While he was down, he said, the crowd surrounded him, cutting him off from other police. "People were pushing and shoving as well as throwing bottles, shoes and eggs," he said. "I was hit with an egg." He used his baton, he said, "in order to shove the crowd aside."

Another officer states that "many rocks and bottles were being thrown at [us]. . . . A house brick struck me on the side of my head after glancing off my helmet." He lost his balance and fell to the pavement. The films fail to show any barrage of missiles at this time, although some may have been thrown.

Just as the police in front of the Hilton were confronted with some sit-downs on the south side of the intersection of Balbo and Michigan, the police unit coming into the intersection on Balbo met the sitting demonstrators. What happened then is subject to dispute between the police and some other witnesses.

The Balbo police unit commander asserts that he informed the sit-downs and surrounding demonstrators that if they did not leave, they would be arrested. He repeated the order and was met with a chant of "Hell no, we won't go." Quickly a police van swung into the intersection immediately behind the police line, the officers opened the door at the rear of the wagon. The deputy chief "ordered the arrest process to start."

"Immediately upon giving this order," the deputy chief later informed his superiors, "we were pelted with rocks, bottles, cans filled with unknown liquids and other debris, which forced the officers to defend themselves from injury. . . . My communications officer was slugged from behind by one of these persons, receiving injuries to his right eye and cheekbone." That officer states: "All this debris came instantaneously, as if it was waiting for the signal of the first arrest."

A sergeant who was on the scene later said that "the hippies behind those sitting down appeared to be the ones doing most of the throwing. . . . Police officers were constantly being hit . . . and were obviously becoming anxious to do something."

A patrolman who was in the skirmish line states that "the order was given to remain in position." But then, he says, one of his fellow officers "ran into the crowd, he was surrounded and I lost sight of him." At this point, the patrolman and other officers in the line "broke into the crowd," using their batons to "push away people who had gathered around" their fellow officer.

He claims they then returned to the line. But another patrolman states that "several police officers were being knocked down by the crowd and several policemen broke formation" to help them "because groups of rioters were attempting to kick and pummel them." At this point, he said, "everything went up for grabs."

The many films and video tapes of this time period present a picture which does not correspond completely with the police view described above. First, the films do not show a mob moving west on Balbo; they show the street as rather clean of the demonstrators and bystanders, although the sidewalks themselves on both sides of the street are crowded. Second, they show the police walking east on Balbo, stopping in formation, awaiting the arrival of the van and starting to make arrests on order. A total of 25 seconds elapses between their coming to a halt and the first arrests.

Also, a St. Louis reporter who was watching from inside the Haymarket lounge agrees that the police began making arrests "in formation," apparently as "the result of an order to clear the intersection." Then, the reporter adds, "from this apparently controlled beginning the police began beating people indiscriminately. They grabbed and beat anyone they could get hold of."

To many other witnesses, it seemed that the police swept down Balbo and charged, with clubs swinging, into the crowd without the slightest pause. What these witnesses may, in fact, have seen was a second sweep of the officers, moving east on Balbo after the first arrest. Once this second action started, the officers did run across the intersection.

"There was just enough time for a few people to sit down before the cops charged," says the law student, quoted earlier. "The guys who sat down got grabbed, and the cops really hit hard. I saw a pair of glasses busted by a billy club go flying through the air."

"The crowd tried to reverse gears," a reporter for a St. Louis paper says. "People began falling over each other. I was in the first rank between police and the crowd and was caught in the first surge. I went down as I tried to retreat. I covered my head, tried to protect my glasses which had fallen partially off, and hoped that I would not be clubbed. I tried to dig into the humanity that had fallen with me. You could hear shouting and screaming. As soon as I could, I scrambled to my feet and tried to move away from the police. I saw a youth running by me also trying to flee. A policeman clubbed him as he passed, but he kept running.

"The cops were saying, 'Move! I said, move, god dammit! Move, you bastards!'" A representative of the ACLU who was positioned among the demonstrators says the police "were cussing a lot" and were shouting, "Kill, kill, kill, kill, kill!" A reporter for the *Chicago Daily News* said after the melee that he, too, heard this cry. A demonstrator remembers the police swinging their clubs and screaming, "Get the hell out of here." . . . "Get the fuck out of here." . . . "Move your fucking ass!"

"People were trying to move but were clubbed as they did" the reporter for the St. Louis paper continued. "I fell to my knees, stumbling over somebody. . . ."

Adds the ACLU representative: "The police kept coming in. . . . The crowd kept trying to get away, but it was so thick that there were many people who seemed . . . to be stuck in the middle and unable to do anything about it. There was a great deal of screaming and yelling. A lot of people were crying and shouting for help. . . . "

The crowd frantically eddied in a halfmoon shape in an effort to escape the officers coming in from the west. A UPI reporter who was on the southern edge of the crowd on Michigan Avenue, said that the advancing police "began pushing the crowd south." A cherry bomb burst overhead. The demonstrators strained against the deputy superintendent of police's line south of the Balbo-Michigan intersection. "When I reached that line," says the UPI reporter, "I heard a voice from behind it say, 'Push them back, move them back!' I was then prodded and shoved with nightsticks back in a northerly direction, toward the still advancing line of police."

"Police were marching this way and that," a correspondent from a St. Louis paper says. "They obviously had instructions to clear the street, but apparently contradicting one another in the directions the crowd was supposed to be sent."

"At first," says the McGovern worker, "the police just pushed the demonstrators with their nightsticks. The demonstrators [nearest the police] tried to move, but couldn't because of the press of the crowd. There was no place for them to go."

The deputy superintendent of police recalls that he ordered his men to "hold your line there" . . . "stand fast" . . . "Lieutenant, hold your men steady there!" These orders, he said, were not obeyed by all.

"Two or three policemen broke formation and began swinging at everyone in sight," the McGovern worker says. The deputy superintendent states that police disregarded his order to return to the police lines—the beginning of what he says was the only instance in which he personally saw police discipline collapse. He estimates that ten to 15 officers moved off on individual forays against demonstrators. But the McGovern worker says "this became sort of spontaneous. Every few seconds more policemen would break formation and began swinging until . . . all the policemen from the original line at Balbo were just swinging through the crowd."

"I turned toward the north and was immediately struck on the back of the head from behind," says the UPI reporter. "I fell to the ground. . . ."

The Clash

Thus, at 7:57 p.m., with two groups of club-wielding police converging simultaneously and independently, the battle was joined. The portions of the throng out of the immediate area of conflict largely stayed put and took up the chant, "The whole world is watching," but the intersection fragmented into a collage of violence.

Re-creating the precise chronology of the next few moments is impossible. But there is no question that a violent street battle ensued.

People ran for cover and were struck by police as they passed. Clubs were swung indiscriminately.

Two Assistant U.S. Attorneys who were on the scene characterized the police as "hostile and aggressive." Some witnesses cited particularly dramatic personal stories.

"I saw squadrols of policemen coming from everywhere," a secretary quoted earlier said. "The crowd around me suddenly began to run. Some of us, including myself, were pushed back onto the sidewalk and then all the way up against . . . the Blackstone Hotel along Michigan Avenue. I thought the crowd had panicked."

"Fearing that I would be crushed against the wall of the building . . . I somehow managed to work my way . . . to the edge of the street . . . and saw police everywhere.

"As I looked up I was hit for the first time on the head from behind by what must have been a billy club. I was then knocked down and while on my hands and knees, I was hit around the shoulders. I got up again, stumbling and was hit again. As I was falling, I heard words to the effect of 'move, move' and the horrible sound of cracking billy clubs."

"After my second fall, I remember being kicked in the back, and I looked up and noticed that many policemen around me had no badges on. The police kept hitting me on the head."

Eventually she made her way to an alley behind the Blackstone and finally, "bleeding badly from my head wound," was driven by a friend to a hospital emergency room. Her treatment included the placing of 12 stitches.

Another young woman, who had been among those who sat down in the intersection, ran south on Michigan, a "Yippie flag" in her hand, when she saw the police. "I fell in the center of the intersection," she says. "Two policemen ran up on me, stopped and hit me on the shoulder, arm and leg about five or six times, severely. They were swearing and one of them broke my flag over his knee." By fleeing into Grant Park, she managed eventually to escape.

Another witness said: "To my left, the police caught a man, beat him to the ground and smashed their clubs on the back of his unprotected head. I stopped to help him. He was elderly, somewhere in his mid-50's. He was kneeling and holding his bleeding head. As I stopped to help him, the police turned on me. "Get that cock sucker out of here!" This command was accompanied by four blows from clubs—one on the middle of my back, one on the bottom of my back, one on my left buttock, and one on the back of my leg. No attempt was made to arrest me or anybody else in the vicinity. All the blows that I saw inflicted by the police were on the backs of heads, arms, legs, etc. It was the most slow and confused, and the least experienced people who got caught and beaten.

"The police were angry. Their anger was neither disinterested nor instrumental. It was deep, expressive and personal. 'Get out of here you cock suckers' seemed to be their most common cry.

"To my right, four policemen beat a young man as he lay on the ground. They beat him and at the same time told him to 'get up and get the hell out of here.' Meanwhile, I struggled with the injured man whom I had stopped to help. . . ."

One demonstrator said that several policemen were coming toward a group in which he was standing when one of the officers yelled, "Hey, there's a nigger over there we can get." They then are said to have veered off and grabbed a middle-aged Negro man, whom they beat.

A lawyer says that he was in a group of demonstrators in the park just south of Balbo when he heard a police officer shout, "Let's get 'em!" Three policemen ran up, "singled out one girl and as she was running away from them, beat her on the back of the head. As she fell to the ground, she was struck by the nightsticks of these officers." A male friend of hers then came up yelling at the police. The witness said, "He was arrested. The girl was left in the area lying on the ground."

The beating of two other girls was witnessed from a hotel window. The witness says, he saw one girl "trying to shield a demonstrator who had been beaten to the ground," whereupon a policeman came up "hitting her with a billy club." The officer also kicked the girl in the shoulder, the witness said.

A *Milwaukee Journal* reporter says in his statement, "when the police managed to break up groups of protesters they pursued individuals and beat them with clubs. Some police pursued individual demonstrators as far as a block . . . and beat them. . . . In many cases it appeared to me that when police had finished beating the protesters they were pursuing, they then attacked, indiscriminately, any civilian who happened to be standing nearby. Many of these were not involved in the demonstrations."

In balance, there is no doubt that police discipline broke during the melee. The deputy superintendent of police states that—although this was the only time he saw discipline collapse—when he ordered his men to stand fast, some did not respond and began to sally through the crowd, clubbing people they came upon. An inspector-observer from the Los Angeles Police Department, stated that during this week, "The restraint of the police both as individual members and as an organization, was beyond reason." However, he said that on this occasion:

> *There is no question but that many officers acted without restraint and exerted force beyond that necessary under the circumstances. The leadership at the point of conflict did little to prevent such conduct and the direct control of officers by first-line supervisors was virtually nonexistent.*

The deputy superintendent of police has been described by several observers as being very upset by individual policemen who beat demonstrators. He pulled his men off the demonstrators, shouting "Stop, damn it, stop. For Christ's sake, stop it."

"It seemed to me," an observer says, "that only a saint could have swallowed the vile remarks to the officers. However, they went to extremes in clubbing the Yippies. I saw them move into the park, swatting away with clubs at girls and boys lying in the grass. More than once I witnessed two officers pulling at the arms of a Yippie until the arms almost left their sockets, then, as the officers put the Yippie in a police van, a third jabbed a riot stick into the groin of the youth being arrested. It was evident that the Yippie was not resisting arrest."

A witness adds: "I witnessed four or five instances of several officers beating demonstrators when it appeared the demonstrators could have been easily transported and confined to police vans waiting nearby."

"Anyone who was in the way of some of the policemen was struck," a UPI correspondent concludes in his statement, "Police continued to hit people in the back who were running away as fast as possible. I saw one man knocked to the street. . . . A policeman continued to poke his stick at the man's groin and kidney area. Several newsmen were struck. Individual incidents of violence were going on over the entire area at once, in any direction you might look.

"In one incident, a young man, who apparently had been maced, staggered across Michigan . . . helped by a companion. The man collapsed. . . . Medical people from the volunteer medical organization rushed out to help him. A police officer (a sergeant, I think) came rushing forward, followed by the two other nightstick-brandishing policemen and yelled, 'Get him out of here; this ain't a hospital.' The medical people fled, half dragging and half carrying the young man with them. . . .

"Another incident I vividly recall is two policemen dragging one protester by one leg, with his shoulders and possibly his head dragging on the pavement as they ran toward a paddy wagon. So much violence was going on at one time. . . ."

A university student who was watching the melee from a hotel window says she saw one young man attempting to flee the police. "Two or three grabbed him and beat him until he fell to the ground." Then, she says, "two or three more policemen were attracted to him and continued to beat him until he was dragged into a paddy wagon."

At another moment, the girl says, she saw another youth "felled by two or three policemen." A medic "dressed all in white and wearing a white helmet" came to aid him. When police saw him giving aid to the downed boy, "they came upon the medic and began to beat him."

"I saw a well-dressed man carrying a well-dressed woman screaming in his arms," said a *Chicago Daily News* reporter. "He tried to carry her to the Hilton Hotel front door and get in. It was secured, so it certainly would have been safe to permit them in. But the police stopped him, and he then carried her back into the crowd. She was hysterical, and I can see no reason for the police treatment of this injured woman." Also during the melee, the reporter says, he saw policemen using sawhorses as "battering rams" against the crowd.

The history professor quoted earlier says, "A number of motorcycle police drove up over the curb on the east side of Michigan and into the crowd." Police also charged demonstrators and onlookers gathered around the old car with the antidraft rally sign which earlier had been taken up to the police line in front of the Hilton.

A series of arrests were made around the antidraft car, some peaceful and some with considerable force. During the course of these arrests, one girl in this group lost her skirt. Although there have been unverified reports of police ripping the clothes from female demonstrators, this is the only incident on news film of any woman being disrobed in the course of arrest.

While violence was exploding in the street, the crowd wedged, behind the police sawhorses along the northeast edge of the Hilton, was experiencing a terror all its own. Early in the evening, this group had consisted in large part of curious bystanders. But following the police surges into the demonstrators clogging the intersection, protesters had crowded the ranks behind the horses in their flight from the police.

From force of numbers, this sidewalk crowd of 150 to 200 persons was pushing down toward the Hilton's front entrance. Policemen whose orders were to keep the entrance clear were pushing with sawhorses. Other police and fleeing demonstrators were pushing from the north in the effort to clear the intersection. Thus, the crowd was wedged against the hotel, with the hotel itself on the west, sawhorses on the southeast and police on the northeast.

Films show that one policeman elbowed his way to where he could rescue a girl of about ten years of age from the viselike press of the crowd. He cradled her in his arms and carried her to a point of relative safety 20 feet away. The crowd itself "passed up" an elderly woman to a low ledge. But many who remained were subjected to what they and witnesses considered deliberate brutality by the police.

"I was crowded in with the group of screaming, frightened people," an onlooker states, "We jammed against each other, trying to press into the brick wall of the hotel. As we stood there breathing hard . . . a policeman calmly walked the length of the barricade with a can of chemical spray [evidently mace] in his hand. Unbelievably, he was spraying at us." Photos reveal several policemen using mace against the crowd.

Another witness, a graduate student, said she was on the periphery of the crowd and could see that "police sprayed mace randomly along the first line of people along the curb." A reporter who was present said a woman cried, "Oh no, not mace!" He said a youth moaned, "Stop it! We're not doing anything!" "Others," recalls another witness, "pleaded with the police to tell them where they should move and allow them to move there."

"Some of the police then turned and attacked the crowd," a Chicago reporter says. The student says she could see police clubbing persons pinned at the edge of the crowd and that there was "a great deal of screaming and pushing within the group." A reporter for a Cleveland paper said, "The police indiscriminately beat those on the periphery of the crowd." An Assistant U.S. attorney put it, "The group on the sidewalk was charged by police using nightsticks." A young cook caught in the crowd relates that:

The police began picking people off. They would pull individuals to the ground and begin beating them. A medic wearing a white coat and an armband with a red cross was grabbed, beaten and knocked to the ground. His whole face was covered with blood.

"The cops just waded into the crowd," says a law student. "There was a great deal of clubbing. People were screaming, 'Help'."

As a result, a part of the crowd was trapped in front of the Conrad Hilton and pressed hard against a big plate glass window of the Haymarket Lounge. A reporter who was sitting inside said, "Frightened men and women banged . . . against the window. A captain of the fire department inside told us to get back from the window, that it might get knocked in. As I backed away a few feet I could see a smudge of blood on the glass outside."

With a sickening crack, the window shattered, and screaming men and women tumbled through, some cut badly by jagged glass. The police came after them.

"I was pushed through by the force of large numbers of people," one victim said. "I got a deep cut on my right leg, diagnosed later by Eugene McCarthy's doctor as a severed artery. . . . I fell to the floor of the bar. There were ten to 20 people who had come through . . . I could not stand on the leg. It was bleeding profusely.

"A squad of policemen burst into the bar, clubbing all those who looked to them like demonstrators, at the same time screaming over and over, 'We've got to clear this area.' The police acted literally like mad dogs looking for objects to attack.

"A patrolman ran up to where I was sitting. I protested that I was injured and could not walk, attempting to show him my leg. He screamed that he would show me I could walk. He grabbed me by the shoulder and literally hurled me through the door of the bar into the lobby. . . .

"I stumbled out into what seemed to be a main lobby. The young lady I was with and I were both immediately set upon by what I can only presume were plainclothes police. . . . We were cursed by these individuals and thrown through another door into an outer lobby." Eventually a McCarthy aide took him to the 15th floor.

In the heat of all this, probably few were aware of the Haymarket's advertising slogan: "A place where good guys take good girls to dine in the lusty, rollicking atmosphere of fabulous Old Chicago. . . ."

During the evening, at least one other window of the Hilton was also broken by crushing crowds.

There is little doubt that during this whole period, beginning at 7:57 p.m. and lasting for nearly 20 minutes, the preponderance of violence came from the police. It was not entirely a one-way battle, however.

Firecrackers were thrown at police. Trash baskets were set on fire and rolled and thrown at them. In one case, a gun was taken from a policeman by a demonstrator.

"Some hippies," said a patrolman in his statement, "were hit by other hippies who were throwing rocks at the police." Films reveal that when police were chasing demonstrators into Grant Park, one young man upended a sawhorse and heaved it at advancing officers.

At one point the deputy superintendent of police was knocked down by a thrown sawhorse. At least one police three-wheeler was tipped over. One of the demonstrators says that "people in the park were prying up cobblestones and breaking them. One person piled up cobblestones in his arms and headed toward the police." Witnesses reported that people were throwing "anything they could lay their hands on. From the windows of the Hilton and Blackstone hotels, toilet paper, wet towels, even ash trays came raining down." A police lieutenant stated that he saw policemen bombarded with "rocks, cherry bombs, jars of vaseline, jars of mayonnaise and pieces of wood torn from the yellow barricades falling in the street." He, too, noticed debris falling from the hotel windows.

A patrolman on duty during the melee states that among the objects he saw thrown at police officers were "rocks, bottles, shoes, a telephone and a garbage can cover. Rolls of toilet paper were thrown from hotel windows. I saw a number of plastic practice golf balls, studded with nails, on the street as well as plastic bags filled with what appeared to be human excrement." He said he saw two policemen, one of them wearing a soft hat, get hit with bricks.

A sergeant states that during the fracas, two men under his command had their plastic faceguards (which they pay for themselves) shattered by bricks or rocks.

A number of police officers were injured, either by flying missiles or in personal attacks. One, for example, was helping a fellow officer "pick up a hippie when another hippie gave [me] a heavy kick, aiming for my groin." The blow struck the officer partly on the leg and partly in the testicles. He went down, and the "hippie" who kicked him escaped.

An attorney who was present also told of seeing demonstrators kick policemen in the groin.

In another instance, a Chicago police reporter said in his statement, "a police officer reached down and grabbed a person who dove forward and bit the officer on the leg. . . . Three or four fellow policemen came to his aid. They had to club the demonstrator to make him break his clamp on the officer's leg." In another case, the witness saw a demonstrator "with a big mop of hair hit a police officer with an old British Army type metal helmet." The reporter said he also heard "hissing sounds from the demonstrators as if they were spraying the police." Later he found empty lacquer spray and hair spray cans on the street. Also he heard policemen cry out, "They're kicking us with knives in their shoes." Later, he said, he found that demonstrators "had actually inserted razor blades in their shoes."

Another type of police difficulty was described by a police captain and mentioned by several other officers in their statements. The captain said that when news cameramen equipped with portable flood lights turned them toward the police, this "caused temporary blindness" and reduced the police effectiveness.

Against the demonstrators' missile throwing and otherwise, police tended to move in groups of eight or ten, regrouping now and then in the street.

Squadrols continually drove into the intersection. "The police kept pulling as many people as they were able to get and taking them into the paddy wagons," says the ACLU representative quoted earlier. The manner in which this was done ranged from restraint to deliberate brutality. In one case, for example, a heavy woman in a muu-muu insisted on using the step at the back of the squadrol as a platform from which to address the crowd. The police repeatedly attempted to move her, but she continued to speak. Finally, a large policeman grabbed her under both arms and lifted her up and into the squadrol.

By contrast, police dragged some persons up the squadrol step, throwing them bodily inside and then hitting them. In one arrest, captured on film, a male demonstrator used his hand to trip one of two policemen carrying him to a paddy wagon. After picking himself up from the pavement, the officer severely beat the demonstrator on the head and chest with his baton. Another policeman joined in, repeatedly jabbing the youth in the groin with his baton.

A man who served as a medical liaison to the demonstration marshals states that he saw the police beat a boy incessantly before putting him into a paddy wagon. He said that the boy looked as if he were already unconscious, but the police continued beating him. According to the university student, quoted earlier about her view from the hotel window, "When an individual was brought to the paddy wagon, two or three policemen stationed at the door would grab the person and continue to beat him."

An Assistant U.S. Attorney who was at the battle reported later: "The arresting officers frequently used their clubs to hit the arrested person in the stomach and kidneys, even though the arrested persons were not in any way resisting arrest or struggling with the police officers." On the other hand, both police officers and a city observer who watched the loading of the paddy wagons state that no excessive force was used in placing nonresisting prisoners in the vans.

Meanwhile, more CTA buses with police reinforcements were pouring into the area. Blue police buses by now were bringing reinforcements into the area. A Chicago attorney who was near the Hilton watched one contingent unload. He says they "gave the finger" to subdued demonstrators in the vicinity and also made obscene remarks, like "Hippies eat shit." Moving quickly through the Balbo-Michigan intersection, they hurried to join their fellow officers pushing north on Michigan.

Says an ACLU representative: "The buses would discharge at the corner of Wabash and Balbo and then the men would form into a line and march down Balbo with their night sticks, chanting, "Kill, kill."

With each new police attack and flurry of arrests, the crowd dispersed farther into the park and east on Balbo.

Peck wound up on the east side of Michigan Avenue. From that vantage point, he said, he thought he saw the deputy superintendent of police and a person in civilian clothes, who he thought was a city official, coming across the avenue in his direction. In a similar situation during the Pentagon confrontation when federal marshals moved in against demonstrators, Peck says, he had been able to obtain a loudspeaker, address himself to commanding authority, calm the crowd and prevent further assaults. With this in mind, he said he went out to "resume negotiations" with the deputy superintendent and the other man. Peck admits he was "probably pretty emotional" at this point, but says he had his senses about him.

Using his hand to emphasize his words, he addressed the deputy: "Why did you have your police move against us when I said we were not violent? Isn't there any way we can get our people to safety?"

At this, Peck insists, they both lunged at him. Peck said he tightened up in "a defensive posture" to break their hold and then ran. Other police came after him. He again assumed the defensive posture and, he claims, was beaten brutally by the officers. Then, Peck says, he was dragged some 200 feet to a police van. Later several stitches were taken on his head, his back and sides were bruised and his genitals were swollen.

A witness to this incident, the Chicago police reporter quoted earlier, says that Peck initiated the trouble by shouting at the deputy: "You're the cause of all this." Then, the witness states, Peck slugged the deputy in the right eye with his fist, knocking his glasses to the street. A police sergeant went after Peck, but was "grabbed by a group of demonstrators who beat the daylights out of him." Finally, another officer made a flying tackle of Peck as he was "trying to escape through the crowd." As Peck was arrested, "the demonstrators broke up a yellow wooden [saw] horse approximately ten or 12 feet long . . . and began throwing [the pieces] at the police." The deputy superintendent, the reporter said, was hit again. The sergeant was rescued from the mob only after several policemen used their batons against the demonstrators. The deputy's version of the incident agrees essentially with this account.

* * *

Police-Media Confrontations

As has been documented, there were ample causes before and during the convention week for media-police hostility. The media representatives felt hampered and frustrated by the convention arrangement difficulties and the ever-present precautions. The police are never enthusiastic about the presence of newsmen in large-crowd situations and their irritation during the week grew for the reasons described above. Police emotions were heightened by their impression, as they listened to radio, watched TV and read newspapers, that the media coverage was anti-Chicago, anti-Mayor Daley and anti-Police.

There is further support for the police view. On August 30, 1968, a National Guard Colonel was interviewed by NBC in connection with the actions of the Guard and the Police Department in clearing the McCarthy staff suite in the Hilton. The Colonel spoke of the "great job" done by the Police Department. As he walked away, he heard one of the technicians or cameramen say to the announcer, "You can't use that.'"

In this emotional climate, with police tempers already shortened by conflicts with demonstrators, it was perhaps inevitable that incidents of police-press violence would occur. They did. We shall only summarize these incidents under the name of the newsman involved. . . .(We have deleted from this report accounts of certain incidents involving newsmen because cases involving them are under active consideration by the United States Department of Justice. The incidents are, however, included in the statistics appearing at the end of this chapter.)

Saturday - Sunday

Lawrence Green

The first instance of violence involving a member of the press in connection with the demonstrators took place Saturday night at about 11:45 p.m., at Clark Street opposite Menomonee Street on Chicago's Near North Side. *Chicago Daily News* reporter Lawrence Green came across some youthful demonstrators on the sidewalk who were shouting at police patrolling the street.

According to Green, he and other newsmen at the scene were ordered "in front" of the police lines and the police then charged the crowd on the sidewalk. Green said he was pushed, then stumbled, and another reporter fell on top of him. Green had his press credentials visible around his neck. As he scrambled to his feet, he said he held out his press card and yelled, "Press! Press! Press!" Nonetheless, a policeman came up to him and clubbed him on the back. Another police officer, seeing his credentials, said, "Fuck your press cards."

Late Sunday night, the Chicago police cleared Lincoln Park of demonstrators. The demonstrators left the park and flowed into the Old Town area of Chicago's North Side and later marched down to the Michigan Avenue bridge. In the process, several clashes with the press occurred.

Howard M. Berliant

Free-lance photographer Howard M. Berliant was standing on the porch of an apartment at 1726 North Clark Street near Lincoln Park, at about 11:45 p.m. Berliant, a friend who lives at that address, and several other people were watching the clash of police and demonstrators. Berliant had two cameras but wore no press identification. As police approached the porch of the apartment building, a policeman said, "Get the man with the camera." He also ordered the group to "move on." Some protested that they lived there and retreated into the outer lobby of the apartment building.

Several police followed them into the lobby, and one of them clubbed Berliant on the head. Berliant was pulled into the inner lobby by his friend. When a policeman threatened with gestures to break the door, it was opened. The police entered the inner lobby, ignored Berliant's plea that they call an ambulance for him, turned and left. Berliant was driven to Henrotin Hospital by his friend. According to hospital records, he was treated for a two-inch laceration of the scalp, requiring seven stitches. The entire incident was observed by several residents of the building.

John Culhane

Newsweek reporter John Culhane was on the east side of Clark Street shortly before midnight as police cleared Lincoln Park. He was accompanied by *Newsweek* trainee Monroe Anderson, III. Culhane asked a policeman where it would be safe to stand and was sent across Clark Street, where he joined a group of reporters in front of the Herman Baptist Church. Police entered the churchyard and called to the reporters, "Walk to us." Culhane shouted, "Press, press." He was wearing a blue helmet, business suit, and press credentials hung around his neck. As the group of reporters left the churchyard, one of the police shouted that the reporters were from *Newsweek*, adding obscene words. The police advanced and Culhane was clubbed on the back of the head. Then, as he moved down the street, he said, another policeman hit him on the right thigh. Several reporters took refuge in a doorway. The police surrounded the doorway, shouting for them to come down. As they did, Culhane was hit again, causing a six-inch bruise on his leg.

* * *

A total of 49 newsmen are described in the above events as having been hit, maced, or arrested, apparently without reason, by the police. Forty-three were hit, three were maced and three were arrested. Of the newsmen involved, 22 were reporters, 23 were photographers and 4 were members of the TV crews.

In ten of these incidents, photographic or recording equipment was deliberately broken; in one, the police intentionally knocked a reporter's notebook out of his hand.

In over 40 instances, the newsman involved was clearly identifiable as such; that is, even aside from photographers carrying the identifying apparatus of their trade, newsmen wore helmets, carried visible press badges or press passes hanging around their necks. In only four situations do the facts indicate that the newsmen were so mixed in with the crowd that the police could have hit them under the mistaken apprehension that they were demonstrators.

Forty-five of the incidents occurred at night, four during the daytime. Fourteen of the newsmen were from Chicago and the balance were from out of town. The average age was about 31 years; 28 were in the 20 to 30 year age bracket; ten were from 31 to 35; seven were over 35. We do not know the ages of the other four.

Ten of the incidents took place on Saturday and Sunday. The greatest number—25—occurred on Monday. None occurred on Tuesday (except for the Dan Rather incident at the Amphitheatre, which is not represented in the above statistics). On Wednesday, however, the violence resumed: there were 14 incidents.

There is evidence of a number of other instances of police-press violence. In 12 of these incidents, newsmen were struck by police batons; in three, their photographic equipment was damaged by police. They are not reported in this chapter either because they took place when the police were moving large crowds (making it possible that any injury to newsmen was accidental) or because we do not have enough information to warrant their inclusion in this report.

* * *

Friday—A Day of Departure

On Friday morning, several hundred demonstrators were in the park, and there were more speeches attacking the "establishment." By noon the crowd had grown again to nearly 1,000, many of whom were curious onlookers, including members of the convention assemblage about to leave Chicago. There were long and serious debates, but there was no physical conflict. A detail of police still guarded the Conrad Hilton Hotel. Throughout Thursday night and Friday, the demonstrators were leaving Grant Park to return home. The convention week was over.

"Elvis the Pelvis" performing at the Arena in Philadelphia, April 1957

GREIL MARCUS

"ELVIS: Presliad" (1976)

When Elvis Presley began his career in the mid-1950s there were suspicions voiced that rock 'n' roll music was a conspiracy to undermine American values. Radio stations competed with each other to get the credit for banning it from their wave lengths. A congressional committee discussed investigating its relationship to "switchblade gangs." Some disliked it as an inducement to promiscuous mixing of the sexes, others hated it even more for mixing races. That it was music of no social or musical value was simply assumed. The best advice seemed to be to wait. Adolescents had adopted it as a badge of defiance; soon they would outgrow this musical acne.

In time people began to realize that rock's appeal stretched farther than adolescence, that it offered a cultural symbol for

a new stage in human life: youth, that long period of preparation in which young Americans interminably consume education to fit them for the complex tasks of a post-industrial economy. People needed an identity of their own during such a long and serious pursuit: they could not be merely prospective adults for so many years and they surely were no longer children.

Greil Marcus insists that we press our understanding of the meaning of rock 'n' roll a step farther. Just as jazz—originally identified only with black Americans—came to symbolize a whole age, so does rock—the music of youth—reach toward the totality of experience of our frightening, distended society. Elvis Presley, the author argues, took the roots of rock music and translated them from the possession of particular sub-cultures—black folk, country folk, young folks—to an American cultural form available on some level to every audience. The scope of this achievement and its costs are the subject of the "Presliad." Whether it is the epic of a hero or a villain poses a large question. Either way, what Marcus writes of Little Richard applies even more to the Big E.: "There is a man who matters. He knows how to rock."

They called Elvis the Hillbilly Cat in the beginning; he came out of a stepchild culture (in the South, white trash; to the rest of America, a caricature of Bilbo and moonshine) that for all it shared with the rest of America had its own shape and integrity. As a poor white Southern boy, Elvis created a personal culture out of the hillbilly world that was his as a given. Ultimately, he made that personal culture public in such an explosive way that he transformed not only his own culture, but America's.

* * *

It was, as Southern chambers of commerce have never tired of saying, A Land of Contrasts. The fundamental contrast, of course, could not have been more obvious: black and white. Always at the root of Southern fantasy, Southern music, and Southern politics, the black man was poised in the early fifties for an overdue invasion of American life, in fantasy, music, and politics. As the North scurried to deal with him, the South would be pushed farther and farther into the weirdness and madness its best artists had been trying to exorcise from the time of Poe on down. Its politics would dissolve into night-riding and hysteria; its fantasies would be dull for all their gaudy paranoia. Only the music got away clean.

The North, powered by the Protestant ethic, had set men free by making them strangers; the poor man's South that Elvis knew took strength from community.

The community was based on a marginal economy that demanded cooperation, loyalty, and obedience for the achievement of anything resembling a good life; it was organized by religion, morals, and music. Music helped hold the community together, and carried the traditions and shared values that dramatized a sense of place. Music gave pleasure, wisdom, and shelter.

"It's the only place in the country I've ever been where you can actually drive down the highway at night, and if you listen, you hear music," Robbie Robertson once said. "I don't know if it's coming from the people or if it's coming from the air. It lives, and it's rooted there." Elegant enough, but I prefer another comment Robbie made. "The South," he said, "is the only place we play where everybody can clap on the off-beat."

Music was also an escape from the community, and music revealed its underside. There were always people who could not join, no matter how they might want to: tramps, whores, rounders, idiots, criminals. The most vital were singers: not the neighbors who brought out their fiddles and guitars for country picnics, as Elvis used to do, or those who sang in church, as he did also, but the professionals. They were men who bridged the gap between the community's sentimentalized idea of itself, and the outside world and the forbidden; artists who could take the community beyond itself because they had the talent and the nerve to transcend it. Often doomed, traveling throughout the South enjoying sins and freedoms the community had surrendered out of necessity or never known at all, they were too ambitious, ornery, or simply different to fit in.

The Carter Family, in the twenties, were the first to record the old songs everyone knew, to make the shared musical culture concrete, and their music drew a circle around the community. They celebrated the landscape (especially the Clinch Mountains that ringed their home), found strength in a feel for death because it was the only certainty, laughed a bit, and promised to leave the hillbilly home they helped build only on a gospel ship. Jimmie Rodgers, their contemporary, simply hopped a train. He was every boy who ever ran away from home, hanging out in the railroad yards, bumming around with black minstrels, pushing out the limits of his life. *He* celebrated long tall mamas that rubbed his back and licked his neck just to cure the cough that killed him; he bragged about gunplay on Beale Street; he sang real blues, played jazz with Louis Armstrong, and though there was melancholy in his soul, his smile was a good one. He sounded like a man who could make a home for himself anywhere. There's so much *room* in this country, he seemed to be saying, so many things to do—how could an honest man be satisfied to live within the frontiers he was born to?

Outside of the community because of the way they lived, the singers were tied to it as symbols of its secret hopes, of its fantasies of escape and union with the black man, of its fears of transgressing the moral and social limits that promised peace of mind. Singers could present the extremes of emotion, risk, pleasure, sex, and violence that the community was meant to control; they were often alcoholic or worse, lacking a real family, drifters in a world where roots were life. Sometimes the singer tantalized the community with his outlaw liberty; dying young, he finally justified the community by his inability to survive outside of it. More often than not, the singer's resistance dissolved into sentiment. Reconversion is the central country music comeback strategy, and many have returned to the fold after a brief fling with the devil, singing songs of virtue, fidelity, and God, as if to prove that sin only hid a deeper piety—or that there was no way out.

By the late forties and early fifties, Hank Williams had inherited Jimmie Rodgers' role as the central figure in the music, but he added an enormous reservation: that margin of loneliness in Rodgers' America had grown into a world of utter tragedy. Williams sang for a community to which he could not belong; he sang to a God in whom he could not quite believe; even his many songs of good times and good lovin' seemed to lose their reality. There were plenty of jokes in his repertoire, novelties like "Kawliga" (the tale of unrequited love between two cigar store Indians); he traveled Rodgers' road, but for Williams, that road was a lost highway. Beneath the surface of his forced smiles and his light, easy sound, Hank Williams was kin to Robert Johnson in a way that the new black singers of his day were not. Their music, coming out of New Orleans, out of Sam Phillips'

Memphis studio and washing down from Chicago, was loud, fiercely electric, raucous, bleeding with lust and menace and loss. The rhythmic force that was the practical legacy of Robert Johnson had evolved into a music that overwhelmed *his* reservations; the rough spirit of the new blues, city R&B, rolled right over his nihilism. Its message was clear: What life doesn't give me, I'll take.

Hank Williams was a poet of limits, fear, and failure; he went as deeply into one dimension of the country world as anyone could, gave it beauty, gave it dignity. What was missing was that part of the hillbilly soul Rodgers had celebrated, something Williams' music obscured, but which his realism could not express and the community's moralism could not contain: excitement, rage, fantasy, delight—the feeling, summed up in a sentence by W. J. Cash from *The Mind of the South*, that "even the Southern physical world was a kind of cosmic conspiracy against reality in favor of romance"; that even if Elvis's South was filled with Puritans, it was also filled with natural-born hedonists, and the same people were both.

> *To lie on his back for days and weeks* [*Cash writes of the hillbilly*], *storing power as the air he breathed stores power under the hot sun of August, and then to explode, as that air explodes in a thunderstorm, in a violent outburst of emotion–in such a fashion would he make life not only tolerable, but infinitely sweet.*

In the fifties we can hardly find that moment in white music, before Elvis. Hank Williams was not all there was to fifties country, but his style was so pervasive, so effective, carrying so much weight, that it closed off the possibilities of breaking loose just as the new black music helped open them up. Not his gayest tunes, not "Move It on Over," "Honky Tonkin'," or "Hey Good Lookin'," can match this blazing passage from Cash, even if those songs share its subject:

> *To go into the town on Saturday afternoon and night, to stroll with the throng, to gape at the well-dressed and the big automobiles, to bathe in the holiday cacaphony . . . maybe to have a drink, maybe to get drunk, to laugh with the passing girls, to pick them up if you had a car, or to go swaggering or hesitating into the hotels with the corridors saturated with the smell of bicloride of mercury, or the secret, steamy bawdy houses; maybe to have a fight, maybe against the cops, maybe to end, whooping and goddamning, in the jailhouse. . . .*

The momentum is missing; that will to throw yourself all the way after something better with no real worry about how you are going to make it home. And it was this spirit, full-blown and bragging, that was to find its voice in Elvis's new blues and the rockabilly fever he kicked off all over the young white South. Once Elvis broke down the door, dozens more would be fighting their way through. Out of nowhere there would be Carl Perkins, looking modest enough and sounding for all the world as if he was having fun for the first time in his life, chopping his guitar with a new kind of urgency and yelling: "Now Dan got happy and he started ravin'—He jerked out his razor but he wasn't shavin' "—

He hollered R-R-RAVE ON *chillen, I'm with ya!*
RAVE ON CATS *he cried*
It's almost dawn and the cops're gone
Let's alllllllll *get dixie fried!*

Country music (like the blues, which was more damned and more honestly hedonistic than country had ever been) was music for a whole community, cutting across lines of age, if not class. This could have meant an openly expressed sense of diversity for each child, man, and woman, as it did with the blues. But country spoke to a community fearful of anything of the sort, withdrawing into itself, using music as a bond that linked all together for better or for worse, with a sense that what was shared was less important than the crucial fact of sharing. How could parents hope to keep their children if their kids' whole sense of what it meant to live—which is what we get from music when we are closest to it—held promises the parents could never keep?

The songs of country music, and most deeply, its even, narrow sound, had to subject the children to the heartbreak of their parents: the father who couldn't feed his family, the wife who lost her husband to a honky-tonk angel or a bottle, the family that lost everything to a suicide or a farm spinning off into one more bad year, the horror of loneliness in a world that was meant to banish that if nothing else. Behind that uneasy grin, this is Hank Williams' America; the romance is only a night call.

Such a musical community is beautiful, but it is not hard to see how it could be intolerable. All that hedonism was dragged down in country music; a deep sense of fear and resignation confined it, as perhaps it almost had to, in a land overshadowed by fundamentalist religion, where original sin was just another name for the facts of life.

Raised Up

Now, that Saturday night caught by Cash and Perkins would get you through a lot of weekdays. Cash might close it off—"Emptied of their irritations and repressions, left to return to their daily tasks, stolid, unlonely, and tame again"—and he's right, up to a point. This wasn't any revolution, no matter how many cops got hurt keeping the peace on Saturday night. Regardless of what a passport to that Southern energy (detached from the economics and religion that churned it up) might do for generations of restless Northern and British kids, there is no way that energy can be organized. But the fact that Elvis and the rest could trap its spirit and send it out over a thousand radio transmitters is a central fact of more lives than mine; the beginning of most of the stories in this book, if nothing near the end of them.

For we are treading on the key dividing line that made Elvis King of Western Bop (they went through a lot of trouble finding a name for this music) instead of just another country crooner or a footnote in someone's history of the blues: the idea (and it was just barely an "idea") that Saturday night could be the whole show. You had to be young and a bit insulated to pull it off, but why not? Why not trade pain and boredom for kicks and style? Why not make an escape from a way of life—the question trails off the last page of *Huckleberry Finn*—into a way of life?

You might not get revered for all time by everyone from baby to grandma, like the Carter Family, but you'd have more fun. Reality would catch up sooner or later—a pregnant girlfriend and a fast marriage, the farm you had to take over when your daddy died, a dull and pointless job that drained your desires until you could barely remember them—but why deal with reality before you had to? And what if there was a chance, just a chance, that you *didn't* have to deal with it? "When I was a boy," said Elvis not so long ago, "I was the hero in comic books and movies. I grew up believing in a dream. Now I've lived it out. That's all a man can ask for."

Elvis is telling us something quite specific: how special he was; how completely he captured and understood what for most of us is only a tired phrase glossing the surfaces of our own failed hopes. It is one thing, after all, to dream of a new job, and quite another to dream of a new world. The risks are greater. Elvis took chances dreaming his dreams; he gambled against the likelihood that their failure would betray him, and make him wish he had never dreamed at all. There are a hundred songs to tell that story, but perhaps Mott the Hoople, chasing the rock 'n' roll fantasy Elvis made of the American dream, said it best: "I wish I'd never wanted then/What I want now twice as much."

Always, Elvis felt he was different, if not better, than those around him. He grew his sideburns long, acting out that sense of differentness, and was treated differently: in this case, he got himself kicked off the football team. Hear him recall those days in the midst of a near-hysterical autobiography, delivered at the height of his comeback from the stage at the International Hotel in Las Vegas: ". . . Had

*EE # 2. May 1972. I read in *Modern Screen* that top GOP politicos are giving *serious consideration* to placing Elvis's name in nomination for the vice-presidency (a plot to get around that $25,000 fee?). The article is illustrated by fifteen-year-old shots of girls waving ELVIS-FOR-PRESIDENT banners. Elvis, the story says, thinks this is a good idea, and has recently addressed a group of Black Panthers in order to test his forensic skills. He told them, and I quote: "Violence is not where it's at. It's a real turn-off, man." I do not know how to take this, especially as I recall it a year later when a TV trailer announces, "Tonight, immediately following the President's speech on Watergate, see Elvis further the cause of rock 'n' roll in *Roustabout*." I am more disoriented by the idea that Elvis could further the cause of *anything* in a movie like *Roustabout* than I am by the missed chance of his involvement in the Watergate scandal. But then, he would have known how to handle it. To Elvis, Watergate would have been something like a cosmic paternity suit.

pretty long hair for that time and I tell you it got pretty weird. They used to see me comin down the street and they'd say, 'Hot dang, let's get him, he's a squirrel, he's a squirrel, get him, he just come down outta the trees.'"

High school classmates remember his determination to break through as a country singer; with a little luck, they figured, he might even make it.

Out on the road for the first time with small-change country package tours, though, Elvis would plot for something much bigger—for everything Hollywood had ever shown him in its movies.

On North Main in Memphis, as Harmonica Frank recalls Elvis, this was nothing to put into words. Talking trash and flicking ash, marking time and trying to hold it off, what did Elvis really have to look forward to? A year or so of Saturday nights, a little local notoriety, then a family he didn't quite decide to have and couldn't support? It would be all over.

Elvis fancied himself a trucker (if there weren't any Memphis boys in the movies, there were plenty on the road), pushing tons of machinery through the endless American night; just his version of the train whistle that called out to Johnny B. Goode and kept Richard Nixon awake as a boy. If it is more than a little odd that what to Elvis served as a symbol of escape and mastery now works—as part of his legend—as a symbol of everything grimy and poor he left behind when he did escape, maybe that only tells us how much his success shuffled the facts of his life—or how much he raised the stakes.

You don't make it in America—Emerson's mousetrap to the contrary—waiting for someone to come along and sign you up. You might be sitting on the corner like a Philly rock 'n' roller and get snatched up for your good looks, but you'll be back a year later and you'll never know what happened. Worst of all, you may not even care. What links the greatest rock 'n' roll careers is a volcanic ambition, a lust for more than anyone has a right to expect; in some cases, a refusal to know when to quit or even rest. It is that bit of Ahab burning beneath the Huck Finn rags of "Freewheelin'" Bob Dylan, the arrogance of a country boy like Elvis sailing into Hollywood, ready for whatever kind of success America had to offer.

So if we treat Elvis's words with as much respect as we can muster—which is how he meant them to be taken—we can see the first point at which his story begins to be his own. He took his dreams far more seriously than most ever dare, and he had the nerve to chase them down.

Cash's wonderful line—"a cosmic conspiracy against reality in favor of romance"—now might have more resonance. Still, if the kind of spirit that romance could produce seems ephemeral within the context of daily life, you would not expect the music it produced to last very long either. Not even Elvis, as a successful young rocker, could have expected his new music to last; he told interviewers rock 'n' roll was here to stay, but he was taking out plenty of insurance, making movies and singing schmaltz. You couldn't blame him; anyway, he liked schmaltz.

Within the realm of country music, the new spirit dried up just like Saturday fades into Monday, but since rock 'n' roll found its own audience and created its own world, that hardly mattered. Rock 'n' roll caught that romantic conspiracy on records and gave it a form. Instead of a possibility within a music, it became the essence; it became, of all things, a tradition. And when that form itself had to deal with reality—which is to say, when its young audience began to grow up—when the compromise between fantasy and reality that fills most of this book was necessary to preserve the possibility of fantasy, the fantasy had become part of the reality that had to be dealt with; the rules of the game had changed a bit, and it was a better game. "Blue Suede Shoes" had grown directly into something as serious and complex, and yet still offhand, still take-it-or-leave-it-and-pass-the-wine, as the Rolling Stones' "You Can't Always Get What You Want," which asks the musical question, "Why *are you* stepping on my blue suede shoes?"

Echoing through all of rock 'n' roll is the simple demand for peace of mind and a good time. While the demand is easy to make, nothing is more complex than to try to make it real and live it out. It all sounds simple, obvious; but that one young man like Elvis could break through a world as hard as Hank Williams', and invent a new one to replace it, seems obvious only because we have inherited Elvis's world, and live in it.

Satisfaction is not all there is to it, but it is where it all begins. Finally, the music must provoke as well as delight, disturb as well as comfort, create as well as sustain. If it doesn't, it lies, and there is only so much comfort you can take in a lie before it all falls apart.

The central facts of life in Elvis's South pulled as strongly against the impulses of hedonism and romance as the facts of our own lives

*EE#3. Elvis's 1973 TV special, *Aloha from Elvis in Hawaii,* was beamed by satellite to one-third of the world's population. Or so his publicity men announced. Perhaps it was that if the one-third of the world—principally the heathen part—had TV sets, they could have watched. It doesn't matter; the conceit of the concept is what matters.

You can see him now, Col. Thomas Andrew Parker, ex-carny barker, the great medical menagerist, tossing helplessly on his bed, scheming—after all these years, still peddling Elvis pens at press conferences, hustling glossies in the aisles at concerts, Colonel Parker does not rest—and what keeps him awake is that *even now there are people who do not know about Elvis Presley!* There are worlds to be conquered! There is work to be done!

Finally, he drops off to sleep. Yes, there are poor beggars somewhere in the Amazon jungle who have yet to get the word (perhaps the King would succeed where dozens of casseroled missionaries have failed—make a note of that), but the Colonel will deal with that tomorrow . . . wait for tomorrow.

Parker dreams.

It is perhaps 1990. Elvis is in his middle fifties now, still young, still beautiful. His latest single—"Baby Let Me Bang Your Box," backed with "My Yiddishe Mama"—has topped all charts. Parker has had his third heart transplant. The world has received the long-awaited actual communication from intelligent beings beyond the solar system. Earth's greatest scientists have assembled in Japan to decipher the message, and after years of error they have succeeded. It consists of only one word, one question on which the fate of ten billion people may rest:

"ELWIS?"

So Colonel Parker rests easy. Age has mellowed him, and his expectations do not go beyond the Milky Way.

do against the fast pleasures of rock 'n' roll. When the poor white was thrown back on himself, as he was in the daytime, when he worked his plot or looked for a job in the city, or at night, when he brooded and Hank Williams' whippoorwill told the truth all too plainly, those facts stood out clearly: powerlessness and vulnerability on all fronts. The humiliation of a class system that gave him his identity and then trivialized it; a community that for all its tradition and warmth was in some indefinable way not enough; economic chaos; the violence of the weather; bad food and maybe not enough of that; diseases that attached themselves to the body like new organs—they all mastered him. And that vulnerability produced—along with that urge to cut loose, along with that lively Southern romance—uncertainty, fatalism, resentment, acceptance, and nostalgia: limits that cut deep as the oldest cotton patch in Dixie.

Vernon Presley was a failed Mississippi sharecropper who moved his family out of the country with the idea of making a go in the city; it's not so far from Tupelo to Memphis, but in some ways, the journey must have been a long one—scores of country songs about boys and girls who lost their souls to the big town attest to that. Listen to Dolly Parton's downtown hooker yearning for her Blue Ridge mountain boy; listen to the loss of an America you may never have known.

They don't make country music better than that anymore, but it's unsatisfying, finally; too classical. This country myth is just one more echo of Jefferson pronouncing that, in America, virtue must be found in the land. I like myths, but this one is too facile, either for the people who still live on the land or for those of us who are merely looking for a way out of our own world, for an Annie Green Springs utopia. The myth is unsatisfying because the truth is richer than the myth.

"King Harvest (Has Surely Come)," the Band's song of blasted country hopes, gives us the South in all of its earthly delight and then snuffs it out. All at once, the song catches the grace and the limbo of the life that must be left behind.

The tune evokes a man's intimacy with the land and the refusal of the land to respond in kind. The music makes real, for the coolest city listener, a sense of place that is not quite a sense of being at home; the land is too full of violence for that. One hears the farmer's fear of separating from the land (and from his own history, which adhering to the land, is not wholly his own); one hears the cold economic necessities that have forced him out. The melody—too beautiful and out of reach for any words I have—spins the chorus into the pastoral with a feel for nature that is *really* hedonistic—

Corn in the field
Listen to the rice as the wind blows cross the water
KING HARVEST HAS SURELY COME*

—and a desperate, ominous rhythm slams the verses back to the slum streets that harbor the refugees of the pastoral disaster: "Just don't judge me by my shoes!" Garth Hudson's organ traces the circle of the song, over and over again.

The earliest picture of Elvis shows a farmer, his wife, and their baby; the faces of the parents are vacant, they are set, as if they cannot afford an unearned smile. Somehow, their faces say, they will be made to pay even for that.

You don't hear this in Elvis's music; but what he left out of his story is as vital to an understanding of his art as what he kept, and made over. If we have no idea of what he left behind, of how much he escaped, we will have no idea what his success was worth, or how intensely he must have wanted it.

Elvis was thirteen when the family left Tupelo for Memphis in 1948, a pampered only child; ordinary in all respects, they say, except that he liked to sing. True to Chuck Berry's legend of the Southern rocker, Elvis's mother bought him his first guitar, and for the same reason Johnny B. Goode's mama had in mind: keep the boy out of trouble. Elvis sang tearful country ballads, spirituals, community music. On the radio, he listened with his family to the old music of the Carter Family and Jimmie Rodgers, to current stars like Roy Acuff, Ernest Tubb, Bob Wills, Hank Williams, and to white gospel groups like the Blackwood Brothers. Elvis touched the soft center of American music when he heard and imitated Dean Martin and the operatics of Mario Lanza; he picked up Mississippi blues singers like Big Bill Broonzy, Big Boy Crudup, Lonnie Johnson, and the new Memphis music of Rufus Thomas and Johnny Ace, mostly when no one else was around, because that music was naturally frowned upon. His parents called it "sinful music," and they had a point—it was dirty, and there were plenty of blacks who would have agreed with Mr. and Mrs. Presley—but Elvis was really too young to worry. In this he was no different from hundreds of other white country kids who wanted more excitement in their lives than they could get from twangs and laments—wanted a beat, sex, celebration, the stunning nuances of the blues and the roar of horns and electric guitars. Still, Elvis's interest was far more casual than that of Jerry Lee Lewis, a bad boy who was sneaking off to black dives in his spare time, or Carl Perkins, a musician who was consciously working out a synthesis of blues and country.

The Presleys stumbled onto welfare, into public housing. Vernon Presley found a job. It almost led to the family's eviction, because if they still didn't have enough to live on , they were judged to have too much to burden the county with their troubles. Elvis was a loner, but he had an eye for flash. He sold his blood for money, ushered at the movies, drove his famous truck, and divided the proceeds between his mother and his outrageous wardrobe. Looking for space, for a way to set himself apart.

Like many parents with no earthly future, the Presleys, especially Gladys Presley, lived for their son. Her ambition must have been that Elvis would take all that was good in the family and free himself from the life she and her husband endured; she was, Memphian Stanley Booth wrote a few years ago, "the one, perhaps the only one, who had told him throughout his life that even though he came from poor country people, he was just as good as anybody."

On Sundays (Wednesdays too, sometimes) the Presleys went to their Assembly of God to hear the Pentecostal ministers hand down a similar message: the last shall be first. This was democratic religion with a vengeance, lower class and gritty. For all those who have traced Elvis's music and his hipshake to his religion (accurately enough—Elvis was the first to say so), it has escaped his chroniclers that hillbilly Calvinism was also at the root of his self-respect and his pride: the anchor of his ambition.

His church (and the dozens of other Pentecostal sects scattered throughout the South and small-town America) was one part of what was left of the old American religion after the Great Awakening. Calvinism had been a religion of authority in the beginning; in the middle-class North, filtered through the popular culture of Ben Franklin, it became a system of tight money, tight-mindedness, and gentility; in the hillbilly South, powered by traveling preachers and their endless revivals, the old holiness cult produced a faith of grace, apocalypse, and emotion, where people heaved their deepest feelings into a circle and danced around them. Momentum scattered that old authority; all were sinners, all were saints. Self-consciously outcast, the true faith in a land of Philistines and Pharisees, it was shoved into storefronts and tents and even open fields, and no less sure of itself for that.

Church music caught moments of unearthly peace and desire, and the strength of the religion was in its intensity. The preacher rolled fire down the pulpit and chased it into the aisle, signifying; men and women rocked in their seats, sometimes onto the floor, bloodying their fingernails scratching and clawing in a lust for absolute sanctification. No battle against oppression, this was a leap right through it, with tongues babbling toward real visions, negating stale red earth, warped privvies, men and women staring from their sway-backed porches into nothingness. It was a faith meant to transcend the grimy world that called it up. Like Saturday night, the impulse to dream, the need to escape, the romance and the contradictions of the land, this was a source of energy, tension, and power.

Elvis inherited these tensions, but more than that, gave them his own shape. It is often said that if Elvis had not come along to set off the changes in American music and American life that followed his triumph, someone very much like him would have done the job as well. But there is no reason to think this is true, either in strictly musical terms, or in any broader cultural sense. It is vital to remember that Elvis was the first young Southern white to sing rock 'n' roll, something he copied from no one but made up on the spot; and to know that even though other singers would have come up with a white version of the new black music acceptable to teenage America, of all that did emerge in Elvis's wake, none sang as powerfully, or with more than a touch of his magic.

Even more important is the fact that no singer emerged with anything like Elvis's combination of great talent and conscious ambition, and there is no way a new American hero could have gotten out of the South and to the top—creating a whole new sense of how big the top was, as Elvis did—without that combination. The others—Carl Perkins, Jerry Lee Lewis, Charlie Rich—were bewildered by even a taste of fame and unable to handle a success much more limited than Presley's.

If Elvis had the imagination to come up with the dreams that kept him going, he had the music to bring them to life and make them real to huge numbers of other people. It was the genius of his singing, an ease and an intensity that has no parallel in American music, that took him from a world he inherited into a world he made.